D1126587

HISTORICAL DICTIONARY

The historical dictionaries present essential information on a broad range of subjects, including American and world history, art, business, cities, countries, cultures, customs, film, global conflicts, international relations, literature, music, philosophy, religion, sports, and theater. Written by experts, all contain highly informative introductory essays of the topic and detailed chronologies that, in some cases, cover vast historical time periods but still manage to heavily feature more recent events.

Brief A–Z entries describe the main people, events, politics, social issues, institutions, and policies that make the topic unique, and entries are cross-referenced for ease of browsing. Extensive bibliographies are divided into several general subject areas, providing excellent access points for students, researchers, and anyone wanting to know more. Additionally, maps, photographs, and appendixes of supplemental information aid high school and college students doing term papers or introductory research projects. In short, the historical dictionaries are the perfect starting point for anyone looking to research in these fields.

HISTORICAL DICTIONARIES OF RELIGIONS, PHILOSOPHIES, AND MOVEMENTS

Jon Woronoff, Series Editor

Orthodox Church, by Michael Prokurat, Alexander Golitzin, and Michael D. Peterson, 1996

Civil Rights Movement, by Ralph E. Luker, 1997

Catholicism, by William J. Collinge, 1997

North American Environmentalism, by Edward R. Wells and Alan M. Schwartz, 1997

Taoism, by Julian F. Pas in cooperation with Man Kam Leung, 1998

Gay Liberation Movement, by Ronald J. Hunt, 1999

Islamic Fundamentalist Movements in the Arab World, Iran, and Turkey, by Ahmad S. Moussalli, 1999

Cooperative Movement, by Jack Shaffer, 1999

Kierkegaard's Philosophy, by Julia Watkin, 2001

Slavery and Abolition, by Martin A. Klein, 2002

Prophets in Islam and Judaism, by Scott B. Noegel and Brannon M. Wheeler, 2002

Lesbian Liberation Movement: Still the Rage, by JoAnne Myers, 2003

Descartes and Cartesian Philosophy, by Roger Ariew, Dennis Des Chene, Douglas M. Jesseph, Tad M. Schmaltz, and Theo Verbeek, 2003

Witchcraft, by Michael D. Bailey, 2003

Unitarian Universalism, by Mark W. Harris, 2004

New Age Movements, by Michael York, 2004

Organized Labor, Second Edition, by James C. Docherty, 2004

Utopianism, by James M. Morris and Andrea L. Kross, 2004

Feminism, Second Edition, by Janet K. Boles and Diane Long Hoeveler, 2004

Jainism, by Kristi L. Wiley, 2004

Wittgenstein's Philosophy, by Duncan Richter, 2004

Schopenhauer's Philosophy, by David E. Cartwright, 2005

Seventh-day Adventists, by Gary Land, 2005

Methodism, Second Edition, by Charles Yrigoyen Jr. and Susan E. Warrick, 2005

Sufism, by John Renard, 2005

Sikhism, Second Edition, by W. H. McLeod, 2005

Kant and Kantianism, by Helmut Holzhey and Vilem Mudroch, 2005

Olympic Movement, Third Edition, by Bill Mallon with Ian Buchanan, 2006

Anglicanism, by Colin Buchanan, 2006

Welfare State, Second Edition, by Bent Greve, 2006

Feminist Philosophy, by Catherine Villanueva Gardner, 2006

Logic, by Harry J. Gensler, 2006

Leibniz's Philosophy, by Stuart Brown and Nicholas J. Fox, 2006

Calvinism, by Stuart D. B. Picken, 2012

Hobbes's Philosophy, by Juhana Lemetti, 2012

Historical Dictionary of the Chinese Communist Party, by Lawrence R. Sullivan, 2012

New Religious Movements, Second Edition, by George D. Chryssides, 2012

Catholicism, Second Edition, by William J. Collinge, 2012

Radical Christianity, by William H. Brackney, 2012

Organized Labor, Third Edition, by James C. Docherty and Sjaak van der Velden, 2012

Islamic Fundamentalism, by Mathieu Guidère, 2012

Witchcraft, Second Edition, by Jonathan Durrant and Michael D. Bailey, 2013

Historical Dictionary of Witchcraft

Second Edition

Jonathan Durrant and Michael D. Bailey

The Scarecrow Press, Inc.
Lanham • Toronto • Plymouth, UK
2012

Published by Scarecrow Press, Inc.
A wholly owned subsidary of The Rowman & Littlefield Publishing Group, Inc.
4501 Forbes Boulevard, Suite 200, Lanham, Maryland 20706
http://www.scarecrowpress.com

10 Thornbury Road, Plymouth PL6 7PP, United Kingdom

British Library Cataloguing in Publication Information Available

Library of Congress Cataloging-in-Publication Data

Durrant, Jonathan B. (Jonathan Bryan)
Historical dictionary of witchcraft. — 2nd ed. / Jonathan Durrant, Michael D. Bailey.
p. cm.
Includes bibliographical references (p.).
ISBN 978-0-8108-7245-5 (cloth : alk. paper) — ISBN 978-0-8108-7512-8 (ebook)
1. Witchcraft—History—Dictionaries. I. Bailey, Michael David, 1971–. II. Bailey, Michael David,
1971–. Historical dictionary of witchcraft. III. Title.
BF1566.B25 2013
133.4'303—dc23
2012021267

Printed in the United States of America

Contents

Editor's Foreword

Does it make sense to publish a book on witchcraft at the beginning of the 21st century? Most definitely so. Without a good knowledge of this presently somewhat unfamiliar subject, one cannot understand earlier periods in Europe and North America where there was a widespread concern about witches intense enough to culminate in witch-hunts and burnings. Nor can one understand the situation in many other ancient and even present-day "primitive" cultures, where the belief in creatures resembling witches was and is quite strong. The information in this book is also instrumental to understanding the emergence of modern witchcraft, also known as Wicca, as well as popular culture's abiding fascination with ghosts and other specters.

Most of the second edition of this *Historical Dictionary of Witchcraft* concentrates on witchcraft in the older, more traditional sense. The dictionary section therefore includes entries on people who strongly influenced the mood of the times: writing about witches and how to find them, bringing them to trial and sometimes having them convicted, or defending them and gradually convincing the broader society that perhaps those persecuted were not actually witches (and perhaps that there was no such thing). Other entries address how it was ascertained if someone was a witch, how confessions were extracted from such a person, what the punishment should be, and why so many witches were women. But the most intriguing entries are often about similar phenomena in other cultures, and about the return of witchcraft in the West—long after it had seemingly disappeared—and in surprising new forms. This trajectory is easier to follow thanks to a brief chronology, easier to understand thanks to a general introduction, and easier to research thanks to a substantial bibliography. Moreover, the information base is expanded in this second edition, building on an already strong first edition, with more entries and related reading.

The authors of both editions of this book are academics rather than practicing witches, as is increasingly the custom. So they have viewed the subject of witchcraft from without and not within, which is often a better and obviously less biased vantage point. Michael D. Bailey studied medieval European history in both Europe and the United States, held positions in several American universities, and is now associate professor of history at Iowa State University. He has written many articles and books, including *Battling Demons: Witchcraft, Heresy, and Reform in the Late Middle Ages* and *Magic and Superstition in Europe: A Concise History from Antiquity to the Present*. The author of this second, expanded edition, Jonathan Durrant, is also a scholar who teaches early modern history and other subjects at the University of Glamorgan in Wales. While focusing mainly on witchcraft in early modern Europe, he has expanded the coverage of this book to other times and places. Over the years, he has written various articles and recently the book *Witchcraft, Gender, and Society in Early Modern Germany*. The two of them have produced something far from hocus pocus, about a topic that has been around for centuries and does not seem quite ready to go away.

Jon Woronoff
Series Editor

Acknowledgments

My thanks go first to Michael Bailey, whose original text provided a sure foundation on which to expand the scope of the entries, and Jon Woronoff, who invited me to undertake this expansion and the several revisions in the light of recent scholarship but who has had to wait very patiently for me to finish them. My thanks also go to my colleagues at the University of Glamorgan, whose work, like mine, has been interrupted by upheaval and uncertainties but who have continued to nurture a productive intellectual environment. As always, I am grateful to Julia and my three boys, William, Adam, and Toben, who have not always understood why I would want to rewrite the dictionary!

Jonathan Durrant

Chronology

ca. 1750 BCE The Code of Hammurabi, one of the first written law codes, contains sections dealing with magic and legal charges of sorcery and witchcraft.

ca. 400 BCE By this time, magicians (*magoi*) come to have a very negative reputation in ancient Greece. They are condemned by Plato, among others.

ca. 150–400 CE Early Christian writers such as Tertullian, Origen, and John Chrysostom condemn magic by associating it with demonic forces, while defending Christian miracles as nonmagical.

375 The Council of Laodicaea forbids Christian clergy from practicing any form of magic.

425 Augustine completes *The City of God*, sections of which become foundational for later Christian demonology and the theory of demonic pacts associated with magic and witchcraft.

438 The imperial law code of Theodosius II prescribes severe penalties for those convicted of practicing magic or divination.

529 The code of Justinian reiterates earlier severe penalties for magic and divination.

789 Charlemagne issues legislation against sorcerers and magicians for his entire kingdom.

ca. 906 An early version of the canon *Episcopi*, describing groups of women who believe that they fly through the night with the goddess Diana, appears in a collection of legal canons made by Regino of Prüm.

1022 The first known burning of heretics in medieval Europe occurs at Orléans.

ca. 1140 Gratian's *Decretum*, one of the first standard texts of medieval canon law, includes several sections dealing with magic, sorcery, and superstition, including a version of the canon *Episcopi*.

1184 Pope Lucius III issues the decree *Ad abolendam*, which orders bishops and other ecclesiastical officials to rigorously investigate cases of heresy.

1215 The Fourth Lateran Council of the church regularizes procedures to be used against heretics.

1231 Pope Gregory IX commissions the first papally appointed inquisitors to hear cases involving heresy.

1233 Pope Gregory IX issues the decree *Vox in Rama*, in which he describes heretics gathering to worship a demon in the form of a toad or a pallid man, and then engaging in sexual orgies, similar to later notions of the witches' sabbath.

ca. 1250–1275 Thomas Aquinas establishes much of the basic scholastic understanding of magic and demonology in his many theological works, including his *Summa contra gentiles* (Summa against the Gentiles) and *Summa theologiae* (Summa of Theology).

1258 Pope Alexander IV orders papal inquisitors not to inquire into matters of sorcery unless the sorcery also involves "manifest heresy," primarily meaning the worship of demons.

1307–1314 Arrest and trial of the Knights Templar in France. Although charges of sorcery do not figure significantly in these events, the trial exhibits many of the features that later characterize the witchcraft trials, including diabolism, conspiracy theories, and forced confessions.

1324–1325 Trial of Lady Alice Kytler in Kilkenny, Ireland, for practicing sorcery with the aid of a demon.

ca. 1324 The inquisitor Bernard Gui writes his handbook *Practica inquisitionis heretice pravitatis* (The Practice of Inquisition into Heretical Depravity), which includes sections on sorcery and demonic magic.

1326 Pope John XXII issues the decretal *Super illius specula*, in which he declares a blanket excommunication on anyone who summons demons or enters into pacts with them for the purpose of performing sorcery.

1376 The inquisitor Nicolau Eymeric writes his highly influential inquisitorial manual *Directorium inquisitorum* (Directory of Inquisitors), in which he proves the necessarily heretical nature of all magic involving the invocation of demons, and hence the legal jurisdiction of ecclesiastical inquisitors over most types of sorcery.

1398 The theological faculty of the University of Paris condemns various forms of superstition and the practice of sorcery in 28 articles.

ca. 1400 One of the earliest known witch-hunts in European history (although in reality the trials probably dealt with simply sorcery and *maleficium*) takes places in the Simme valley in the western Alps.

1426 The Franciscan preacher and moral reformer Bernardino of Siena witnesses an early trial for witchcraft in Rome.

1427–1436 First major witch-hunts in Europe are carried out in Savoy, Dauphiné, and the Valais; they are discussed at the Council of Basel (1431–1449).

ca. 1428 The Lucerne chronicler Hans Fründ describes witchcraft in the diocese of Sion in the western Alps.

ca. 1436 Claude Tholosan, a secular judge in the French region of Dauphiné, writes a treatise *Ut magorum et maleficiorum errores manifesti ignorantibus fiant* (That the Errors of Magicians and Witches may be made Clear to the Ignorant), detailing the practices of witchcraft based on trials he had conducted in Dauphiné and arguing that secular courts should have jurisdiction over this crime. Also around this time, an anonymous clerical author writes *Errores Gazariorum* (Errors of the Gazarii), a brief but extremely lurid description of witchcraft and the witches' sabbath.

1436–1438 The Dominican theologian Johannes Nider writes his *Formicarius* (The Anthill), a long moralizing treatise containing some of the most extensive early accounts of witchcraft to appear in Europe.

1440–1442 The French critic Martin Le Franc writes the long poem *Le Champion des Dames* (Defender of the Ladies), which includes a section on witchcraft.

1458 The French inquisitor Nicholas Jacquier writes the influential treatise *Flagellum haereticorum fascinariorum* (Scourge of Heretical Witches), one of the first major treatises devoted exclusively to witchcraft and witch-hunting.

1474 Heinrich Kramer (Institoris) is made inquisitor in southern Germany, where he presides over numerous witchcraft trials.

1478 The Spanish Inquisition is established.

1484 Pope Innocent VIII issues the bull *Summis desiderantes affectibus*, ordering that inquisitors in German lands should not be hindered or prevented from exercising their authority in matters of sorcery and witchcraft. The bull is later included in the *Malleus maleficarum*.

1486 *Malleus maleficarum* (Hammer of the Witches) is written by the Dominican inquisitor Heinrich Kramer.

1487 *Malleus maleficarum* is published in the first of many printed editions.

ca. 1500–1575 The steady rise in the number of witchcraft trials, evident since the early 15th century levels off, in this period, and in many areas the number of witchcraft trials actually declines.

1523 The *Carolina* legal code is enacted for all lands of the German Empire. It deals, in part, with matters of witchcraft.

1542 The Roman Inquisition is established by Pope Paul III.

1563 A Statute ordering the death penalty for witches is passed in England. Stringent witchcraft laws are also passed in Scotland. Johann Weyer publishes *De praestigiis daemonum* (On the Deceptions of Demons), a treatise that is skeptical of various aspects of witchcraft.

1566 The first major witchcraft trials in England take place at Chelmsford, Essex.

ca. 1575–1675 Witch-hunting reaches its height in most regions of Europe.

1580 The French political philosopher Jean Bodin publishes his very influential treatise on demonology and witchcraft, *De la démonomanie des sorciers* (On the Demonomania of Witches).

1582–1594 A series of witch-trials take place in the archbishopric and electoral principality of Trier in the German Empire.

1584 The skeptical English thinker Reginald Scot publishes his *Discoverie of Witchcraft*.

1589 Dietrich Flade, vice governor of Trier, is executed for witchcraft; he is the highest ranking victim of any witch-hunt in Europe. Peter Binsfeld, suffragan bishop of Trier, writes a *Tractatus de confessionibus maleficorum et sagarum* (On the Confessions of Witches), defending the necessity of witchcraft trials and the procedures used in them.

1590–1591 A group of supposed witches from North Berwick, Scotland, are put on trial; the Scottish king takes part in the proceedings.

1593 The skeptical theologian Cornelius Loos, who had criticized a recent wave of witch-hunting in Trier, is forced to recant publicly. He is then exiled from Trier to Brussels.

1595 The French magistrate and important demonologist Nicolas Rémy publishes his *Daemonolatria* (Demonolatry).

1597 King James VI of Scotland (from 1603 also James I of England) publishes his *Daemonologie* (Demonology).

1599 The first edition of the Jesuit Martin Del Rio's *Disquisitiones magicarum* (Disquisitions on Magic) is published.

1604 A new witchcraft act is passed in England, establishing harsher penalties for the crime.

1608 The Italian friar Francesco Maria Guazzo publishes his *Compendium maleficarum* (Handbook of Witches), which becomes the most important and influential such manual used in Italy. In England, William Perkins' *Discourse on the Damned Art of Witchcraft* is published posthumously.

1609–1614 A major outbreak of witch-hunting occurs in the Basque lands in southwestern France and northern Spain.

1611–1633 Intense witch-hunting takes place in several Catholic territories in southern Germany, including Bamberg, Eichstätt, and Würzburg.

1631 The German Jesuit Friedrich Spee publishes the *Cautio criminalis* (Warning for Prosecutors) anonymously. It is a harsh critique of the procedures by which most witchcraft trials are conducted.

1633–1634 A famous case of mass possession occurs among nuns in a convent at Loudun, France.

1645–1646 The infamous witch-hunter Matthew Hopkins directs the most intense witch-hunt in English history, primarily in the counties of Essex and Suffolk, leading to the execution of more than 200 victims.

1661–1662 During the "great Scottish witch-hunt," hundreds of trials and executions occur throughout the country.

1669 Severe witch-hunts occur in Mora in central Sweden. These in turn help to trigger hunts in other areas of the country.

ca. 1675–1750 In this period, most regions in Europe see a steady reduction and end of witch-hunting.

1682 Following the "Affair of the Poisons," King Louis XIV reclassifies the crime of witchcraft in France as mere "superstition," no longer warranting capital punishment, effectively ending legally sanctioned witch-hunting in the country.

1689 Cotton Mather preaches about the dangers of witchcraft in Boston, Massachusetts.

1692 The famous witchcraft trials of Salem, Massachusetts, take place.

1712 Jane Wenham becomes the last witch convicted and sentenced to death in England. She is reprieved.

1736 The Witchcraft Act of 1604 is repealed in Great Britain, effectively decriminalizing witchcraft in that country.

1782 Anna Göldi is executed in the Swiss Canton of Glarus. This is the last execution for witchcraft carried out under full and unequivocal legal sanction in Europe.

1793 Local courts sentence to death two convicted witches in Posnan (now in Poland, then under Prussian authority). If they had been able to act, higher authorities would almost certainly have prevented the executions.

1828 The German scholar Karl-Ernst Jarcke advances the argument that historical witchcraft was actually a pre-Christian, pagan religion.

1888 The Hermetic Order of the Golden Dawn, an elite secret society devoted to ritual magic, is founded in England.

1899 The amateur folklorist Charles Leland publishes *Aradia, or the Gospel of the Witches*, an account of the history and beliefs of the supposedly ancient religion of witchcraft in Italy.

1921 The British academic Margaret Murray publishes *The Witch-Cult in Western Europe*, the first of three studies in which she argued that historical witchcraft was actually a form of ancient pagan fertility religion.

1935–1943 The Nazi Hexen-Sonderkommando (Special Witch Command) collates information about witches persecuted in Germany in an attempt to prove that witchcraft was a pagan cult persecuted by Christian authorities.

1937 British anthropologist E. E. Evans-Pritchard publishes *Witchcraft, Oracles and Magic among the Azande*, a very influential study of African systems of magic and witchcraft.

1944 The mediums Helen Duncan and Jane Yorke become the last people to be tried and convicted under the British Witchcraft Act of 1736.

1951 The British Witchcraft Act of 1736 is repealed in the Fraudulent Mediums Act.

1954 Gerald Gardner publishes *Witchcraft Today*, laying the foundations for modern witchcraft, or Wicca.

1962–present Witch-hunting occurs throughout Africa, claiming many thousands of victims, notably in Tanzania, South Africa, Zambia, and the Central African Republic.

1966 Anton Le Vey founds the Church of Satan in San Francisco, the most important group within modern Satanism. The movement is not, however, associated in any direct way with modern Wicca.

1971 Keith Thomas publishes *Religion and the Decline of Magic*, marking the beginning of a new historiography of witchcraft "from below."

1972 In a decision by the Internal Revenue Service, the Church of Wicca becomes the first Wiccan organization to achieve official federal recognition in the United States.

1989 The British academic Tanya Luhrmann publishes *Persuasions of the Witch's Craft*, the first major study of modern witchcraft done outside the movement.

1999 Ronald Hutton publishes *The Triumph of the Moon*, the first major academic study of modern witchcraft and neo-paganism.

2005 Three Angolans are jailed in England for their involvement in the torture of an eight-year-old girl whom they believed to be a witch.

2009 Daniel Bogado releases his documentary *World of Witchcraft* about witch trials in the Central African Republic.

Introduction

Witchcraft has proven an important, if difficult, historical subject to investigate and interpret over the last four decades or so. Modern historical research into witchcraft began as an attempt to tease out the worldview of ordinary people in 16th- and 17th-century England, but quickly expanded to encompass the history of witchcraft in most cultures and societies that have existed. Much has been written, and remains to be written, about the great European witch-hunts of the period from the early 15th into the 18th centuries, but scholarly studies now extend back to the time of earliest law code that punished sorcery, the Babylonian Code of Hammurabi (1792–1750 BCE), and forward to the last witchcraft cases in England, those of Helen Duncan and Jane Yorke, tried in 1944. There has also been a significant amount of interest in the development of the modern religion of witchcraft, or Wicca, as various forms of neo-paganism continue to attract adherents.

The importance of studying witchcraft has been highlighted by recent events in Africa. In parts of sub-Saharan Africa, secular authorities and evangelical church leaders have been punishing alleged witches on a scale that dwarfs that of the early-modern witch-hunts. There are a lot of similarities between the two series of hunts, despite their appearance on different continents: As in Europe, the dominant church, in this case the evangelical church, has promoted witch accusations and witch-hunting in some African countries; it has been supported by laws and justice systems; in hard times, people have rejected providential or natural reasons for the inexplicable misfortunes they suffer, preferring to see themselves as the victims of evil; the marginalized (mainly women and children) have become the main victims of the hunts; lynchings are common; and skeptics and opponents are harassed and accused of witchcraft in their turn. The major difference between witch-hunting in Europe and Africa is in the volume of executions. In Africa, accused witches are generally believed to be possessed and are therefore exorcized; in western and central Europe, convicted witches were often burned at the stake (or hanged in England and its colonies). Despite the scale of witch-hunting in Africa and the similarities to the European experience, there has, unfortunately, been little media interest in it.

Although one can point to continuities and similarities in the history of witchcraft across the world, definitions of witchcraft remain partial. It has not always been easy to identify where witchcraft differs from the low forms of magic employed by cunning men and women, the religious practices of priests, or the high, ritual magic of the learned, which might include alche-

1

my, astronomy, or divination. Even influential theologians from the time of the Church Fathers down to the present have struggled to separate different means of dealing with occult, or hidden, spiritual forces. Historically—and anthropologically—witchcraft is often regarded as the manipulation of evil forces, like demons, by someone who was born with, or had been taught, the necessary power to do it. This definition does not include practitioners of love magic or magical healing, or shamanistic groups like the *benandanti* of early-modern Italy. While these people believed that they could manipulate the spirit world, they regarded themselves as Christian and benevolent, and often stated in witchcraft trials that they could unwitch, but not bewitch, their neighbors. Such a definition also excludes alleged witches in early-modern Spain and its territories, for example, where witchcraft continued to be treated as a delusion, produced by the devil, long after demonologists in western and central Europe had accepted that witchcraft was a heresy that needed to be eradicated. The Spanish Inquisition therefore handed down only light punishments for the sin of witchcraft. In modern times, witchcraft has been regarded by its practitioners, but not by some of the more fundamentalist Christian groups, as a benevolent practice in tune with the natural world.

The scope and complexity of historical witchcraft makes the writing of a dictionary on it quite difficult. The original focus of the first edition of this dictionary was "the historical phenomenon of witchcraft as defined and constructed in Europe during the era of the great witch-hunts." In general, this focus has been preserved in the present edition. After all, in a European and New World context, witchcraft was a significant phenomenon. It has been estimated that there were about 100,000 witchcraft trials in later medieval and early-modern Europe and its colonies, and that the number of executions for the crime exceeded 50,000. Friends, family, and neighbors would have been touched in some way by these events, as would the vast number of people who came to know them through the news media of the day. Many of these trials and executions were concentrated on the emerging nation-states that came to dominate the history of the modern era: Germany, France, and Great Britain. On the other hand, quite small outbreaks have become an important part of the history of other nations. The Salem witch trials ended in only 19 executions, but are probably among the most well-known in the world, and are integral to the story of the United States not least because they offered Arthur Miller an analogy for the McCarthyite trials of the 1950s.

The geography of witch-hunting demands an explanation: why did it occur in western and central Europe rather than its south and east? The chronology of witch-hunting, beginning in the Renaissance, continuing throughout the Protestant and Catholic Reformations and the Scientific Revolution, and ending during the Enlightenment, also needs to be explained. Witchcraft beliefs can no longer be thought of as an aberration, the remnants of pagan beliefs that had survived in obscure corners of Europe. Why, then, did quite rational thinkers like Jean Bodin ignore the few skeptics who did exist and write on the demonomania of witchcraft as if it were a potent threat? And why did women make up such a high proportion—about 75 percent—of those accused of the crime? Indeed, why were men sometimes also prosecuted as witches, in some places in large numbers? This dictionary cannot hope to answer any of these questions adequately, but it does attempt to show where research is being done and what interpretations are being offered in witchcraft historiography.

While entries relating to the European witch-hunts continue to dominate this edition of the dictionary, primarily because they have increased in number to reflect a larger scope of research, more entries on witchcraft and related practices in other parts of the world have been included to give greater context. In part, this knowledge, especially where it has been derived from anthropological scholarship, has enabled historians to understand how witchcraft beliefs are structured and function. It is also important, however, because syncretic religions like Voodoo have become part of western culture. Not only have they migrated from the Caribbean and parts of South and Central America to urban centers in the United States, they originated in European Catholicism and the slave trade, and have come to stand, wrongly, for evil or the occult in films and pulp fiction. Indeed, witchcraft has been a common theme in art, fiction, and plays since witch-hunting began, and in opera and popular music of the modern era. The merging of witchcraft elements from different cultures in a more global environment, fed by the ease with which people can gain an eclectic range of knowledge from television and the Internet, means that a broader scope of entries is needed to help readers negotiate and understand the history of witchcraft. The arts, literature, and music are also the primary routes by which some people come to be interested in the subject of witchcraft, although they tend to offer a simplistic understanding of historical witchcraft and the different cultural perceptions of the subject.

DEFINITIONS

At one level, the presence of something like witchcraft across all recorded human history suggests that it is fundamental to understanding human societies and cultures, and the fears and cosmologies of individuals or groups of people. The problem with this level of understanding is that one might assume that a definition of witchcraft will be relatively fixed and unchanging. In fact, the concept of witchcraft does change depending on the historical period in question, the place in which it has been located, and the individual opinions of those who recorded its presence. There were, for example, no witch-hunts before the early 15th century in Christian Europe. At a basic level, all medieval and early-modern witches were guilty of following the devil, and at least believing that they manipulated occult forces for their own nefarious purposes. The 10th-century canon *Episcopi*, however, described witchcraft as a delusion created by the devil. The followers of Diana, its author stated, were deceived into believing that they performed harmful sorcery. Their only crimes were to allow themselves to be tempted by the devil and to endanger the souls of other women whom they might deceive into doing the same; it was for these that they had to be punished.

By the end of the 14th century, Nicolau Eymeric had argued, convincingly for many, that sorcery necessarily involved apostasy, idolatry, and therefore heresy. Shortly after, the first witch heretics were persecuted in Switzerland and parts of France and Italy, and the new stereotype of heretical witchcraft—a diabolical sect of sinners, mainly women, who worshiped the devil at sabbaths and really harmed their neighbors and crops—had arrived. Witches were no longer deluded; they were a potent threat to the lives and souls of Christians. It was this stereotype that became the foundation of later witchcraft persecutions in Europe, supported by a series of demonologies beginning with the work of Johannes Nider in the early 1400s. Once printing became commonplace, other texts, like Heinrich Kramer's *Malleus maleficarum* (ca. 1486), developed and disseminated the idea of the female witch sect. The witch trials that did occur only served to reinforce this conception of witchcraft, at least in parts of western and central Europe. As the notion of the witch sect spread, so too did the Latin and vernacular vocabularies used to describe it, helping to link diabolical witchcraft with local versions of witchcraft, magic, and sorcery.

Not all theologians or other thinkers in Europe shared this understanding of witchcraft, however. Throughout the period of the great witch-hunts, there existed a strong line of skeptics who argued that the witches were deluded or ill, that the biblical injunction "Thou shalt not suffer a witch to live" and the story of the Witch of Endor were based on mistranslations, that torture forced the innocent to confess to acts that they had never done, or that witchcraft simply did not exist. Skepticism was also evident in the plays written and produced in Jacobean England, and the verdicts arrived at by juries in places like Essex that were as likely to be "not guilty" as "guilty." Complete skepticism about the power and danger posed by witches increased markedly after the mid-17th century, and, as it became more prevalent, witchcraft trials died out, followed shortly by the repeal of much witchcraft legislation. Witchcraft beliefs did, of course, persist at all levels, and there were instances of lynchings in many places and large-scale persecutions in 18th-century Hungary, but the last European witch was executed in Switzerland in 1782.

The definitions of witchcraft used in the later Middle Ages and the early-modern period meant that witch-hunters were predisposed to find witches among certain groups of people, and treat witchcraft in very specific ways. Early demonology, based on ancient associations of women with harmful sorcery in myth and legend, assumed that witches would usually be women rather than men. Women on the margins of society, particularly elderly, poor women, tended to be more vulnerable to witchcraft accusations because they lacked the protection of male relatives. Such women were on the increase in early-modern Europe because of the intensification of the so-called Little Ice Age and the agrarian crises and inflationary cycles that it produced, notably in the late 16th and early 17th centuries when witch-hunting was at its height. The treatment of witchcraft as a *crimen exceptum* (exceptional crime) in many jurisdictions meant that accusations against individual women could escalate into a full-blown witch persecution. In these jurisdictions, the normal restraints on torture were removed, witnesses who would not otherwise be able to testify (notably children and known enemies) were allowed to give evidence, and, on occasion, spectral evidence was accepted. Witch-suspects could therefore be forced to confess to all elements of the diabolical version of witchcraft and name the accomplices they had seen at the witches' sabbaths. In these circumstances, witchcraft trials could continue until the authorities tired of persecution or other events, such as invasion by enemies, intervened. The confessions of witches produced at the height of the witch-hunts provided witch-hunters with confirmation of the extent of the witch sect's activities and further details about its practices.

PRECEDENTS: MAGIC AND RELIGION IN THE ANCIENT AND MEDIEVAL WORLDS

The early 15th-century figure of the witch as someone who worshiped demons and the devil, and performed harmful sorcery through the agency of demons had precedents in the ancient world. The Babylonian Code of Hammurabi recognized that individuals might practice malevolent forms of sorcery to harm or injure people and their property. In Europe, at least by the fifth century BCE, the beginning of the golden age of the Greek city-states, religion was being defined in relation to magic, opposing the public and communal cults of the states with other private, secretive, or anti-social systems for accessing supernatural power. While priests would engage with deities and the spirit world for the greater civic good, and functioned to maintain stability and social order, magicians in ancient Greece tended to be private individuals working for their own gain or selling their magical services to neighbors who needed supernatural aid. Like the Christians who were later to adopt the classical pagan terms *lamia* and *strix* as words for witch, the ancient Greeks aligned magical practice with alien cultures, notably that of the Persians: The Greek word *mageia* derived from the Greek name for the Persian priestly cast. Magic was a practice of the other, the outsider in Greek society. The Greeks also used the word *goeteia* to describe lower forms of magic, even further removed from religious ritual than *mageia*, and this concept is perhaps the closest ancient approximation to later European witchcraft. In practice, the distinction between religion and magic in Greek religion and mythology was blurred and ambiguous. The demigoddesses Medea and Circe were both associated with magic and witchcraft while each retaining her spiritual status. Such blurring of the boundaries between religion and magic allowed medieval Christians to transform Medea and Circe into witches that would contribute to the development of the later idea of witchcraft.

The ancient Greek definition of magic as harmful, anti-social and associated with the priests of foreign religions was mirrored in ancient Hebrew tradition. In the Book of Exodus in the Bible, Moses and Aaron confront the Pharaoh during the Israelites' captivity in Egypt (Exodus 7:8–12). Commanded by the Pharaoh to demonstrate the power of the Hebrew god, Aaron casts down his staff and it turns into a serpent. Using enchantments, the Pharaoh's priests (called "wise men," "sorcerers," and "magicians" in the King James' version of the Bible) replicate the miracle, but their serpent is devoured by Aaron's, thus proving the superiority of divine power. Later, in 1 Kings 18:20–40, the prophet Elijah challenges the priests of Baal, who have been corrupting the people of Israel, to built an altar upon which to sacrifice a bullock and pray to their gods to light the sacrificial fire. Although they try for many hours, their gods do not provide fire. Elijah then builds his altar and douses his bullock in water, but at his prayer, a great fire descends from heaven and consumes the sacrifice. Apart from these demonstrations of the divine power of the Hebrew god over the magic of foreign priests, the Israelites were commanded not to permit a sorcerer or seer (Hebrew *kashaph*) to live, rendered famously, if inaccurately, in the 17th-century King James' translation: "Thou shalt not suffer a witch to live" (Exodus 22:18). The magic of these sorcerers or seers was considered criminal because it was believed to be harmful. King Saul is described as acting on this command in 1 Samuel 28:3, driving out all the sorcerers and diviners from his kingdom because they threatened its stability. It was for this reason that the Witch of Endor feared meeting the king when he came to ask her to conjure up the spirit of Samuel.

Despite the stories and commandments recorded in the Old Testament, Judaism did not develop a clearly defined concept of the devil. This only occurred in early Christianity. Evil did not then exist as an ontological concept; it was merely an absence of good. The devil could not therefore create evil. Rather, the devil was permitted by God to tempt people into sin (and away from God's grace) as a punishment or test of their faith. He and his demons were also permitted to work wonders in contrast to the miracles performed by holy men and women with the aid of God, but these demonic wonders were really only illusions. In the apocryphal rivalry between the apostle Peter and the magician Simon Magus, first alluded to in Acts 8:9–24, Simon Magus was reported to have tried to fly up to heaven. At a word from Peter, however, Simon Magus crashed to the ground. Simon Magus's transport was, it transpired, merely an illusion created by the invisible demons who were carrying him; Peter's power over them was miraculous.

As demonology developed, the devil and his demons began to play a regular and more consistent role in the world. Saint Augustine of Hippo, who lived from 354 to 430 CE, described the world in terms of a struggle between divine and demonic forces in his most influential work *The City of God*, although he was careful not to allow the devil the power to create evil in the world without God's permission. In this struggle, harmful sorcery was demonic. Human magicians had to make a pact with the devil, renouncing their faith, and worship him in place of God. At this stage, however, redemption was still possible, as the legend of the sixth-century Saint Theophilus of Adana was to show. He had made a pact with the devil, but, showing repentance, was released from it by the intercession of the Virgin Mary. The sorcery caused by a magician or a witch was also likely to be illusory, the result of the devil deluding his follower into believing that he or she had caused events that God had already ordained would happen anyway.

This concept of sorcery as a delusion was repeated in the canon *Episcopi*, first collected in the 10th century. Although this canon warned bishops to be vigilant in the eradication of *sortilegium* (divination) and *maleficium* (harmful sorcery) in their dioceses, and described the groups of women who were believed to ride with the pagan goddess Diana across the night sky, it did not advocate the execution of witches. Punishments for sorcery in late Christian Antiquity were therefore relatively mild—involving penance and correction—as the church authorities sought to win back the soul for Christ rather than eradicate a sect of heretical magicians. This seems to have been the approach taken by the church authorities when they first had to deal with the influx of pagan Germanic tribes into the territories of the Western Roman Empire: The conversion of pagans, the correction of erroneous beliefs, and the eradication of superstitions. In this context, demonic power was not regarded as a serious or organized threat to faithful Christians.

Where sorcery was prosecuted in the early Middle Ages, trials tended to be conducted by secular authorities. In Germanic law codes, as in ancient ones, harmful sorcery was defined as a felony and practitioners were punished not for their apostasy or heresy (which were left to the church courts), but for the harm they had done. They were not, however, generally accused of belonging to a devil-worshiping cult and acting in concert with other sorcerers. The existence of such laws against harmful sorcery indicate that secular authorities rejected the concept of sorcery as a delusion and regarded it as one possible means to commit crime against persons or their property. Trials seem, however, to have been rare, and the persecution of sorcerers even rarer. It may be that the foundation of law and justice in the early-medieval period, accusatorial procedure, limited the number of accusations of sorcery and witchcraft against suspected individuals.

In accusatorial procedure, private individuals brought cases against each other, and plaintiffs were responsible for prosecuting a case and providing evidence of the guilt of the person accused. It was particularly difficult to offer hard evidence or reliable witnesses for crimes that were secretive by nature, such as poisoning or sorcery. To determine these cases, judicial ordeal, or for the elites trial by combat, was permitted. Judicial ordeal placed the judgment of a case in the hands of God, who would protect those accused who were innocent. The accused might be made to grasp heated iron for a length of time. The wound was then observed over a period of days, and, if it was judged to have healed sufficiently, the person was declared innocent. Apart from being unreliable as a means of determining innocence, accusers might have been reluctant to bring forward cases of sorcery because the law of *talion* would be applied if they could not prove their case. The law of *talion* was designed to prevent frivolous cases being prosecuted by applying the punishment for the crime to the unsuccessful accuser in instances where the ordeal proved the innocence of the accused. It is, however, difficult to determine how much of a barrier to prosecution this law was in practice.

Around the 12th century, Roman law was rediscovered across Europe, and states began to replace accusatorial procedure with the new legal method of inquisitorial procedure. Private persons could still bring accusations under this system, but judges could now also initiate inquests themselves. In either case, after the initial accusation, the responsibility for prosecuting the case lay with the judges or magistrates. Ordeal was replaced with more rational methods of investigation, like the examination of witnesses, the interrogation of suspects, and the collection of other material evidence. In secretive crimes, like sorcery, the problem of evidence and witnesses remained, making prosecutions difficult unless the accused confessed. It was assumed that people would lie to protect themselves and the judges were therefore permitted to use torture. It was also recognized, however, that excessive torture could force virtually anyone to confess, and restrictions were placed on the types of torture and the frequency with which they could be employed. In cases of witchcraft, these restrictions were sometimes ignored or they were relaxed, but not to the extent that happened in central Europe toward the end of the Middle Ages.

During the medieval period, the legal basis and methods for persecution without serious consequences for the accuser had been laid, but witch-hunts could not happen if there was not also a belief that a widespread sect of diabolical witches existed as a real threat to society. This belief began to coalesce in the 12th century just as Roman law began to replace local legal systems. The so-called Renaissance of the 12th century saw the rediscovery and study of classical Greek and Roman, Hebrew, and Arabic texts among the educated, mainly clerical, elites of Europe. These texts included learned treatises on magical arts, alchemy, astrology, and divination, often performed through the invocation of spirits or demons. They confirmed what scholars already knew from the works of early church fathers, like Saint Augustine, that demonic magic did exist as a force in the world. Scholars and papal inquisitors could even read about or see the effects of demonic activity in the church's encounters with heretical sects, principally the Cathars and the Waldensians. By the middle of the 13th century, the great scholastic authority Thomas Aquinas was devoting a significant proportion of his major theological works to the exploration and explanation of the power of demons. Over time, Aquinas's works became influential at the highest levels of the church hierarchy. Pope John XXII, who held the post from 1316 until 1334, ordered papal inquisitors to take action against demonic sorcery, and he passed an automatic sentence of excommunication on anyone who engaged in such activities. It was only in the late 14th century, however, that the theologian and inquisitor Nicolau Eymeric crafted the definitive theological and legal argument that because demonic sorcery involved pacts with the devil and the worship of demons, and therefore both apostasy and idolatry, it was always heretical. Heresies, of course, usually flourished among groups of like-minded people, so the stage was now set to turn harmful sorcery performed by individuals into the witch sect.

THE EMERGENCE OF WITCHCRAFT AND THE AGE OF EUROPEAN WITCH-HUNTS

In the early 15th century, the fully developed idea of European witchcraft as a conspiracy of demonic sorcerers who worshiped the devil as part of a diabolical witch cult began to emerge. The first true witch-hunts took place at this time in and around the western Alps. Here, accusations of harmful and malevolent sorcery increased significantly, and the local judicial authorities, drawing on the idea of sorcery as a heresy, began to add their own notions of diabolism and demonic conspiracy, as well as local beliefs about everyday witchcraft and sorcery, into the trial processes and the witchcraft narratives they produced. The trials in this part of Europe also roughly coincided with the difficult Council of Basel, which met from 1431 until 1449. Basel was not far from the location of the witch-hunts, and interest in them may have been piqued more than usual by Pope Eugenius IV's accusations that Amadeus VIII, duke of Savoy, was tolerant of witches and witchcraft. Amadeus was defended by his secretary Martin Le Franc in *Le champion des dames* (The Defender of Ladies) and was duly elected anti-pope, Felix V. Several delegates to the Council, including Johannes Nider and Nicholas Jacquier, went on to write about the witch-hunts in the western Alps, drawing on the stories they had from witch-hunters, clergymen, and chroniclers.

Information about diabolical witchcraft was disseminated by men associated with the Council of Basel, and the witch-hunts gradually spread into other parts of Europe during the course of the late 15th century. This initial phase of the witch-hunts culminated in the publication of the most notorious medieval witch-hunting manual: the *Malleus maleficarum* (Hammer of the Witches), written by the Dominican inquisitor Heinrich Kramer Institoris in Latin and first printed in 1487. The *Malleus* never served as the definitive source on all aspects of witchcraft and demonology, but it did become very popular, and circulated widely in numerous editions. Unlike the work of such predecessors as Johannes Nider, on whom Kramer drew, the *Malleus* benefited from the new technology of printing. It also seemed to be endorsed by Pope Innocent VIII, who had issued the bull *Summis desiderantes affectibus* in 1484 demanding that local authorities support Kramer, Jakob Sprenger, a senior Dominican friar often cited as the co-author of the *Malleus*, and the University of Cologne, to which the spurious notarial approval appended to the *Malleus* was attributed.

As the *Malleus maleficarum* was being written, the individual witch trials and small-scale witch-hunts characteristic of the 15th century were beginning to die away. In fact, despite its later notoriety and widespread publication, no edition of the *Malleus* was published between 1521 and 1576. Kramer himself had sought papal support for his activities and written the *Malleus* in response to the opposition he had received from local clerical and secular authorities. This opposition arose, in part, from jealousy over the local jurisdictions that could be ignored by inquisitors like Kramer, but it may also have been informed by Renaissance humanism that was then influential across Europe. Many humanists were skeptical of witchcraft and the existence of a diabolical witch sect, although, like earlier skeptics such as the author of the canon *Episcopi*, they believed in the devil as well as God, and demons as well as angels. The Protestant Reformation may also have influenced the hiatus in witch-hunting during the early 16th century. Like the Renaissance humanists who remained in the Catholic church, Protestant theologians challenged the authority of late-medieval scholastic writings, but they did not deny the existence of the devil or demons. Over time, they did become more concerned with the devil and demons than many of their Catholic counterparts. In the short term, however, the Reformation gave European Christians on all sides new heretical enemies to deal with, enemies who genuinely threatened the political and spiritual stability of Europe, especially in the German Empire.

As well as developing a strong demonology of their own, Protestant theologians did what Kramer had advocated in the *Malleus maleficarum*, and handed authority over many spiritual crimes to the secular courts. During the course of the 16th century, especially after 1560, witchcraft was dealt with by secular laws in Protestant areas. This did not mean that church courts relinquished all control over witchcraft as a crime. In England, for example, the consistory and other church courts continued to prosecute witchcraft as an act of idolatry long after the Witchcraft Act of 1563, and some individuals were prosecuted in both church and secular courts. In general, however, witchcraft had become a felony in the Protestant lands of central and western Europe, and witches were prosecuted for the physical harm that they had allegedly caused to their neighbors. In Catholic territories the extent of secular jurisdiction over witchcraft was mixed. In France, the crime tended to be treated as a felony and prosecuted in the secular courts. In the Catholic territories of the German Empire, witch-hunting became part of the Catholic or Counter-Reformation agenda in ecclesiastical principalities and bishoprics, or places like the duchy of Bavaria ruled by very devout princes. In Spain, the Spanish Inquisition asserted its authority over witchcraft as a crime, and continued to treat it as a relatively minor error into which women were deluded by the devil; witchcraft was not therefore believed to pose a real physical threat to people, although it might still pose a spiritual threat to the souls of the weak.

The type of authority that oversaw witch trials had a direct impact on the extent of witch persecution. In Protestant England, juries tended to be cautious and often found witch-defendants not guilty; in Civil-War England and Puritan Salem, Massachusetts, the failure of the justice system led to outbreaks of witch-hunting in the 1640s and 1692 respectively. In France, appeals to the higher courts of the *parlements*, which often upheld appeals against convictions for witchcraft, limited the number of executions for the crime, while the rigor of witch persecution in Catholic Germany was the direct result of using specially-appointed witch commissions. In Spain, very few witch executions occurred because the Spanish Inquisition did not treat witchcraft as a *crimen exceptum* (exceptional crime), kept to its rules of prosecution, and sought mainly to correct errors of belief rather than eradicate a witch sect.

While the gradual adoption of Roman law and inquisitorial procedure, the evolution of a new demonology, the secularization of the crime of witchcraft in many parts of the continent, and the Catholic Reformation created structures that permitted the prosecution of heretical and harmful witches on a large scale, accusations of witchcraft arose out of more immediate changes and problems in 16th-century Europe. The most intense period of witch-hunting, from about 1560 to about 1630, coincided with the intensification of the Little Ice Age and increased religious warfare, particularly in France and the German Empire. Early-modern Europeans were engulfed by agrarian crises, inflationary cycles, wage depression, social dislocation, and constant stories, if not experiences, of war that only served to deepen the insecurities brought about by the Protestant and Catholic Reformations. These insecurities found a number of outlets ranging from popular revolt to witchcraft accusations.

In their turn, as the number and intensity of witch trials increased, demonologists on all sides resumed the publication of treatises on the subject. The *Malleus maleficarum* was reprinted in 1576 and several times thereafter, while contemporary works by Jean Bodin in 1580, Nicolas Rémy in 1595, Martín Del Rio in 1599, and Francesco Maria Guazzo in 1608, among many others, proved even more popular and influential. By the mid-17th century, however, witchcraft prosecutions began to decline sharply across much of Europe. There were some late outbreaks that occurred in particular local circumstances in Scotland and Sweden in the 1660s and 1670s respectively, in Salem in 1692, and Poland and Hungary in the 18th century. It was not until 1782 that the last witch, Anna Göldi, was executed in Switzerland. For the most part, however, witchcraft trials had ceased in western and central Europe by the 1640s and 1650s, and witchcraft legislation was repealed in the later 17th century (in 1682 in France) or early 18th century (in 1736 in England).

GENERAL NATURE OF WITCH-HUNTS

Although witch-hunts were common across Europe in the 16th and 17th centuries, it is difficult to generalize about them. The first observation to make is that the intensity of witch-hunting in a limited number of territories meant that most Europeans were not caught up in it. They were also unlikely to have any first-hand knowledge of isolated witchcraft trials. Early-modern England and Wales, for example, consisted of several thousand parishes, and large urban centers, like London where about a tenth of the population lived. There were constant witch trials in the counties surrounding London, notably in Essex, and in East Anglia, but those living in London itself or further afield rarely witnessed a witch trial, much less witch-hunting on the scale of that conducted by Matthew Hopkins during the Civil War. In fact, despite the numerous historical studies of witchcraft cases, ordinary people were slow to accuse their neighbors of using harmful sorcery to hurt them. They could draw upon many other well-versed explanations for misfortune, not least providence and nature. A related observation is that in areas where witchcraft was not prosecuted as a *crimen exceptum* (exceptional crime), such as England, Rothenburg ob der Tauber (in the German Empire), or Spain, neither juries, councillors, nor inquisitors were generally credulous of witchcraft. They may have believed in the existence of witches, and they may have read with fear the reports of witchcraft trials and witch-hunting in other places, but they had to be convinced by the best available evidence that their neighbors who were suspected of witchcraft had actually caused the harm of which they stood accused. Nevertheless, it seems that individual trials, based on the interpersonal animosities that are a characteristic of small, tightly-knit communities, especially those under the additional strain of agrarian and economic crises, could sometimes escalate into a full-blown hunt for witches.

An investigation into accusations against an individual witch-suspect could reveal long-standing suspicions that he or she had been responsible for a series of events over a number of years or, frequently, decades. It is not always clear how genuine these suspicions were; neighbors may well have manipulated and re-evaluated past misfortunes, perhaps subconsciously, only after a suspected witch was arrested. In many cases, however, the investigation would usually end in the conviction or acquittal of the suspect. A convicted witch would be executed, banished, made to perform a penance, or given some other punishment, depending on local laws and practices, and that would generally be the end of the matter. In some places, however, the authorities were less concerned with the harm perpetrated by the witch, and more interested in identifying other members of a heretical witch sect that they had determined to eradicate. In these places, like the prince-bishoprics in the German Empire, the normal restraints on the use of torture and types of witness were disregarded by specially-appointed witch commissions, staffed by jurists and clerics. The commissions established interrogatories, standard lists of questions, which would lead a suspect from a basic confession of immorality and witchcraft to pacts with the devil, diabolical baptisms, acts of sacrilege, and attendance at witches' sabbaths. Acts of harm against neighbors formed only a small section of these interrogatories. At each stage, but especially during the questions about the witches' sabbaths, a suspect was asked to name her accomplices.

To help extract all of this detailed information, the suspects were tortured in extreme ways, for long periods of time, and over many consecutive sessions of interrogation. Tortures included the thumbscrews and the strappado (including the innovative use of weights and pulleys to create more pain). The idea of torture in these instances was to create sufficient pain to produce a confession without permanently, or at least visibly, harming the suspect's body, but in some places more brutal and damaging forms of torture, such as the boots, were used; the use of the boots led to irreparably crushed bones such as tibiae and fibulae. Witch-suspects, fearful of execution by burning alive and for their souls, could withstand a surprising amount of torture, but eventually in places like Bamberg, Würzburg, and Eichstätt, they would submit. At this point, and over subsequent sessions, they would name their accomplices who were generally women they associated with as kin, friends, or close neighbors. After two or three investigations, the witch commissioners who used such techniques had an almost inexhaustible supply of suspected witches to interrogate.

The interrogatories drawn up by witch commissioners reflected their reading of demonology. They asked about all the stereotypical acts that witches were supposed to commit, and the confessions they obtained only served to confirm that the witches did really participate in them. Ordinary people certainly read about these acts, notably in the broadsheets and pamphlets that reported many of the witch trials, but they rarely accused witch-suspects of performing them. They no doubt understood that such accusations could easily arouse suspicions about their own status: how could one view a secret witches' sabbath by accident? It also seems that very few witch persecutions developed into witch panics. Once a witch-hunt began, ordinary people did not usually take the opportunity to accuse other neighbors of harm by witchcraft. Even high profile witch-suspects, like Dietrich Flade, who had created many enemies tended to be accused by suspects faced with torture rather than their unmolested enemies in the communities.

Lack of public interest in witch-hunting was not, however, the reason why witch persecutions died out. Witch-hunting reached a peak in the 1620s in the German Empire, but by 1630 most of the aggressive witch-hunters were either dead or in exile, having been driven out of their territories by the Swedish invasion of the empire. Their principal defender, Maximilian I, duke of Bavaria, was distracted by the Thirty Years War, and the university at Ingolstadt, which had advocated the persecution of witches, was now dominated by a new generation of Jesuits, like Adam Tanner, who were skeptical of the use of torture in witchcraft trials. Once the political situation had settled in Germany, it appeared that there was no appetite to renew witch-hunting. There were, of course, later witch persecutions, and, although one could argue that they occurred in territories with weak central government or that were experiencing political or religious conflict, as happened in the German Empire, England during the Civil War, or Salem (which had been left temporarily without a governor), they tended to flare up for particular local reasons.

DECLINE OF WITCH-HUNTING AND SURVIVAL OF WITCHCRAFT BELIEFS

Witch trials and witch-hunting declined in different parts of Europe at different times. In England, where witchcraft prosecutions were mild, they had largely ceased by the beginning of the reign of King James I in the early 17th century; in the German Empire, where most witch trials and executions took place, they were over by about 1630. The main reason why the witch persecutions ended was because judicial authorities, whether ecclesiastical or secular, were no longer willing or able to continue them. There had always existed a reasonably high level of skepticism about the reality of witchcraft or the procedures used to prosecute witches. As the witch-hunters of the late 16th and early 17th centuries died off or were distracted by other matters—ruling two countries in the case of James VI of Scotland and I of England, or the needs of war in the case of the Catholic witch-hunters in Germany—this skepticism came to dominate the attitudes of the governing and learned elites toward witchcraft. Perhaps the most influential form of skepticism at this time was that concerning the legal procedures used to prosecute witches. The Jesuit Friedrich Spee articulated this viewpoint in his anonymous *Cautio criminalis* (A Warning on Criminal Justice, 1631). He was critical of the torture used to force confessions of witchcraft and the names of accomplices, and, while he did not deny the reality of witchcraft, he asserted that all of the witches whose spiritual confessions he had heard in Würzburg were innocent. This was a view shared by the Jesuits at the influential university in Ingolstadt. There was also a general incredulity about witchcraft. English juries did not always convict suspected witches, the councillors in Rothenburg ob der Tauber refused to bow to pressure to begin a witch-hunt, the French *parlements* often upheld appeals against witchcraft convictions, and Londoners watched plays that were clearly skeptical of the reality and power of witchcraft. Other forms of early skepticism, including the belief that witchcraft was a delusion created by the devil or illness, and that the term had been mistranslated in the various editions of the Bible, were less influential.

By the end of the 17th century, some authorities had become completely skeptical of witchcraft and were prepared to dismantle the legislation that had allowed witchcraft trials to occur. The English Witchcraft Act of 1604, for example, was repealed by the legislation of 1736 that made it a criminal act to fraudulently claim witchcraft or other supernatural powers. Before then, Francis Hutchinson had already written of the history of witchcraft as if it was a bygone phenomenon. While lawmakers, judges, and bishops no longer believed in the reality of witchcraft, however, others continued to do so, as the later witch persecutions in Poland and Hungary demonstrate. These believers included scholars like Joseph Glanvill, a member of the Royal Society, as well as ordinary people who continued to make accusations where they were legally able to, or lynch suspected witches were they could not. Over time, however, witchcraft as a potent spiritual and physical threat has receded in the popular imagination.

WITCHCRAFT IN THE MODERN WORLD

Despite the decline of witch prosecution in Europe, and a general level of skepticism about its reality, witchcraft remains an important phenomenon in the modern world. In the West, witchcraft, or Wicca, exists as an attractive religion for many, even though it is only modeled on pagan traditions and rituals, rather than being a continuation of an ancient pagan fertility religion as both Margaret Murray, the early 20th-century British Egyptologist and anthropologist, and Gerald Gardner, the founder of modern witchcraft, both believed. They presented this theory in Gardner's *Witchcraft Today*, for which Murray provided an introduction. The growth of witchcraft as a modern religion, influenced by the writings of the politically-active witch Starhawk, notably *The Spiral Dance* (1979), has been particularly strong in America. With its emphasis on worshiping the Goddess and equality of the sexes, its environmental concerns, and its structural flexibility, it offers an alternative spirituality to that of many mainstream religions.

Sorcery and magic also play a significant role in the syncretic religions of South America and the Caribbean, such as Santería and Voodoo (more accurately called Voudou or Vodou), which grew among slaves as a fusion of Christian elements with the African religions that the first slaves brought with them. While much magical activity is considered by the adherents of these religions to be neutral, witchcraft is often regarded as an evil force. In Africa in recent times, there have been some large-scale witch persecutions promoted by the evangelical church and aided by laws against witchcraft and the harm that witches are believed to cause. They generally end in exorcism rather than execution, but the victims of the persecutions tend to be the poor and displaced persons on the margins of societies ravaged by economic crisis and warfare.

The myths and legends of Antiquity, the stories of the Bible and folklore, and the witch trials themselves, have exerted a strong influence on European cultural productions and traditions. William Shakespeare, Johann Wolfgang von Goethe, Lord Byron, Robert Burns, and Arthur Miller are just some of the many playwrights and poets who have produced works with witchcraft as a theme or feature. They have been followed by composers of classical music and operas, novelists, particularly those who write for teenage readers, artists, popular musicians (notably in the 1960s) and filmmakers. The celebrations of Halloween and, in parts of Europe, Walpurgisnacht, long-standing historical traditions in themselves, reinforce stereotypes of the witch with her pointy hat, ugly features, black clothes, broomstick, black cat familiar, and cauldron, all features that would have been recognizable, but perhaps also feared, by early-modern Europeans. The more dangerous characteristics of the European witch stereotype also feature in the stories of witches found in other cultures, ranging from the Caribbean to Malaysia and Japan. These non-European stories have their own histories, of course, in many cases dating back to the very early Babylonian Code of Hammurabi. Despite the range of witch stories, and the volume of witchcraft historiography that began hesitantly in the 18th century, grew slowly throughout the 19th and early 20th centuries with the work of Jules Michelet, Jakob Grimm, Henry Charles Lea, Joseph Hansen, and C. L'Estrange Ewen, and began in earnest in about 1970 with studies of English witchcraft by Alan Macfarlane and Keith Thomas, it is still the basic watered-down cultural stereotype that dominates the popular conception of witchcraft today. Such a simplistic conception muddles history and devalues a shared cultural heritage. This is why the present volume is necessary.

ACCUSATORIAL PROCEDURE. This refers to the basic system of criminal procedure used in most courts of law in medieval Europe prior to the 13th century. Under this procedure, legal actions were initiated by private individuals who felt themselves afflicted or injured in some way. Accusers, however, did more than just initiate trials. They also acted as prosecutors and were responsible for proving the guilt of the person or people who they had accused. If the accused did not confess their guilt, and if no other positive proof could be provided, the matter was placed in the hands of God. Most often the accused would then be made to undergo an ordeal. They might be dunked in water, or made to put a hand in boiling water, or forced to hold hot irons. If they were able to stay immersed in the water for a sufficient period of time in the first case, or if their wounds healed reasonably well in the second or third, they were judged to be innocent. Nobles, instead of undergoing an ordeal, might have access to trial by combat in which, in theory, God would ensure that the innocent won and the guilty lost. If an accused person was judged innocent, the accuser became subject to the law of *talion* and was punished for bringing a false accusation. The punishment was usually the same as the accused would have received if they had been found guilty.

For crimes such as **sorcery** or, later, **witchcraft**, which were secretive by their very nature, positive proof was very difficult to obtain. Thus almost all cases would have been decided by ordeal. Fear of divine judgment and severe punishment probably prevented many specious accusations. Moreover, even when accusers honestly suspected that sorcery was being used against them, the extremely secretive and indirect nature of the crime meant that complete certainty was probably rare. Thus the threat of legal repercussions for false or unproven accusations helped keep the number of trials for sorcery low.

After ordeal was abandoned in the early 13th century, many European lands began to adopt **inquisitorial procedure**, first in the ecclesiastical courts but eventually in the secular ones as well. This procedure made prosecuting crimes like witchcraft much easier and so provided a necessary condition for the emergence of **witch-hunting** in the late-medieval and early-modern periods. Where accusatorial procedure was retained (in **England**, **Scotland**, **Sweden**, Denmark, and **Hungary**), it was adapted from a private to a communal procedure, including, for example, the use of juries to act in the role of the accuser, and the punishments for false accusations were made less severe. These adaptations removed some of the anxieties that may have prevented medieval accusers from bringing cases against sorcerers or witches. This helps explain why witchcraft prosecution became possible in these territories.

See also SWIMMING.

ADLER, MARGOT (1946–). An American journalist, author, and practicing **pagan**, Adler wrote the first important study of the emergence of **neo-paganism** and modern **witchcraft**, or **Wicca**, in America. Her book, *Drawing Down the Moon*, published in 1979, the same year as **Starhawk**'s *The Spiral Dance*, became an important text for modern witchcraft. From a historical perspective, in particular, it recognized that much, if not all, of modern witchcraft's connection to the historical witchcraft of the medieval and early-modern periods was fictitious.

Raised in New York City in a non-religious household, Adler studied at the University of California at Berkeley and at Columbia University's School of Journalism. She began a career in broadcast journalism and was also active in political, environmental, and feminist causes. She was introduced to modern neo-paganism in the early 1970s while in England investigating the history of the druids. Returning to New York, she entered a coven and began practicing modern witchcraft as established by **Gerald Gardner**. Approached to write a book about modern witchcraft, she began researching the origins and development of the movement.

Adler soon realized that many of the claims made by Gardner, that modern witchcraft was directly linked to the witches of the medieval and early-modern periods, and that witchcraft represented a genuine preservation of an even more ancient, pre-Christian religion, were false. Nevertheless, she recognized that most religious beliefs ultimately rested on pseudo-history in which real historical fact and myth were merged to meet the needs of belief. Modern Wiccan and neo-pagan groups could recognize the largely mythical nature of this pseudo-history, she argued, and still retain the force and value of their beliefs. These ideas, among others, were set out in *Drawing Down the Moon*.

See also FEMINISM AND WITCHCRAFT.

AFFAIR OF THE POISONS. A scandal involving several prominent members of the court of Louis XIV of **France**, including his official mistress Madame de Montespan. The affair began in late 1678 with an investigation into a plot to **poison** the king. It quickly uncovered a magical underworld of poisons, **love magic**, and **black masses** said over the body of Montespan. By the end of the affair in 1682, 36 people had been executed, 4 were sent to the galleys, and 34 others were exiled; about 60 suspects were never tried, but placed in solitary confinement. Louis XIV's royal edict closing the affair regulated the sale of poisons, declared magical practices to be fraudulent, and threatened banishment for practitioners.

AFRICA, WITCH-HUNTS IN. Witch-hunts in Africa are not a new phenomenon and they still occur today. In 1914, the British authorities in Northern Rhodesia (now Zambia) had to intervene against the increasing severity of professional witch finders and communities toward suspected witches. They issued a witchcraft ordinance in 1914 prescribing punishment for making accusations of **witchcraft** or using certain forms of **magic** to discover supposed witches. Between 1970 and 1988, there were reportedly about 3,000 witchcraft-related killings in northern Tanzania. These killings were perpetrated by vigilante groups and focused mainly on **women**. Recently, since the 1990s, there have been regular reports of hunts for and executions of alleged witches across all parts of sub-Saharan Africa. The numbers of people killed or displaced as alleged witches during these actions is difficult to determine, but seem to run into the thousands. A significant proportion of these people are **children** in areas riven by war or AIDS. Some of these hunts have their roots in traditional fears of witchcraft in African societies and a few are politically or economically motivated. The most widely reported, however, have been those orchestrated by evangelical church leaders who cite the **Bible** as their authority. **Laws** against witchcraft in some parts of Africa validate these responses toward suspected witches.

Like **muti killings**, attacks on suspected witches have occurred in African communities in the West. In 2005, three Angolans were jailed in **England** for their involvement in the torture of an eight-year-old girl whom they believed to be a witch.

See also AFRICAN WITCHCRAFT.

AFRICAN WITCHCRAFT. The experience of **witchcraft** in sub-Saharan Africa is varied, and generalizations are difficult to make. This is because the continent is large, the communities are diverse, and the types of witch beliefs held by communities are adaptable to social and cultural change. Like witchcraft in the West, African witchcraft also has a complex history. Most research into African witchcraft has been conducted by anthropologists from the West, beginning in the early 20th century. This has led to a problem of terminology, with *sorcery* and *witchcraft* being used to gloss local words and give false impressions about specific witch beliefs in the societies studied.

The anthropologist whose work has had the most influence on the historiography of **witch-hunting** in early-modern Europe is E. E. Evans-Pritchard. His study of the Azande of southern Sudan revealed three distinct categories of magic among these people. Good **magic** was used by **witch doctors**, diviners, and oracles to predict the future and to protect against harmful magic. **Evil** sorcery was used to harm other people. This form of magic often involved using material objects in the performance of spells and typically targeted individuals. A third category that Evans-Pritchard labeled witchcraft, entailed an internal, hereditary power passed down from fathers to sons and more often mothers to daughters. It manifested, supposedly, in the witch's stomach as a small black swelling. Witches were to some extent organized and gathered at secret meetings to practice their magic. They could attack individual people, but were also responsible for all manner of hardships and afflictions suffered by the entire community, including crop failures, lack of game, infertility, and even poor government. Other African societies make similar distinctions. For example, the Bechuana of Botswana distinguish between "day sorcerers" and "night witches." Day sorcerers might work magic either to help or to harm people, but do so on an individual basis and for specific reasons, often for pay. Night witches are more inherently malevolent. They are typically pictured as old **women** who seek to harm the entire community.

The categories of magic identified among the Azande are reminiscent of the historical European concept of witchcraft as a diabolical conspiracy directed at the entire Christian world. On the basis of such parallels, Evans-Pritchard suggested that anthropologists and historians should exchange ideas about witchcraft. Keith Thomas and Alan Macfarlane took up the challenge and wrote anthropologically inspired studies of witchcraft in early-modern **England**. Fellow historians criticized Thomas's work in particular because the large, complex society and culture of Renaissance England could not be made comparable to the small Azande tribe. Thomas and Macfarlane were clear, however, that they were not adopting the interpretations of anthropologists. Instead, they were adapting the approaches of these scholars to find out about the function of witchcraft beliefs and accusations in the specific English context. These approaches paved the way for a new history of witchcraft in the West from the point of view of the witch suspects and their victims.

Other anthropological studies, often using approaches different than Evans-Pritchard, have shown that witchcraft beliefs and experiences in Africa vary over time and according to the type of social structure developed by the society being studied. These beliefs have been adapted to deal with increasing commercialization and social dislocation. They are sustained by the teachings of some evangelical church leaders, reports about **muti killings** perpetrated by witches, and the existence of witchcraft **laws** in some parts of the continent.

Older African beliefs and systems of magic have also influenced some modern religions that incorporate a significant amount of what could be labeled magical rituals. In particular, African slaves brought to the Americas and forced to convert at least nominally to Christianity retained many of their traditional beliefs. African deities and other supernatural entities were merged with Christian saints to produce a number of syncretistic belief systems. The modern religions of **Santería** and **Voodoo** are prominent examples of this syncretism. These religions are practiced in the **Caribbean**, Latin America, and Hispanic communities in **North America**.

See also AFRICA, WITCH-HUNTS IN.

AGE, CORRELATION WITH WITCHCRAFT ACCUSATIONS. By far the most common image of a witch is that of an old hag. From surviving evidence, it seems clear that the majority of people accused of **witchcraft** throughout the historical period of the European **witch-hunts** were old **women**. There is also an opposite stereotype of the witch as young seductress, but this seems to have been more common in literary representations of witchcraft (the models being classical figures like **Circe** and **Medea**) than in actual accusations. It was often assumed, however, that old women suspected of witchcraft in the medieval and early-modern periods were sexually voracious and therefore sexually driven. **Children** were also sometimes accused of witchcraft in large numbers at the height of the European witch persecutions. They are frequently accused of witchcraft in modern **Africa**.

The reasons why so many elderly women were accused of witchcraft in the early-modern period are complex. During the 16th century, the elderly were marginalized economically and socially as demographic pressures and agrarian crises put a strain on the provision of basic necessities. Widows were particularly vulnerable to this marginalization. If old women lacked the protection of a supportive family, they could easily become scapegoated as witches for inexplicable misfortunes in a village. Sometimes they had a history of strange or threatening behavior that developed over many years into suspicions of witchcraft. This behavior may have become more evident in some women after menopause. Where torture was used on suspects, they tended to name as accomplices neighbors of the same social status, gender, and age as themselves. This process reinforced the social and demonological stereotypes of the witch as elderly and female.

See also DEMONOLOGY; MALE WITCHES; SEXUALITY AND WITCHCRAFT.

AGRIPPA VON NETTESHEIM, HEINRICH CORNELIUS (1486–1535). Agrippa was one of the most influential magicians and occult philosophers of the early-modern period. He was born and educated in Cologne in the **German Empire** but spent much of his life at various universities, city administrations, and royal courts across Europe. His occult philosophy was based on his readings of the Kabbalah, neo-platonism, and **Hermetic magic**. He completed his major work on magical knowledge, *De occulta philosophia* (On Occult Philosophy), in 1510, but it was only published in its final form in 1533. It was denounced as heretical by the inquisitor of Cologne.

In 1518, Agrippa was appointed legal advisor to the city of Metz, now in **France**. In this position he successfully defended a **woman** accused of **witchcraft**. The grounds for the accusation were that the woman's mother had been convicted as a witch and executed. Agrippa argued that a person had to make a deliberate and voluntary **pact** with the **Devil** to become a witch. A witch's power could not simply be inherited from another person.

Agrippa's student **Johann Weyer** reported that his teacher died in 1535. After his death, stories began to circulate about Agrippa's life as a practitioner of demonic **magic**. He was rumored to be able to reanimate corpses with his magic. It was also said that he had kept a demonic **familiar** disguised as a black dog, a form that Johann Wolfgang von Goethe gave to Mephistopheles in his version of the **Faust** legend.

ALBERTUS MAGNUS (ca. 1190–1280). Born in the **German** region of Swabia, Albertus Magnus (Albert the Great) was a Dominican friar and an important medieval philosopher and theologian. He taught theology at the university in Paris, where his most famous student was **Thomas Aquinas**, and later went to the Dominican *studium* at Cologne. Albertus viewed some **magic** as a form of natural science, distinct from demonic **sorcery**. In the area of **demonology**, however, he helped to develop notions of explicit and tacit **pacts** that humans might enter into with **demons**. His student Aquinas would develop this position more fully, and such ideas formed an important basis for later notions of **witchcraft**. Like many famous medieval scholars, Albertus himself developed a popular reputation as an **alchemist**, astronomer, and sorcerer. While he certainly did engage in the study of certain occult sciences, which he viewed as legitimate, he thoroughly condemned demonic sorcery.

ALCHEMY. An occult science that developed in **Antiquity** and was rediscovered in Europe, along with other forms of learned **magic** and occult practices, in the 12th century, alchemy involved the manipulation of the secret properties of chemicals and other natural materials. Above all, alchemists sought to discover the so-called philosopher's stone, which would allow them to transmute lead or other common materials into silver and gold. As a clearly learned form of magical practice, like **astrology**, alchemy had little direct connection to **witchcraft**. Alchemists might, however, as a result of the secretive nature of their work, become suspected of practicing more sinister forms of magic.

ALEXANDER IV, POPE (?–1261). By the 1250s, papal inquisitors, whose purpose it was to investigate cases of **heresy**, were increasingly dealing with matters of **sorcery**, and questions were being raised as to whether such matters properly fell under their jurisdiction. In 1258, Alexander IV (pope from 1254 to 1261) ruled that sorcery was not a matter of concern for papal inquisitors, unless the sorcery involved acts that "manifestly savored of heresy" (*manifeste saperent haeresim*). Since any case of sorcery that involved the invocation or worship of **demons** met this condition, Alexander's ruling provided an important basis for later inquisitorial action against sorcerers and witches.

See also INQUISITORIAL PROCEDURE.

ALEXANDER V, POPE (ca. 1340–1410). Alexander V reigned as pope for less than a year from June 1409. During this time he sent a letter to the Franciscan inquisitor Pontus Fougeyron in which he announced his concern over the existence of many people, both Christians and **Jews**, who performed demonic **sorcery** and worshiped **demons**. In particular, he stated that people were forming "new sects" (*novas sectas*). The use of this phrase was not original to Alexander and does not make direct reference to **witchcraft**. It did, however, lay the foundation for the belief in a new and dangerous sect of witches previously unknown to the church. Descriptions of this new witch sect were soon provided by **Johannes Nider** in his *Formicarius* (The Anthill, 1437–1438).

See also INQUISITION.

ANTIQUITY, WITCHCRAFT IN. The prosecution of **witchcraft** in the later-medieval and early-modern periods was influenced by the treatment and understanding of the topic in Antiquity. Witchcraft, and the related activities of **sorcery**, **necromancy**, and some forms of **divination**, were the subject of numerous ancient **laws**, including the Code of Hammurabi (1792–1750 BCE), and the Old Testament of the **Bible**, notably Exodus 22:18, which was commonly translated as stating that witches should be executed. As well as Scripture, Renaissance scholars knew the various Roman laws that proscribed these activities. Often in Antiquity the punishment for these crimes was **execution**. Roman law also gave late-medieval jurists the **inquisitorial**

procedure, which allowed authorities rather than individuals to prosecute alleged criminals and replaced the drama of the ordeal used in **accusatorial procedure** with the drama of **torture**. These changes meant that victims of witchcraft could come forward without fear of the law of *talion*, by which they would receive the punishment for the alleged crime if the plaintiff was found innocent, and that individual witchcraft episodes could escalate into full-scale **witch-hunts**.

Ancient and classical myths also provided models of witchcraft through the stories of goddesses, sorceresses, and malevolent **women**, such as **Lamashtu**, Isis, **Lilith**, **Diana**, **Circe**, **Medea**, **Hecate**, and the **Witch of Endor**, and descriptions of the Roman **Bacchanalia** and the Germanic **Wild Hunt**. The ancient Egyptian deity Isis was one of many goddesses who were patrons of the magical arts. Witchcraft, and particularly harmful sorcery, tended to be associated with women in Antiquity, although some men like Apuleius of Madaura, were prosecuted for similar activities. Many demonic creatures and deities of Antiquity were able to **metamorphose** into humans or animals just as later witches were sometimes thought to do. The gatherings of **heretics** and the witches' **sabbaths** described in late-medieval **demonologies** resembled the Bacchanalia with its sexual **orgies** and other excessive rites that tended to be performed at night. The Wild Hunt was explicitly associated with witchcraft in the **canon** *Episcopi* of the early 10th century in which witches were said to be followers of **Diana** with whom they rode at night. This **pagan** belief evolved into the **night flight** undertaken by witches on their way to a sabbath. The scholarly terms *maleficium* (harmful sorcery or witchcraft), *lamia* (used for witch), and *strix* (also used for witch), as well as *veneficium* (originally meaning both a **poisonous** substance and sorcery or witchcraft), originated in the demonologists' reading of classical mythology.

APOSTASY. Referring to a complete renunciation of the basic principles of faith, apostasy was considered to be one of the chief crimes entailed in **witchcraft**, along with **idolatry**, during the medieval and early-modern periods. Upon entering a heretical cult of witches, usually at a witches' **sabbath**, new witches were generally believed to be required to renounce the Christian faith entirely and pledge themselves to the service of the **devil**. Unlike normal **heresy**, which involved errors of belief or practice that could be corrected, apostasy was often seen as an unforgivable crime, a kind of treason against God that required the most severe form of punishment possible.

AQUINAS, THOMAS (ca. 1225–1274). A Dominican friar and one of the most important theologians of the Middle Ages, Aquinas was born in **Italy** and studied in Paris and Cologne under the direction of the Dominican scholar **Albertus Magnus** (Albert the Great). Aquinas later became a professor of theology at Paris and in Italy. In numerous works, most notably his *Summa contra gentiles* (Summa against the Gentiles) and *Summa theologiae* (Summa of Theology), he systematized medieval theology according to scholastic logic. Although his works were at first controversial, they later became widely accepted as authoritative, especially by other Dominican authors. Many early clerical authorities who wrote on **witchcraft** cited Aquinas heavily, including the Dominicans **Johannes Nider**, **Jean Vineti**, and **Heinrich Kramer**, author of the *Malleus maleficarum*.

Aquinas did not write about witchcraft himself—he lived centuries before the idea of diabolic witchcraft fully developed in Europe—but he did discuss the operations of **sorcery** and the power of **demons** in several of his works. He worked out a logical system to explain how demons, as **evil** spiritual beings, could affect the physical world, including how demons operating as succubi and **incubi** could impregnate **women**, and how they might influence human actions. He argued that demonic sorcery always entailed at least a tacit pact between the human sorcerer and the demon that the sorcerer invoked. Demons submitted to carry out the wishes of sorcerers in order to ensnare and corrupt them. While Thomas's works influenced later **demonology**, he was more ambiguous than his successors on some important points. In keeping with the **canon** *Episcopi*, he rejected the idea that demons could physically transport humans (the basis for the belief in the witches' **night flights**). In summarizing his theology, he also did not suggest that practitioners of sorcery should be punished for their activities or **heresies**.

ART, WITCHCRAFT IN. **Sorcery** and **witchcraft** have been the subject of art in various media in **Antiquity** and in Europe from the 15th century. Depictions of **Lilith**, **Circe**, **Medea** and **Hecate** appear infrequently in vase-paintings, frescoes, sarcophagi, statuary, and bas-reliefs of the Old Babylonian, Ancient Greek, and Roman periods. The influence of Homer's *Odyssey* and Apollonius of Rhodes's *Argonautica* on European culture during the Renaissance saw a revival of interest in Circe, Medea, and sorceresses generally, but not Lilith or Hecate. Whether these witch figures were painted by the Lower Rhenish Master in the late 15th century or the Pre-Raphaelites and their followers at the turn of the 20th, they are usually represented as beautiful, seductive enchantresses. Such images remain common and have inspired both Gustav Doré's **Witch of Endor** (1866), for example, and the witches of fantasy or comic-book art. If they are not given new names, like the Scarlet Witch, these modern versions are often given alternate ones drawn from **folklore** (such as **Morgan le Fay**) or, in their darker incarnations, from Antiquity (such as Lilith).

The **stereotypical** image of the old hag only began to appear in the early 16th century, often alongside the younger, sexier witches. These early images are now most commonly associated with **Albrecht Dürer** and **Hans**

Baldung Grien. Recent innovations in printing meant that they circulated widely as woodcut illustrations to treatises and legal manuals by men like **Ulrich Molitor** and **Johann Weyer**. The witchcraft represented in these images tended to be stereotypical, incorporating **night flying, sabbaths**, weather magic, sexual **orgies** with **demons**, the **obscene kiss, cannibalism** and disorderly dancing. These elements had their origins in the propaganda against the Cathars and **Waldensians**. As the witch persecutions progressed, these sabbath images became more elaborate, most famously in the book illustrations by Jan Ziarnko (1613) and Michael Herr (1626). As **skepticism** about witchcraft increased, the old hag became useful as a shorthand for popular superstitions in, for example, William Hogarth's cartoon *Credulity, Superstition and Fanaticism: A Medley* (1762) and the work of **Francisco Goya**. The old hag continues to be the stereotype of the witch used at **Halloween**.

See also STORMS AND STORM-RAISING.

ASIAN WITCHCRAFT. Witches and similar malevolent creatures exist in the **folklore** and belief systems of many cultures across Asia. Like their counterparts in Europe, **Africa**, and the **Caribbean**, they tend to be **women**, or disguise themselves as women. They include various types of spirit **foxes**, known in Japan, for example, as *kitsune*, which practice **magic** and **divination**, are known to possess people and houses, and, in the appearance of a beautiful woman, can drain a man of life through aggressive sexual activity. Vampiric creatures also feature in Asian folklore, and include the Malaysian **penanggal**, a woman who seeks out the blood of pregnant women or infants, and inflicts a wasting disease on her victims. The **mangkukulam** is a more conventional type of witch who practices magic and **sorcery** in Filipino folklore. Despite the wide spread of these witch-like creatures, accounts of witchcraft trials and **witch-hunts** are much less common in Asia than in late-medieval and early-modern Europe or modern Africa.

See also POSSESSION, DEMONIC; SEXUALITY AND WITCHCRAFT; VAMPIRES.

ASTROLOGY. Throughout ancient, medieval, and early-modern Europe, most people believed that the stars and planets exerted influence on many aspects of the terrestrial world, including human beings, and that stellar bodies could be used to predict the future. Astrology, the study of the stars and their effects, was practiced as a real, if often occult, science by educated elites, but many forms of astrology were also practiced at a popular level. Perhaps the most common use of astrology was the practice of making horoscopes to predict the future and divine the destiny of individual people. This practice was sometimes proscribed by secular **law**, such as the Elizabethan

Act of 1580–81 "against seditious words and rumours uttered against the Queen's most excellent majesty." Astrology also entered into many other forms of magical and occult operations, since the power of the stars was thought, for example, to affect **alchemy** and even demonic invocations. Astral **magic**, which claimed to draw down and manipulate the power of heavenly bodies, was obviously intimately connected to astrology. There was, however, little direct connection between astrology and **witchcraft**.

AUGUSTINE OF HIPPO, SAINT (354–430). The most important of the so-called Latin Fathers of the Christian church, and probably the most important intellectual figure in the history of Western Christianity, Augustine's writings on **demonology** and the nature of **magic** provided a basis for all further consideration of these subjects throughout the Middle Ages and early-modern Europe. Above all, his ideas about demonic involvement in most forms of magic and the necessity of **pacts** between the magician and the **demon** were essential to later concepts of **sorcery** and **witchcraft**.

Born in North Africa, Augustine studied in Carthage and **Italy**. Although his mother was a Christian, Augustine was influenced by the Manichean sect and did not convert to Christianity until 385. He then returned to North Africa, where he became a priest and later bishop of the city of Hippo (now Annaba in Algeria). For the rest of his life, Augustine devoted himself to demonstrating the superiority of Christianity to **pagan** religions. Of particular importance to the history of magic and, later, witchcraft were his arguments that pagan deities were in fact demons and that pagan religious practices were empty superstitions. His theology of **evil** was also to influence later views on how witchcraft operated. Augustine's *De divinatione daemonum* (On the Divination of Demons), written in 406, was devoted to a discussion of the nature of demons, and he returned to the subject in other works including sections of his greatest work, *The City of God*, written from 413 to 425. He distinguished sharply between magic performed with the aid of demons and legitimate Christian miracles performed by divine power. Because demons were inherently evil, he reasoned, they would not serve humans who invoked them unless those sorcerers entered into pacts and worshiped them.

B

BABA YAGA. Baba Yaga is a famous witch of Slavic, especially **Russian**, **folklore** who also appears in the work of the poet Alexander Pushkin (1799–1837), the composer Modest Mussorgsky (1839–1881), and the novelist Isaac Bashevis Singer (1902–1991). In most Slavic languages *Baba* means "grandmother" or "old woman," and Baba Yaga is usually represented as an old hag who lures people to her home where she cooks and devours them. Like the witch in the Western European folk story of Hansel and Gretel, she prefers to eat young **children**. She lives in a hut beyond a river of fire. The hut is surrounded by stakes set with human skulls and built on chicken legs so that it can move at her command. In the various tales about her, she flies through the air in either a mortar carrying a pestle and **broom** or an iron **cauldron**. She is clearly related to other **night-flying**, child-devouring monsters that later became associated with witchcraft in Western European witchcraft, such as the Roman **strix**.

See also CANNIBALISM; CLASSICAL MUSIC, WITCHCRAFT IN; FICTION, WITCHCRAFT IN.

BACCHANALIA. A religious celebration in honor of the Roman god of wine, Bacchus, the rites, real or supposed, of the Bacchanalia became an important basis for the idea of the witches' **sabbath** in later medieval Europe. In ancient Greece, worshipers of the god of wine and fertility, Dionysos (who later became the Roman Bacchus), gathered at night, often in secluded wilderness areas. Their celebrations usually involved a number of **women** led by male priests, and the representation of the god as a horned **goat**, a traditional symbol of fertility. The rites performed by the followers of Dionysos included the consumption of wine, ecstatic dancing, animal sacrifice, and sexual frenzy. In Roman times, the Bacchanalia became so associated with **orgies** of uncontrolled revelry, sexuality, and immorality that it was outlawed by the Roman Senate in 186 BCE. Descriptions of Bacchanalia can be found in Euripides's *Bacchae* (5th century BCE) and Livy's *History of Rome* (c. 10 CE).

See also ANTIQUITY, WITCHCRAFT IN.

BACON, ROGER (ca. 1213–1291). An English Franciscan philosopher and scholar, Bacon was one the most important natural scientists of the Middle Ages. In particular, he studied **alchemy, astrology**, mathematics, and optics. He developed a popular reputation as a sorcerer because of his unconventional scientific experiments and his pursuit of occult learning. There is no evidence, however, that Bacon was ever significantly interested in matters of demonic **sorcery** or ritual **magic** (as some medieval scholars were), and he certainly was never associated with **witchcraft** in any way.

BALDUNG GRIEN, HANS (1484–1545). A south **German** artist who developed the iconography of the witches' **sabbath**, Baldung produced several images that remained influential until the 17th century. The first of Baldung's witchcraft woodcuts, "Witches' Sabbath" (1510), brought together naked witches, including old hags, a **cauldron**, weather magic, **night flight**, **goats**, a **cat**, references to the castration of men (limp sausages), the sexual voracity of the witch (flowing hair), and disorderliness (riding a flying goat backward). Some of this iconography had its origins in the propaganda against the **Waldensians** and in the *Malleus maleficarum*. Other elements were borrowed from his contemporaries, such as Baldung's former master **Albrecht Dürer**. Baldung developed the witchcraft scenes in later woodcuts and paintings, and other artists borrowed heavily from them. The woodcut of 1510 formed the basis for another of 1516 that was used to illustrate works by **Ulrich Molitor, Johann Geiler von Kaysersberg**, and **Johann Weyer**.

 See also ART, WITCHCRAFT IN; SEXUALITY AND WITCHCRAFT; STORMS AND STORM-RAISING.

BAMBERG WITCH TRIALS. Bamburg was the scene for some of the most severe **witch-hunts** in the **German Empire**. The persecution of witches in and around the Catholic city of Bamberg was particularly intense during the reign of Bishop Johann Georg Fuchs von Dornheim, the so-called *Hexenbischof* or witch-bishop, from 1623 to 1633. The witch-hunts under Dornheim and his predecessor Bishop Johann Gottfried von Aschhausen (1609–1622) were provoked by crop failures, but soon became part of a process to enforce moral reform. Dornheim established a large staff to carry out the hunt for witches. This staff included his Suffragan Bishop Friedrich Förner, who supported Dornheim's actions in 35 sermons published in 1626. Förner was also instrumental in the building of the *Hexenhaus* (witch house) in which to hold and interrogate the witch suspects. Here the suspects were subjected to new, sadistic forms of **torture**. As the hunts in Bamberg spiraled out of control, many prominent citizens were accused. Eventually, the situation became so bad that an appeal was made to the emperor Ferdinand II. In 1630 and 1631, he issued mandates that proper legal procedures should be more carefully adhered to in all cases of suspected **witchcraft** in accordance with the **Carolina law code**. From this point, and especially after the death of Dornheim and other important persecutors, the number of trials in Bamberg gradually decreased.

See also DEMONOLOGY; EICHSTÄTT WITCH TRIALS; STORMS AND STORM-RAISING; WÜRZBURG, WITCH TRIALS AT.

BAPHOMET. An image of the **devil** or a **demon** as a horned, half-**goat** creature, Baphomet is of medieval origins. The word may be a corruption of the name of the Islamic prophet Muhammad (often incorrectly rendered as Mahomet in medieval Christian sources), conceived by Christian authorities as a demon or idol. In the early 14th century, the **Knights Templar** were accused of possessing an idol shaped like the head of Baphomet that they supposedly worshiped. In the 19th century, the image of Baphomet was revived among occultists and enthusiasts of ritual **magic**. Perhaps the most famous image of the horned goat-devil was drawn by the French occultist Eliphas Lévi, and the well-known British occultist **Aleister Crowley** took the name Baphomet at one point in his career. In the 20th century, a version of the image of Baphomet—a goat's head inscribed in an upside-down **pentagram**—was adopted by the **Church of Satan** as its official symbol, and practitioners of modern **Satanism** continue to use similar images. The image has also often been associated with **witchcraft**, but no practitioners of **Wicca** or other forms of modern **neo-paganism** use the image in any way.

BASEL, COUNCIL OF (1431–1449). This great church council, held in the city of Basel in the first half of the 15th century, was an important center for the early diffusion of the idea of **witchcraft** across Western Europe. Several of the most important early theorists of witchcraft were present at the council or associated with it in some way, and clearly many clerics first learned of witchcraft while at Basel.

In the early 15th century, full-fledged demonic witchcraft, that is, witchcraft that involved not just the practice of harmful **sorcery** (*maleficium*) against others, but also the worship of **demons** or the **devil**, **apostasy** from the faith, gatherings at a **sabbath**, and all the attendant horrors that implied, was a fairly new and localized phenomenon. Some of the earliest true witch trials were only just beginning to take place, mainly in the lands in and around the western Alps. They were most notable in the dioceses of Lausanne and Sion, and the territories of Dauphiné and Savoy. The Council of Basel brought churchmen from across Europe together just to the north of these regions.

Several of the first learned authorities to write on witchcraft were present at the Council of Basel. Perhaps the most important among these men was the Dominican theologian **Johannes Nider**. In his major work on witchcraft, the *Formicarius* (The Anthill), he included several accounts of witches in the Simme Valley in the Bernese *Oberland*, that is, the alpine territory of the city of Bern, and elsewhere in the diocese of Lausanne. He also wrote about the supposed witchcraft of **Joan of Arc**, about whom he learned while at the council from clerics who had come from Paris. The French cleric and poet **Martin Le Franc** was also at Basel, and there composed his poem *Le champion des dames* (The Defender of Ladies) in which he included a long section about witchcraft. Moreover, there is strong evidence to suggest that the anonymous clerical author of the *Errores Gazariorum* (Errors of the Gazarii), another important early description of witchcraft, was associated with the council in some way.

Many ecclesiastical authorities involved in the prosecution of witches were present at the Council of Basel. Both the inquisitor Ulric de Torrenté, who conducted some of the earliest witch trials in the diocese of Lausanne, and George de Saluces, bishop of Lausanne from 1440 until 1461, attended the council. Most famously, **Nicholas Jacquier**, later a witch-hunting inquisitor in northern **France**, attended the council in 1432 and 1433. He wrote the important treatise on witchcraft *Flagellum hereticorum fascinariorum* (The Scourge of Heretical Witches) in 1458.

See also SWITZERLAND, WITCHCRAFT IN.

BASQUE LANDS, WITCHCRAFT IN. The Basque lands comprise a small region in southwestern **France** and northern **Spain**, lying on either side of the Pyrenees. They were the scene of some of the most intense **witch-hunting** in both countries. The major Basque witch-hunt began in 1609. In France, the judge **Pierre de Lancre** was appointed to the Pays de Labourd and began to investigate cases of **witchcraft**. He quickly became convinced that the entire region was infested with witches. He wrote of thousands of witches gathering at great **sabbaths**, and he is often credited with executing up to 600 supposed witches, although in all likelihood the figure should be under 100. In Spain, cases of witchcraft fell under the jurisdiction of the Spanish **Inquisition**, and in 1609 the inquisitor **Alonso de Salazar Frías** was appointed to the regional tribunal at Logroño. Unlike Lancre, he was skeptical of many of the charges being made in the courts. In 1611 and 1612, he conducted a thorough investigation of the procedures being employed in witch trials in the region. He found many lapses in procedure and became convinced that many of the convictions being obtained were false. Based on his report, the central council of the Spanish Inquisition in Madrid, the *Su-*

prema, established much stricter oversight and guidelines for witch trials. By 1614, the severe outbreak of witch-hunting on both sides of the Pyrenees was over and the region was returning to normal.

See also SKEPTICISM.

BAVARIA, WITCH TRIALS IN. The duchy of Bavaria (from 1623 an electorate) was the dominant Catholic state of the **German Empire** at the height of the European witch persecutions. Both pro and anti **witch-hunting** parties were strong in the territory. The pro witch-hunting party was dominated in the late 16th and early 17th centuries by Jesuit theologians at the University of Ingolstadt and Jesuit-trained officials at the ducal court. These theologians and officials urged Dukes Wilhelm V (r. 1579–1597) and Maximilian I (r. 1598–1651) to hunt witches using **Peter Binsfeld**'s work and the *Malleus maleficarum* as guides. The persecution of witches was to be part of the social and moral reform of Bavaria. They also corresponded with other demonologists (like **Nicolas Rémy** and **Martín Del Rio**) and local witch-hunters (like the prince-bishop of **Eichstätt**).

When the anti witch-hunting party came to prominence in about 1600, it insisted, citing the **Carolina law code**, that **witchcraft** cases had to be referred to the university in Ingolstadt before further **torture** could be used on suspects. The law faculty in Ingolstadt denied the legality of torture in these cases. The university was also coming under the influence of skeptical Jesuits like **Adam Tanner** and his students who supported the courtiers opposed to witch persecution and criticized witch-hunters in neighboring territories like Eichstätt. The opposition view was strengthened by opinions received from foreign universities. The opponents of witch-hunting ensured that trials in Bavaria were only sporadic and never reached the scale of events in **Bamberg**, Eichstätt, and **Würzburg**.

See also BAVARIAN WAR OF THE WITCHES; DEMONOLOGY; SKEPTICISM.

BAVARIAN WAR OF THE WITCHES. The War of the Witches was the name given to the debate about the reality of **witchcraft** provoked by Don Ferdinand Sterzinger, a Theatine father, in his skeptical "Academic Lecture about the Prejudice That Witchcraft Can Produce Effects." The lecture was delivered in 1766 in honor of the birthday of the **Bavarian** prince-elector Max III Joseph (r. 1745–1777), and the subsequent debate lasted for the next five years. It was conducted in sermons, satires, and treatises across Central Europe and **Italy**. Skeptics, supported by Max III Joseph and the pillars of the Enlightenment, ridiculed witch beliefs as backward. They drew on the **skepticism** that had found its voice in the work of **Christian Thomasius** and **Balthasar Bekker** and coalesced around the execution of the subprioress

Maria Renate Singerin in 1749. Defenders of witch trials, led by the religious orders, notably the Jesuits, refuted the critics using outmoded **demonological** arguments. The patronage enjoyed by the skeptics and the positions they held in Bavarian political, academic, and religious life ensured that they won the intellectual argument.

BAYLE, PIERRE (1647–1706). An important philosopher, born in **France** and later professor at the university in Rotterdam, Bayle was a strong advocate of liberalism and religious toleration. He treated the subject of **witchcraft** at length in his *Résponse aux questions d'un provincial* (Responses to the Questions of a Provincial), written in 1703. He did not deny the potential reality of **sorcery** or witchcraft, or the power of the **devil**. Instead he advocated a more moderate form of **skepticism**, arguing that many acts attributed to witchcraft could also arise from natural causes, and that human authorities could rarely, if ever, be certain in assigning blame to witches. He also felt that the excessive use of **torture** led to many false convictions in cases of witchcraft, that many convicted witches were in fact deranged or confused, and that authorities should not place so much credence in popular beliefs and concerns.

BEKKER, BALTHASAR (1634–1698). One of the most important and perhaps the most thorough opponent of **witch-hunting** in the 17th century, Balthasar Bekker was a Dutch clergyman and rationalist thinker who followed the model of the French philosopher René Descartes. In 1691, he published the first volumes of his *De Betoverde Weereld* (The Enchanted World) that was soon translated into German, English and French. In this work, Bekker exhibited a complete **skepticism** about the very existence of **witchcraft**, unlike many other opponents of the witch-hunts who chose to criticize only the faulty procedures of witch trials that they felt were producing numerous false confessions. Drawing on a new mechanistic understanding of the universe, Bekker did not deny that **demons** could exist, but he did deny that they could exert any influence or power over the natural world or human affairs. Rather than resort to credulous interpretations of misfortune as the product of witchcraft, Bekker argued that one should seek natural explanations. He also argued that witchcraft and **sorcery** were fraudulent acts. Equally, because demons lacked any real power in the world, there was no basis for the supposed **pact** between witches and the **devil**. Despite the popularity of his work, Bekker was labeled a **heretic** and ultimately expelled from the Dutch Reformed Church.

BENANDANTI. The apparent remnants of an ancient fertility cult, the *benandanti* were men and **women** in the northern **Italian** region of Friuli who practiced a form of archaic **shamanism**. The name *benandanti* translates as "those who go well" or "well-doers," and they regarded themselves as defenders of the Christian faith. Each of the *benandanti* had been born with the caul, the inner fetal membrane, still intact and covering their bodies. Such births are taken as a sign of supernatural power in many cultures. Upon reaching maturity, the *benandanti* were initiated into their cult. On certain days they were summoned, while they slept, to travel in spirit form to battle witches, also in spirit form. The *benandanti* traveled as smoke or small animals or they rode supernatural **goats**, roosters, or **cats**. They were armed with fennel stalks and the witches with sorghum stalks. If the *benandanti* were victorious, the fertility of the land and abundant crops in the coming season were assured. When awake and in their physical forms, the *benandanti* were also thought to have certain supernatural powers, especially the power to perform magical **healing**.

In 1574, the *benandanti* first came to the attention of the ecclesiastical authorities. By 1749, the **Inquisition** had conducted 85 proceedings against them. Initially, the inquisitors were interested in the night battles with witches, but later they were concerned mainly with the *benandanti*'s healing abilities. By the mid-17th century, some, but certainly not all, *benandanti* had been induced to confess to flying to witches' **sabbaths** and practicing **witchcraft**. Only 15 sentences were, however, issued against them and they were punished with admonitions, abjurations, imprisonment or banishment, but not **execution**. It seems that, far from dying out after these trials, the *benandanti* survived in modified forms until very recently, contacting the dead and performing therapeutic functions in their communities. This is not surprising as scholars agree that the beliefs and practices of the *benandanti* are among the best examples of the adaptability of ancient cultural traits to new cosmologies.

See also NIGHT FLIGHT.

BERKELEY, WITCH OF. The story of the witch of Berkeley supposedly took place around the time of the Norman conquest of **England** in 1066. The chronicler **William of Malmesbury** included it in his history of the kings of England, the *Gesta regum*, and the story continued to circulate throughout the medieval and early-modern periods. A powerful sorceress lived at Berkeley. She performed demonic **magic** and had clearly entered into some sort of **pact** with the **devil**. Upon receiving a premonition of her own death, she asked her children, since they could not save her soul, at least to try to protect her body after death by sewing it into the skin of a stag and placing it on a stone coffin fastened by three chains inside a church. On the first two nights after her death, **demons** assailed the church in which she lay and broke two of the chains. On the third night, the devil himself appeared and commanded the woman's corpse come with him. The body replied from inside the coffin that it could not, at which point the devil broke the third chain and carried off the corpse on an enormous black horse. Although horrific in its description of the connection between **sorcery** and ensnarement of a human soul by demons, the story of the witch of Berkeley does not contain any overt descriptions of the worship of demons or other elements of **diabolism** that would later come to comprise the stereotype of **witchcraft**.

BERNARDINO OF SIENA (1380–1444). One of the most popular preachers in the early 15th century, Bernardino was a Franciscan friar who was active across northern **Italy**. He was particularly concerned with matters of immorality that he felt threatened to corrupt the entire community in which they were found, especially **sorcery** and **witchcraft**, sodomy, and toleration of **Jews**. In fiery sermons, he called for the extirpation of these supposed sins. He witnessed an early witch trial in Rome, probably in 1426 (some sources give 1424 or other years). He later tried to instigate trials for witchcraft in his native Siena in 1427, and was associated with a witch trial in Todi in 1428. Through his sermons, Bernardino can be seen as helping to begin the spread of concern over sorcery and witchcraft that would soon escalate into the earliest **witch-hunts** in Europe.

BIBLE, WITCHCRAFT IN. The most famous reference given to **witchcraft** in the Bible is the passage from Exodus 22:18, given in the 17th-century King James' Version as "Thou shalt not suffer a witch to live." Throughout the period of the European **witch-hunts**, this passage served as the biblical justification for the execution of witches. In fact, the original text referred to sorceresses or diviners, one of many observations of Christian translations of the Bible made by the **skeptic Reginald Scot**, but ignored by demonologists, judges, and accusers. Another biblical passage of significance for the later history of witchcraft was the story of the **Witch of Endor** (again originally described only as a soothsayer) to whom King Saul went to consult with the spirit of the dead prophet Samuel. This story suggests that there had been a recent witch-hunt: the soothsayer was frightened of Saul because he had had magicians driven out of Israel. In other Old Testament stories, **Moses** and Aaron defeated the magicians of the Egyptian pharaoh and Elijah the priests of Baal in magical contests. Like the soothsayer of Endor, these magicians and priests of **pagan** religions were later held to have worked their magic by summoning demons. The victory of God's prophets in these contests was used to show the superiority of divine miracle to demonic **sorcery** or witchcraft.

Elsewhere, the Old Testament prohibits various other magical practices, including several forms of **divination** or **astrology**, casting spells, consulting **familiar** spirits, and **necromancy**. These practices are often associated with other vices. In the same chapter of Exodus where it prescribes death for a "witch," the penalties for a range of deviant behavior—from poor husbandry and a lack of hospitality to bestiality and blasphemy—are also described. Similarly, Jezebel is described as practicing both "whoredomes" and "witchcrafts."

Sorceresses and witchcraft were not features of the New Testament. Magical practices did, however, continue to be associated with deviant behavior in this part of the Bible, for example in Mark 7:22 and Revelation 22:15. The apostles of Christ also encountered magicians. Peter refused **Simon Magus** of Samaria's request to buy his power, while Paul blinded Bar-Jesus and converted many magical practitioners in Ephesus. In later apocryphal literature, the rivalry between Simon Magus and Peter (also called Simon Peter) was elaborated, and Simon Magus became the archetype for practitioners of demonic sorcery throughout the Middle Ages. In the stories of **exorcism**, Jesus and his disciples demonstrated how the Church could deal with people who were possessed. The three magi (probably astrologers) who traveled to see the child Jesus in Bethlehem present a similar positive image of occult practice.

See also DEMONOLOGY; POSSESSION, DEMONIC.

BINSFELD, PETER (1546–1598). A theologian and suffragan bishop of **Trier**, Binsfeld was an influential **German** authority on **witchcraft**. He played an important role in the severe outbreak of **witch-hunting** that took place in Trier in the late 1580s and 1590s and informed his *Tractatus de confessionibus maleficiorum et sagarum* (Treatise on the Confession of Witches), first published in 1589. His purpose in the treatise was to justify the witch trials at Trier, and in particular to defend the value of the confessions made by accused witches as evidence against other witches. He drew on the major Catholic works on witchcraft, such as the *Malleus maleficarum* and the treatises by **Alfonso de Spina** and **Jean Bodin**, and he criticized more **skeptical** authorities such as **Johann Weyer**. He also opposed **Cornelius Loos**, who had written a treatise criticizing the severe witch-hunts he had witnessed in Trier. Binsfeld was cited as an authority in the **Bavarian** witch trials.

BLACK MASS. Generally conceived as an elaborate, but serious perversion of the Catholic mass usually celebrated by a Catholic priest, very few examples of the Black Mass exist. Although the witches' **sabbath** involved inverted Catholic rites (such as the **obscene kiss** instead of the kiss of peace), trampling on or otherwise desecrating the host, sexual **orgies**, and worshiping the **devil**, these acts were mockeries of Christian practice. They were not performed for spiritual or material profit. In 1586, however, the Sicilian **Inquisition** investigated claims that four men (two priests and two students) had performed Black Masses for their own gain. Three of the defendants were sent to the galleys. A century later, the defendants in the **Affair of the Poisons** were accused of attending Black Masses celebrated by a Catholic priest, although Madame de Montespan, the mistress of Louis XIV of **France**, was cleared of any involvement in them. The descriptions of these masses tended to be titillating rather than horrific.

Some secret and possibly occultist organizations of the 18th century, such as the infamous Hellfire Club in England, were also rumored to perform Black Masses, but these were most likely irreverent and libertine revels that were exaggerated by gossip. These exaggerations were probably helped by the notoriety of the erotic **fiction** of the contemporary libertine, the Marquis de Sade, in which priests, monks, and the pope celebrate these rites. In fact, the Black Mass has remained in the public consciousness because novelists and filmmakers have been attracted by its combination of eroticism and horror. More recently, "La Messe Noire" published in Anton LaVey's *The Satanic Rituals* (1972) has led to the belief that his foundation, the **Church of Satan**, performs the Black Mass as a magical ceremony. LaVey and his followers have, however, explicitly rejected the mass as anything other than a parody of Christian ceremony or a psychodrama. Although most **satanists** and practitioners of modern **witchcraft**, or **Wicca**, and other forms of **neopaganism** do not perform rituals resembling the Black Mass, erroneous stereotypes of this sort persist.

See also FILMS, WITCHCRAFT IN.

BODIN, JEAN (1529/30–1596). One of the greatest political thinkers of the 16th century, Bodin is most famous for his *Six livres de la République* (Six Books of the Republic), published in 1576. Here, he presented one of the first modern arguments about the nature of political sovereignty, maintaining that ultimate sovereignty lay with the people who comprised a state. This work established Bodin as one of the most progressive political thinkers of his time. In terms of the history of **witchcraft**, however, he is most well known for his work *De la démonomanie des sorciers* (The Demonomania of Witches). First published in 1580, this book went through 10 editions before 1604, and for the remainder of the period of the **witch-hunts** stood as one of the preeminent authoritative sources on witchcraft. Nowhere near as liberal on this subject as he was in other areas of political theory, Bodin argued forcefully for the real danger posed by witchcraft and the need for authorities to uncover and destroy this crime.

Born in Angers, **France**, Bodin became a Carmelite monk, but left the monastery to pursue a university education at Toulouse, where he excelled in classics, philosophy, economics, and above all law. Eventually, he became a professor of law. In 1561, he went to Paris in the service of the King Charles IX until the publication of *Six livres* lost him royal favor and he became a provincial prosecutor in Laon. His *Démonomanie* was based, in part, on his own experience of witch trials. Bodin was convinced of the reality and threat of witches, arguing at length against such **skeptics** as **Johann Weyer**. His theories on witchcraft may be linked to his larger political thought in that he saw in political authority a reflection of divine order on earth. Thus, he was convinced that secular magistrates had to take all measures necessary to protect this order from the diabolical threat of witchcraft.

BOGUET, HENRI (ca. 1550–1619). A lawyer and author of a well-known legal treatise on **witchcraft** in early-modern Europe, Boguet based his writings on his own experience of witch trials, including his personal examinations of witches in Franche-Comté. In his *Discours des sorciers* (Discourse on Witches), published in 1602, he not only described witchcraft but collected existing legal statutes and codified the procedures legal authorities should take against witches. The book did not, however, contribute more than local color to the existing **demonology** in either **France** or Europe more widely, especially as it was neither translated into Latin nor re-published throughout the remainder of the **witch-hunts** after the third edition of 1610. It was therefore only as a brief practical handbook for dealing with witchcraft that the *Discours* gained a short-lived influence in France.

BONAE MULIERES. Literally meaning "good **women**," *bonae mulieres* was a common term by which authorities writing in Latin described various women or female creatures found in many European folk legends who flew or otherwise traveled at night and often needed to be placated with offerings of food and drink. Aspects of the *bonae mulieres* are reflected in the women who were thought to ride with the pagan goddess **Diana**, as described in the **canon *Episcopi*** and other sources, as well as older beliefs in malevolent, female, nighttime **demons** such as the **strix** or **lamia**, or the Germanic concept of the **Wild Hunt**. All of these notions came to inform the developing stereotype of witchcraft in various ways, contributing most especially to the notion of the **night flight** of witches to a **sabbath**.
See also FOLKLORE.

BONIFACE VIII, POPE (ca. 1235–1303). As pope from 1294 to 1303, Boniface came into contact with many powerful European rulers, such as the English king Edward I and especially the French monarch Philip IV. After

Boniface died, his political enemies continued to struggle against his successors in the papacy. As part of this conflict, servants of the French crown posthumously accused Boniface of **heresy**, murder, and sodomy; of performing ritual **magic**; and of being in league with **demons**. Although the magic the pope was accused of performing was more akin to learned **necromancy** than **witchcraft**, and although the charges against him were clearly politically motivated, the case, along with the similar trial of the **Knights Templar** at about the same time, served to some degree as a harbinger of later developments, culminating ultimately in the earliest **witch-hunts**.

BOOK OF SHADOWS. In modern **witchcraft**, or **Wicca**, collections of magical rituals, prayers, spells, beliefs, and teachings are called Books of Shadows. They are the basic texts (or **grimoires**) of the Wiccan religion. The original Book of Shadows was composed by the founder of modern witchcraft, **Gerald Gardner**, and his chief assistant **Doreen Valiente**. Nevertheless, there is no definitive Book of Shadows for the entire Wiccan tradition, which is very fragmented and decentralized. Gardner himself continually rewrote and modified his Book of Shadows, incorporating material from the *Key of Solomon*, Freemasonry, and the works of **Aleister Crowley** and **Charles Leland**, as well as developing his own. After breaking with Gardner, Valiente authored her own rituals as well. Among modern witches, most **covens**, the basic groupings in which the religion functions, have their own Book of Shadows modified to meet their needs and beliefs. Some ceremonies of modern witchcraft can be practiced alone, and some modern witches are entirely solitary, not part of any organized group or coven, so that individual witches can also have their own personalized Books of Shadows.

BORDELON, LAURENT (1653–1710). A French abbé and prolific satirist, Bordelon's popular *L'histoire des imaginations extravagantes de Monsieur Oufle* (The Story of the Extravagant Imaginations of Monsieur Oufle) was first published in both Paris and Amsterdam in 1710. *Oufle* is an anagram of *le fou* (crazy), and Bordelon's work is highly **skeptical** of **astrology**, **witchcraft**, **lycanthropy**, and the existence of **demons**. Among his adventures, Monsieur Oufle attended a witches' **sabbath**. This scene is illustrated in the satire and is almost an exact copy of Jan Ziarnko's depiction of the sabbath in **Pierre de Lancre**'s account of his **witch-hunting** activities. In Bordelon's publication, however, the event is presented as one of Oufle's "extravagant imaginations" rather than as reality. Bordelon's skeptical attitude was mirrored in artistic works by near contemporaries like William Hogarth.

See also ART, WITCHCRAFT IN; FICTION, WITCHCRAFT IN.

BORROMEO, SAINT CARLO (1538–1584). As archbishop of Milan, Carlo Borromeo regarded the prosecution of **magic** and **witchcraft** as part of his Catholic reform agenda, which also aimed to eradicate superstitious practices. Perhaps the most important witchcraft case in which Borromeo became involved was the prosecution of some **women** from Lecco by his own tribunal in 1569. This case provoked a controversy between Borromeo and the more cautious Roman **Inquisition** that crystallized the Inquisition's moderate approach to witchcraft cases for the remainder of the 16th and into the 17th century. Despite the dispute with Rome, Borromeo and his immediate successors in Milan continued to involve themselves in witchcraft prosecutions. Borromeo was canonized in 1611.

See also ITALY, WITCHCRAFT IN.

BRITISH ISLES, WITCHCRAFT IN. *See* ENGLAND AND WALES, WITCHCRAFT IN; IRELAND, WITCHCRAFT IN; SCOTLAND, WITCHCRAFT IN.

THE BROCKEN. Also known as Blocksberg or Bocksberg, The Brocken is the highest peak in the Harz mountains, **Germany**. During the early-modern period it became the imaginary focus of the witches' **sabbaths** in Germany. An illustration to **Johannes Praetorius**'s *Blockes-Berges Verrichtung* (1668), written after the end of the major period of **witch-hunting**, depicts a large-scale sabbath on the mountain involving all its stereotypical elements. In 1808, Johann Wolfgang von Goethe described witches celebrating **Walpurgisnacht** on The Brocken in *Faust*. Two rock formations on the mountain, the *Teufelskanzel* (**Devil**'s Pulpit) and the *Hexenaltar* (Witches' Altar), and the phenomenon of the Brocken specter (the shadow of the observer magnified when cast upon the surfaces of clouds around the mountain) continue to reinforce the cultural association of the mountain with witchcraft and the supernatural.

See also ART, WITCHCRAFT IN.

BROOMS. One of the most commonly recognized images of **witchcraft** has been the **night flights** of witches astride brooms. The first images of witches on brooms date from the 15th century, most famously those that illustrate the description of witchcraft in *Le champion des dames* (The Defender of Ladies) by the French poet **Martin Le Franc**. Like other early sources, such as the *Errores Gazariorum* (Errors of the Gazarii), *Le champion* also describes witches flying on staffs and other common household or farming implements as well. In other descriptions of flight, such as that found in the **canon Episcopi**, witches rode on animals or **demons** in the form of animals. It was the broom, however, that became generally associated with the witch and her flight, even today during celebrations of **Walpurgisnacht** and **Halloween**. It was, after all, an item almost all **women** would have once had to hand in their homes. To enable flight, witches were thought to anoint themselves or the broom with potions or **ointments**. Often these would be supplied to them by the **devil** at a witches' **sabbath**.

BUCKLAND, RAYMOND (1934–). Born in London, Buckland was the person initially most responsible for the introduction of modern **witchcraft**, or **Wicca**, to the United States. While still living in **England**, Buckland became interested in the study of religions and the occult. He was drawn to the notion of witchcraft as a revived ancient religion by the writings of **Margaret Murray** and **Gerald Gardner**. In 1962, he emigrated to the United States and, a year later, while back in England, met Gerald Gardner by whom he was initiated into modern witchcraft. Thereafter, Buckland became Gardner's principal agent in **North America**. Eventually, Buckland broke with Gardner's variety of witchcraft and founded his own, called *Seax-Wicca*, based more closely on ancient Anglo-Saxon traditions. A prolific author, Buckland has written many books and for a long time conducted a correspondence school in witchcraft from his home.

BURNING TIMES. Coined by **Gerald Gardner**, the Burning Times refers to the period of the European **witch-hunts**. The term has been adopted by both **neo-pagans** (like the witch **Starhawk**) and **feminists** (notably Mary Daly) to highlight the persecution and oppression of **pagan** religions and **women** in general. The term is misleading in several respects. Not all convicted witches were **executed**, and in **England** and Wales condemned witches were hanged rather than burned. It also suggests an active discrimination against the practices of **cunning men and women** or a violent misogyny on the part of patriarchal authorities. In fact, cunning folk were not a particular target group of the witch-hunts and, while European society was generally misogynistic, witch trials were sporadic, involved women as accusers and, occasionally, focused on **male witches**. The claim made by some feminists that the Burning Times are comparable to the Holocaust cannot be sustained. There was never any attempt to rid the world of women in the way that the Nazis tried to murder all **Jews**.

C

CAESARIUS OF HEISTERBACH (ca. 1180–1250). A well-known Cistercian abbot of Heisterbach in the Rhineland, Caesarius was a theologian and the author of numerous treatises on religious subjects. His most famous work was the *Dialogus miraculorum* (Dialogue on Miracles), composed in the 1220s and 1230s. In this long, moralizing work, he included several stories of **demons** and demonic **sorcery**, particularly **necromancy**. He stands as an example of the increasing concern over such matters on the part of clerical authorities in the late 12th and 13th centuries.

CALVIN, JEAN (1509–1564). After **Martin Luther**, Calvin was the leading figure of the Protestant **Reformation**. While Calvin did believe that witches existed and could perform harmful **magic**, he interpreted most of the magical practices listed in the key chapters of the **Bible** as **divination**, a form of **sorcery** that did not directly harm people or their property. In his doctrine, the power of witches was a diabolical illusion that God permitted the **devil** to create. Calvin did not incorporate the diabolical **pact**, **incubi**, **night flight**, or the **sabbath** into his **demonology**. This interpretation helped foster the Calvinist "disenchantment" of the world and formed the basis for later Calvinist opposition to witch trials. Calvin did, however, support the death penalty for witches because of their **apostasy**. This stance allowed **witch-hunts** to occur in places like **Scotland** that were Calvinist.

CANNIBALISM. One of the more horrible aspects of the witch stereotype, cannibalism, especially the cannibalizing of babies and young **children**, has a long association with **sorcery**, **heresy**, and **witchcraft**. In ancient and classical mythology, nocturnal monsters such as **Lamashtu**, the **strix**, and **lamia** were believed to kill and often devour children. Such monstrous **women** also include **Baba Yaga** and **Yama-uba**. During the Middle Ages, **Jews** were sometimes suspected of murdering Christian children and eating their flesh in a dark parody of the Christian Eucharist. Later, the killing and eating of babies was thought to be a standard element of the witches' **sabbath**, reinforced by its reappearance in the many images of witchcraft in the early-modern period. Ironically, the association of cannibalism with unorthodox and clandestine religious assemblies probably began with the rise of Christianity itself. In the Roman Empire, when Christianity was seen as a dissident sect, authorities often condemned Christian gatherings as orgiastic festivals, and they sometimes sought to equate the consumption of the Eucharist, which is the flesh of Christ in Christian doctrine, with cannibalism.

See also ANTIQUITY, WITCHCRAFT IN; ART, WITCHCRAFT IN.

CANON *EPISCOPI*. One of the most important legal texts regarding **sorcery**, superstition, and later **witchcraft**, the earliest version of the canon appeared in the 10th century in the legal collection of Regino of Prüm. It was incorporated into later collections of canon law, including the influential *Decretum* of Gratian in the 12th century. The canon took its name from the first word of its text in Latin, and commanded bishops and their officials to eradicate sorcery and harmful **magic** in their dioceses. It went on to describe "certain **women**" who believed that they flew at night in large assemblies with the goddess **Diana** and obeyed her commands. Like other authorities, the canon was careful to state that these women had been deluded by the **devil** to whom they had given themselves. He imposed the illusion of **night flight** on their minds. While these women were presented more as victims than servants of Satan, they posed a threat to the souls of other women whom they might seduce into the same errors. The canon therefore prescribed banishment for the followers of Diana if they persisted in their beliefs.

The canon and the popular beliefs it describes formed an important basis for the later concept of the night flight of witches to a **sabbath**. It was also suggestive of the spiritual weakness of women that was to be reiterated at length in the *Malleus maleficarum* (ca. 1486). In stating that the night flight and other activities of the followers of Diana were illusions, however, the canon presented later authorities who believed in the existence and power of witches with a dilemma. The canon had to be reconciled with the emerging stereotype of the witch and her activities. Some writers, like **Martin Le Franc** and **Johannes Nider**, simply denied the possibility of transvection. Defenders of the belief in night flight noted that the canon was referring to a single case (the followers of Diana) and not a general principle. After all, a **demon** had transported Jesus through the air (Matthew 4:1–11). Witches were also believed by Pope **Alexander V** and **Nicholas Jacquier**, for example, to be a new sect to which older descriptions did not apply specifically. The Spanish and Roman **Inquisitions**, on the other hand, tended to retain the view that witchcraft acts were illusions, errors that needed correction. Many **skeptics** and opponents of the **witch-hunts** found the illusory nature of witchcraft and the non-capital punishments described in the canon useful in their arguments.

CARIBBEAN WITCHCRAFT. A range of practices and beliefs derived from the European and **African** origins of the people of the Caribbean contribute to a variety of complex occult systems in the region. **Sorcery**, such as **Obeah**, and **witchcraft** are found independently of and blended into **Santería** and what the West tends to term **Voodoo**, but that should more accurately be called *Vodou*. There are also **folkloric** traditions in the Caribbean that incorporate **soucouyants**, **Ole Higue** and **Loogaroo**, vampiric old hags who practice sorcery or witchcraft. The first important reference to witchcraft that may have had its origins in the region comes from the **Salem** trials of 1692. Tituba, the slave who confessed to witchcraft at the beginning of these trials, but who escaped capital punishment, may have had links to the Caribbean. Her ethnicity cannot be proven, but the available evidence suggests that she may have come from or through the islands, perhaps from **South America** or even Africa, on her way to Salem. The witchcraft she confessed to was, however, a European version that her Puritan owners had brought with them from **England**. Recently, between 1999 and 2001, there have been minor panics about sorcery and witchcraft in Dominica. Like some European **witch-hunts**, these panics coincided with severe economic problems. Such panics are, however, much rarer than in parts of Africa.

CAROLINA LAW CODE. A criminal **law** code for all the lands of the **German Empire** was introduced at the Reichstag in Regensburg in 1532 under the authority of the emperor Charles V. The code therefore derives its name from his (*Carolus* in Latin). The Carolina code, in theory, governed **witchcraft** prosecutions in the German Empire for the remainder of the period of the **witch-hunts**. However, given the political fragmentation of the empire, local courts could generally apply the law as they saw fit. For example, in the severe witch trials in **Bamberg** in the early 17th century, victims of the trials actually appealed to the emperor that he should enforce the proper application of the Carolina code.

CASTAÑEGA, MARTÍN DE (EARLY 16th CENTURY). A Franciscan friar in **Spain**, Martín witnessed a series of witch trials in Pamplona in 1527. In response, he wrote a *Tratado muy sotil bien fundado de las supersticiones y hechicerías* (Treatise . . . on Superstition and Witchcraft). Published in 1529, this was the first work on **witchcraft** to be printed in the Spanish vernacular. Martín adopted a qualified **skepticism** toward witchcraft. He accepted that some witches really existed, but avoided any discussion of the more extreme elements of the witch stereotype, such as **night flight** and the witches' **sabbath**. He also argued that many events attributed to witchcraft could be caused by other, natural, means, and he was concerned that many people accused of witchcraft were actually mentally ill.

CATS. Cats have long been associated with **magic** and **witchcraft**. The ancient Egyptians venerated cats and associated them with **Isis**, the mother goddess and lunar deity who was also patron of the magic arts. In Christian Europe, **heretics** and later alleged witches, including the **Knights Templar**, were often thought to worship cats, or **demons** that had transformed themselves into cats. In early descriptions of the witches' **sabbaths**, the **devil** was sometimes depicted as a black cat rather than a **goat**. Cats were also common among the many animal forms that a demon could take when it became a witch's **familiar**, and this association of cat with demon was occasionally made explicit, for example, in the **Chelmsford witches'** case in which the cat familiar was named Satan. There is little evidence, however, that cats believed to be familiars were burned alongside their witch mistresses or, indeed, that they were massacred at times of famine and epidemic because they were believed to be **evil**.

CAULDRON. Alongside the **broom** and the pointed hat, the cauldron has become one of the everyday items most commonly associated with witches. It is simply a pot used for boiling food, but its size lends itself to the idea that large objects like humans, adults or **children**, might be cooked in it. In classical mythology, the cauldron was used by **Medea** to create her potions and restore Jason to life by boiling his body parts in it. Cauldrons were also used for regeneration, as well as divination, in Celtic and Germanic mythology. **Johannes Nider** introduced the stories of witches boiling children in their cauldrons to make magical **ointments** in his *Formicarius* (The Anthill) of the late 1430s. Nider got these stories from his informant, the Swiss magistrate Peter of Bern, and they were repeated in both the **witch-hunting** manual *Malleus maleficarum* (ca. 1486) and the **skeptical Johann Weyer**'s *De praestigiis daemonum* (1563). At about the same time, the cauldron became part of the stereotypical image of the witches' **sabbath**. It is to be seen in the illustrations to the works of **Ulrich Molitor** and **Pierre de Lancre**, and in the much imitated **witchcraft** scenes by **Hans Baldung Grien**. The cauldron remains a staple of **Halloween** imagery.
    See also ART, WITCHCRAFT IN.

CHELMSFORD WITCHES. The first major witch trial in **England** occurred at Chelmsford, Essex, in 1566. No witch suspects had been tried under the first English statute against **witchcraft** passed in 1542 and repealed in 1547. Before a new **law** was passed in 1563 early in the reign of Elizabeth I, two individuals were tried before the assize courts in Essex (in 1560 and 1561) and a further three were brought before them in 1564 and 1565. The 1566 case was, however, the first significant one to be tried because it involved four **women**, all from the village of Hatfield Peverel, and it became the subject of the first English witchcraft **pamphlet**. This pamphlet reported the confessions of the suspects Elizabeth Francis, Agnes Waterhouse, and Agnes's daughter Joan, but ignored the case against Lora Winchester. Elizabeth confessed that she had learned witchcraft from her grandmother, who had given her a **cat** named Sathan (Satan) as a **familiar**. During the 16 years she had the cat, it committed murder, abortion. and physical harm on her behalf. Elizabeth then gave the cat to Agnes, who confessed to turning it into a toad and instructing it to commit further acts of *maleficium*. Joan said she called up Sathan, who appeared in the form of a dog, to scare a girl who would not give her bread and cheese. He did so only after Joan had promised herself body and soul to him. Agnes was convicted and hanged. Elizabeth received a lighter sentence, but, after appearing before the assize court twice more on charges of witchcraft in 1572 and 1579, was finally executed. Joan was acquitted.

The Chelmsford case is typical of English witchcraft. The diabolical **pact** is not as developed as it was in Europe and there is no hint of anything resembling a witches' **sabbath**. This is because English law tried witchcraft as a felony rather than a **heresy**, and a suspect had to be accused of committing an act of harm against another person or his property to be indicted. The demonic is reduced to a familiar that does the harm on behalf of the witch. As a county town and seat of the Essex assize court, Chelmsford was the site of many later witch trials, including the infamous trial of 23 women instigated by **Matthew Hopkins** in 1645.

CHILDREN, WITCHCRAFT AND. Historically, children have featured in **witchcraft** events in several ways. On occasion, children could be accused of witchcraft, although this was generally only the case in large-scale **witchhunts** like those in **Würzburg** during which 41 children, mostly boys, were executed between 1627 and 1629. Many of these boys were fellow students and simply named friends as accomplices under **torture**. Other children were vulnerable to accusations because a close relative had been arrested as a witch. In his investigations into witchcraft in the **Basque country**, **Alonso de Salazar Frías** listened to confessions from well over a thousand child and adolescent witches. It is not clear why these children came forward. In **Africa**, many of the victims of the recent witch-hunts have been children displaced from their homes by warfare or economic crisis.

Children also played an important role as accusers and witnesses in witchcraft cases. They could bring charges directly, or they could begin a panic among adults by exhibiting symptoms of bewitchment or demonic **possession**. Their adult relatives would then begin making accusations of witchcraft, perhaps directed by the children. The most famous case of a major series of trials being generated by the accusations of children occurred in **Salem**, Massachusetts, in 1692. A similar case occurred in **Mora**, Sweden, in the 1660s. In **England**, as elsewhere, the exceptional nature of witchcraft meant that child witnesses were called even when their testimony was not permissible. Children were called as witnesses against both the **Chelmsford** and **Saint Osyth** witches.

Most frequently, however, children featured in witchcraft cases purely as victims. Witches were regularly accused of committing **infanticide**, killing their neighbors' babies or infants, or causing pregnant women to miscarry. In **demonology** and iconography, witches were described sacrificing babies and small children to the **devil** as part of the **cannibalistic** rituals at their sabbaths. This sacrificial element has its origins in **Antiquity, folklore** and the blood libels against **Jews**, especially from the 12th to the 20th centuries, that asserted that they ritually murdered children of the Christian faith. The idea that witches make such sacrifices persists today and there have been unfounded allegations that practitioners of modern witchcraft, or **Wicca**, and **Satanism** ritually abuse and murder children.

CHRONOLOGY OF WITCH-HUNTING. The intensity of **witchcraft** prosecution was not constant in Europe. Before the 15th century, cases involving **sorcery** or witchcraft, like the trials of the **Knights Templar** or **Alice Kyteler**, were sporadic. It was only as the full witchcraft stereotype began to develop from the early 15th century, in the work of **Johannes Nider** for example, that **witch-hunts** began to occur in parts of **Switzerland** and the Alpine areas of **Italy** and **France**. Although influential treatises on witchcraft, notably by **Heinrich Kramer** and the more cautious **Ulrich Molitor**, followed and circulated widely via the new printing presses, witch-hunting did not spread or intensify until about 1560. Localized witch trials were conducted, but **Martin Luther** was able to observe that witches did not seem so common as they had in his youth. This lull in witch-hunting resulted from the continuing resistance to external interference in episcopal affairs encountered by Kramer and the **skepticism** of Renaissance **humanists**, like **Erasmus** and **Agrippa**. It is also possible that the religious divisions created by the **Reformation** diverted the attention of theologians and secular authorities away from witchcraft.

By the time **Johann Weyer** had published his skeptical work in 1562, witch trials and new **demonologies** were increasing in number. They intensified in central and western Europe throughout the late 16th century and reached their peak in the ecclesiastical principalities of the **German Empire** (**Bamberg, Eichstätt**, Ellwangen and **Würzburg**) in the 1620s. This intensification coincided with a combination of other problems. By the mid-16th century, the population of Europe had begun to outstrip its resources resulting in social immobility, wage depression, inflationary cycles, and widespread unemployment and vagrancy. The so-called Little Ice Age, which was particularly bad from about 1560 to about 1630, caused persistent harvest failures that exacerbated these problems. In these circumstances, attitudes toward the poor changed, and able-bodied beggars were no longer regarded as blessed and deserving of alms. In themselves, these factors were not sufficient to provoke witch persecution. Southern and Eastern Europe did not experience the same intensity of witchcraft prosecution. This may have been because theologians and **inquisitors** there retained the view that witchcraft acts were illusory, and they did not experience at first hand the political and social tensions caused by the Protestant and Catholic Reformations.

Witch persecution began to decline sharply in about 1630 with the end of the Little Ice Age and the deaths of the main Catholic witch-hunters in the German Empire. The Thirty Years War also reached the part of the empire most affected by witchcraft persecution at the same time and the ecclesiastical princes therefore had other concerns than moral reform. There were outbursts of witch-hunting in **France** and **England** in the 1640s, **Scotland** and **Sweden** in the 1660s, **Salem** in 1692, and **Hungary** in the 18th century. Generally, however, witch prosecution was on the decline and skepticism about its very existence increasing among theologians and judges. The last known person to be executed for witchcraft in Europe was **Anna Göldi** in **Switzerland** in 1782. Witch-hunts have been rare in the rest of the world with the exception of parts of modern **Africa**.

See also BLACK MASS.

CHURCH OF SATAN. Founded by Anton Szandor LaVey [real name Howard Stanton Levey], the Church of Satan is the leading organization for modern **Satanism**. LaVey engaged in a variety of professions, but was always deeply interested in matters of **magic** and the occult prior to the foundation of the church in San Francisco in 1966. His major publications, *The Satanic Bible* (1969) and *The Satanic Rituals* (1972), have been influential far beyond his own church. Most other Satanist groups adhere to LaVey's basic principles, even if they do not accept all aspects of the Church of Satan's particular structure and forms.

Modern Satanism, as conceived by LaVey, has little to do with the traditional Satanism thought to exist in the past (and still believed by many to exist in the modern world). To begin, LaVey's Satanism does not really involve the worship of Satan, at least not in the traditional sense in which Satan is seen as the Christian **devil**, the representation of **evil**. The Church of Satan does not (in its own view) advocate immorality or evil. Rather, it adheres to a philosophy of strong individualism and hedonism, so long as the well-being of other people is not adversely affected. The church advocates personal freedom and the pursuit of worldly pleasure, above all physical and especially sexual pleasure, which it maintains have been falsely proclaimed to be evil by Christianity. In this basic philosophy, as well as in his continued interest in occult learning and ritual magic, LaVey can be seen as following in the footsteps of such famous 19th-century figures as **Aleister Crowley**. Thus the Church of Satan does advocate and adhere to its own well-defined, if non-Christian, ethical code. In particular, the use of illegal narcotics is strongly disapproved, and the torture or sacrifice of animals is strictly forbidden (in contrast to many popular images of Satanist activity).

Despite the use of magical rituals in the Church of Satan, and the frequent popular association of Satanism with **witchcraft**, the church is in no way associated with any aspect of modern witchcraft, or **Wicca**. Modern witches strongly deny any aspect of Satanism in their religion. For their part, members of the Church of Satan and most other Satanist groups reject any association with Wiccan, **neo-pagan**, or other New Age groups. In particular, they would object to the strong **feminist** element of much modern witchcraft. It should be noted that the Church of Satan is extremely small, certainly not more than a few thousand members, and other Satanist groups are even smaller.

CHURCH OF WICCA. One of the oldest organizations of modern **witchcraft**, or **Wicca**, in the United States, the Church of Wicca was also the first such organization to receive official recognition as a religion. The church was founded in 1968 by Gavin and Yvonne Frost. The Frosts then set about trying to attain official tax-exempt religious status from the Internal Revenue Service. This came in 1972 and was the first ruling to give Wicca the status of a federally recognized religion. Subsequently, the Church of Wicca became the first Wiccan organization to have its status as an officially recognized religion upheld in court as a result of a federal appeals court affirmation of a prisoner's rights case in Virginia.

The church follows most of the usual beliefs and rites of Wiccan practice, with one notable exception. The church holds that the nature of the deity is not definable, as opposed to the typical emphasis on the female **Goddess** in most other forms of modern witchcraft. The church also maintains a School of Wicca, the oldest correspondence school for modern witchcraft in the United States.

CIRCE. Along with **Medea**, Circe was one of the great female sorceresses in classical mythology. She was often thought to be the daughter of **Hecate**, goddess of **magic**, and so was herself a demigoddess. She is most famous for having turned the crew of the adventurer Odysseus into swine when they came to her island. Odysseus forced her to reverse her spell, but became enamored with her and stayed on her island for a year. In the medieval and early-modern periods, Circe became a literary archetype of the witch, especially for the notion of witches as dangerous seducers of men.

See also ANTIQUITY, WITCHCRAFT IN; SEXUALITY AND WITCH-CRAFT.

CLASSICAL MUSIC, WITCHCRAFT IN. Witches, **witchcraft**, and **magic** have occasionally been the subject of classical music. "The Sorcerer's Apprentice" by Paul Dukas, and Modest Mussorgsky's "Night on Bald Mountain," his tone poem on a witches' **sabbath**, were made popular by Disney's animated **film** *Fantasia* (1940). The witches' sabbath has also been the subject of pieces by Hector Berlioz and Edward MacDowell. Like his Russian contemporaries, Mussorgsky incorporated **folklore** about **Baba Yaga** into other compositions. Several other composers have turned well-known stories about witchcraft and magic into music. These include Piotr Tchaikovsky's version of Lord Byron's *Manfred*, and the many reworkings of various parts Johann Wolfgang von Goethe's *Faust*, by, for example, Ludwig von Beethoven, Franz Liszt, and Richard Wagner. "Hedwig's Theme," John Williams's composition for three films of the Harry Potter series, is named after Potter's owl **familiar**.

See also ART, WITCHCRAFT IN; FICTION, WITCHCRAFT IN.

COLONIAL AMERICA, WITCHCRAFT IN. *See* NORTH AMERICA, WITCHCRAFT IN; SOUTH AMERICA, WITCHCRAFT IN.

COMO, BERNARD DE (?–1510). A Dominican friar and inquisitor who conducted a number of witch trials at Como in northern **Italy**, Bernard wrote a brief *Tractatus de strigiis* (Treatise on Witches). The treatise has most often been dated to the early 16th century, but may have been written as early as the mid-1480s at about the same time as the *Malleus maleficarum*. It was later reprinted in several editions, often with the *Malleus*.

COVEN. In modern **witchcraft**, or **Wicca**, a coven refers to an organized and set group of witches who practice together. The traditional number of people in a coven is 13, consisting of a leader and 12 members; in practice, however, the number varies widely. As modern witchcraft is a very unstructured religion, covens are self-regulating and determine what rites and ceremonies they will follow. Historically, the term can be traced at least to trials in the mid-17th century in **Scotland**, and of course the idea that witches met in groups to worship the **devil** and perform harmful **sorcery** was always a basic element of the idea of witchcraft. However, despite the claims of some modern witches to be members of extremely old covens, some up to 800 years, there is no historical connection between the modern ritual coven and the sorts of gatherings and witches' **sabbaths** that were thought to take place in the period of the **witch-hunts**.

THE CRAFT. An alternate term for the rites and beliefs of modern **witchcraft**, or **Wicca**.

CRIMEN EXCEPTUM. Witchcraft was considered a *crimen exceptum* (excepted crime) by **Heinrich Kramer** and later **demonologists**. An excepted crime was usually one that involved treason, **heresy, apostasy**, or **idolatry**. The exceptional nature of crimes like witchcraft meant that the usual rules of evidence were relaxed to permit prosecution testimony from **women, children**, servants, and others who were not normally allowed to testify in criminal cases. **Witch-hunters** were also able to exploit witchcraft's status as an exceptional crime by introducing innovative forms of **torture** and applying them persistently until a witch suspect confessed. This was most common in places like the prince-bishopric of **Eichstätt**.

CROWLEY, ALEISTER (1875–1947). One of the most famous occultists and practitioners of ritual **magic** in modern times, Crowley is idolized by some and vilified by many others. He himself carefully cultivated a dark reputation and seemed to enjoy the approbation of others. His connections to **witchcraft** are tangential at best, but still important.

Born in Warwickshire, **England**, into an intensely religious family, Crowley came to reject Christianity entirely. He became interested instead in many varieties of occultism prevalent in England in the late 19th century and remained so throughout his life. In 1898, he joined the **Hermetic Order of the Golden Dawn**, one of the most important occultist organizations in England, but his rapid rise within the order led to conflict with some members in its hierarchy and schism within the organization. Crowley claimed to have experienced many special revelations and to be the incarnation of several historical occult figures, including an ancient Egyptian priest of the 26th pharaonic dynasty. His *Book of the Law*, written in 1904, claimed that the Christian era was past and espoused a new religion based on esoteric and magical knowledge. His most famous work, *Magick in Theory and Practice* (1929), viewed ritual magic as a means toward union with God (Crowley used the spelling "magick" to distinguish real, mystical magic from illusion or trickery).

Although by no means himself a witch or neo-pagan, Crowley did exert some influence over modern witchcraft, or **Wicca**, and other forms of **neo-paganism**. At the very end of his life, Crowley briefly met **Gerald Gardner**, the founder of modern witchcraft, and many elements of Crowley's magical philosophies and rituals found their way into some of Gardner's early writings on witchcraft. Many of the more explicit elements were, however, later removed by Gardner and especially his chief disciple **Doreen Valiente**. Nevertheless, Crowley's most basic philosophical principle, known as the

"Law of Thelema," has proven very influential on modern witchcraft and other varieties of neo-paganism. The "Law of Thelema" is expressed in *The Book of the Law*: "Do what thou wilt shall be the whole of the law." This is not meant to express complete immorality, but rather profound individuality and respect for human free will. The basic "Wiccan Rede" developed by Gerald Gardner ("an' it harm none, do what ye will") is probably a direct borrowing of Crowley's statement and remains part of the creed common to modern Wicca and most neo-pagan groups.

CUNNING MEN AND WOMEN. Also called wise men or wise **women**, witch doctors, or sometimes white witches or wizards, cunning men and women were people who engaged in a variety of activities, such as magical **healing**, fortune telling, and **divination**. Their activities were generally regarded as good or helpful, as opposed to the harm, or *maleficium*, caused by witches. Cunning men and women claimed to derive their power in various ways. Many maintained that they possessed a hereditary form of power passed down through their family. Others might claim power due to some special occurrence at birth or later in life. Being the seventh son of a seventh son, for example, or being born with the caul were considered signs of supernatural power.

Typically, the activities of cunning men and women included performing magical as well as non-magical healing, fertility rituals, or **love magic**. They also acted as fortune tellers and performed other types of divination, such as identifying thieves, locating lost or stolen items, or reporting on the condition of loved ones far away. Cunning folk were often consulted in cases of perceived bewitchment, either to undo it or to identify the witch who had supposedly cast the spell. A few cunning men and women dabbled in more clearly learned forms of magic or divination, such as **astrology**. In short, they offered all the magical services common in pre-modern European society.

Although cunning folk were not often identified as witches by most people since their **magic** was beneficial rather than harmful, they could nevertheless fall under suspicion on occasion. Also, during the late-medieval and early-modern periods, when authorities were more concerned with the supposedly demonic nature of almost all magic, rather than the particular ends to which it might be employed, cunning men and women could easily find themselves charged with witchcraft.

D

DANEAU, LAMBERT (ca. 1530–1595). A French Calvinist minister, Daneau wrote a short work on **witchcraft** while resident in Geneva, **Switzerland**. While it is often asserted that the Latin edition *De veneficiis* (Witches) was first published in 1564, this was in fact a translation of the French original *Les sorciers* published in 1574. *Les sorciers* was presented as a dialogue, a popular format preferred by the English Puritan **George Gifford**. It was written to counter **skepticism** about witchcraft. As the Latin title suggests, Daneau believed that witches used poisonous **magic** to harm others or their property. Like **Heinrich Kramer** before him, Daneau argued that secular judges should be authorized to punish witches by death. The dialogue was subsequently translated into English and German.

See also CALVIN, JEAN (1509–1564); POISON.

DEE, JOHN (1527–1608 or 1609). The most renowned learned magician in Elizabethan **England**, Dee pursued studies in various branches of mathematics, science, and **magic**, including **astrology**, **alchemy**, **hermeticism** and scrying (crystal gazing). Dee was arrested for casting Queen Mary of England's horoscope in 1555, but acquitted of the charge of treason. Although the casting of horoscopes was linked to **witchcraft** in an Elizabethan **law** of 1580, Dee himself did not have a reputation for witchcraft. In fact, as both princess and queen, Mary's half sister Elizabeth employed Dee as an astrologer. He built up an important library of magical and scientific works at his house at Mortlake, including many items of European **demonology** collected during his travels across the continent in the 1580s. These demonologies were not, however, used to influence the course of **witch-hunting** in England. After Queen Elizabeth's death in 1603, Dee spent the last few years of his life in relative poverty.

DEL RIO, MARTÍN (1551–1608). A famous Jesuit scholar, Del Rio authored the *Disquisitiones magicarum* (Disquisitions on Magic), first published in 1599–1600 and frequently republished throughout the 17th century. This work became probably the most important and most cited treatise on **magic** and **witchcraft** in the 1600s.

Del Rio was born into a distinguished Spanish family in Antwerp (then part of the Spanish Netherlands). He was an intellectual prodigy and had published an edition and commentary on the tragedies of Seneca by the time he was 19. At 24, he was appointed attorney general for the region of Brabant. In 1580, however, he chose to enter the Jesuit order, after which he studied and taught at numerous Jesuit centers around Europe. It was at Louvain that he composed his *Disquisitiones*. This wide-ranging work began with a discussion of magic in general before focusing on demonic magic and witchcraft. Del Rio also included a discussion of harmful **sorcery** and *maleficium*, and a section of instructions to judges about how they should handle cases of witchcraft, as well as discussing subjects such as prophecy, fortune telling, and **divination**, and the role of priestly confessors in dealing with these activities. In many ways the most comprehensive learned treatise on witchcraft in the early-modern period, the *Disquisitiones* was also extremely popular, surpassing such works as the *Malleus maleficarum* and **Nicolas Rémy**'s *Daemonolatria*.

DEMONOLOGY. Referring to the scholarly study of **demons** and the **devil**, demonology has always existed in Christianity as a counterpart to theology, the study of God. As early as the second century CE, Christian monks in the deserts of Egypt were writing about nature of demons, which they thought were assailing them constantly. The early church fathers were also demonologists, and the great **Saint Augustine of Hippo** wrote extensively about the nature of demons in some of his major works, including *De divinatione daemonum* (On the Divination of Demons) and sections of *The City of God*. After late **Antiquity**, few major works were written about demons until about the 12th century, when the study of demons began to revive as part of the general revitalization of education and intellectual life in Europe known as the "Renaissance of the 12th Century." In the 13th century, the important medieval theologian **Thomas Aquinas** discussed the nature and powers of demons in several of his works.

Throughout the period of major **witch-hunting** in Europe, from the 15th to the 17th centuries, witches were believed to have entered **pacts** with the devil and to cause harm, or *maleficium*, through the power of demons. Thus virtually every treatise on **witchcraft** was really a treatise on demonology, or at least contained large sections of demonological material. The knowledge, or supposed knowledge, about the nature, variety, and number of demons was refined as never before. As fallen angels, the demons were thought to retain their rank respective to one another based on the order of angels in heaven (in ascending order: seraphim, cherubim, thrones, dominions, principalities, powers, virtues, archangels, and angels). Lucifer, the devil, was the prince of all demons. Chief demons under him included Asmodeus, Astaroth, Baal, Beelzebub, Belial, and Leviathan. These demons were derived principally from the **Bible** and had generally been **pagan** deities worshiped by tribes and nations encountered by the ancient Israelites. Christian authorities considered all such pagan gods to be demons.

Demonologists spent a great deal of effort calculating the number of demons, which was known from the Bible to be "legion." In the 15th century, **Alfonso de Spina** estimated that one-third of all the angels in heaven had sided with Lucifer when he fell, and by various calculations he determined this number to be 133,306,668 demons. Other figures were based on the association of the number six with the devil. In the 16th century, one authority determined that there were 66 princes in hell commanding 6,660,000 demons. **Johann Weyer**, who was actually **skeptical** about many aspects of witchcraft, calculated that there were 1,111 legions in hell, each with 6,666 demons, for a total of 7,405,926 demons commanded by 72 princes.

DEMONS. As **evil** spirits that could be commanded by humans, demons were essential to **witchcraft** as conceived in Christian Europe in the medieval and early-modern periods, since it was through the agency of demons that witches were believed to perform harmful **sorcery** and cause *maleficium*. In exchange for the ability to command demons, witches were thought to have offered worship to the demons or to the **devil** himself. For this act of **apostasy** and the harm they caused, many Christian authorities believed witches posed such a threat to society that they needed to be eradicated at all costs. Witchcraft therefore became a *crimen exceptum*, permitting **witch-hunters** to use extreme methods of investigation and execution in their pursuit of its practitioners.

Most pre-modern cultures have believed in the existence of powerful spirits that could be controlled by human beings for magical purposes. In ancient Greece, such creatures were known as *daimones*. These creatures were not, however, necessarily evil; some had good or ambivalent intentions toward human beings. Good and evil spirits also existed in the ancient Jewish **demonology** that informed early Christian theology and later the Jewish Kabbalah of the medieval and early-modern periods. As Christianity developed, however, its demonology became far more rigid. In the early fifth century, **Saint Augustine of Hippo** defined the essential nature of the world as being one of conflict between the forces of good, represented by the Christian church, and the forces of evil, led by Satan, In Christian demonology, demons became associated with the fallen angels who rebelled with Satan and were cast out of heaven. The church also transformed the gods and goddesses of classical,

Celtic and Germanic mythology into figures of evil. By the 16th century, a literary genre of *Teufelsbücher* (devil books) emerged in Germany in which each vice was presided over by its own demon. Christian demons were therefore evil, and humans who became involved with them in any way were believed to be **heretics** or apostates.

Augustine's view that magicians made **pacts** with the demons they sought to control was later extended to witches hunted in the medieval and early-modern periods. These witches were believed to have sex with their demon lovers at the witches' **sabbaths** and on other occasions.

See also ANTIQUITY, WITCHCRAFT IN.

DEVIL. In Christian cosmology, the devil is the personification of the principle of **evil**. The origins of the devil are vague. He is a composite of several figures in the Hebrew **Bible**, including the serpent that tempted Eve in the Garden of Eden, Lucifer, the rebellious angel who was cast out of heaven, and Satan, who appears in the Book of Job. He also incorporates elements of characters who appear in the Jewish Apocryphal literature of the period 200 BCE to 100 CE. In the New Testament, the devil is usually referred to by the Greek *diabolos* or the Hebrew *satan*. *Diabolos* can mean accuser or slanderer.

In early Christianity, the devil was a tempter and a deceiver who worked on earth with God's permission. For **Saint Augustine of Hippo**, however, the devil became a more powerful and feared figure. He was an angel who used the free will given him by God to rebel and become the commander of both the fallen angels who followed him and those humans he tempted away from God. These sinners he would torment in hell. As Augustine's view began to dominate Christian theology, bestial and foul features were attributed to the devil, including black or red coloring and a **goat**- or dragon-like appearance. Encounters with heretical groups like the Cathars of the 12th century who believed that the devil was lord over all matter and therefore a creative (rather than passively tempting) force on earth reinforced the power of the devil for theologians. Popular Protestant and Catholic reformers, with their claims that their opponents were agents of the devil, spread fear of the devil more widely.

Some **demonologists** came to believe that witches were not merely **women** who had been tempted by the devil to believe that they flew at night with **Diana** or a similar goddess or who performed harmful **sorcery** through the agency of **demons**. They also accused witches of worshiping the devil. After they had been seduced by the devil and made a **pact** with him, witches would worship him at their **sabbaths** in a manner that mirrored Christian rites in a grotesque way.

Although it is entirely probable that at least some people accused of **witchcraft** during the period of the **witch-hunts** did in fact practice some form of sorcery, and a few of them may even have worshiped the devil and believed that they gained power from him, there is no evidence that any large cults of devil-worshiping sorcerers ever really existed in Europe. Likewise, although some people continue to accuse practitioners of modern witchcraft, or **Wicca**, of worshiping the devil, this is not the case. Modern witches are **neopagans** who do not adhere to the principal elements of Christian belief; they do not seek to undermine Christianity as **heretics** or **apostates**. Even groups that practice modern **Satanism** do not worship the devil as he is understood by Christians.

DEVIL'S MARK. During the period of the **witch-hunts**, many authorities believed that the **devil** marked all witches as a sign of their service to him. This mark could take many forms and, in practice, once a person became suspected of **witchcraft** almost any blemish, scar, or bodily mark might serve as evidence. Witches were routinely searched for such marks when they were arrested and brought to trial through a procedure known as **pricking**. The devil's mark should not be confused with the **witch's mark** that was believed to be the spot on the flesh where witches would suckle their demonic **familiars**.

DIABOLISM. **Witchcraft** as conceived in the Christian European context during most of the medieval and early-modern periods, and certainly during the age of the most intense **witch-hunting** in the 15th, 16th, and 17th centuries, was comprised of two essential elements: *maleficium* (the harm caused to human beings, their livestock or their property); and a range of activities that focused on the supposed worship of the **devil** and supplication of **demons** entailed in the performance of that sorcery. These latter elements are often referred to collectively in modern scholarship as diabolism.

Essential to the diabolical aspect of witchcraft was the basic belief, firmly held by most Christian authorities at least since the time of the great church father **Saint Augustine of Hippo** in the fifth century, that most if not all forms of sorcery relied on demonic agency, and that this entailed a heretical **pact** made between the demon and the human sorcerer. The sorcerer would offer or promise to offer the demon certain signs of worship in exchange for which the demon would perform certain acts. Although notions of demonic pacts are rooted in early Christianity, however, the linkage of this concept to the performance of acts of *maleficium* was slow to develop. Even in the late 14th century, the inquisitor **Nicolau Eymeric** had to prove that demonic sorcery necessarily entailed **idolatry** and the worship of demons. Thereafter, however, the full range of diabolism evident in later witchcraft quickly developed, and by the early 15th century the stereotype was already fairly complete.

Witches, in addition to simply entering into pacts with certain demons or offering them worship in exchange for magical power, were believed to have entered into complete **apostasy** from the true faith and to have surrendered their souls to the devil himself. They were members of an organized, conspiratorial, satanic cult, and gathered regularly at secret nocturnal gatherings known as witches' **sabbaths** where they would worship the devil; desecrate the cross, Eucharist, and other holy objects; and perform other abominable acts, such as killing and **cannibalizing** babies and small **children** and engaging in sexual **orgies** with each other, with various demons, and with the devil.

DIANA, GODDESS. A pagan goddess of the moon and the hunt, Diana is the Roman incarnation of the Greek Artemis. As a lunar goddess, she was associated even in ancient times with secret, nocturnal activities. Particularly as part of a trio of lunar goddesses including Selene and **Hecate**, Diana was sometimes associated with dark **magic** and **witchcraft**.

As Europe became Christian, Diana, like all **pagan** gods and goddesses, came to be regarded as a **demon**, at least by ecclesiastical authorities. In the early Middle Ages, a belief developed that Diana led large groups of **women** on nocturnal journeys through the night sky. This belief seems based not in any element of traditional mythology surrounding Diana, however, but on the Germanic notion of the **Wild Hunt**, a band of ghosts or spirits who would haunt the countryside at night, destroying and killing as they went. The leader of the hunt was most commonly a female spirit named Berta or **Holda**, but was typically translated as Diana (and sometimes **Herodias**) by ecclesiastical authorities when they wrote in Latin. The most famous image of Diana leading a group of women on a nocturnal flight is contained in the 10th-century **canon** *Episcopi*. Such ideas clearly influenced the later development of ideas of **night flight** and the witches' **sabbath**.

In modern witchcraft, or **Wicca**, Diana remains an important figure. Early in the 20th century, **Margaret Murray** used the long association of Diana with witchcraft to claim, without any real evidence, that historical witchcraft was in fact a direct survival of ancient paganism long into the Christian era. Most Wiccans today recognize that Murray's theories are groundless and maintain that Wicca is, at most, a creative revival of certain pre-Christian religious beliefs and in no way a direct surviving remnant of such religions. However, they still revere Diana as an important pagan goddess. As a lunar deity, she continues to be associated with magic; as a virgin goddess and goddess of the hunt, she is an archetype for the strong **feminist** and naturalist elements in modern witchcraft.

See also ANTIQUITY, WITCHCRAFT IN.

DIVINATION. Referring to the practice of revealing hidden knowledge or foretelling the future by magical means, divination is one of the most common forms of **sorcery** around the world and throughout human history. The English word *sorcery* in fact derives from the Latin *sortilegium*, meaning fortune telling or divination, specifically by casting lots. This became the French *sorcellerie*, which meant both sorcery and, eventually, demonic **witchcraft**. In **Antiquity**, although the practice of divination was widespread, diviners were often viewed with suspicion, either because they were thought to be charlatans or, if genuine, because they were thought to traffic with **evil** forces. The marginal status of divination in the ancient world is well illustrated in the **biblical** story of King Saul, who expelled sorcerers and diviners from his kingdom, but then felt compelled to consult the **Witch of Endor** (actually a seer rather than a maleficent witch) before a crucial battle with the Philistines.

For Christian authorities in medieval and early-modern Europe, divination was a crime because, like many other forms of **magic**, it was thought to involve the invocation of **demons**. In addition, attempting to foretell the future was seen as an affront against the power of God, who alone could know such things. Nevertheless, divination remained common and was widely practiced by professional **cunning men and women** across Europe. Such people were often viewed with suspicion by the authorities and could become targets for accusations of witchcraft. However, in most cases the penalties for simple divination were not as severe as for actual harm, or *maleficium*. The practice of divination, of course, extends long after the main period of **witch-hunting** ended in Europe and even today, the wide array of horoscopes, tarot readings, and other means of divination attest to the continued practice of what might be the most common and enduring form of magical activity in history.

DUNCAN, HELEN (1897–1956). The most famous of the last people prosecuted in **England** under the Witchcraft Act of 1736, Helen Duncan, also known as Hellish Nell, was a Scottish medium who worked across Great Britain during the Second World War. British naval authorities became interested in Duncan in November 1941, when she indicated to the audience at a séance she was conducting that HMS *Barham* had been sunk. At the time, only the relatives of those on board had been informed of the incident. Fearing that her fraudulent activities could lead her to reveal further classified information, and that she was exploiting bereaved or anxious relatives of military personnel, the naval authorities had her, and three of her associates, arrested in January 1944. Duncan was charged first under the Vagrancy Act of 1824, and then under the Witchcraft Act that had been introduced two centuries earlier to control the fraudulent activities of self-confessed witches. Duncan was convicted and imprisoned; she was released in 1945.

Although another medium, Jane Yorke, was convicted under the same Act later in 1944, it was the public interest in Duncan's case that led to the repeal of the Witchcraft Act in the Fraudulent Mediums Act of 1951.

See also LAWS AGAINST WITCHCRAFT, EUROPEAN.

DÜRER, ALBRECHT (1471–1528). Albrecht Dürer was born in Nuremberg and is regarded as one of the greatest of all **German** artists. In 1497, he produced the engraving known as *Four Naked Women*. The presence of a **devil** in the background and a skull and bone at the **women**'s feet has led some historians to see the women as witches. Dürer's later engraving known as *Witch Riding Backwards on a Goat* (ca. 1500) is clearly a depiction of a witch and influenced **witchcraft** iconography throughout early-modern Europe. It shows an old crone, naked with flowing hair, riding backward on a **goat**, an animal commonly associated with the devil. In the corner, weather magic is represented by a hailstorm that would destroy crops. These elements of disorder, inversion, and destruction were reproduced by Dürer's contemporaries and students, like **Hans Baldung Grien**, and elaborated by later European artists into the full-blown image of the witches' **sabbath** as it appears in, for example, **Johannes Praetorius**'s *Blockes-Berges Verrichtung* (1668).

See also ART, WITCHCRAFT IN; STORMS AND STORM-RAISING.

E

EICHSTÄTT WITCH TRIALS. The small southern **German** prince-bishopric of Eichstätt experienced three intense waves of **witch-hunting** between 1590 and 1631, in 1590–1592, 1603, and 1617–1631. The first wave was held up as an example for the new duke of **Bavaria**, Maximilian I, to follow. Of the victims of the hunts (between 240 and 279 individuals), however, three-quarters were arrested during the last and most prolonged outbreak. Most of these victims were **women** and almost all were either **executed** or died in custody. While the final wave of witch-hunting in Eichstätt played on fears about malevolent witchcraft activity raised in the previous outbreaks, it was primarily an extension of the Catholic reform agenda promoted by the prince-bishop Johann Christoph von Westerstetten. Westerstetten had previously been responsible for a witch persecution in Ellwangen when he was prince-provost there. The Eichstätt witch trials were notable at the time for the prolonged use of extreme forms of **torture**, such as the **strappado**, and the long list of leading questions adopted by the witch suspects' interrogators. These methods ensured that the witch-hunts in the principality, like those in neighboring **Bamberg** and **Würzburg**, fell most heavily on the women of the local elite. A large number of men were also implicated in witchcraft through this process, but the prejudices of the interrogators meant that they preferred to concentrate on the women named as accomplices.

See also MALE WITCHES; REFORMATION.

ENDOR, WITCH OF. A famous witch of the **Bible**. In 1 Samuel 28, King Saul, who has exiled all the sorcerers and seers from his kingdom, nevertheless seeks supernatural guidance before a battle against the Philistines. Because God will not answer him, he goes to consult a "witch" (she is actually described as a seer or medium) living in Endor. She summons the spirit of the dead prophet Samuel for the king.

Later theologians in the medieval and early-modern periods generally argued that the Witch of Endor could not have summoned the spirit of Samuel. Rather she, like other witches and supposed seers, actually summoned a **demon** who appeared in the form of Samuel. Thus, she became a model for the involvement of witches in demonic **magic** and in the spreading of demonic deception. Opponents of belief in **witchcraft** also used the story of the Witch of Endor, seeing in it an example of simple human deception. The **skeptical** author **Reginald Scot**, for example, in his *Discoverie of Witchcraft*, argued that the Witch of Endor had no supernatural powers of any sort, but simply fooled Saul with the aid of a human accomplice.

ENGLAND AND WALES, WITCHCRAFT IN. Despite the importance of the English experience of **witchcraft** in two of the most influential works in the historiography of the subject, Alan Macfarlane's *Witchcraft in Tudor and Stuart England* (1970) and Keith Thomas's *Religion and the Decline of Magic* (1971), relatively few witch trials were conducted in England and Wales. There were, perhaps, fewer than 500 executions for the crime throughout the early-modern period, most of them concentrated in the southeast of England (but not in the capital London). In the Home Circuit of the assize courts (that is, the counties of Essex, Hertfordshire, Surrey, Sussex, and Kent), less than half of those tried were convicted of the crime, and only half of those convicted were hanged (the usual form of **execution** for witches in the country), while the rest received lesser punishments. In other parts of the kingdom, such as Wales, there seem to have been very few witch trials indeed. Additional cases of witchcraft could be prosecuted in the church courts, but the punishments they could hand down to convicted witches were minor. The vast number of English witchcraft cases occurred during the reigns of Queen Elizabeth I and **King James I**, with a further outbreak conducted by **Matthew Hopkins** and John Stearne between 1645 and 1647.

Witchcraft became a secular crime in the Witchcraft Act of 1542, but this legislation was ineffective and repealed in 1547. The Elizabethan Witchcraft Act of 1563 made witchcraft a felony. It only applied the death penalty for murder by witchcraft in the first instance, or for injuring people or killing animals in the second instance (the first such offense was punishable by a year's imprisonment and four sessions in the pillory). Under James I, the punishments were made more harsh in an Act of 1604, but by this time witch trials in England and Wales were on the decline. The last witch prosecuted under the 1604 Act was **Jane Wenham**. She was convicted in 1712, but reprieved, and the legislation was repealed in the Witchcraft Act of 1736 that made it a crime of fraud to claim to have supernatural powers.

The lack of witchcraft convictions in England and Wales resulted from four factors. First, witchcraft was treated mainly as a felony or serious misdemeanor, and the accuser therefore had to prove that murder or injury had actually been committed. It was not material to the case whether or not the accused had made a pact with the **devil**, attended witches' **sabbaths**, and committed **heresy**. That was a matter for a church court. Second, English justice followed a modified **accusatorial procedure**. After the magistrate had examined the accused and the witnesses, the case was passed up to the assize court at which a grand jury would determine whether there was a case to answer, and a petty jury would hear the evidence and come to a verdict. The juries consisted of men from the parishes of the county who might not be so credulous of their neighbors' accusations as witch-hunters elsewhere. Third, **torture** was not permitted in English witchcraft cases and there was little chance that an individual witchcraft episode would escalate into a full-blown **witch-hunt**, although local fears might result in accusations against a number of alleged witches, as happened in **Saint Osyth** in 1582. Finally, despite the large volume of **demonological** literature that circulated in the country, there seems to have been considerable skepticism about witchcraft as shown not only in the relative incredulity of the juries, but also the work of **Reginald Scot**'s *Discoverie of Witchcraft* (1584), and plays like *The Witch of Edmonton* (1621). When the justice system was put under strain, however, as happened in the late 1640s during the English Civil War, Hopkins was able to act on his religious convictions in his pursuit of witches, torturing them until they confessed.

Apart from the mildness of witchcraft prosecution in England and Wales, the cases are notable for the number of **familiars** that appear in the confessions.

See also LAWS AGAINST WITCHCRAFT, EUROPEAN.

ERASMUS, DESIDERIUS (1466–1536). Erasmus was born in the Netherlands, at Rotterdam, and studied at the University of Paris, among other places. He was a scholar of the classics as well as the **Bible** and the early church fathers, especially Saint Jerome, and became the most important figure in the history of northern **humanism**. Erasmus's interest in **witchcraft** was, however, slight. The only episode of witchcraft that he related in his correspondence really concerned ritual **magic**, or **sorcery**, and an early version of the **Black Mass** that had occurred near Orleans, **France**. While he did not deny the power of sorcery in his letter to the abbot of Saint Bertin, he appeared to be **skeptical** of the confessions of the accused parties in this case—a man, his wife and their daughter—and also of the motives of the friar who brought the charges against them. Erasmus thought the sorcery described in this episode was novel rather than rooted in Scripture and theology.

ERICTHO. In Roman literature, Erictho appears in *Pharsalia*, Lucan's epic poem about the civil war between Julius Caesar and Pompey. Unlike some of the other beautiful, if dangerously powerful sorceresses of classical mythology and literature, such as **Circe** and **Medea**, Erictho is portrayed as a hideous, almost semi-demonic figure. Erictho lives in Thessaly, a land long associated with **sorcery** in ancient times. In a story that resembles that of the **Witch of Endor** in the **Bible**, on the eve of the decisive battle of Pharsalus, the son of Pompey comes to consult with Erictho, asking her to **divine** the outcome of the battle by summoning the spirits of the dead. She picks the body of a slain youth whom she reanimates to answer the questions asked of it. Later, Erictho appears in Dante's *Divine Comedy* and among the witches in Johann Wolfgang von Goethe's *Faust*.

See also ANTIQUITY, WITCHCRAFT IN.

ERRORES GAZARIORUM. The "Errors of the Gazarii" was written in Savoy in the late 1430s and is a brief but extremely lurid tract describing the activities of a heretical sect. While the anonymous author does not use the word *witches*, preferring a common term for heretics derived from *Cathars*, historians include the text among the first writings about the **witchcraft** sect because of its date, the diabolical activity it describes, its subtitle—"those who have been convinced that they ride a **broomstick** or rod"—and its subsequent popularity. It survives in two manuscript versions of about the same date and incorporates material from the **Council of Basel**.

The tract describes the seduction and initiation of heretics, their meetings at **sabbaths** (here termed "synagogues"), why they might fall into **heresy**, and a list of **evils** they commit. At the sabbaths, the heretics renounced the Christian faith, worshiped the **devil** (usually in the form of a black **cat** or other animal), practiced **cannibalism** by devouring babies and small **children**, and engaged in sexual **orgies**. The acts of harm, or *maleficium*, performed by the heretics included producing **poison**, murder, causing infertility, and raising destructive **storms**. The importance of the text, however, is that it is one of the earliest sources to accept the **night flight** of witches as reality. In many respects, therefore, heretical activity as it is depicted in the *Errores* is similar to that found in early writings on witchcraft by **Johannes Nider, Claude Tholosan, Hans Fründ**, and **Martin Le Franc**.

ESTONIA, WITCHCRAFT IN. The northern and southern halves of Estonia came under **Swedish** rule in 1561 and 1621 respectively, but despite attempts to convert the local population to an orthodox Lutheranism, **pagan** beliefs persisted in the country throughout the early-modern period. Of the 205 defendants who came before the Estonian courts between 1520 and 1725, fewer than one-third of them were executed, even though their **sorcery** was grounded in the local pagan traditions that the Swedes wanted to eradicate, and many Estonian sorcerers, whether male or female, could turn themselves into wolves or, sometimes, bears. The Estonian trials are also remarkable because over 60 percent of the accused were men. This proportion of men among the accused reflects local pagan beliefs about the supernatural power they possessed in the local culture.

See also MALE WITCHES; METAMORPHOSIS; WEREWOLVES.

EUGENIUS IV, POPE (1383–1447). Eugenius reigned as pope from 1431 until 1447, during a period when the full stereotype of **witchcraft** was just beginning to emerge as a clearly defined concept. At this time, the first real **witch-hunts** were taking place in the lands in and around the western Alps, and the first treatises and authoritative accounts describing witchcraft were being written. Eugenius was constantly in conflict with the **Council of Basel** to the extent that it eventually deposed him in favor of the duke of Savoy, Amadeus VIII, who became the anti-pope Felix V.

Like previous popes, such as **John XXII** and **Alexander V**, Eugenius concerned himself directly with matters of **witchcraft**, **magic**, and **sorcery**. In 1434, he wrote to the Franciscan inquisitor Ponce Fougeyron (possibly the author of *Errores Gazariorum*) about Christian and Jewish practitioners of various occult arts. In 1437, he issued a letter to all papal **inquisitors** in which he described the acts of the many people he believed to be practicing demonic sorcery throughout Christendom. These acts included contracting **pacts** with **demons** and worshiping them, **night flight**, weather magic, and the desecration of the Eucharist. In 1440, Eugenius denounced Felix V to the Council of Basel for his toleration and patronage of witches. In this denunciation, Eugenius used the vulgar terms *stregule*, or *strogonos*, as well as the more formal *Waudenses* (the name once given to the heretics of the Vaudois). Felix's secretary, **Martin Le Franc**, responded to the denunciations with his *Le champion des dames*.

See also STORMS AND STORM-RAISING; WALDENSIANS.

EVIL. For **Saint Augustine of Hippo**, evil was a principle rather than a thing; it did not exist by itself, but represented a lack of good. Having chosen to rebel against God, the **devil** was permitted to tempt people away from God and from good. Like the devil, humans could exercise their God-given free will to act on these temptations, and in doing so fell into evil. The influence of Augustine's theology of evil meant that the fall into temptation became the means by which the devil was understood to lure humans into **heresy** or **apostasy**, including **witchcraft**. In the case of witchcraft, **demonologists** like **Heinrich Kramer** believed that **women** were much weaker than men intellectually and emotionally. In order to persuade women into a **pact**, the devil merely had to offer them something that they needed, for example money, rather than appeal to reason. The devil was helped by the alleged lustfulness of women and their need for emotional fulfillment through sex.

The dominant view of harmful **sorcery** by witches in the medieval period was that its effects were illusory. The witch was tempted by the devil to believe that her sorcery had caused the harm she intended. As only God had power over health and death, the event that was seen by the witch as harmful would have happened anyway without her sorcery. The witch's main sin, according to the **canon** *Episcopi*, for example, was that she drew other women into the heresy and imperiled their souls as well as her own. By the time of the **witch-hunts** of the early-modern period, the devil and his **demons** were much more potent figures. They had become the agents by which the witches were believed to perform their harmful sorcery. Although the devil and demons still required God's permission to act, they did so in much more creative and intrusive ways than merely tempting people to sin. While evil remained intangible, it was written of as if it had an existence by itself. Witches could therefore be entirely evil rather than simply lacking in good, and consequently posed such a threat to both lives and souls that they needed to be eradicated.

EVIL EYE. Also known as fascination, the evil eye refers to the power of witches to effect harm simply through their gaze or the glance of their eyes. This is surely one of the most widespread of all forms of folk magic, and the **evil** power of glances or stares is known in many historical and world cultures. For example, in Europe alone it exists in **France** as *mauvais oeil*, in **Germany** as the *böse Blick*, and perhaps most famously in **Italy** as the *mal occhio*. The term itself arises from the **Bible**, Mark 7:21–22, where Christ states: "from within, out of the heart of men, proceed evil thoughts, adulteries, fornications, murders, thefts, covetousness, wickedness, deceit, lasciviousness, an evil eye, blasphemy, pride, foolishness" (this from the King James' Version; the term is *oculus malus* in the medieval Latin Vulgate).

Drawing on pre-modern scientific thought that the eye saw by emitting rays rather than receiving them, theories of natural **magic** held that the evil eye might work by transmitting harmful intentions along these rays, thereby affecting the person held in the gaze. **Demonological** theories maintained that witches simply signaled to **demons** by the glance of their eyes the victims whom they sought to afflict. Fairly common among folk beliefs was the idea that the evil eye might be either intentional or unintentional. That is, some witches might deliberately seek to harm through the glance of their eyes, but others might be unaware that their gaze contained such power, or at least be unable to control or deliberately employ such power. Many forms of amulets and charms were devised for protection from the evil eye.

EXECUTIONS. At the height of the period of the European **witch-hunts**, condemned witches were executed either by burning or by hanging. The popular misconception that some witches were punished by drowning comes from accounts of **swimming** suspected witches as an ordeal to determine guilt, and from accounts of lynchings that fell outside normal justice. In most of Europe, witchcraft was prosecuted as a **heresy**, a crime punishable by burning. In northern Europe, notably in **Germany** where the witch-hunts were most intense, the authorities tended to take the view that the witch sect was so powerful and dangerous that all of its adherents should be executed, even if they confessed and reconciled themselves to God. In some places, like **Eichstätt**, penitent witches might be beheaded before they were burned. In southern Europe, where the **inquisitions** tended to treat **witchcraft** as a delusion, the aim was to reconcile convicted witches to the church and reha- bilitate them into the Christian community; like other minor heretics, they were only executed by burning if they persisted in their views. In **England** and its colonies, including those in **North America**, witchcraft was prose- cuted as a felony, a crime punishable by hanging. The rites and practices of suspected witches were unimportant. Rather, actual harm against a person or his property had to be proven to find a suspect guilty. These different ap- proaches to the crime of witchcraft and its punishment account in large measure for the varying intensity of witch execution across Europe. In all cases where execution took place, it was a public spectacle designed to warn other witches and deter anyone else from falling into the crime of witchcraft.

EXORCISM. Referring to the casting out of demonic spirits and curing cases of demonic **possession**, the practice of exorcism in the Christian tradi- tion is based on such **biblical** passages as Luke 9:1 ("Then Jesus called the 12 together and gave them power and authority over all demons"). Very early in the history of Christianity, the office of exorcist became one of the minor orders of the church. Exorcism then became a rite, performed by a cleric who had been instituted as an exorcist, with an officially recognized ceremony. Although the Roman Catholic church has abandoned the minor order of exorcist, it still prescribes an official rite for exorcism for priests to use. In Protestant denominations, rites for exorcism have largely been abandoned, but exorcisms are still sometimes performed.

While exorcism is used generally to describe the act of expelling a **demon**, it is properly a form of adjuration, an earnest command that the **devil** or demon possessing a body name himself and do what the exorcist requires of him. It is in this sense that exorcism appears in texts on **witchcraft** and **demonology**. This formal definition also brings exorcism close to illicit ritu- al **magic** and conjuration in which a magician commands a demon to do as he requires. For this reason, theologians and demonologists like **Martin de Castañega**, **Desiderius Erasmus**, and **Heinrich Kramer** found exorcism problematic. During the **Reformation**, the similarities between exorcism and ritual magic did make it an easy target for the reformers to hit. Later in the early-modern period, exorcism became a site of spiritual struggle between Catholics and Calvinists in **France** as each side tried to show that God was on their side by demonstrating his power over a demon through them.

As both a means of expulsion and a form of adjuration, exorcisms became important throughout the entire period of the **witch-hunts**. The official rite of exorcism was sought as a cure for demonic possession, which could be brought about by witchcraft. A legitimate exorcism could also be performed by any faithful Christian as a defense against witchcraft or remedy for bewitchment. Because witches performed all of their harmful **sorcery** through the power of demons, afflicted people could invoke the power of Christ to ward off or overcome demonic assault. Other actions also had an exorcizing effect. Identifying a witch, taking her to court, and executing her would relieve a victim of witchcraft-induced possession.

While exorcism has been dissociated from witchcraft in mainstream Christian churches in the Western world, it is still used in witchcraft cases in **Africa**. Most commonly, **children** accused of witchcraft in Africa are forcibly exorcised by the evangelical pastors by whom they have been identified.

EYMERIC, NICOLAU (ca. 1320–1399). A Dominican friar and inquisitor in the Kingdom of Aragon, Eymeric wrote his most important work, the inquisitorial manual *Directorium inquisitorium* (Directory of Inquisitors), in 1376 while in exile at the papal court in Avignon. Like the *Practica inquisitionis haeretice pravitatis* (Practice of Inquisition into Heretical Depravity) of the inquisitor **Bernard Gui** half a century earlier, Eymeric's treatise was a general handbook of procedures to be used in conducting an **inquisition**. As such, it included sections on **sorcery** and demonic invocation. In terms of the development of learned clerical thought about **magic**, however, Eymeric's handbook is even more important than Gui's, for Eymeric established the basic argument that demonic invocation necessarily entailed the worship of **demons**. Thus, all demonic magic was de facto heretical and subject to the jurisdiction of ecclesiastical courts and papal inquisitors.

As an inquisitor, Eymeric seems to have been particularly interested in sorcery and demonic magic. Several years prior to writing his more general *Directorium*, he wrote a *Tractatus contra daemonum invocatores* (Treatise against Invokers of Demons), which served as a basis for the sections on sorcery and demonic magic in his later manual. Eymeric presented long, theological arguments to demonstrate that demons could not be summoned or commanded for magical purposes without some form of worship being offered to them. Ultimately, he argued that simply to invoke a demon for supernatural aid, when a true Christian should turn in prayer to God, was to show the demon a form of adoration (*latria*) due only to God. This amounted to **idolatry** (*idolatria*), and meant that all demonic magic could be considered a form of **heresy**. Eymeric's arguments formed the basis of the church's position against demonic sorcery for the rest of the Middle Ages and into the early-modern period. Eymeric never discussed **witchcraft** in his writings, and clearly was concerned primarily with learned demonic magic, or **necromancy**. His argument that all demonic magic involved the worship of demons, however, obviously had important consequences for the development of the concept of witchcraft and the persecution of witches in later years.

See also SPAIN, WITCHCRAFT IN.

F

FAMILIARS. Various lesser **demons** who were thought to attend witches in an assumed animal form were generally known as familiar spirits or, more simply, as familiars. This aspect of the witch stereotype is somewhat unique in being more developed in **English**, Irish, and **Scottish** sources than in continental ones. A demonic familiar might appear in almost any animal form. Toads, owls, rats, mice, and dogs were all common, but **cats** were especially associated with familiar spirits. A witch might be given a familiar by the **devil**, or might inherit one from another witch, as happened in the case of the **Chelmsford witches**. The demon then attended the witch and performed magical services for her. The witch, in turn, cared for her familiar much as one would care for a household pet, which is of course what many supposed familiars probably were. In particular, witches were thought to feed their familiars with their own blood, which the familiar might suck from a small protuberance somewhere on the witch's body, the so-called **witch's mark**.

One of the earliest examples of a demon resembling a familiar appears in the case of **Alice Kyteler**. Accused of **witchcraft** in **Ireland** in 1324, Alice was supposedly attended by a demon known as Robert or Robin Artisson, who could appear as a cat, a shaggy dog, or an Ethiopian. Unlike witches with later familiars, Alice would have sexual relations with Robert and would sacrifice animals to him, especially roosters. Such accusations seem to lie somewhere between the later concept of the familiar and the worship of demons and sexual **orgies** that typified the witches' **sabbath**, over which demons or Satan himself would typically preside in the form of a black cat, **goat**, or other animal.

FASCINATION. *See* EVIL EYE.

FAUST. Perhaps the most famous story of a human entering a pact with the Satan is that of Faust. Faust was not a witch but rather the archetypal learned magician of the Renaissance period. The legend appears to have been based originally on the life of a Georg or Johann Faust, who seems to have been a traveling magician in southern Germany. This Faust was attacked in print by the humanist theologian **Johannes Trithemius**, who modeled his version of the man on **Simon Magus**. Over the remainder of the 16th century, the legend of Faust developed and circulated through the writings of **Martin Luther**, **Johann Weyer**, and Johann Fischart, the translator of **Jean Bodin**'s *Démonomanie* into German, among others. By the time the first "Faustbook" appeared in Germany in 1587, the legend had acquired elements from the stories of **Theophilus of Adana**, **Paracelsus**, and **Agrippa**. Faust's legend inspired Christopher Marlowe's **play** *Dr Faustus*, written in 1588, and Johann Wolfgang von Goethe's *Faust* of the early 19th century. The many later versions of the Faust legend by novelists and composers have usually been based on Goethe's masterpiece.

In the basic legend, Faust sold his soul to the **devil** in exchange for magical knowledge and power. He was served by a **demon** named Mephistopheles, who sometimes accompanied him as a **familiar** in the form of a black dog with fiery eyes. Aided by Mephistopheles, Faust pursued worldly pleasure and arcane knowledge. At end of his life, however, the devil came to claim his soul, killing him in a terrible manner.

See also CLASSICAL MUSIC, WITCHCRAFT IN; FICTION, WITCHCRAFT IN; MAGIC.

FEMINISM AND WITCHCRAFT. The history of **witchcraft** has lent itself to feminist political agendas in a variety of fruitful ways. The basic fact that **women** were by far the most frequent victims of witch accusations during the early-modern period allowed some feminists to argue that witch-hunting was women-hunting on the part of a patriarchal elite. This argument was emphasized in the exaggerated claims made by a few influential feminists about the number of women executed as witches during the period of the **witch-hunts**, or **Burning Times**. The American suffragette Matilda Joslyn Gage claimed that it was 13 million, the radical feminist theologian Mary Daly that it was 9 million. While these figures are implausible, the idea that witch-hunting was women-hunting inspired both historical scholarship and cultural representations of witchcraft. Barbara Ehrenreich and Deirdre English argued in 1974 that witch-hunting was focused on female midwives and herbalists, who were persecuted on behalf of the male medical establishment. This interpretation found its way into such works as Caryl Churchill's **play** *Vinegar Tom* (1976). Other feminists, such as Anne Sexton, Sylvia Plath, and Adrienne Rich, explicitly identified with the witch as the victim of sexual repression by men. Still others found Keith Thomas's and Alan Macfarlane's class-bound theories of the function of witchcraft accusations useful in demonstrating the subjugation and oppression of women in economic terms. While feminist historians of witchcraft now tend to distance themselves from the idea of witch-hunting as women-hunting, focusing instead on the issues that dominate the witches' confession narratives (the body, motherhood, and household and gender relations), and mainstream feminism seems to avoid the subject, witchcraft as a practice often informs feminist lifestyles. **Starhawk**, for example, roots her witchcraft in feminist and environmental concerns.

FICTION, WITCHCRAFT IN. The storytelling in **folklore**, pamphlets from the period of the **witch-hunts**, and early witch **plays** has formed the basis for a large and eclectic volume of **witchcraft** fiction aimed at adults and children. There were, of course, also influential stories of witchcraft, **sorcery**, **magic**, and related matters in the literature of **Antiquity** and the Middle Ages, such as the myths of **Circe** and Odysseus, and Apuleius of Madaura's comic tale *The Golden Ass* (second century). Fernando de Rojas in *La Celestina* (1499) and Miguel de Cervantes in several works in the 16th century built on these various traditions. In neither case, however, did they portray the stereotypical witch of the *Malleus maleficarum*. Celestina is a prostitute who dabbles in **love magic** (although she has to perform this with the aid of **devil**), while Cervantes, like the Spanish **inquisitors**, appears to have been **skeptical** of a witch's actual power. Later British stories that introduced witchcraft, such as Robert Burns's *Tam O'Shanter* (1791) and Lord Byron's *Manfred* (1816–1817), tended to be dramatic poems in which the witches were illusory or allegorical, but not maliciously powerful.

Since then witchcraft stories have become staples of both literary and pulp fiction. The **Lancashire** witchcraft case of 1612 was fictionalized in William Harrison Ainsworth's novel of 1849; and Eveline Hasler's novel about **Anna Göldi**, the last witch to be executed in Europe, was published in 1982. Modern witches appear in, for example, Mikhail Bulgakov's satire *The Master and Margarita* (1966–67) and as the main characters in John Updike's pair of novels about the witches of Eastwick (1984 and 2008). Recently, there has been a trend for strong witch characters in the work of female novelists such as Anne Rice and Alice Hoffman. *Weird Tales* magazine (1923–1954; revived 1988) has served the pulp fiction market, as did prolific novelists like Carter Brown.

Witch figures for **children** and young adults are much more varied, ranging from L. Frank Baum's witches in *The Wonderful Wizard of Oz* (1900) to Celia Rees's *Witch Child* (2000), taking in creations by C. S. Lewis, Marvel Publishing, Roald Dahl, Terry Pratchett, and J. K. Rowling along the way. Like the stories for adults, many of these have been adapted for **film**.

FILMS, WITCHCRAFT IN. Stories about **witchcraft** and **magic** offer a combination of history, fantasy, and horror that filmmakers can play with on screen. Early films were adaptations of familiar stories or real events, such as the **Faust** story that Georges Méliès's borrowed for his short *Le manoir du diable* in 1896. Of these earlier fictional stories, William Shakespeare's *Macbeth* (1605) has proven the most durable, the iconic cinematic portrayal of the three witches of this **play** coming from Orson Welles's version of 1948. The tradition of depicting real witchcraft events also began in the early years of cinema. **Joan of Arc**'s trial and execution featured in a number of short films and were the subject of Carl Theodore Dreyer's feature *The Passion of Joan of Arc* (1928). Dreyer was later to film the story of **Anne Pedersdotter**'s trial in *Day of Wrath* (1943). There have been several film versions of the **Salem** witch trials, including two adaptations of Arthur Miller's *The Crucible* (1953) by Raymond Rouleau and Jean-Paul Sartre in 1957 and Nicholas Hytner in 1996. On occasion, historical events have shaded into horror in, for example, *The Witchfinder General* (1968), about **Matthew Hopkins**, and films about executed witches returning to haunt the descendants of their prosecutors.

Witches feature in other films as diverse as *Snow White and the Seven Dwarves* (1937), *The Wizard of Oz* (1939), *Fantasia* (1940), *The Seventh Seal* (1957), *The Last Valley* (1970), *The Witches of Eastwick* (1987), and, more recently, the Harry Potter series. In many cases, these films are adaptations of **folklore** or novels, particularly those written for children. Toward the end of the 20th century, the Western stereotype of the **Halloween** witch found its way into the Japanese genre of anime.

Witchcraft events and practices have also been the subject of several documentaries. The earliest, *Häxan* (1922), mixed documentary with both fantasy and horror. Gary Foxcroft's award-winning film *Saving Africa's Witch Children* (2008) highlights the plight of alleged child witches in Nigeria.

See also AFRICA, WITCH-HUNTS IN; FICTION, WITCHCRAFT IN.

FINLAND, WITCHCRAFT IN. *See* SWEDEN, WITCHCRAFT IN.

FLADE, DR. DIETRICH (1534–1589). Probably the highest-ranking victim of any **witch-hunt** in European history, Flade was a prominent citizen of **Trier**, an archbishopric and also at that time an independent electoral principality of the **German Empire**. He actively opposed the spread of Protestantism in the region on behalf of the prince-archbishop and became head of the criminal court. From 1580 to 1583, he also acted as vice governor of Trier, and, in 1586, he was appointed rector of the university there even though he was a layman and not a cleric. In the 1580s, the number of witch trials in Trier began to escalate, influenced by a period of bad weather, agrarian failures, and economic difficulties. At first, the criminal court, under Flade's direction, was hesitant and cautious in cases of **witchcraft**, although Flade was not an opponent of witch trials. The court's stance, however, roused the opposition of more zealous witch-hunting authorities, notably the suffragan bishop of Trier, **Peter Binsfeld**. Eventually, Flade himself was accused of witchcraft and denounced by witch suspects under torture. He was an easy popular target because he was considered greedy and ambitious. Flade fled from Trier twice, but was captured and returned to the city. He was arrested in April 1589 and finally executed in September of the same year. Flade's case was mentioned by **Cornelius Loos** and **Martín Del Rio**, as well as Binsfeld.

FLYING. *See* NIGHT FLIGHT.

FOLKLORE. Witches and sorcerers, or sorceresses, appear in the myths and legends of cultures dating back to **Antiquity**, and, in many cases, they continued to exist independently of the **demonology** that sought to demonize them as anti-Christian during the medieval and early-modern periods. In these myths and legends, one finds many goddesses who used witchcraft or sorcery, among them **Lilith, Hecate, Circe, Medea, Diana**, and **Holda**. There are also mythical sorceresses like **Morgan le Fay** and **Baba Yaga**, and, in Japan, **Yama-uba**. It was from folklore that elements of the **night flight** and the witches' **sabbath** were drawn. Both the **Wild Hunt** of the followers of Holda and the **shamanistic** transvection of the *benandanti* contributed to, or reinforced, the notion of the witches' flight on **brooms** and animals. The sites at which the witches were alleged to meet, such as **The Brocken** in **Germany** or simply open spaces beyond town or village boundaries, usually had folkloric associations. The **cauldron** and the **cannibalism** of **children** also feature in folklore and myth. In addition, the ability to control weather, love, and fertility through **magic** are common themes of folkloric tales, as are some of the ways of identifying witches, such as **pricking**. The witches of folklore continue to shape modern conceptions of the witch, usually through retellings of the stories, like Hansel and Gretel, that were collected by Jacob Grimm in the 19th century.

See also STORMS AND STORM-RAISING.

FOXES. In Asian **folklore** and legend, foxes have a long association with **magic, divination**, and the **possession** of human beings. In China, they are called *huli jing*, in Korea, *kuminho*, and in Japan, *kitsune*. These foxes have similarities to several European spiritual beings: they can be either benevolent or maleficent, like European fairies; they can tempt and possess human beings, like **demons**; they can be controlled in much the same way as a witch's **familiar** or a magician's demon; and they are sometimes worshiped, as **heretics** were supposed to have worshiped **cats** or **goats**. As well as being able to divine the future, they were also thought to possess land and dwellings in much the same way as ghosts or poltergeists. In several stories, fox women seduce young men, either by taking on the form of a beautiful young **woman** (after working hard for several centuries to achieve this power) or by possessing one. In a characteristic reminiscent of the lustful old crone of European **demonology**, the fox woman then drains the man whom she has seduced of life by aggressive **sexual** activity.

See also ASIAN WITCHCRAFT.

FRANCE, WITCHCRAFT IN. The most populous state in early-modern Europe, France witnessed trials for demonic **sorcery** and **witchcraft** from the early 14th century to the end of the **Affair of the Poisons** in 1682. Estimates of the number of witches executed reach 4,000. In 1307, the **Templars** in the country were accused by King Philip IV of **heresy** and worshiping **demons**, among many other crimes, as part of his successful attempt to have the order suppressed and take its wealth for himself. Shortly after the execution of the order's Grand Master Jacques de Molay in 1314, **Pope John XXII** ordered the inquisitors in Toulouse and Carcassonne to prosecute anyone suspected of invoking or worshiping **demons** in magical rituals. **Inquisitions** against heretics, notably the **Waldensians**, continued in southern France and its Alpine regions, Savoy, and parts of **Switzerland**, and in the early 15th century, some of these evolved into the first proper witch-hunts in Europe, provoking debate at the **Council of Basel** and a spate of influential witch-hunting manuals and **demonologies** by men like **Johannes Nider** and **Claude Tholosan**.

At the height of the great **witch-hunts** in Europe, France was notable for the relatively high proportion of **men** accused of witchcraft (up to 75 percent in some regions), and the lenience with which the *parlement* of Paris treated witches who appealed to it. Some legal authorities, including **Jean Bodin** in his *De la démonomanie des sorciers* (The Demonomania of Witches, 1580), did, however, support witch-hunting and remained influential among witch-hunting judges. One of the most intense witch-hunts in France occurred in 1609 in the **Basque**-speaking Pays de Labourd in the south of the country. **Pierre de Lancre**, a lawyer and royal official, was sent there to investigate witchcraft. He had about 80 witches executed before he handed the matter over to the *parlement* of Bordeaux, although he was later to claim that he had executed over 600 witches. The *parlement* proved **skeptical** and reluctant to prosecute any more cases; Lancre responded with a detailed description of the trials he had conducted, *Tableau de l'inconstance de mauvais anges et démons* (Description of the Inconstancy of Evil Angels and Demons, 1612), the first of three he was to write on witchcraft. *Tableau* was illustrated with a full-blown image of the witches' sabbath by Jan Ziarnko. Possession also became a feature of French witchcraft trials at about this time. Among such cases, that of Urbain Grandier and the nuns of **Loudun** in the early 1630s has become the most well known, notably through Ken Russell's **film** *The Devils* (1971) and Aldous Huxley's novel *The Devils of Loudun* (1952) on which it was based. By the time of the Affair of the Poisons and King Louis XIV's edict declaring magical practices to be fraudulent, witchcraft prosecution was already dying out in France.

See also ART, WITCHCRAFT IN; CHRONOLOGY OF WITCH-HUNTING; FICTION, WITCHCRAFT IN.

FRÜND, HANS (ca. 1400–1469). A civic chronicler from Lucerne, Hans Fründ was the author of a brief report on **witchcraft** derived from the witch trials that occurred in 1428–1430 in the Alpine region of Valais in the diocese of Sion. It is one of the earliest reports of full-fledged witchcraft in European history. Fründ was a layman and his account may therefore be closer to actual witch beliefs than those of other early authorities, most of whom were clerics and whose understanding of witchcraft was colored by learned **diabolism**. Fründ described a sect of witches that had been persuaded to reject Christianity by an evil spirit who appeared to them in animal form (a bear or a ram). The **pact** they made with this spirit contracted them to pay an annual fee in kind and promise a limb to the spirit on their death. The witches gathered together at meetings similar to a **sabbath** to which they flew at night. At the meetings they feasted, practiced the **cannibalism** of **children**, engaged in sexual **orgies**, and worshiped **demons**. They also learned how to cause acts of harm, or *maleficium*, and how to metamorphose into wolves and become invisible. Fründ's report is in many ways similar to other accounts of witchcraft from the early 15th century, such as the *Errores Gazariorum*, and those by **Johannes Nider** and **Claude Tholosan**. This indicates that a basic understanding of witchcraft was quick to establish itself in the course of the 1420s and 1430s.

See also DEVIL; METAMORPHOSIS; NIGHT FLIGHT; SWITZERLAND, WITCHCRAFT IN.

G

GARDNER, GERALD (1884–1964). The founder of modern **witchcraft**, or **Wicca**, Gardner claimed that he had been initiated into a **coven** of hereditary witches in **England**, a group that supposedly followed practices that had been passed down from the time of historical witchcraft during the period of the great **witch-hunts** and even before. In fact, Gardner claimed that witchcraft actually represented an ancient, pre-Christian fertility religion. In a deliberate attempt to revive this religion, he published *Witchcraft Today* in 1954, and thus launched the movement that would evolve into modern Wicca.

Gardner was born into a well-off family near Liverpool, England. He later moved to East Asia where he worked for many years in Ceylon (now Sri Lanka), Borneo, and Malaysia. He became deeply involved in the study of eastern religions and occultism. In 1936, he retired from his position as a colonial civil servant for the British government and returned to England, where he continued to pursue his interest in esoteric religions and the occult. He became an amateur archeologist, both in Great Britain and in the Middle East, and joined the Folklore Society, where he collaborated with **Margaret Murray** on a paper on historical witchcraft. In 1938, while living in Hampshire, he joined the Fellowship of Crotona, a mystical, quasi-Masonic group. Within this group, supposedly, was a secret inner circle whose members styled themselves as hereditary witches. Gardner claimed that he was initiated into this group in 1939. The Witchcraft Act of 1736 made it a crime in England to claim to be a witch, and Gardner only began to go public with his supposed discovery of an ancient religion after its repeal in 1951. His first book, *Witchcraft Today*, aroused tremendous interest and immediately made him a celebrity. Over the next few years, he and his most important disciple, **Doreen Valiente**, wrote several works on the nature and rituals of modern witchcraft. These writings became the basis for what became known as the Gardnerian tradition of witchcraft. The principal text of the rituals is the so-called **Book of Shadows**, of which Gardner produced several versions.

Although Gardner's writings (some of the most important of which were collaborations with Valiente) provided the basis for modern witchcraft, other traditions soon began to emerge. Valiente herself formed a second coven, and by 1957 this group had broken with Gardner, upset over the level of publicity and media attention that he continually sought. Other groups followed. In the 1960s and 1970s, the practice of witchcraft had grown significantly, and many different, independent Wiccan groups came into existence in both Europe and **North America**. Gardner's notion, based on the theories of Margaret Murray, that modern witchcraft was a direct survival of an ancient fertility religion, has been thoroughly disproved and is no longer accepted by many Wiccans today. The development of Wicca has been influenced by other factors, above all **feminist** ideologies, and other texts, such as **Starhawk**'s *The Spiral Dance*, have become as important, if not more so, than Gardner's original *Witchcraft Today*. Nevertheless, all branches of modern witchcraft owe something to Gerald Gardner.

See also LAWS AGAINST WITCHCRAFT, EUROPEAN.

GEILER VON KAYSERSBERG, JOHANN (1445–1510). A theologian who studied at Freiburg and Basel, Johann Geiler von Kaysersberg served as a preacher in Strasbourg from 1478. His *Die Emeis* (The Ants) is a collection of Lenten sermons delivered in 1508 and published in 1516 and 1517. Twenty-six of the sermons deal with **witchcraft** and were influenced by Geiler's reading of **Johannes Nider**'s *Formicarius* (The Anthill); another sermon treats of lycanthropy, the transformation of people into **werewolves**. *Die Emeis* was intended for a wide audience. It was one of the first major works on witchcraft to be published in the **German** vernacular. It was also richly illustrated with images that took inspiration from the work of Geiler's contemporaries like **Hans Baldung Grien**.

GERMAN EMPIRE, WITCHCRAFT IN. The Holy Roman Empire of the German Nation, or German Empire, was the heartland of witch-hunting during the early-modern period. It was an extensive empire that, at various times, stretched from the Baltic Sea down into northern **Italy**, and from Flanders on the North Sea to Silesia in the west. It was comprised of numerous autonomous or semi-autonomous states, of which the most important were the seven electorates (the Palatinate of the Rhine, the kingdom of Bohemia, Saxony, Brandenburg, and the archbishoprics of Cologne, Mainz, and **Trier**) to which **Bavaria** was added in 1623. These electors voted in the new emperor, although by the time of the great **witch-hunts** this position had become the office of the Habsburg family. The electorates, and the duchies, counties, prince-bishoprics, imperial free cities, and other states that made up the empire, had their own traditions, legislatures, law codes, judiciaries, and from 1555, right to impose a religion on their subjects. The **Carolina Law Code** of 1532 did not have much impact on local **laws**. The empire therefore included territories that were able to become independent, such as **Switzerland**, and others that were easily claimed by **Spain**, **France**, and other nations.

The general consensus among historians is that over half of those executed for **witchcraft** in the European witch-hunts, some 26,000 people, were tried in territories of the German Empire. Not all German territories did, however, witness a witch persecution. Witch-hunting tended to be concentrated in certain principalities, such as **Bamberg**, Bavaria, Cologne and Westphalia, **Eichstätt**, Trier and **Würzburg**, and took place mainly in the period 1580 to 1630, especially in the 1620s. Places like Rothenburg ob der Tauber saw few witch trials, primarily because the authorities there were more skeptical about witchcraft and did not use **torture** during the trials of suspected witches. Several explanations for the intensity of witch-hunting in parts of Germany have been put forward. These areas were particularly hard hit by the so-called Little Ice Age, which reached its height between 1560 and 1630, and also the ravages of the Thirty Years War (1618–1648). There may also have been a fear of old **women** at about this time that made them particularly vulnerable. Witch-hunting was certainly part of the Catholic **Reformation** agenda developed by the Bavarian dukes and their clients like the prince-bishops of Eichstätt whose diocese included the lands belonging to the Lutheran free city of Nuremberg and the Calvinist Elector Palatine.

The rigor with which witchcraft was prosecuted in the German Empire meant that witch persecution reached relatively powerful men like **Dietrich Flade** as well the more conventional marginalized old women. The diversity of approaches to witchcraft also meant that a range of opinions on the reality, extent, and appropriate punishment of witchcraft could coexist. **Heinrich Kramer** was the most famous of the many German church figures who promoted witch-hunting. On the other hand, his contemporary **Agrippa** was a skeptic, although his brand of **skepticism** differed from later figures like **Friedrich Spee** and **Adam Tanner**. The debates about the existence of witchcraft were finally played out in the **Bavarian War of the Witches** in the late 1760s. The experiences of witchcraft, and related activities like **sorcery** and **magic**, in the empire have formed the basis of works of German **art** by **Albrecht Dürer** and **Hans Baldung Grien**, for example, literature, notably Johann Wolfgang von Goethe's *Faust*, and music.

See also EXECUTIONS; PLAYS, WITCHCRAFT IN.

GERSON, JEAN (1363–1429). A prominent late-medieval theologian and chancellor of the university at Paris, Gerson wrote several works condemning **sorcery** and superstition. These included *Le miroir de l'âme* (Mirror of the Soul) and *De erroribus circa artem magicam* (On Errors in the Magic

Arts), in which he argued that all uses of **magic** and the seeking of advice from sorcerers were acts of **apostasy** and **idolatry**. Gerson's argument placed the prosecution of magicians, sorcerers, and their clients firmly in the hands of the **Inquisition**. He did not, however, write about a witch sect.

GIFFORD, GEORGE (?–1620). A preacher at Maldon in Essex, where some of the most intense **witch-hunts** in **England** took place in the late 16th century, Gifford wrote two important treatises on **witchcraft**, *A Discourse of the Subtle Practices of Devils by Witches and Sorcerers* (1587) and *A Dialogue Concerning Witches and Witchcrafts* (1593). In these works, he adopted a position of moderate **skepticism** toward witchcraft. That is, Gifford felt that the **devil** was the true enemy of Christian society, and that the devil was powerful enough to work his **evil** in the world without the cooperation of human witches. Focusing too much on witches, he felt, distracted authorities from the real source of evil in the world. Nevertheless, Gifford did support the execution of witches for trafficking with **demons** and the devil.

GILLES DE RAIS (1404–1440). A French nobleman and Marshal of **France**, Gilles de Rais rose to prominence for his military accomplishments during the course of the Hundred Years War. A companion of **Joan of Arc**, he was later tried and executed on charges of **heresy** and murder. Like Joan, he is often regarded as having been executed for **witchcraft**, although in reality he was never accused of this crime, and even the charges of demonic **magic** made against him were somewhat tangential to his ultimate conviction. Having become extremely powerful in the course of the war, Gilles made many political enemies. He also incurred significant debts in the course of the 1430s, and was forced to begin selling off his land. His enemies seem to have conspired against him largely because, if he were convicted of heresy, they could confiscate rather than purchase his lands. Gilles was brought up on a number of particularly terrible and graphic charges. Before an ecclesiastical court, he stood accused of performing **alchemy** and demonic magic, of summoning and worshiping **demons** and making pacts with them, and sacrificing **children** to them. He was also tried before a secular judge for the sexual murder of over 100 children.

By the time of his trials, Gilles had certainly developed a dark reputation that his enemies were able to exploit. Although most of the charges against him were clearly fabricated by his political opponents, he may well have been a murderous pedophile, and it is certainly possible that he turned to alchemy or even darker magic in an attempt to alleviate his financial problems. Ultimately, he confessed to practicing alchemy and murdering children. His case, however, was hardly one of typical witchcraft.

GLANVILL, JOSEPH (1636–1680). The chaplain of King Charles II of **England**, Glanvill attempted to prove the existence of **witchcraft** and other supernatural and occult phenomena in his *Saducismus triumphatus* (Sadducism Overcome). He felt that those who were **skeptical** of such phenomena were merely trying to disguise their own atheism, since to deny witchcraft one had to deny the reality of the **devil**'s power, and ultimately, for Glanvill, this meant denying the power of God as well. His work became popular not so much for its learned reasoning as for its collection of colorful stories and examples of witchcraft.

GOATS. After **cats**, goats were the animals most typically associated with **witchcraft** in medieval and early-modern Europe. They appear most commonly in images of the witches' **sabbath**, beginning with those by **Hans Baldung Grien** and **Albrecht Dürer**, as the form that a **demon** or the **devil** adopted when presiding over the gathering. Witches had to kneel before the goat, worship it, and often give the *osculum infame*, the **obscene kiss**, to its hindquarters. This image of a goat demon was borrowed from medieval stereotypes of **heresy** in which the heretics would worship demons in the form of goats. In turn, this stereotype had its origins in stories of the **pagan** worship of certain horned deities with goat-like features, such as the Greek Pan and the Celtic Cernunnos. Pan and Cernunnos were both fertility gods, and the goat has a long history as a symbol of fertility. For medieval and early-modern **demonologists**, however, goats were the wicked counterpart to the good sheep in the **Bible** and commonly associated with lust rather than fertility. It was only with **Margaret Murray**'s thesis that witches were in fact followers of an ancient fertility cult that the goat-like god Pan was returned to a more positive role. Since then, modern witchcraft, or **Wicca**, has adopted the **Horned God** to worship as the male counterpart and consort of the **Goddess**. The goat, and especially the goat-headed image of the devil known as **Baphomet**, also remains a prominent symbol among practitioners of modern **Satanism**.

THE GODDESS. In modern **witchcraft**, or **Wicca**, the Goddess is the primary deity. She is the companion of, and generally seen as superior to, the God or **Horned God** who represents the male aspect of the divinity. Although a supreme deity, the Goddess is above all a nature and fertility deity. She is regarded as being the Earth itself and embodies all creative and productive forces, particularly **magic**. She is in some ways a conglomeration of all early **pagan** mother deities.

The worship of powerful fertility goddesses is ancient and seems to have existed in almost all human cultures. Modern witches identify the Goddess with such ancient female fertility deities and mother goddesses as the Sumerian Inanna, Babylonian Ishtar, Egyptian Isis, Phoenician Astarte, and Greco-Roman Demeter. Also particularly associated with the Goddess are the Greco-Roman triad of moon goddesses **Diana** (Artemis), Selene, and **Hecate**, all of whom, especially Hecate, were associated with magic in **Antiquity**. Inanna, Ishtar, Isis, and Astarte were also lunar deities associated with magic and, frequently, the underworld.

GÖLDI, ANNA (1734–1782). The last person known to be executed for the crime of **witchcraft** in Europe was the servant Anna Göldi; she was executed by beheading in the Swiss canton of Glarus. In late 1781, following an argument between Göldi and one of the daughters of the house in which she was then a servant, pins were found in the girl's breakfast milk. Göldi was dismissed and fled, but the girl became bedridden and spat up pins, bits of wire and nails, much as the victims of **possession** were sometimes seen to. Göldi was found and arrested, and made to heal the girl. Göldi and her alleged accomplice Rudolf Steinmüller were then put on trial. Eventually, under the threat of **torture**, Göldi confessed to giving the girl a piece of cake containing the seeds of the metal bits that grew inside her. Göldi was convicted of **poisoning** the girl and sentenced to death in 1782; Steinmüller hanged himself in jail. Occurring long after the period of the **witch-hunts** had ended and many states had repealed their **laws** against witchcraft, the case caused outrage across Europe. In 1982, the case became the subject of a novel by Eveline Hasler.

See also EXECUTIONS; FICTION, WITCHCRAFT IN; SWITZERLAND, WITCHCRAFT IN.

GOYA Y LUCIENTES, FRANCISCO JOSÉ DE (1746–1828). After the illness that caused his deafness in 1792, the great Spanish artist Goya turned his attention to darker subjects than he had painted or engraved before. Goya's scenes of **witchcraft** or **magic** formed part of the series *Caprichos* (Caprices), completed in 1799, and others are included among his later *Black Paintings*. The *Caprichos* engravings are satires of Catholicism, in which the witchcraft scenes are critical of superstition, clerical hypocrisy, and the **Inquisition**'s involvement in the Logroño trials of 1610. The *Black Paintings* reveal a grotesque, disorderly world that cannot be forced into the categories favored by the early Enlightenment. While Goya's work is **skeptical** of the reality of witchcraft, it does not reject its imaginative role in highlighting the juxtaposition of intellect and experience.

See also ART, WITCHCRAFT IN.

GREGORY IX, POPE (ca. 1170–1241). Gregory reigned as pope from 1227 to 1241. In 1233, he issued the decretal letter *Vox in Rama* (A Voice in Rama) to the archbishop of Mainz and the bishop of Hildesheim. In it, Gregory described a heretical gathering presided over by a **demon** in the shape of a giant toad. New members of this heretical sect had to kiss this creature, and also a pallid man whose kiss was as cold as ice. The **heretics** then feasted until a large black **cat** appeared, which the heretics also had to kiss on its hindquarters, and afterward engaged in a sexual **orgy**. Although *Vox in Rama* does not describe **witchcraft**, it did contribute to later accounts of the witches' **sabbath**. The alleged heretics described in the letter were being pursued by the Dominican **inquisitors** established by Gregory, notably in the Languedoc where they hunted out the remaining Cathars. It was Dominican friars and inquisitors, like **Johannes Nider** and **Heinrich Kramer**, who were among the most vigorous **witch-hunters** of the 15th century.

See also OBSCENE KISS.

GRILLANDUS, PAULUS (LATE 15th TO 16th CENTURY). A papal judge who presided over several witch trials around Rome in the early 16th century, Grillandus wrote a *Tractatus de haereticus et sortilegiis* (Treatise on Heretics and Witches) around 1525. It was frequently reprinted, and, after the *Malleus maleficarum*, was one of the most important and influential treatises on **witchcraft** written prior to the major rise in **witch-hunting** in the later 16th century.

GRIMOIRE. The practical written or printed manual of a magician, witch, or **cunning man or woman**, a grimoire provides advice on vestments, rituals, spells, and other matters relevant to the practice of **magic**, **witchcraft**, or **healing** using herbs and charms. They are often associated with **hermetic** writings, and the authorship or content of many grimoires has been attributed, fictitiously, to many biblical and historical characters, such as Aristotle, **Moses**, Solomon, **Albertus Magnus**, various medieval popes, and **Faust**. **Martín Del Rio** claimed that witches received books of magic as part of their **pact** with the **devil**, although most were probably illiterate. Cunning folk certainly continued to use grimoires as handbooks and several of these survive, notably in Wales. More recently, the witches' grimoires have been revived in the form of the **Books of Shadows** adopted by **covens** and solitary practitioners of **Wicca**.

GUAZZO, FRANCESCO MARIA (? TO EARLY 17th CENTURY). An Italian friar of the order of Saint Ambrose, which specialized in **exorcisms**, Guazzo wrote the encyclopedic *Compendium maleficarum* (Handbook of Witches) at the request of **Carlo Borromeo**, archbishop of Milan, in 1605.

Although the *Compendium* was based, in part, on his experiences in Milan, where he served as a consultant on **witchcraft** trials, and Cleves-Jülich, **Germany**, where he attended the bewitched duke, most of its content was drawn from existing Catholic demonologies. These included the treatises of **Johannes Nider** and **Heinrich Kramer** as well as the more recent work of **Nicolas Rémy** and **Martín Del Rio**. Guazzo's work added nothing to early-modern **demonology** but became well known because of its anecdotal style and the series of images that illustrate it.

See also ART, WITCHCRAFT IN.

GUI, BERNARD (ca. 1261–1331). A Dominican friar and papal inquisitor in the southern French region of Languedoc, Gui is most well known as the author of one of the first major inquisitorial manuals, *Practica inquisitionis haereticae pravitatis* (The Practice of the Inquisition into Heretical Activity), completed by 1324. In this work, Gui included some sections on **sorcery** and **divination**, as well as on clearly learned demonic **magic**, or **necromancy**. He never described diabolic **witchcraft** per se, but his writings were an important basis for later inquisitorial thought in this area.

Born in Limousin, Gui entered the Dominican order in 1279. He studied theology at Montpellier and then served as prior of several Dominican convents in Languedoc until 1307, when he was appointed a papal inquisitor and began operating from Toulouse. He remained in this office until 1324, when he became bishop of Lodève. Throughout his tenure as an inquisitor, Gui seems never to have conducted an **inquisition** into a case of sorcery personally. Nevertheless, sorcery was becoming a concern for religious authorities in southern **France** at this time. In 1320, **Pope John XXII** ordered the inquisitors of Toulouse and Carcassonne to take action against those who invoked or worshiped **demons** as part of magical ceremonies. In his *Practica*, Gui included several sections of procedures to be used specifically against clerics who engaged in demonic invocation, including a long description of complex necromantic ritual magic. He also included a section on sorcery and divination generally. While Gui clearly assumed all such magic was demonic in nature, he actually described acts quite different from the overtly demonic practices of learned magic. Instead, he discussed what seems to be a much more common sort of magic, aimed at **healing**, discovering thefts, locating lost objects, or inspiring love, and performed via everyday objects and simple rituals. Gui's association of such common magic with demonic invocation was fundamental for the later prosecution of sorcery and eventually witchcraft in inquisitorial courts.

H

HALE, SIR MATTHEW (1609–1676). An English judge, and later chief justice of the King's Bench, Hale is most well known for conducting the trial of two witches at Bury Saint Edmunds in 1662. In this notorious case, which began when several **children** exhibited signs of bewitchment and accused two old **women** of causing them, he allowed hearsay and unsupported **spectral evidence**. He also refused to give credence to clear evidence of fraud and perjury on the part of some of the children in his zeal to obtain convictions. The alleged witches were sentenced to be hanged, and the case was later reported in *A Tryal of Witches Held at Bury St. Edmunds* (1682). One of the ministers present at the **Salem** trials in 1692, John Hale, noted in his *A Modest Enquiry into the Nature of Witchcraft* (1702) that Matthew Hale's handling of the Bury Saint Edmunds case, particularly his use of spectral evidence, served as a model for the New England judges.

See also ENGLAND AND WALES, WITCHCRAFT IN; NORTH AMERICA, WITCHCRAFT IN.

HALLOWEEN. The period around Halloween has long carried supernatural significance and has often been associated with death and the spirits of the dead. The Celtic tribes of Europe celebrated the feast of **Samhain**, their New Year and the beginning of winter, on 1 November. On the night before this festival, the boundaries between the material world of the living and the supernatural world of the dead were believed to be particularly weak. The Romans, who by 43 CE had conquered most Celtic territory in Western Europe, combined two of their own holidays with the Celtic Samhain: the feast of Feralia, which commemorated the dead, and the feast of Pomona, goddess of apples and other fruits, which celebrated fertility and rebirth. In the seventh century, Pope Boniface IV, seeking to Christianize these **pagan** holidays and incorporate them into the church's liturgical calendar, declared 1 November to be All Saints' Day, to honor Christian saints and martyrs. Later, around 1000, the church declared 2 November to be All Souls' Day, commemorating all the Christian dead. All Saints' Day was also known as All Hallows', and so the night before became Hallows' Eve and eventually Halloween.

Throughout the early-modern period, Halloween was not widely celebrated across Europe, nor was it regarded as a time when witches were abroad. Other festivities, like **Walpurgisnacht** (Saint Walburga's Night, 30 April) were associated with witches; and in Lutheran countries, 31 October was celebrated as "Reformation Day." Even where Halloween was celebrated, in Britain and **Ireland**, for example, the customs tended to be local rather than uniform. It was only with the popularization and commercialization of Halloween in the United States during the 20th century that most of the activities associated with it became standardized. It was at this time that the witch figure became a feature of Halloween celebrations.

These modern activities did, however, have historical origins. The tradition of trick-or-treating may have had its roots in the medieval celebration of All Souls' Day, when people would give pastries and other food to the poor in exchange for their promise to pray for the souls of the gift-givers' dead relatives. It might also have a connection with the "mumming" or "souling" popular in medieval Ireland and **England**. The "mummers" reveled in outlandish costumes on All Hallows' Eve and threatened wealthy neighbors with mischief unless they received a sufficient bribe. Even older was the tradition of leaving offerings of food and wine for the spirits of the dead thought to roam free on this night.

In modern times, and especially in the United States, certain religious groups have tried to associate Halloween with **witchcraft** and **Satanism**. In some cases, following the Puritan opposition to Halloween in early-modern **England** and colonial New England, some fundamentalist Christians have called for the suppression of this festivity, believing it, inaccurately, to be inspired by the **devil**. Halloween has also become a real witches' holiday, as practitioners of modern witchcraft, or **Wicca**, as well as practitioners of other forms of **neo-paganism** have revived the celebration of the Celtic Samhain.

See also NORTH AMERICA, WITCHCRAFT IN.

HAND OF GLORY. In medieval and early-modern sources, witches were often described as taking the limbs of corpses, and especially their hands, for magical purposes. The Hand of Glory was one particular use to which such a limb could be put. The hand of a hanged murderer was removed from the corpse, often while it still hung on the gallows, then pickled and dried. It was then used to hold candles or the fingers themselves could be lighted. Supposedly, the hand had the power to immobilize or incapacitate anyone within a house, and was often employed by thieves.

HARTLIEB, JOHANN (ca. 1410–1468). Court physician to Duke Albrecht III of **Bavaria**, Hartlieb was one of the first authorities to write on **witchcraft** in a vernacular language. Around 1456, at the invitation of the alchemist Margrave Johann of Brandenburg-Kulmbach, he wrote his *Buch aller verbotenen Kunst* (Book of All Forbidden Art). It is primarily a study of **magic** and **divination** in which the reader is warned of the dangers of forbidden arts. Yet, in its second part, Hartlieb describes in detail how to perform them. In the book, Hartlieb, unlike other 15th-century **demonologists** such as **Johannes Nider**, accepted the reality of **night flight**, including a description of the **ointments** used by witches, and the witches' **sabbath**. Hartlieb also wrote elsewhere on such matters as chiromancy (palm reading).

HEALING, MAGICAL. Curing diseases and healing injuries have historically always been among the principal functions of common **magic**. Across Europe in the Middle Ages and early-modern period, a wide variety of healers and **cunning men and women** practiced such magic. In common culture, for the most part, such people were easily distinguished from witches, who performed harmful magic and who were typically believed to cause disease rather than cure it. Authorities, however, especially clerical authorities, often did not recognize such distinctions. They placed less importance than most average people on the effects of magic and were more concerned with the means by which magic supposedly operated. Because they believed that most magical operations depended on invoking demonic power, such acts were still **evil** even if (occasionally) used to achieve beneficial ends. Many authorities believed, for example, that witches might cause a disease or injury only to cure it later. They supposedly did this not out of compassion for their neighbors, but in order to corrupt their souls by involving them in operations of demonic power.

In practical terms, because most witch trials began with acts of *maleficium*, magical healers, who were not commonly seen to perform such harmful **sorcery**, were generally safe. If a **witch-hunt** developed, however, and accusations increasingly came to be directed by authorities rather than arising naturally, magical healers and cunning folk were certainly at risk. Authorities, who at best regarded them as frauds and charlatans, could become convinced that they were witches, and as the level of panic generated by a hunt increased within a community, common people, too, could begin to become suspicious of the nature of magical healers' supposed power.

See also WITCHCRAFT.

HECATE. An Anatolian goddess of childbirth who also protected liminal spaces, like thresholds, which made buildings or borders vulnerable to **demons** and ghosts, Hecate became associated in Greek mythology with **mag-**

ic, **witchcraft**, the dark phases of the moon, crossroads, and the underworld. She was therefore regarded by the Greeks as a dangerous and often **evil** deity, worshiped for her power over the dead. Hecate was imagined by them as a three-faced spirit that haunted crossroads and roamed about at night, visible only to dogs (a dog's howl was taken as a sign that Hecate was near). She caused nightmares, insanity, and untimely deaths. The mythical sorceresses **Circe** and **Medea** were sometimes believed to be daughters of Hecate. In the Christian Middle Ages, when **pagan** deities were transformed into demons, many of Hecate's terrifying attributes and her strong association with witchcraft were transferred to the more general figure of **Diana**. She appears as one of the three witches in Shakespeare's *Macbeth*.

See also ANTIQUITY, WITCHCRAFT IN; PLAYS, WITCHCRAFT IN.

HELLISH NELL. *See* DUNCAN, HELEN (1897–1956).

HERESY. Any belief contrary to a formally established doctrine of the church is considered a heresy. In the Middle Ages, the practice of demonic **sorcery** was deemed to be heretical because clerical authorities decided that such acts must entail the worship of **demons** and were thus considered a form of **idolatry**, a violation of the first commandment. The most influential figure in establishing an argument for the heretical nature of demonic sorcery was the 14th-century theologian and inquisitor **Nicolau Eymeric**. Because witches were thought to perform sorcery by demonic means, they were also considered heretics. Many aspects of **witchcraft**, and especially many aspects of the witches' **sabbath**, derived from earlier medieval stereotypes of heretics, notably the **Waldensians** and Cathars, and their assemblies. Heretics were commonly described as worshiping demons, often in the form of an animal such as a **cat** or **goat**, murdering **children**, desecrating the sacraments, and engaging in sexual **orgies** with one another. All of these stereotypical elements were later transferred on to witches through demonologies and treatises like the ***Errores Gazariorum*** (Errors of the Gazari). During the period of the **witch-hunts**, many authorities argued that denying the reality of witchcraft or the existence of witches was also heretical, because the church had declared such things to be real.

HERMETIC MAGIC. A major source of magical and occult knowledge in European history was the body of writings traditionally ascribed to Hermes Trismegistus (the Thrice-Great Hermes) and referred to collectively as the *Corpus Hermeticum*. Thrice-Great Hermes was a mythical figure—a blend of the Greek god Hermes and the Egyptian god of wisdom, Thoth. He stood as a personification of arcane, magical knowledge, and supposedly wrote over 20,000 books containing his wisdom. In fact, the *Corpus Hermeticum* was composed by various authors over several centuries. Much of it was lost in ancient times, but some writings remained known throughout the Middle Ages, and more were rediscovered in the Renaissance of the 14th and 15th centuries. Hermetic writings became a basis for much learned or high **magic**, including **astrology** and **alchemy**, in the Renaissance and continued to be a basis for systems of learned magic and occult science in Europe thereafter. **Agrippa**, for example, was influenced to some extent by hermeticism. In the 19th century, when occultists in England organized into a group, they designated themselves the **Hermetic Order of the Golden Dawn**. The rites and rituals of such groups have had some effect on modern **witchcraft**, or **Wicca**, but historical hermetic magic, always regarded as a highly learned system and limited to a small elite, had little to do with witchcraft in the medieval and early-modern periods.

HERMETIC ORDER OF THE GOLDEN DAWN. Founded in England in 1888, the Golden Dawn was an elite, secret society, along the lines of earlier Masonic and Rosicrucian groups. Unlike those groups, however, the purpose of the society was to promote the study and practice of ritual **magic** among its members. Although the founders initially claimed that the order was of ancient origin, the rituals and practices of the Golden Dawn were in fact a loose assembly of ancient Greco-Roman, Egyptian, and Hebrew systems of magic and mysticism, and medieval and modern Christian beliefs. The members of the Golden Dawn could justify mingling different belief systems because they accepted the notion, perhaps most famously articulated in the writings of the British anthropologist James Frazer, that all historical religions were built upon a single, underlying mythic system. Such ideas also influenced **Margaret Murray** and others to conceive of historical **witchcraft** as an ancient, pre-Christian fertility cult.

The members of the Golden Dawn, which included such luminaries as W. B. Yeats and the famed occultist **Aleister Crowley**, were not especially interested in witchcraft, which they considered to be a form of low magic. By merging systems of ritual magic into a kind of **neo-pagan** structure of belief, however, the order did help establish a basis for the development of modern witchcraft, or **Wicca**. The principal founder of modern witchcraft, **Gerald Gardner**, was drawn to the sort of occult studies that the Golden Dawn promoted. Significantly, he was inducted by Aleister Crowley into the *Ordo Templi Orientis*, another occult society that Crowley headed after his expulsion from the Golden Dawn.

HERNE THE HUNTER. In Germanic legend, Herne was a male spirit (also given as Herlechin, Harlequin, or Berthold) sometimes thought to lead the **Wild Hunt** instead of the female spirit **Holda** or Berta. He was pictured wearing an antlered headdress. Christian authorities in the Middle Ages frequently associated him with the **devil**. In modern **witchcraft**, or **Wicca**, he is associated with the **Horned God**.

HERODIAS. In the **Bible**, Herodias was the wife of Herod who demanded the head of John the Baptist. Although she became the embodiment of female **evil** in the Middle Ages, her association with **witchcraft** seems quite coincidental. In the Germanic concept of the **Wild Hunt**, a group of spirits was led in nocturnal flight by a female deity most typically named **Holda** or Berta. Authorities writing in Latin tended to transform this deity into the classical **Diana**, even though it was **Hecate** who led spirits through the night in classical mythology. Some authorities, however, gave this deity the name Herodias instead, apparently working from the Germanic Ber- (alternately Her-) beginning of the original name to provide a similar-sounding biblical one. The image of the Wild Hunt later became an important basis for the idea of **night flight** of witches to a **sabbath**.

HOBBES, THOMAS (1588–1679). The most important English political philosopher of his day, Hobbes is best known for his extremely important and influential treatise on government, *Leviathan* (1651). He treats **witchcraft** only tangentially in this work, but demonstrates a complete **skepticism** about the reality of witches and witchcraft. For Hobbes, spirits—either angels or **demons**—had no real existence or power in the world. **Biblical** passages referring to such spirits he interpreted metaphorically. Without the real presence of demons in the world, the entire basis for the reality of witchcraft was removed.

HOLDA. A Germanic goddess, also known as Hulda, Holle, Holt, Berta, Bertha, or Perchta, she was associated with fertility, the moon, and the hunt. For these reasons, she was often equated by medieval authorities with the classical goddess **Diana**. Holda was believed to lead the **Wild Hunt**, a group of spirits and ghosts who roamed through the night. This Germanic legend became an important basis for the later Christian notions of the **night flight** of witches to a **sabbath**.
See also HERODIAS.

HOODOO. While it is based on a similar syncretization of beliefs originating in **African** and Native American traditions and Christianity, Hoodoo differs from **Voodoo** in that it is not a religion. It seems to have begun among either **Irish** seamen or African slaves in the American South and developed into a collection of remedies and practices that might generally be called folk magic. Although there is no separate theology, the **Bible** is used as a talisman, and the European apocryphal **grimoire** the *Sixth and Seventh Books of Moses* sustains the belief that **Moses** was a conjurer.

See also NORTH AMERICA, WITCHCRAFT IN.

HOOPOE (*UPUPA EPOPS*). A type of bird common in Europe and throughout much of Africa and Asia, hoopoes are distinguished by the fanlike crests on their heads. Historically, they have long been associated with magic and supernatural powers. The blood of the hoopoe, as well as its brains, tongue, and heart, were all regarded as being particularly efficacious when used in spells, charms, and conjurations, and the hoopoe itself was often used by magicians as a sacrifice when invoking **demons**. Certain modern devotees of magic continue to regard the hoopoe as a sort of totem.

HOPKINS, MATTHEW (?–1647). Born the son of a Puritan minister in Suffolk, Hopkins became, briefly, the most notorious and successful witch-hunter in English history. In less than two years, from 1645 to 1646, he oversaw investigations into as many as 250 cases of suspected **witchcraft** in eastern **England**. At least 100 of the witch suspects Hopkins investigated as the self-styled "Witchfinder General" were executed. His methods proved too extreme, however, and he quickly found himself faced with criticism and significant opposition from local authorities. His **witch-hunting** activity ended in 1646, as rapidly as it had begun. In 1647, he published a brief treatise entitled *Discoverie of Witches*, defending himself and his procedures. He died in obscurity later that year.

The motivations for Hopkins' zeal in persecuting witches are difficult to determine. He may have been alarmed by the witchcraft accusations around his property in Manningtree, Essex, in the winter of 1644–45. At about the same time, Essex had become a stronghold of the Parliamentarian side in the English Civil War. The Parliamentarians had acted to get rid of scandalous clergymen who fell short of the exacting spiritual standards demanded by Puritanism, and Hopkins may have regarded witchcraft as undermining those standards. Whatever his motivations, Hopkins and his associate John Stearne were soon offering their services as witchfinders for a modest fee. Their first success came in the series of witch trials prosecuted in **Chelmsford**, Essex, in 1645. Thereafter, their reputation spread, and they hired more staff and conducted numerous trials throughout Essex, Norfolk, Suffolk and other counties in eastern England. Although **torture** was illegal in England, except in cases of high treason, Hopkins did apply "watching" (a form of sleep deprivation) to obtain confessions. The use of "watching," and a reliance on **King James'** s *Daemonologie*, help explain why the trials conducted by Hopkins and his associates focused more on **heresy** than previous English cases had. The use of extreme practices, alongside the charging of fees and the questionable legality of the investigations by people who were not magistrates and therefore not authorized to look into criminal cases, helped rouse opposition against Hopkins and bring his career to an end.

HORNED GOD. In modern **witchcraft**, or **Wicca**, and other forms of **neo-paganism**, the Horned God is the male aspect of the supreme deity, and consort to the **Goddess**. Although the Goddess is held to be superior, the Horned God is very important in modern neo-pagan rituals. The god is often associated with such historical **pagan** deities as the Celtic Cernunnos, the Greek Pan and Roman Faunus, and the Celtic and Germanic figure of **Herne the Hunter**. All of these beings are depicted as horned, and often appeared in half-animal forms. Following the theories of **Margaret Murray**, some modern witches believed that historical witchcraft was an actual survival of an ancient, pre-Christian religion, and that during the Middle Ages, Christian authorities had mistakenly (or deliberately) transformed the witches' worship of the Horned God into worship of the Christian **devil**. Murray's theories have long since been disproved, however, and most Wiccans see their religion as a creative revival of historical pagan beliefs, not as the continuance of a long, clandestine tradition.

HUMANISM. Describing a program of humanistic studies that developed in **Italy** in the late 14th and 15th centuries and then spread to the rest of Europe, humanism is often seen as one of the defining elements of the Italian Renaissance. The term was first coined in the 19th century. As a program of study, it stressed attention to the literature of classical **Antiquity**, both Latin and Greek, and placed more value on rhetoric than on dialectic logic in argumentation. It developed as an intellectual system in opposition to medieval scholasticism. Regarding **witchcraft**, humanist scholars were often inclined to a certain degree of **skepticism**. This might have been partly because of their natural suspicion of much scholastic thought that had formed the basis of medieval **demonology**. Also, because of their closer attention to ancient texts, humanists often realized that the **Bible** and other ancient sources did not really describe witchcraft as it was conceived in the 15th and 16th centuries. Nevertheless, humanists did not deny the reality of the **devil** or his potential power in the world, and humanism as a system of thought was in no way antithetical to belief in witchcraft.

HUNGARY, WITCHCRAFT IN. **Witch-hunting** in the ethnically and confessionally mixed kingdom of Hungary was a late phenomenon. Just over 4,000 people seem to have been accused of **witchcraft** in the country, over 2,250 of them in the early 18th century, when witchcraft trials had died out elsewhere and some countries, like **England**, were repealing their witchcraft **laws**. By far the majority of those accused of witchcraft were ethnic Hungarians, followed in number by Germans and Croatians, then Romanians, and to a much lesser extent Slovaks, Gypsies, Ruthenians, and Serbs. About half of those accused were executed. It seems that this late reception of the diabolical notion of witchcraft and persecution of witches resulted from the relatively late introduction of the witches' **sabbath** and **pact** with **demons** into Hungarian **demonology** and law. Once these concepts, and the precepts of Benedict Carpzov's legal treatise *Practica nova imperialis Saxonica verum criminaliam* (New Rules for Criminal Cases for Imperial Saxony, 1635), had become established in Hungary, witch prosecution increased until it reached its peak in the early 1700s. Empress Maria Theresa personally intervened in witch prosecution in Hungary after she had examined an accused witch and concluded that all witchcraft accusations were false. Her **skepticism** was given voice in a royal decree of 1768 that halted the further **execution** of witches.

Once introduced into Hungary, western ideas of witchcraft could merge with older concepts of demonic **magic** that had been prosecuted throughout the medieval period, the activities of the *táltos* (a local **shamanistic** figure), and regional fairy beliefs. A local, popular variant of witchcraft therefore evolved that resonated with the peoples of Hungary. After Maria Theresa's intervention, **vampires** and **werewolves**, about which local traditions already existed, replaced witches as aggressive demonic figures.

HUTCHINSON, FRANCIS (1660–1739). A curate of Bury Saint Edmunds, Suffolk, Hutchinson wrote the **skeptical** *An Historical Essay Concerning Witchcraft* (1718) in response to the last English **witchcraft** case, that of **Jane Wenham** in 1712, and the work of Richard Boulton, which continued to treat the spiritual threat of witchcraft and **magic** as a reality. Hutchinson argued that many cases of witchcraft were improbable, and much evidence for the crime was the product of mental illness, imposture, and **torture**. In this latter claim, Hutchinson followed influential skeptics like **Johann Weyer**, **Reginald Scot**, **Friedrich Spee**, and **Balthasar Bekker**, as well as opponents of **Joseph Glanvill**, such as **John Webster**. Although it does not seem to have been read widely, Hutchinson's *Essay* did reflect the distance that had grown in intellectual circles from what were now generally regarded as the superstitious beliefs of the ignorant. Shortly after the publication of the *Essay*, Hutchinson was invested as the bishop of Down and Connor.

I

ICELAND, WITCHCRAFT IN. As in **Hungary**, witch persecution arrived late in Iceland. Between 1593 and 1720, just over 180 individuals from a very small population of about 50,000 were accused of **witchcraft**. Of these only 22 were burned at the stake. Two facts mark these trials out from most other places in Europe, except perhaps **Estonia** and **Finland**: of these 22 witches all but one was **male**; and the Icelandic term for them translates as **cunning men**. Most of the Icelandic trials occurred against the backdrop of local introduction of the **Reformation** and in an area of the country presided over by two zealous **witch-hunters**.

See also EXECUTIONS.

IDOLATRY. Idolatry is the worship of false gods or their images, and regarded as a serious form of **heresy**. Along with **apostasy**, it was considered by most authorities throughout medieval and early-modern Europe to be the main crime entailed in **witchcraft**. Rather than focus on the supposed harm that a witch might achieve through her **sorcery (*maleficium*)**, first ecclesiastical authorities and then increasingly secular ones as well considered the real **evil** of witchcraft to lie in the witches' involvement with **demons**. They developed theories that defined how most, if not all, demonic sorcery, such as witches were believed to perform, required that worship be offered to demons, or that they be invoked in some way that set them equal to or above divine power. The inquisitor **Nicolau Eymeric** developed an extended and detailed argument about the idolatrous nature of demonic **magic** in the late 14th century, and thereafter, demonic magic and witchcraft were often classified by authorities as a violation of the first commandment.

IMP. Any type of small **demon** or demonic creature might be called an imp. In medieval and early-modern Europe, sorcerers were often thought to keep imps imprisoned in jewels, vials, or glass jars to serve them. Particularly in **England**, **Scotland**, and **Ireland**, witches were also thought to keep imps in animal form as **familiars**.

INCUBI AND SUCCUBI. In medieval and early-modern Europe, people believed that **demons** could take substantial form and engage in sexual activity with humans. Demons who took male form were called *incubi* and those who took female form were called *succubi*. Early Christian authorities tended to doubt that demons, as spiritual creatures, could assume solid material form in order to engage in sexual intercourse with humans. By the 13th century, however, the idea that this was possible for demons had gained ground sufficiently that **Thomas Aquinas** described how demons could collect semen from men by having sex with them as succubi, preserve its potency, and then use it to inseminate **women** by having sex with them as incubi. The child that resulted from sex between a woman and an incubus would often be a mixture of human and animal. In the 14th century, **Alice Kyteler** was accused of having sex with an incubus called Robert, son of Art. By the late 15th century, **Heinrich Kramer** was observing in his *Malleus maleficarum* that women now offered themselves to incubi rather than suffer their assaults. Throughout the period of the **witch-hunts**, witches often confessed that they sealed the **demonic pact** with sexual intercourse with a demon or the **devil** (who was frequently described as having an ice cold penis), and that they also had sex with demons during the **orgies** at their **sabbaths**.

While Christian authorities originally doubted the corporeal existence of incubi and succubi, they did exist in mythology, legend, and **folklore**. Romulus and Remus (the founders of Rome), Merlin, and **Martin Luther** were just a few of the many legendary or historical figures who were believed, by some, to have been born of a woman and an incubus. The fairy tale Beauty and the Beast is also a version of this kind of story. Similarly, succubi have ancestors in the ancient Sumerian spirit called *Ardat Lili* or *Lilitu*, a monstrous female demon with wings and talons who could fly through the night, seduce men, and drink their blood; the Hebrew demon **Lilith**; and the Greco-Roman creatures **strix** and **lamia**. In Christian **demonology**, they were thought to tempt religious men to stray from God. Because witchcraft was regarded mainly as a female **heresy** and demonologists regarded women as emotionally and intellectually weak, incubi appear much more frequently in the stories of later medieval and early-modern witchcraft than succubi.

INFANTICIDE. A major crime historically associated with **witchcraft** has been the killing, in various ways and for various purposes, of babies and small **children**. As far back as classical **Antiquity**, creatures like the **strix** and **lamia** were believed to fly through the night and prey on children. Such nocturnal female monsters later contributed to the stereotype of witchcraft. In medieval and early-modern Europe, witches were thought to kill children in several ways. One standard act of harm, or *maleficium*, by witches was to cause fatal diseases in children. Witches were also believed to be able to cause miscarriages and abortions of unborn fetuses. The murder of children also played an important role in typical images of the witches' **sabbath**, where witches were thought to use parts of babies' bodies in their magic spells, to sacrifice children to the **devil**, and to **cannibalize** babies as part of their general feasting and revelry.

One obvious explanation for the longstanding connection of witchcraft with infanticide is the extremely high mortality rate of infants and young children in the pre-modern world. Accusations of witchcraft provided a ready explanation for such misfortune. Historians used to think that **midwives** were frequently accused of witchcraft for this reason, but this theory has since been largely discredited and it now seems clear that in fact very few midwives were accused of the crime. Some people still suspect that practitioners of modern witchcraft, or **Wicca**, engage in infanticide, although the ritual murder of children is more often associated with **Satanism**. In fact, no Wiccan or Satanist groups engage in or promote any activity like this, and there has never been any substantial, credible evidence that organized groups of any nature exist that focus on the ritualistic abuse or murder of children. Nevertheless, this longstanding myth shows few signs of abating in the modern world.

INNOCENT III, POPE (1160/61–1216). One of the most important popes of the medieval period, reigning from 1198 until 1216, Innocent played a critical role in the introduction of **inquisitorial procedure** to Western Europe. In 1215, the Fourth Lateran Council, under the pope's direction, regularized legal procedures used against heretics, and, importantly, allowed judges to initiate inquests into **heresy** themselves, even when no accuser was present. In later centuries, such procedures would be essential to the spread of **witch-hunts**.

INNOCENT VIII, POPE (1432–1492). In the first year of his pontificate, which lasted from 1484 until 1492, Innocent VIII issued what is sometimes regarded as the most important papal pronouncement concerning **witchcraft**, the bull *Summis desiderantes affectibus* (the title comes from the document's opening words in Latin: "Desiring with Supreme Ardor"). Having been alerted by the papal inquisitors **Heinrich Kramer** and **Jakob Sprenger** to the existence of numerous witches throughout the lands of the **German Empire**, the pope expressed his grief that so many Christians had fallen into such grave error and **heresy**, sacrificing their souls to the **devil** and performing harmful **sorcery** and causing *maleficium* in his service. The pope then noted that many local authorities had not given Kramer and Sprenger the assistance they required to conduct their **inquisitions** effectively and root out this particularly terrible error. He commanded that papal inquisitors should have full authority to investigate and prosecute this crime in all territories, and that local authorities should give all necessary assistance and offer no impediments to such action. Although sometimes regarded as marking the official start of **witch-hunting** in Europe, the bull is actually fairly typical of papal pronouncements on sorcery and witchcraft throughout the late-medieval period, at least since the pontificate of **John XXII** in the early 14th century. The bull was later included in the infamous late-medieval witch-hunting manual *Malleus maleficarum*, written by Heinrich Kramer and first published in about 1486. Although the bull pre-dated the *Malleus* and was not directly connected to it, its inclusion seemed to lend papal approval to the witch-hunting manual.

INQUISITION. Although it is often regarded as some sort of supreme, repressive legal organ of the church, there never was, in fact, anything like a coherent and centrally controlled "Inquisition" in medieval Europe. Beginning in the 13th century, there were individual, papally appointed inquisitors who were responsible for helping to combat **heresy**, and in later periods there were certain standing Inquisitions. However, neither individual inquisitors nor organized Inquisitions played a significant role in matters of **witchcraft** or **witch-hunting**. Papal inquisitors were important in some of the earliest trials in the 15th century, but thereafter, and throughout the period of the great witch-hunts, witchcraft was generally classified as a secular crime and tried in secular courts (albeit in courts operating according to **inquisitorial procedure**).

The Latin term *inquisitio*, taken in the legal sense, merely meant an inquiry; in cases of heresy, this inquiry was originally conducted by episcopal courts because the enforcement of correct religious belief and observance was the responsibility of local bishops. In 1231, however, **Pope Gregory IX** responded to the perceived rise in heresy at that time by issuing the bull *Ille humani generis*. In this bull, Gregory commissioned the Dominican convent in Regensburg to form an inquisitorial tribunal independent of the local bishop and directly under papal authority. This was the *inquisitio haereticae pravitatis* (inquisition into heretical depravity), and is generally taken to mark the creation of "the Inquisition" in Europe. However, papal inquisitors, although in theory under the control of Rome, still acted largely as independent agents, and certainly there was no inquisitorial structure or organization that could be called the "Inquisition" at this time. In 1252, Pope Innocent IV permitted inquisitors to use **torture** to help detect heretics. Previously, torture had been excluded from church law.

Inquisitors seem rather quickly to have begun cases involving sorcery. In 1258, however, **Pope Alexander IV** specifically forbade papal inquisitors from trying such cases unless there was evidence that the acts of **sorcery** were also heretical in nature. In practice, this might not have represented much of a limitation on inquisitorial authority because the church assumed that most sorcery relied on the agency of **demons**, and involvement with demons or **pacts** made with them could clearly be construed as heresy. In 1320, **Pope John XXII** specifically ordered the inquisitors of Toulouse and Carcassonne in southern France to take action against any sorcerers who were invoking or worshiping demons as part of their magical rites. In 1326, John then issued the bull *Super illius specula*, which declared a sentence of automatic excommunication on any sorcerer who invoked demons, worshiped them, or entered into pacts with them. Later that century, in 1376, the inquisitor **Nicolau Eymeric** wrote his *Directorium inquisitorum* (Directory of Inquisitors) in which he proved by theological argument that all magic involving demonic invocation entailed **idolatry**. This was a form of heresy, and therefore subject to inquisitorial authority.

In the 15th century, papal inquisitors played an important role in early witch trials and the production of some of the earliest literature on witchcraft. The author of one of the most lurid early accounts, the *Errores Gazariorum* (Errors of the Gazarii), may have been the Franciscan inquisitor Ponce Fougeyron. **Heinrich Kramer**, author of the infamous *Malleus maleficarum*, was also an inquisitor in southern **Germany** for several years and conducted many witch trials before he wrote this important treatise on witch-hunting. Despite such important inquisitorial contributions to the emergence of witch-craft prosecution, however, one of the basic elements of the crime, namely the practice of harmful sorcery to cause *maleficium*, had always been under the jurisdiction of secular authorities. Thus witch trials were from the start conducted in both secular and ecclesiastical courts. During the period of the most intense witch-hunting in the 16th and 17th centuries, the majority of trials were conducted in secular courts in most European lands.

It is notable, in fact, that in the lands of southern Europe, where witchcraft remained more often under ecclesiastical jurisdiction, witch-hunts were relatively light and in particular the number of executions for witchcraft was significantly lower than in many other areas. **Italy** and **Spain** are also the only two regions of Europe that actually had Inquisitions in the sense of large, centralized, bureaucratic organizations that oversaw the actions of inquisitorial courts. The Spanish Inquisition was founded in 1478 as an instrument of the Spanish royal government, not the pope in Rome. The Holy Office of the Roman Inquisition was founded by Pope Paul III in 1542. Both of these institutions were notably lenient in matters of witchcraft. There are several reasons for this. First, inquisitorial courts in general regarded witch-craft as a form of heresy and, traditionally, death sentences were only imposed on recalcitrant heretics. If the accused were willing to confess and formally renounce their errors, then a less severe punishment could be imposed. Cases of witchcraft were often somewhat different, because the heresy involved was so extreme, but in general, inquisitorial courts proved more willing to impose lesser sentences than secular ones. In addition, the inquisitors tended to err on the side of caution, preferring to regard acts of witch-craft as illusions perpetrated on the witches by the **devil**. In this view, the witches neither attended **sabbaths** nor caused harm to individuals or their property. The inquisitors' job was to reconcile the suspect to true belief rather than punish a nonexistent heresy or felony. Inquisitors were also dissuaded from acting on the names of accomplices given by witch suspects under investigation.

The centralization of the Inquisitions prevented witchcraft cases from escalating into full witch-hunts. The most severe witch-hunts took place in regions, like the German Empire, where local authorities had significant autonomy. Local judges were often swept up in the panic that could follow several accusations of witchcraft and therefore allowed certain legal procedures and safeguards, such as those that governed the use of torture, to lapse. Centralized courts, like Inquisitions, on the other hand, were less susceptible to local conditions and tended to stress the proper application of procedure and the careful evaluation of evidence. The Inquisitions could impose their will on areas where witch-hunts threatened to get out of control, as happened in Navarre in 1611 when the Spanish Inquisition acted on the report of its inquisitor **Alonso de Salazar Frías** and prevented the trials from continuing. Throughout Europe, in lands where legal systems were largely centralized or at least overseen by a central authority, prosecutions and especially executions for witchcraft were generally low. This was true for both the centralized Inquisitions in Spain and Italy and the lesser Inquisitions in Portugal and Venice.

INQUISITORIAL PROCEDURE. This refers to a system of legal procedure that came to be used increasingly in European courts of law, both ecclesiastical and secular, after the 13th century, in place of the older **accusatorial procedure**. It was in many ways a more rational procedure than the earlier method, and was based to some extent on the recovery of Roman legal texts and principles of jurisprudence in the course of the 11th and 12th centuries. In terms of the potential to try cases of **sorcery** and **witchcraft**, however, the introduction of inquisitorial procedure had dire consequences. Certain aspects of the accusatorial procedure, above all the potential for punishment of the initial accuser if an accused person was proven innocent, tended to restrict the frequency of accusations for particularly secretive or difficult to prove crimes, of which sorcery was certainly one. Inquisitorial procedure, on the other hand, by placing responsibility for the prosecution of a trial in the hands of the court itself, paved the way for more frequent accusations, and the use of **torture** allowed under inquisitorial procedure ensured frequent confession to even the most fantastic crimes.

Under inquisitorial procedure, cases were still often initiated by accusations made by private people who felt themselves injured or afflicted in some way. However, judges were also given the power to call people before their courts on their own initiative, often based only on some general ill repute (*infamia*). However cases began, the most important aspect of inquisitorial procedure was that the judges themselves were responsible for the investigation and prosecution of the case. They did this usually by interrogating the accused person and other potential witnesses. For serious crimes, the level of proof needed was testimony from two reliable witnesses or a confession. This was in many respects a far more rational and advanced method of conducting trials than the older accusatorial procedure that had often relied on trial by ordeal to determine guilt or innocence. However, for crimes like sorcery or witchcraft, judges faced a particular problem in that, because of the secretive and clandestine nature of such acts, reliable witnesses could rarely be found. This meant that much more weight came to rest on the testimony of the accused themselves.

Because it was assumed that people would lie to protect themselves, torture was allowed under inquisitorial procedure in order to obtain a full confession. Judges were fully aware that torture could also be used to produce false confessions, and regulations were put in place to ensure that this did not occur. However, for crimes like witchcraft, which were regarded as particularly terrible, such regulations were often set aside. This was especially true if one or more of the initial accusations began to produce an atmosphere of panic in the community, to which the judges were often not immune. Thus, inquisitorial procedure facilitated the rise of accusations for witchcraft by eliminating the potential legal repercussions on private individuals for false accusations and by allowing the courts themselves to initiate trials. Also, in cases of witchcraft, especially where it was designated a *crimen exceptum*, inquisitorial procedure and its reliance on confessions produced through torture provided the courts with a method that could virtually ensure conviction. For these reasons, widespread witch-hunting would have been practically inconceivable if inquisitorial procedure had not been gradually adopted by almost all European courts by the end of the Middle Ages.

See also INQUISITION.

INSTITORIS, HEINRICUS. *See* KRAMER (INSTITORIS), HEINRICH (ca. 1430–1505).

IRELAND, WITCHCRAFT IN. Witchcraft trials in Ireland were very rare. The most well-known case, that of **Alice Kyteler**, was prosecuted in 1324. For the early-modern period, details are only extant for two trials, one in 1661 and another in 1711, while a further seven cases are known to have been prosecuted. It is unclear why so few witchcraft trials were conducted, especially as the existing witchcraft statute of 1586 repeated the English Witchcraft Act of 1563, and many Scots who had witnessed the **witch-hunts** of the 1590s in their own country migrated to Ireland in the early 17th century. It seems that, apart from the colonial divide between native Irish and their colonial rulers, Irish society was not as fractured economically or socially as in **England** or politically as in lowland **Scotland**, and that arbitration was a more frequent method of resolving issues than prosecution.

See also LAWS AGAINST WITCHCRAFT, EUROPEAN.

ISIDORE OF SEVILLE, SAINT (ca. 560–636). A major scholar of the Visigothic kingdom in **Spain** in the seventh century, Isidore's most important work was the 20 volumes of his *Etymologies*. Because he was convinced that most things were best understood by exploring the origins of their names, he organized this work as a study of the roots of words. In fact, it was a virtual encyclopedia of all the knowledge available to him, including a great deal of Greek and Roman learning, hence he makes a suitable patron saint of the Internet. Isidore did not specifically focus on matters of **magic** or **witchcraft**, but he preserved much information on these subjects from Ancient, **Jewish**, and early Christian sources, including **Saint Augustine of Hippo**. His work was very popular and became a standard reference source and basis for later medieval scholars on all subjects, including magic and the occult.

See also ANTIQUITY, WITCHCRAFT IN.

ISIS. In Ancient Egyptian cosmology, Isis assimilated the goddess Serket to become the goddess of **magic** as well as motherhood and fertility. Like **Hecate**, **Lilith**, and other deities of **Antiquity**, she was also associated with the dead and, therefore, the Underworld. In one of the more important stories in Egyptian mythology, based on the annual cycle of the seasons, Isis used magic to resurrect her brother-husband Osiris and fashion a new penis for him after he had been killed by Set. Worship of Isis continued among the Greeks and Romans, many of whom remained interested in Egyptian mythology and religion.

ISLAM, WITCHCRAFT AND MAGIC IN. As in Christian societies, **magic** and **witchcraft** have been the subject of scripture, law, and culture throughout Islamic history. In the Quran, God is presented as the refuge from sorcerers, who are considered **evil**, and those who possess the **evil eye**. These sorcerers performed their **magic** through the tying of knots and by controlling *jinns*, spiritual beings that could be good, like angels, but are most often regarded as evil and akin to **demons**. Pre-Islamic Egypt was regarded as the cradle of **sorcery** and the story of **Moses** defeating the Egyptian sorcerers demonstrates the power of God over **pagan** gods and superstitions. Despite the insistence that sorcery and **divination** are evil, and the Prophet Muhammad's denunciation of tribal soothsayers in pagan Arabia, the Quran, like the Bible, has been misused for sortilege. There were some early attempts to eradicate magicians on the basis that Muhammad had a sorcerer who had tried to cast a spell on him killed, but Islamic authorities did not develop a **demonology** similar to that of late medieval and early-modern Christian theologians. They did not describe sects of female witches who were alleged to make **pacts** with and worship the **devil**. Sorcerers tended to be regarded as either male or female and tended to work alone. This view accounts for the lack of **witch-hunting** in Islamic societies.

In Islamic culture, particularly in **folklore** and story collections like the *Arabian Nights*, sorcerers and diviners were believed to harm people, provide talismans, use **astrology**, locate treasure, perform **love magic**, shapeshift, and fly through the air. Most Islamic commentators regarded these practices and stories as survivals of pre-Islamic pagan culture or imports from outside the Islamic world.

In recent years, there have been sporadic prosecutions for witchcraft and sorcery in Arab countries, but no prosecutions on the scale of those in parts of modern **Africa**.

See also METAMORPHOSIS; NIGHT FLIGHT.

ITALY, WITCHCRAFT IN. The **witch-hunts** in Savoy in the early 15th century, which provoked debate about **witchcraft** at the **Council of Basel**, and the sermons against witches, heretics, and sodomites delivered by **Bernardino of Siena** at about the same time, threatened to turn Italy into an early heartland of witch persecution. Witchcraft prosecution in the peninsula was, however, very mild. The years 1580 to about 1650 did see a much more intense phase of prosecution, but nothing like that experienced in the **German Empire**. As in **Spain**, the population of Italy was almost uniformly Catholic and the authorities did not feel threatened by large, neighboring territories of Protestants; they could concentrate on correcting superstitions, like those of the *benandanti* of the Friuli, rather than eradicating **heresy**. While the authorities certainly numbered magical beliefs among these superstitions, ordinary folk did not. For them, low magic usually had practical, beneficial purposes, including **healing**, locating items that had been lost or stolen, or finding love. Witch trials also tended to be overseen by the Roman **Inquisition** that had been created in 1542, laid out strict rules for the conduct of all inquisitions (including limitations on the use of **torture**), and, from 1588, prohibited the prosecution of people whom alleged witches claimed to have seen at their **sabbaths**, mainly because it tended to follow the **skeptical**

view of the **canon *Episcopi***. A convicted witch was likely to receive only a minor punishment. The key factors that lay behind most witch-hunts elsewhere in Europe were, therefore missing from Italy.

See also LOVE MAGIC.

J

JACQUIER, NICHOLAS (ca. 1400–1472). A Dominican friar who was active at the Council of Basel in 1432 and 1433, Jacquier was later an inquisitor in northern **France**, where he participated in some witch trials; in Bohemia from 1466 to 1468; and at Lille from 1468 until his death. In 1458, he wrote a treatise entitled *Flagellum haereticorum fascinariorum* (Scourge of Heretical Witches). Here, he argued that witches represented a new form of **heresy**, worse than any that had been seen in the past. The famous **canon** *Episcopi*'s dismissal of **night flight** as an illusion, for example, did not apply to this new heresy. Jacquier based his discussions on his own experiences and witchcraft and magic trials, such as that of **Gilles de Rais**, as well as the works of his near contemporaries **Nicolau Eymeric**, **Jean Vineti**, and **Johannes Hartlieb**. He was therefore among the first authorities to systematically address the reality of night flight and the witches' **sabbath** and include **apostasy** and **idolatry** among the crimes of the witches. The *Flagellum* gained further influence among later **demonologists** after it was printed as a supplement to a 1581 edition of the ***Malleus maleficarum***.

JAMES VI AND I, KING (1566–1625). King first of **Scotland** (as James VI, 1567–1625) and then later also of **England** (as James I, 1603–1625), James owed his long reign to the fact that his mother, Mary Queen of Scots, was accused of murdering her husband and was forced to abdicate her throne in 1567 in favor of her infant son, then just 13 months old. Regents governed the kingdom until the early 1580s, when James was old enough to take up his personal rule of a country that was divided and relatively unstable. A Witchcraft Act had been passed in 1563 in Scotland, during the reign of Mary, but only sporadic cases of witchcraft were prosecuted before 1590. In that year, however, the affair of the **North Berwick Witches**' began. A group of alleged witches were put on trial in Edinburgh and, under questioning and **torture**, confessed to attempting to kill the king by various methods, including raising **storms** at sea in an attempt to drown him on his journey to Denmark to collect his new queen, Anne. As the North Berwick case involved treason against James and was possibly instigated by his cousin Francis Stewart, Earl of Bothwell, the king took an interest in it, questioning some of those accused.

James seems to have been ambivalent about the confessions of the North Berwick witches, but his interest in witchcraft as a form of treason, against God as well as himself, was piqued and he began to read about the subject. He became alarmed at the **skepticism** expressed in the works of **Johann Weyer** and **Reginald Scot** and, in response, he wrote his own *Daemonologie* (Demonology), a defense of the belief in **witchcraft** based partly on his reading of **Jean Bodin**'s *De la démonomanie des sorciers*. James's *Daemonologie* was first published in 1597 as the large-scale prosecutions that followed those of North Berwick were coming to an end. After James acceded to the English throne on the death of Elizabeth I in 1603, his **demonology** was issued in a new edition and he ordered copies of Scot's *Discoverie of Witchcraft* to be burned throughout England. In 1604, Parliament passed a new witchcraft act strengthening the legislation against witches already passed under Elizabeth I. Despite these actions, the number of witch trials in England continued to decline sharply during his reign.

Although James was the only early-modern ruler to write a treatise on witchcraft, many of his contemporaries shared his interest in the subject, as is shown by the **laws** and extent of **witch-hunting** in parts of early-modern Europe. In fact, his interest was entirely proper in a Renaissance prince who believed he ruled by divine right. As God's representative in the "great chain of being," the witches' treason against God through their **heresy** and **apostasy** was equally treason against the king, and upset the order of both cosmos and kingdom.

JEWS. Although often persecuted by Christian authorities in medieval and early-modern Europe, and always marginalized within Christian society, Jews were only rarely accused of being witches. **Witchcraft**, insofar as it was believed to be predicated on a **pact** with the **devil** and the worship of **demons**, was regarded by Christian authorities as a **heresy**; Jews, as non-Christians, could not be found guilty of heresy because they were not Christians in the first place. Despite injunctions in the **Bible** against witchcraft and certain forms of **divination** and **sorcery**, Jews shared little of the Christian concern over witchcraft. The concept of the devil was not as developed in Judaism as it became in Christianity, and the idea that humans worshiped him and did his bidding in the form of sects was rare, although some religious leaders like Shimon ben Shetah were reported to have executed large numbers of witches on occasion. Later Jewish commentators on the **witch-hunts** in early-modern Europe, such as Rabbi Menasseh, sometimes accepted learned Christian witch beliefs, although their commentaries did not provoke witch-hunting in Jewish communities. Similarly, Jewish **demonology** allowed for the existence of good as well as **evil** spirits that could be called upon to perform **magic**, by biblical characters and rabbis as much as ordinary men and women who claimed the powers of **healing**, divination, or mediumship. Not all forms of magical practice in Jewish tradition were therefore linked as thoroughly to evil as they were by Christian authorities. These differences in attitudes toward magical beliefs enabled some early-modern Christian intellectuals to justify the use of the Jewish Kabbalah.

In Christian minds, however, Judaism was often believed to be very similar to witchcraft in a number of ways, and at times virtually identical to it. Christian authorities typically considered Jews to be a significant threat to the faith, similar to witches, and often conceived of elaborate, conspiratorial plots by Jews to undermine Christian society, just as they suspected that witches were engaged in an organized conspiracy directed by Satan. Christian stereotypes about Jews that had developed in the Middle Ages were often carried over and applied to witches as well. For example, in the earliest documents from the late Middle Ages, secret gatherings of witches are referred to not as **sabbaths** but as synagogues. The image of witches murdering **children** and devouring them also derives partly from earlier anti-Jewish stereotypes. Jews were often accused of murdering Christian children, draining their blood, or eating them in a parody of the Eucharist.

JOAN OF ARC, SAINT (ca. 1412–1431). Often regarded as one of the most famous victims of accusations of **witchcraft**, Joan was burned at the stake in the city of Rouen in Normandy on 30 May 1431. In fact, although Joan was charged with certain crimes relating to witchcraft, these proved incidental, at best, to her final conviction and **execution**, which in any event was a foregone conclusion because of the highly politicized nature of her trial during the Hundred Years War fought between the English and the French.

Joan was born in Domrémy in Champagne and began to hear voices while still quite young. She became convinced that these voices were those of the Archangel Michael and the Saints Margaret and Catherine, and that they were commanding her to save **France** from the invading English. Accepted by the French dauphin, Charles VII, as a genuine messenger from God, she was allowed to lead a force to the relief of the city of Orléans, besieged by the English. She broke the siege and inflicted a major defeat on the English. Just over two months later, on 17 July 1429, she was present when Charles VII, having won several other victories, was crowned king in the cathedral of Reims. She led several more campaigns, but in May 1430, she was captured and turned over to the English by their allies the Burgundians. She was put on trial in Rouen, deep in English-held territory.

Joan was accused of a wide range of crimes and **heresies**. Her voices were assumed by her judges to be demonic, and she was charged with consorting with fairies, summoning **demons**, worshiping them, performing **sorcery**, and making **pacts** with the **devil**. Such charges are similar to those that make up many cases of witchcraft, but they do not represent a clear accusation of that crime. Moreover the charges of sorcery made against Joan were withdrawn for lack of evidence before her final conviction, which was entirely based on charges of false beliefs and heresy. Nevertheless, for her supposed involvement with demons and her apparently supernatural accomplishments, many contemporary authorities did regard Joan as something very akin to a witch. The early authority **Johannes Nider** included Joan in his discussion of witchcraft in the fifth book of his large treatise *Formicarius* (The Anthill), although he consistently termed her a magician (*maga*) and not a witch (*malefica*).

The story of Joan of Arc has been dramatized in **plays** by William Shakespeare, Friedrich von Schiller, Jean Anouilh, Berthold Brecht, and George Bernard Shaw, and **operas** by Giuseppe Verdi, and Piotr Tchaikovsky. Voltaire wrote a poem on it, and Mark Twain a novel. It has been filmed repeatedly since the early years of cinema, most recently by Luc Besson in 1999. Joan was canonized in 1920 and is one of the patron saints of France.

See also FICTION, WITCHCRAFT IN; FILMS, WITCHCRAFT IN.

JOHN XII, POPE (1244–1334). As one of the most important and powerful popes of the early 14th century, John, who reigned from 1316 until 1334, contributed significantly to the development of ecclesiastical concern over demonic **magic**. He ordered papal **inquisitors** to begin taking action against suspected demonic **sorcery** because this was deemed to be a form of **heresy**, and he issued a sentence of automatic excommunication against any Christian who practiced such magic. His bull *Super illius specula* remained an important ruling against practitioners of demonic magic for the remainder of the Middle Ages.

Born Jacques Duèse in the French city of Cahors in 1244, John studied both theology and canon law. He came to the papal throne only after a hotly contested election during which the papacy had been vacant for nearly two years. From the very beginning of his pontificate, John was especially concerned with matters of sorcery and demonic magic. He feared that his opponents both within and outside the church were trying to assassinate him through sorcery. In 1317 he had Hugues Géraud, the bishop of Cahors, arrested on such charges, and other arrests were to follow. From 1320 to 1325, charges of sorcery were brought against many of John's political enemies in **Italy**, especially members of the Visconti family, the powerful rulers of Milan.

Although it is clear that John often used accusations of sorcery in an entirely cynical way as a political tool, he seems also to have been genuinely concerned about such practices, both because of the perceived threat to his own safety and because of the heresy involved in dealing with demonic forces. In 1320, he instructed William, Cardinal of Santa Sabine, to order that the papal inquisitors of Toulouse and Carcassonne in southern **France** begin taking action against anyone who engaged in demonic invocation or sorcery. Later, in 1326, he issued the bull *Super illius specula*, in which he declared a sentence of automatic excommunication on any Christians who invoked or worshiped **demons** in order to perform any kind of magic. Although John was clearly more concerned with learned demonic magic, or **necromancy**, than with common *maleficium* of the sort later associated with **witchcraft**, his rulings formed an important basis for later inquisitorial jurisdiction over cases of witchcraft.

K

KNIGHTS TEMPLAR. *See* TEMPLARS.

KRAMER (INSTITORIS), HEINRICH (ca. 1430–1505). A Dominican friar and papal **inquisitor**, Kramer (in Latin, Institoris) is best known as the author of the infamous late-medieval **witch-hunting** manual *Malleus maleficarum* (Hammer of Witches), first published in 1486. Although **Jakob Sprenger**, also a Dominican inquisitor, has traditionally been cited as the co-author of the manual, the existing evidence points to Kramer as the sole author.

Kramer was born in Sélestat (Schlettstadt), in Alsace, then in the **German Empire**, and educated in the city's Dominican monastery. He was appointed to the office of papal inquisitor in 1474 and promoted to inquisitor of upper (southern) Germany in 1478. As an inquisitor, Kramer investigated claims of the ritual murder of Christian children by **Jews**, and cases of **witchcraft**, notably in the Rhineland, Ravensburg, and Innsbruck in the 1480s, and Nuremberg in 1491. In the Rhineland, Kramer encountered opposition from the local ecclesiastical authorities, including the bishop of Strasbourg, and had to obtain the bull *Summis desiderantes affectibus* from **Pope Innocent VIII** to insist on their cooperation. Kramer also encountered opposition in Innsbruck and was formally asked to leave the Tyrol region by the bishop of Brixen. Much of this opposition focused on Kramer's dubious methods, including intimidation and the irregular use of **torture**. In response, Kramer wrote the *Malleus maleficarum* to justify his actions and advise other witch-hunters, both ecclesiastical and secular, on the conduct of witch trials. The second edition of 1487 brought together Innocent's bull and Kramer's text, giving the latter indirect papal authority. Adding Sprenger as an author and appending a spurious notarial approval from the theological faculty of the University of Cologne served the same purpose.

As it became increasingly clear that Kramer was the primary, if not the sole, author of the *Malleus maleficarum*, many scholars have sought to link elements of that work to Kramer's own personality. He has been depicted as emotionally disturbed, an almost pathological hater of **women**, and prone to strange sexual fantasies. He was certainly an arrogant and ruthless man who aroused much opposition from local authorities. In 1490, he was censured by the Dominican order for his irregular and excessive activities. In 1500, he was dispatched to combat **heresy** and witchcraft in Bohemia, where he died.

KYTELER, ALICE (?–ca. 1324). A wealthy woman of Kilkenny, **Ireland**, Lady Alice married four husbands, three of whom died under mysterious circumstances. When her fourth husband, Sir John le Poer, began to sicken, several of her **children** began to accuse her of using **sorcery** to bewitch their fathers into leaving all their wealth to her and her favorite son by her first marriage, William Outlaw. In 1324, the case was taken up by Bishop Richard Ledrede, an appointee of **Pope John XXII**. Ultimately, Alice and five other **women**, including one servant who was burned at the stake, were accused of renouncing the Christian faith, worshiping **demons** and sacrificing to them at crossroads, and performing harmful sorcery. Alice supposedly had a demon **familiar** named Robert or Robin, Son of Art, who would appear to her in the form of a **cat**, a black dog or an Ethiopian, with whom she had sexual intercourse. The case did not proceed smoothly because Lady Alice had powerful relatives and friends who put up resistance and Bishop Ledrede does not appear to have been well liked (after the case, he had to flee Ireland for Avignon). Nevertheless, Alice was eventually condemned for **heresy**. She only escaped punishment by fleeing to **England**, where she probably spent the rest of her life.

The Kyteler case was the first trial involving *maleficium* (by harmful sorcery) and heretical **diabolism** in Ireland, and no other case would occur until the 17th century; it is also one of the earliest in Europe in which heresy and sorcery were explicitly linked together, in this instance by a bishop who was attempting to introduce the inquisitorial apparatus favored by John XXII into Ireland. It is, however, difficult to determine how important the case was to the development of witch beliefs and **witch-hunting** practices in Europe. It certainly resembles later witch trials in several ways, including the treatment of the accused as an organized group and the accusation that Alice had sexual intercourse with her familiar. It was, however, an isolated event and was only reported in the manuscript known as *Narrative*, probably written by Ledrede himself, which did not circulate widely.

See also INQUISITION; SEXUALITY AND WITCHCRAFT.

L

LAMASHTU. A monster, **demon**, or goddess of Mesopotamian mythology, Lamashtu was willfully malevolent, especially toward pregnant **women** and newborn babies, whom she attacked and devoured, drinking their blood like a **vampire**. She was also said to eat men, cause nightmares, destroy the fertility of the land, **poison** rivers, and bring sickness and disease. She was depicted as a hybrid of lion, donkey, and bird and was described as the "seven witches" in incantations because of her seven names. She is related in character to **Lilith**, **Lamia**, and other witch-like characters of **Antiquity**.

See also CANNIBALISM; CHILDREN, WITCHCRAFT AND.

LAMIA. In classical mythology, Lamia was a queen of Libya whom Zeus, the king of the gods, loved. Hera, Zeus's queen, took revenge on Lamia by killing her **children**. She in turn became a monster who roamed the night seeking to kill the children of others. Over time, the individual Lamia became a whole category of **demons** or monsters, all called *lamia* (plural *lamiae*), that preyed on children. They were believed to be **vampires** who sucked the blood from their victims. They contributed to the medieval and early-modern image of the witch as a **woman** who performed **evil** at night and especially sought to harm babies and small children. Some classical authors also said that they seduced young men in order to eat them. Through the work of **Isidore of Seville**, who mistakenly derived the word *lamia* from the Latin *laniare* ("to tear, savage, mutilate"), and later authors as diverse as **Ulrich Molitor**, **Johann Weyer**, and **Martín Del Rio**, *lamia* became a common term for witches in many areas of Europe during the era of the major **witch-hunts**.

See also ANTIQUITY, WITCHCRAFT IN; LILITH; SEXUALITY AND WITCHCRAFT.

LANCASHIRE WITCHES. Term sometimes applied to the Pendle witches, whose trial in **England** occurred in 1612 in Lancashire. In all, some 19 people were accused and put on trial, but the case originated with the accusation of an old **woman**, Elizabeth Sowthern, who was about 80 years old. She not only confessed but also accused another old woman as well as her own granddaughter. From this point, the search for other witches grew. The case itself can be seen as fairly typical of English **witchcraft**, apart from the evidence of Grace Sowerbutts that included the killing of a child and the exhumation of its body to be eaten, attending a witches' **sabbath**, and having sexual intercourse with **demons**; her evidence was rejected. The significance of the case, like that of **Saint Osyth**, lies in the records that it produced. The court clerk kept a detailed and semi-official record of the proceedings, and this was subsequently published in 1613 as a chapbook entitled *The Wonderful Discovery of Witches in the County of Lancashire*. In turn, this chapbook became the inspiration for William Harrison Ainsworth's novel of 1849.

There was a further outbreak in 1633–1634 in the same area. No trials were held, although as many as 60 individuals may have been suspected of witchcraft. The instigator of the first accusation, Edward Robinson, confessed that he had made it up to avoid punishment from his father. This case became the subject of Thomas Heywood and Richard Brome's **play** *The Late Lancashire Witches* (1634).

See also AGE, CORRELATION WITH WITCHCRAFT ACCUSATIONS; CANNIBALISM; CHILDREN, WITCHCRAFT AND; FICTION, WITCHCRAFT IN; SEXUALITY AND WITCHCRAFT.

LANCRE, PIERRE DE (1553–1630). A French lawyer and royal official, Lancre was appointed by King Henry IV to investigate **witchcraft** in the Pays de Labourd, a **Basque**-speaking region in the southwest of **France**. He conducted intense investigations and trials in 1609, but the *parlement* of Bordeaux refused to deal with the cases that remained after his commission had expired. In response to the **skepticism** of his parliamentary colleagues, he published an extensive account of these trials, *Tableau de l'inconstance de mauvais anges et démons* (Description of the Inconstancy of Evil Angels and Demons) in 1612, as well as later works, *L'incredulité et mescréance du sortilège* (The Incredulity and Misbelief of Witchcraft) and *Du sortilège* (On Witchcraft), in 1622 and 1627 respectively. These works did not influence the attitude of the parliamentary judges toward the question of witchcraft.

Lancre was extremely credulous when it came to accusations of witchcraft. He accepted the testimony of **children**, and many of the witch suspects he tried were in fact minors to whom he offered clemency because they had merely attended witches' **sabbaths**. According to his accounts, the Basque lands were the center of the most intense witchcraft in Europe. He believed that huge witches' sabbaths were held in this region, with sometimes up to 2,000 witches supposedly attending. Ultimately, he became convinced that almost the entire population of the region, some 30,000 people, including all the local clergy, were tainted by witchcraft. Many accounts state that Lancre executed 600 people during the course of the trials, but this figure is certainly grossly inflated. A more reasonable estimate would be around 80 **executions**.

LaVEY, ANTON. *See* CHURCH OF SATAN.

LAWS AGAINST WITCHCRAFT, AFRICAN. Laws against the practice of **witchcraft** exist at national, regional, and local levels in several **African** countries. These laws were originally introduced by colonial or, in the case of South Africa, racist governments to undermine traditional **magical** practices under a loose definition of witchcraft. While the national South African Suppression of Witchcraft Act (1957), for example, makes it illegal to accuse someone of being a witch, it also prohibits the knowledge and practice of witchcraft. In post-Apartheid South Africa, the Ralushai Commission (1995) defined witchcraft as an "**evil**" activity distinct from traditional practices and therefore changed the emphasis of the Act. In Zimbabwe, the influential National Traditional Healers Association lobbied successfully for amendments to the existing Witchcraft Suppression Act in 2006. These amendments have made it easier to accuse someone of harming people or property by witchcraft. The application of laws against witchcraft in the Central African Republic has been the subject of Daniel Bogado's documentary *World of Witchcraft* (2009).

See also AFRICA, WITCH-HUNTS IN.

LAWS AGAINST WITCHCRAFT, EUROPEAN. Although **witchcraft** was punishable by death in the ancient Mesopotamian Code of Hammurabi (1792–1750 BCE) and later laws of Middle Eastern societies, it is difficult to trace the early development of legislation against witchcraft, **sorcery**, and related practices in Europe. In the ancient Greek world there were certainly instances of witches and users of **love magic**, for example, being executed, but it may be that they were punished for their intent (treachery or causing harm) rather than their beliefs or procedures. The legal situation of witchcraft and sorcery in ancient Rome is better known. The *Twelve Tables* of 451 BCE proscribed the singing of **evil** incantations and the charming of crops from one field into another. In 186 BCE, **magic**, **divination**, and foreign cults were conflated with treason in the Senatorial Decree on Bacchanals that allegedly saw 5,000 people executed for using sorcery. Thereafter, the state undertook periodic expulsions and **executions** of suspected astrologers and sorcerers, and several early emperors banned divinatory practices that might have fueled conspiracies against them. A later law of 81 BCE, *Lex Cornelia de sicariis et veneficiis* (Law of Cornelius on Assassins and Poisoners/Sorcerers), seems to have outlawed the trading and possession of harmful drugs as well as their use. When Apuleius of Madaura was tried under this law in the second century CE, he was also accused of activities like the use of **Voodoo** dolls and divination. In the fourth century, the Christian Emperor Constantine legislated against soothsaying and magic, especially love magic, but exempted healing practices and weather magic for the benefit of agriculture. In 357 and 358, Constantius II extended the list of practices proscribed by law to include **astrology**, divination, augury, and the activities of seers, Chaldeans, mages, and evildoers generally. Further codification of the existing laws against sorcery and witchcraft, with the encouragement of the Church, occurred in the *Codex Theodosianus* (438) and *Codex Justinianus* (529).

In the Middle Ages, secular authorities tended to legislate against the practical effects of magic, notably harmful sorcery, or *maleficia*, and the destruction of crops; ecclesiastical authorities tended to issue canons and penitentials against the heretical elements of witchcraft. Early medieval punishments prescribed by secular legislation were generally light, usually fines, whippings, or public humiliation; in the case of the Visigothic Code, a perpetrator could be enslaved. Only in rare instances did legislators set down the death penalty for the use of harmful sorcery. It was, however, unusual for a witch to be condemned to death, partly because, in **accusatorial procedure**, the law of *talion* prevented spurious accusations (the accuser would suffer the punishment for the crime if his suit failed), partly because individuals accused of harmful sorcery were not usually suspected of murder or another felony, and partly because rulers like King Coloman of Hungary (ca. 1074–1116; r. 1095–1116) tended to believe that witchcraft was a **pagan** superstition and that witches did not, therefore, exist.

While the **Bible** forbade any magical activity and, in Exodus 22:18, stipulated that witches should not be permitted to live, medieval canons, like the **canon** *Episcopi* (early 10th century), and penitentials also took the view that witchcraft and related practices were superstitions or illusions into which witches had been deluded by the **devil**. These ecclesiastical instruments punished both alleged practitioners of witchcraft and sorcery and those who believed that witches could do the fantastical things, like **night flight**, ascribed to them. In these cases, a person guilty of **apostasy** or **heresy** could be reconciled to the Church after a minor punishment and a period of penance. This did not mean that a persistent or unrepentant heretic could not be executed when the Church ran out of patience, or that suspected witches were never accused of doing something so terrible that the Church had to act, but it did mean that ecclesiastical law did not facilitate **witch-hunting**. It was only with the introduction of **inquisitorial procedure** into the **Inquisition**'s attacks on heretical groups in the later Middle Ages that **demonology** was altered to portray witches as more of a threat than they had been. At this time laws were beginning to emerge that created an environment suitable for witch persecution. The *Schwabenspiegel* of ca. 1240 brought together the crimes of sorcery and apostasy through the **pact** with the devil, a fusion adopted by **Jean Gerson** in 1398 and Duke Amadeus VIII in his *Statuta Sabaudie* (1430) that he promulgated in response to the witch-hunts in the 1420s in Savoy. At the end of the 15th century, **Heinrich Kramer** sought, in the Third Part of the *Malleus maleficarum* (c. 1486), to hand jurisdiction over heretical witchcraft to all courts, whether ecclesiastical or secular.

Throughout the 16th century, legislation against witches increased across much of Europe, regardless of whether the states in question were Catholic or Protestant. The process was not, however, a uniform one. The *Constitutio Criminalis Carolina* (**Carolina Law Code**) of 1532, which applied to the whole **German Empire**, and the witchcraft statutes enacted in 1563 in **England** and **Scotland**, followed medieval practice in punishing harmful sorcery and reserving execution for felonious acts of harm and murder by witchcraft. Once the period of intense witch-hunting began in the late 16th century, witchcraft legislation in some states, like Württemberg, Saxony, and **Bavaria**, emphasized the spiritual crime of apostasy, punishing it by death. As witch-hunting reached its peak, several territories found it necessary to introduce laws to curb persecution and limit its consequences. These included places like **Trier** that saw very intense and prolonged witch persecution. After witch-hunting died down, European states tended to allow witchcraft legislation to lapse. It was only rarely, as in England in 1736, that this legislation was formally repealed.

Not all early-modern territories took responsibility for the prosecution of witches from the Church, and others enshrined a generally **skeptical** view of witchcraft in their laws. In southern Europe, the Inquisition asserted its role in the extirpation of witchcraft beliefs. In Nuremberg (in 1536) and the Tirol (in 1544) sorcery became punishable as a fraudulent activity rather than as a real threat to their citizens.

See also ANTIQUITY, WITCHCRAFT IN; POISON; STORMS AND STORM-RAISING.

LE FRANC, MARTIN (1410–1461). One of the most important French poets of the 15th century, Martin Le Franc included a section on **witchcraft** in his long poem *Le champion des dames* (The Defender of Ladies), written between 1440 and 1442. The poem finds its larger context in the late-medieval *querelle des femmes*, the literary discussion of the virtues of **women**. *Le champion* was one of many responses, including another by **Jean Gerson**, to the 13th-century misogynistic poem *Roman de la rose*. In the poem, the "Adversary" raises the issue of witchcraft to attack women. In the ensuing debate, he cites various recent cases of **sorcery** to reproduce the new view of witchcraft. Alongside **night flight** and **cannibalism**, the "Adversary" introduces **apostasy**, **idolatry**, sexual **orgies**, including sex with **demons**, and sorcery to cause *maleficium*. He also cites the stories of **Simon Magus**, Apuleius of Madaura, and **Circe**, and the work of **Saint Augustine of Hippo** and **Albertus Magnus** to show that such harm may be caused by God's permission. The "Defender's" argument follows the **skeptical** line of the **canon** *Episcopi* (early 10th century) that the activities of witches are mere illusions or delusions and could not really have happened. He also points out that many learned demonic magicians are men.

Le Franc composed his poem while he was at the **Council of Basel** in the service of Duke Amadeus VIII of Savoy, later elected anti-pope Felix V by the council as part of its struggle against **Pope Eugenius IV**. The Council of Basel was an important center for the early development and transmission of the idea of witchcraft, and Le Franc seems to have been influenced by its environment. The poem can also be read as a response to Eugenius IV's attack on Duke Amadeus and his alleged toleration of witches. A later manuscript of the poem, copied for Philip the Good, Duke of Burgundy, is illustrated with the first images of witches flying on **broomsticks**. Le Franc's poem stands along with the accounts of **Johannes Nider**, **Claude Tholosan**, **Hans Fründ**, and the anonymous author of the *Errores Gazariorum*, as one of the earliest sources describing the developing idea of witchcraft in the early 15th century.

LELAND, CHARLES (1824–1903). A wealthy **North American** author and amateur anthropologist, Leland devoted his life to studying **folklore**, **magic**, and the occult. His major contribution to the emergence of modern **witchcraft**, or **Wicca**, in the 20th century came with the publication of *Aradia, or the Gospel of the Witches* in 1899. While traveling in **Italy**, Leland claimed to have met a traditional, hereditary witch named Maddalena. She revealed to him that witchcraft was in fact an ancient, **pagan** religion that had been persecuted by religious authorities in the medieval and early-modern periods and driven underground, but that still survived. She claimed to trace her own hereditary powers back to Etruscan roots. She described the beliefs and practices of this religion to Leland, who subsequently published them as *Aradia*. In fact, the doctrines and supposed history outlined in *Aradia* are heavily indebted to 19th-century anthropology and historical studies such as those by Jules Michelet, who argued that historical witchcraft was in fact a form of popular resistance against oppressive religious authorities. Either Leland invented the supposed witch religion himself or Maddalena simply told her wealthy patron what he wanted to hear. A similar interpretation of historical witchcraft was later advanced in the more influential writings of **Margaret Murray**.

LILITH. In Jewish **demonology**, Lilith was the first wife of Adam but refused to accept the authority God had given him over her and left him. She became a demonic creature who stalked the night, either appearing as a beautiful **woman** and seeking to seduce men, or trying to kill babies and small **children**. Like other mythological creatures, such as the **lamia** or **strix**, as well as demonic **succubi**, she became an archetype of female **evil**. The only potential reference to Lilith in the **Bible** (Isaiah 34:14) was translated as *lamia* in the Latin Vulgate version authorized by the medieval Church. As such, she contributed to the later image of the witch in Christian demonology, especially to the notions of the female witch as sexually driven and as a murderer of young children.

See also JEWS; SEXUALITY AND WITCHCRAFT.

LOOGAROO. Like **Baba Yaga**, **Ole Higue**, **Yama-uba**, and the stereotypical witch of the early-modern period, Loogaroo is conceived as an old **woman**. In the **folklore** of the **Caribbean**, Loogaroo makes a **pact** with the **devil**, but she can only retain her magical powers if she pays him in blood every night. Each night she therefore sheds her skin, assumes the form of a fiery ball, and searches for suitable victims whom she attacks like a **vampire**. It is possible to protect oneself against Loogaroo by leaving a pile of rice or sand outside the front door (which Loogaroo feels compelled to count grain by grain) or stealing her skin that she hides under the cotton silk tree or "Devil's Tree." Beliefs in Loogaroo are a mixture of French folklore (her name is perhaps a corruption of the French **werewolf** Loup-garou) and African **Voodoo**, or **Voudun**.

See also AFRICAN WITCHCRAFT; FRANCE, WITCHCRAFT IN.

LOOS, CORNELIUS (1546–1593). A Catholic priest and scholar, Loos was a strong opponent of **witch-hunting** who ultimately suffered condemnation as a **heretic** for his beliefs. Born in Gouda in the Netherlands, Loos studied at Louvain and Liège and then taught at Mainz and **Trier**, which was a center of witch-hunting at the time. He grew increasingly concerned about the nature of the trials taking place and attempted to stop them, writing a treatise *De vera et falsa magia* (On True and False Magic). He not only argued that excessive use of **torture** led to false confessions in witch trials, but also that **demons** could not assume physical bodies to operate in the world. In particular, Loos criticized **Peter Binsfeld**, the suffragan bishop of Trier and a strong proponent of witch-hunting. He was imprisoned on the grounds that failure to accept the reality of **witchcraft** was heresy, his writings were suppressed, and in 1593 he was forced to recant his beliefs. He was then banished to Brussels but refused to remain silent on matters of witchcraft and so was arrested and imprisoned as a relapsed heretic. He probably would have been executed had he not died of natural causes shortly thereafter.

LOUDUN, POSSESSIONS AT. The most famous of four related cases of convent **possessions** in early-modern **France**, that in Loudun began in September 1632 and culminated in the death of a local priest, Urbain Grandier, in August 1634. The possession of the Ursuline nuns of Loudun began with the apparition of their deceased religious director who begged them for prayers, and soon manifested itself in erotic and immoral behavior. The nuns claimed that their **demons** aroused love for Grandier, their new religious director, and that he came to them at night, encouraging them to sin. The convulsions and immodest behavior, including blasphemy, exhibited by the nuns was typical of possessed individuals. During **exorcism**, the nuns' demons blamed Grandier for causing their possessions; the mother superior, Jeanne des Anges, even managed to vomit up the **pact** he had made with the **devil**. The exorcisms soon became public, attracting crowds of up to 2,000 spectators, and the case was referred to King Louis XIII and Cardinal Richelieu. Eventually, on 18 August 1634, Grandier was convicted as a **sorcerer** and burned at the stake before thousands of people.

The story behind the possessions is unclear. Grandier had been a parish priest in Loudun since 1617 and had a reputation as a libertine. It was only in about 1630, however, that he began to make enemies of the more powerful local families. It may well be that the Tricant family who were involved in the exorcisms and had the case referred to the king were taking revenge on Grandier for the seduction of one of their daughters. It is not certain, however, that the nuns were acting as part of a plot. The continuation of the possession cases after Grandier's death suggests that they may have been genuinely sick. It is also remains unclear why Louis XIII and Richelieu concerned themselves with this case.

The case has been the subject of Aldous Huxley's novel *The Devils of Loudun* (1952), which was the basis for Ken Russell's **film** *The Devils* (1971). The story of the possession has also been turned into an **opera** by Krzysztof Penderecki (1969).

See also EXECUTIONS; FICTION, WITCHCRAFT IN.

LOVE MAGIC. Producing affection or arousing discord between people, as well as increasing or impeding sexual fertility, have always been among the principal uses to which **magic** has been put throughout history. In medieval and early-modern Europe, such love magic took the form of a wide variety of popular spells and charms. **Witchcraft** was often strongly associated with the negative aspects of love magic. Witches were thought to be able to arouse enmity, jealousy, and hatred between people. Most especially they were thought to afflict sexual fertility. The harm, or *maleficium*, that witches caused by their **sorcery** was believed to be able to cause impotence in men and prevent conception in **women**. Witches were also thought to cause miscarriages and stillbirths. The infamous **witch-hunting** manual *Malleus maleficarum*, in particular, contains extensive discussion of the sexually destructive aspects of witchcraft.

LUTHER, MARTIN (1483–1546). The primary figure responsible for launching the Protestant **Reformation** in the early 16th century, Luther challenged ecclesiastical authority and traditional medieval theology in many ways. On the question of **witchcraft**, however, he accepted the real existence of witches and all the aspects of medieval theology and **demonology** that underlay the idea of witchcraft, although he did reject the ideas of **night flights**, **metamorphosis**, and the **sabbath**. In fact, the great stress he laid on the power of the **devil** to tempt and assail humans might have disposed him to be more concerned about witchcraft than many earlier religious authorities. He rarely wrote about witchcraft or **sorcery** exclusively, but did discuss such matters in sermons and biblical commentaries. He made clear on many occasions that he believed witches were a serious threat to Christian society, and that they needed to be rooted out and destroyed.

LYCANTHROPY. *See* **METAMORPHOSIS; WEREWOLVES.**

M

MACUMBA. Like **Voudun**, Macumba is a syncretic religion combining elements of **African** spirit worship and European Catholicism. It has its origins among the slaves of early-modern Brazil, where it is still practiced and sometimes called **Quimbanda**. Spirits are asked to grant requests for financial gain, **love magic**, and **divination**. The spirits might require the use of spells, rituals, and animal sacrifice, as well as payment to both the priest and the spirit. Over time, some practitioners rejected the black magic and animal sacrifice associated with Macumba and established Umbanda. The term *macumba* can be used pejoratively to mean **witchcraft** or black **magic**.

See also SOUTH AMERICA, WITCHCRAFT IN.

MAGIC. Magic is a difficult concept to define. It is found in most cultures of the world from **Antiquity** to the present and can cover the use of spells and charms; the practices of **alchemy**, **astrology**, or **divination**; and the attempts of early scientists to uncover the occult (or hidden) forces of the world. In most cases, magic involves the invocation and manipulation of spirits. There are therefore close links between religion and magic. For ordinary medieval and early-modern Christians magical practices, and those of the **Caribbean** and **South America** who practice one of the syncretic religions that have evolved there, prayers to the saints, **witch bottles**, or the workings of **cunning men and women** (or priests) were a means of exerting control over an uncertain world. **Love**, **healing**, and protective magic were the most commonly used forms, although some people did resort to black magic to avenge themselves of a wrong. In some communities, certain people, such as the *benandanti* of the Friuli in **Italy**, worked to protect crops from destruction by witches.

In the late-medieval and early-modern periods, church authorities everywhere tried to correct the superstitions that led to low magic, but their primary concern was the **necromancy**, or demonic **sorcery**, practiced in learned magic. Early magicians believed that they could call up and command **demons** because the apostles and early church fathers were able to do so, mainly as a form of exorcism in cases of **possession**. In the late 14th century, however, **Nicolau Eymeric** argued in his *Tractatus contra daemonum invocatores* (Treatise against Invokers of Demons) that necromancy necessarily involved the worship of demons and, therefore, **idolatry**. Eymeric's argument became one of the foundations on which **witchcraft**, which was believed to involve harmful sorcery, or *maleficium*, was prosecuted as a **heresy**. Today, beneficent magic is an important part of modern witchcraft, or **Wicca**, and other forms of **neo-paganism**.

MALEBRANCHE, NICOLAS (1638–1715). A French philosopher born in Paris, Malebranche studied theology at the university there. In 1660, he entered the Catholic religious order of the Oratorians, intending to pursue his studies of the early church father **Saint Augustine of Hippo**, until he encountered the highly rationalist philosophy of René Descartes. In his major work, *De la recherche de la verité* (The Search after Truth), published in 1674, Malebranche espoused a near-complete **skepticism** about **witchcraft**. The **devil**, he argued, had very little real power in the world, and so most of the alleged crimes of witchcraft could not be real. When not based on completely false accusations, they arose from delirium, mental instability, and an inability to distinguish delusion from reality on the part of those who confessed to such crimes.

MALE WITCHES. Although the European **witch-hunts** of the early-modern period are usually associated with **women**, as many as 6,000 men were also executed for the crime of **witchcraft**. **Demonologists** from the early-14th century onward did not, of course, reject the idea that men might also be seduced into the new emotional **heresy** of witchcraft. It was just harder for them to imagine that men could be vulnerable to irrational temptations based on sex and money into which women were believed to fall. Some male witches, like **Dietrich Flade** in **Trier** or Urbain Grandier in **Loudun**, were clearly accused of the crime by their enemies; some were simply related to female witches; still others were accused of witchcraft by their neighbors in the same way that many women were. In some hunts, like that in **Eichstätt**, men tended to denounce other men under **torture** and eventually an accumulation of such denunciations against an individual could not be ignored by the interrogators. It was, however, in the marginal areas of Europe, like Finland and **Estonia**, that men were accused in larger numbers. In the **pagan** religions that persisted in these regions, **sorcery** was traditionally associated with men. In the processes of colonization and Christianization, these sorcerers or **shamans** were demonized as witches and punished accordingly.

MALEFICIUM. In the broadest terms, the crime of **witchcraft** as it was conceived in late-medieval and early-modern Europe may be said to have consisted of two elements: harm inflicted through occult means, known as *maleficium*; and the practice of demon worship, **idolatry**, **apostasy**, and **heresy**, usually described collectively as **diabolism**. While diabolism was unique to witchcraft in the Christian West, *maleficium* is the defining characteristic of witchcraft in most cultures around the world. In Christian **demonology** from the late-medieval period on, where witchcraft was considered a real threat (rather than a delusion), *maleficium* was often understood to involve at least an implicit **pact** with the **devil** and the invocation of **demons**; it had, therefore, to be heretical.

In the historical European context, *maleficium* could be inflicted through harmful **sorcery** or a witch's body (notably the **evil eye**), words, or gestures. In typical late-medieval or early-modern witchcraft cases, witch suspects were accused by their neighbors of causing harm to human beings, especially **children**, or their livestock and other property. This harm might include murder, disease, and impeding the fertility of people as well as their livestock and crops. In such cases, the death, disease, or destruction caused to the victim was generally regarded as inexplicable in natural or providential terms; instead, the witch suspects were believed to have caused the *maleficium* out of enmity. The punishment of the convicted witch was thought to give relief from the *maleficium* in cases where the harm could still be remedied. Witch suspects were also sometimes accused of causing pestilence or famine, often by raising **storms** or hail, and performing **love magic** to arouse affection or enmity between people.

Maleficium was a feature of both secular and ecclesiastical witchcraft trials in the early-modern period. For most ecclesiastical authorities, diabolism was the main crime of the witches, and their acts of harm, frequently confessed under **torture**, were merely further evidence of their true nature. Although secular judges might have shown a personal interest in diabolism, they could usually only prosecute the witches' *maleficium*. In **England** and other regions of Europe where witches were generally prosecuted in secular courts and the focus was mainly on *maleficium*, **witch-hunting** was noticeably less severe. In early-modern **Spain**, witchcraft continued to be defined as a delusion. The *maleficium* attributed to witches by ordinary people was therefore regarded by the Spanish **Inquisition** as an illusion that was not punishable in law.

MALLEUS MALEFICARUM. The most notorious treatise on **witchcraft** and **witch-hunting**, the *Malleus maleficarum* (Hammer of Witches), was written in 1486 and first published in or before 1487. Until the 19th century, it was assumed that the *Malleus* was co-authored by two Dominicans, **Heinrich Kramer**, an inquisitor, and **Jakob Sprenger**, a theologian and head of the Teutonic (or German) province of the order. Since then, however, Sprenger's role has been disputed, and he may, in fact, have been an opponent of Kramer's activities, driving the inquisitor from his province. The appearance of Sprenger's name in both the foreword to the *Malleus* and the papal bull *Summis desiderantes affectibus* that was published as part of the text did, however, lend the treatise additional authority.

Kramer wrote the *Malleus maleficarum* in response to the opposition he encountered during his **inquisition** in Innsbruck in 1485. Kramer's unorthodox methods of interrogation, including the use of intimidation and excessive **torture**, led the local bishop of Brixen, Georg II Golser, backed by the citizens, clergy and nobility of the Tyrol, to stop the investigations and free all the **women** suspected of witchcraft; Kramer was forced to leave the territory in February 1486. Despite this failure, Kramer used his presence in Innsbruck to suggest that he had been aided by Bishop Golser and the archduke of Tyrol. Like the use of Sprenger's name and the publication of the bull *Summis desiderantes affectibus* issued on Kramer's behalf by **Pope Innocent VIII** prior to the events in Innsbruck, this was a piece of manipulation designed to enhance the authority of the *Malleus*. He added to the luster of the treatise by referring to a letter of approbation issued by the University of Cologne (denied by two of the alleged authors) and suggesting that King Maximilian I, later the **German** Emperor, backed the work (which he did not). Kramer clearly understood how to manipulate the new technology of printing to give credence to a treatise that he knew would be controversial.

The *Malleus maleficarum* itself consists of three parts. The first addresses theological issues, arguing that witchcraft was a threat to Christianity. Kramer based much of this part of the *Malleus* on his reading of **Saint Augustine of Hippo** and **Thomas Aquinas**, emphasizing the necessity of God's permission and the witch's free will. It conformed to the new **demonology** that had emerged from about 1400 in the work of **Jean Gerson, Johannes Nider, Claude Tholosan**, and **Hans Fründ**, as well as in the *Errores Gazariorum*, in which witchcraft had become a **heresy** rather than a mere superstition. In this part, Kramer also argued that **women** were more likely to fall into the heresy of witchcraft than men because they were emotionally weaker. The **devil** did not have to tempt them away from God through rational argument; he only had to offer to meet their emotional or everyday needs. The second part of the *Malleus* deals with protection against witchcraft and how to cure bewitchment. The final part of the treatise hands jurisdiction over witchcraft cases to all courts, ecclesiastical and secular as well as inquisitorial, and was designed as a manual of procedure and formula. It set witchcraft aside as a *crimen exceptum* (exceptional crime) that was not subject to the normal limits on the types of witnesses who could testify in such cases or the amount of torture that could be applied to the accused under interrogation.

The influence of the *Malleus maleficarum* over the prosecution of witch-craft at the height of the witch-hunts is disputed. The text offers a detailed and comprehensive, if contradictory, set of arguments and information about the new witch sect as one inquisitor understood it. As one of the earliest printed demonologies, it also achieved a wide circulation throughout Europe. That does not mean, however, that it was widely read or that it directly influenced later works or the actions of witch-hunters. Sixteenth-century demonologists, judges, and legislators did sometimes reference the *Malleus*, but they tended to draw on a wide range of other texts as well and to defer to contemporary authorities like **Jean Bodin**, **Peter Binsfeld**, or **Martín Del Rio**. The **Reformation** also reduced the influence of the *Malleus* in areas that did not remain Catholic.

MAMBABARANG. A type of **mangkukulam**, or witch, from the Philippines, the mambabarang kills using black **magic**. He takes a strand of his victim's hair and ties it to insects or worms. These insects or worms are then pricked and the victim's body becomes infested with creatures that will eventually kill them.

MANDRAKE. A herb native to the Mediterranean region, mandrake has long been thought to possess magical powers and has been used in a wide variety of medicines, spells, and potions. The ancient Greeks associated the plant with the semi-divine sorceress **Circe**. The mandrake contains atropine, hyoscyamine, and scopolamine, all of which have medical uses today. In small doses, these drugs in the medicines and **poisons** made from the mandrake can induce hallucinations or a feeling of lightness associated with out-of-body experiences like astral-planing. They can also be used to bring on a coma or as an anesthetic. In large doses, the mandrake is highly poisonous and can be used to harm people.

The power of the mandrake was attributed to its root, which can appear as a small, human-shaped figure. Supposedly, the mandrake will shriek loudly when uprooted and will kill whoever digs it up. Anyone wanting to use the mandrake root was therefore advised to dig up most of the plant but not fully remove it from the ground. A dog was then tied to the plant with a rope, and its master would leave. As the dog tried to follow, it would pull the mandrake from the ground and, in doing so, be killed. The master could then return to collect the root. Witches were said to pick the root from beneath gallows trees, where it supposedly grew from the blood or semen of hanged criminals. The striking visual appearance of the root and the myths that surrounded it made the mandrake a central feature in the work of several 17th-century artists who painted pictures of witches' **sabbaths**, including Frans Francken the Younger, Jacques de Gheyn, and David Teniers the Younger.

See also ART, WITCHCRAFT IN; MAGIC.

MANGKUKULAM. A witch or sorcerer in the Philippines, a mangkukulam uses spells, curses, and potions to harm his or her victims. In more recent times, mangkukulams have been accused of using **Voodoo** dolls to inflict pain and injury on people. They are mostly associated with areas of the Philippines where traditional healers are commonly consulted because illness there is often regarded as being supernatural in origin. Victims will sometimes seek out the mangkukulam and bribe him to remove the spell. Mangkukulams are sometimes known as "bruho" (male witch) or "bruha" (female witch) from the Spanish words *brujo* and *bruja*.

See also MAMBABARANG.

MAP, WALTER (ca. 1140–1208/10). An English cleric who served as a royal justice under King Henry II, from about 1182, Map recorded various stories, anecdotes, and observations in a work entitled *De nugis curialium* (On the Folly of Courtiers). Here, he included accounts of diabolical **pacts**, demonic activity, **sorcery**, and **heresy**. He described a heretical sect known as *Publicans* or *Patarines*, the members of which gathered secretly to feast, celebrate, and worship a **demon**, who appeared in the form of a large black **cat**. Although Map did not describe them in any way as witches, his account of their activities, and the stereotypes of heretics upon which it drew, would obviously influence the later image of the witches' **sabbath**.

MATHER, COTTON (1663–1728). The son of the important Puritan minister **Increase Mather**, Cotton himself became a leading minister in the Massachusetts colony and was more closely involved in matters of **witchcraft** than his father. Influenced by the works of **William Perkins** and **Joseph Glanvill**, among others, he was firmly convinced of the reality of witches and the dangerous satanic threat that they supposedly represented, especially in New England. He therefore supported witch trials and **witch-hunting** in his sermons and writings. In 1689, he recounted the dangers of witchcraft in *Memorable Providences, Relating to Witchcraft and Possessions*, based on his experience of the Goodwin case of the previous year. The book helped to set the stage for the major outbreak of witch-hunting in **Salem**, Massachusetts, in 1692. Once these trials began, Mather met with other Boston ministers to discuss the matter. Although they were concerned about the difficulty in determining a true case of witchcraft, especially when only **spectral evidence** was available, Mather and many of his fellow ministers encouraged local authorities to seek out and prosecute witches vigorously. In 1693, he wrote *The Wonders of the Invisible World*, justifying his support for the trials in Salem.

Shortly after the trials in Salem, a backlash against rampant witch-hunting in the New England colonies began and public opinion started to turn against Mather, who remained firm in his convictions regarding the dangerous threat that witches posed. His reputation suffered, and, as a result, he was passed over several times for the presidency of Harvard College. In reaction to this perceived insult, Mather began to take an interest in the Connecticut College School, and in 1718 he wrote an impassioned letter to Elihu Yale urging him to endow this institution that would thereafter bear his name. Although Yale seems to have been moved more by other pleas for support, the founding of Yale University ranks among the few positive actions to be associated, however distantly, with the Salem witch-hunts.

MATHER, INCREASE (1639–1723). A prominent Puritan minister in colonial Massachusetts and president of Harvard College (1685–1701), Increase Mather was educated at Harvard and Trinity College, Dublin. He served as a minister in the Church of England until 1661, when he returned to Massachusetts. In 1684, he published *An Essay for the Recording of Illustrious Providences* in an attempt to counter the religious laxity he had found in the New England colonies. The essay recorded a variety of supernatural occurrences, including **witchcraft** and demonic **possession**, and became popular among Mather's fellow Puritans. During the outbreak of **witch-hunting** at **Salem** in 1692, Mather was commissioned by the leading ministers in Massachusetts to write *Cases of Conscience Concerning Evil Spirits Personating Men* (published in 1693) in response to the judges' use of **spectral evidence**. Mather argued for greater caution in prosecuting witchcraft because **demons** could impersonate innocent and upright people who might then be wrongly prosecuted as witches. He concluded, however, in support of all the convictions at Salem. He also added a postscript denying that his work was at odds with *The Wonders of the Invisible World*, written in support of the trials in Salem by his son **Cotton Mather**. Like Cotton Mather and his contemporary **Joseph Glanvill**, Increase Mather's later works tried to prove the existence of the spirit world in an effort to counter the **skeptical** "Sadducees."

See also NORTH AMERICA, WITCHCRAFT IN.

MEDEA. One of the great sorceresses of classical mythology, Medea was the daughter of the king of Colchis, and a priestess of **Hecate**, the ancient Greek goddess of **magic** and **witchcraft**. She was also sometimes depicted as the niece of the sorceress **Circe**. When Jason came to Colchis in search of the Golden Fleece, Medea fell in love with him and aided him with her magic. She protected Jason with **ointments**, and helped him during his adventures with her spells, herbs, and **poisons**. In Greece, she used magic to kill Pelias, the usurper of Jason's kingdom. But Medea could also be selfishly cruel. In some stories she killed and dismembered her brother to delay her father's pursuit of Jason. She later murdered a rival for Jason's love with the gift of a poisoned robe that burst into flames when she put it on. Medea then killed her own **children** by Jason and fled in a dragon-drawn chariot.

In the medieval and early-modern periods, she became a literary archetype of the witch, especially of the notion that witches were motivated by carnal passions and associated with weather magic, graveyards, necromancy, and the night. She has also been the subject of **operas** and paintings (particularly those by artists associated with the Pre-Raphaelite Brotherhood), and appeared as a character in **films** such as *Jason and the Argonauts* (1963).

See also ANTIQUITY, WITCHCRAFT IN; ART, WITCHCRAFT IN; LOVE MAGIC; STORMS AND STORM-RAISING.

METAMORPHOSIS. Among the powers that witches were commonly believed to possess was that of metamorphosis, the ability to alter their own shape, usually into that of some kind of animal. In particular, witches were often thought to be able to turn themselves into **werewolves**, and there is a strong historical connection between **witchcraft** and lycanthropy. Authorities in medieval and early-modern Europe differed as to the reality of such transformations, however. For example, **Jean Bodin** accepted its reality, while the *Malleus maleficarum*, following the arguments of **Thomas Aquinas** on the nature and extent of demonic power, held that such changes were just illusions created by **demons** and not real alterations of substance.

MIDWIVES. A great deal of modern scholarship on **witchcraft** maintains that midwives were especially vulnerable to accusations of this crime, and figured prominently in many witch trials. As healers, they were widely believed to have access to spells for **magical healing** and other occult remedies, and they could easily become suspect of wrongdoing if a birth did not go well. Much **feminist** scholarship in particular has focused on the idea of the supposed midwife witch. Observing that midwives occupied one of only a few positions of public power and authority open to **women** in premodern Europe, these scholars have argued that the tarring of midwives with accusations of witchcraft was an attempt by male authorities to reduce or eliminate powerful, independent roles for women in society. Recently, however, the entire premise of such arguments has been called into serious question. Careful study of trial records reveals that very few midwives were ever actually accused of witchcraft. Rather than vulnerable and marginal members of society, they had to be respectable and trusted in order to succeed in their profession. It now seems clear that many historians have been led astray by a few spectacular cases, by the extended references to midwife witches in the infamous **witch-hunting** manual *Malleus maleficarum* (noted for a level of misogyny that is not, in fact, present in many other major treatises on witchcraft or **demonology**), and by a tradition of association that originated in the now-discredited work of **Margaret Murray**.

MODERN WITCHCRAFT. *See* WICCA.

MOLITOR, ULRICH (1442–1508). An early author on witchcraft, Molitor was born in the southern **German** city of Constance. He was educated at the universities of Basel and Pavia, where he received his degree in canon law. He then served as an official in the episcopal court in Constance before entering the service of Duke Sigismund of Tyrol. Following **Heinrich Kramer**'s unsuccessful attempt to prosecute witch suspects in the Tyrol in 1485, the duke asked Molitor to investigate the matter of **witchcraft**. In 1489, Molitor published his conclusions in the treatise *De lamiis et phitonicis mulieribus* (Concerning Witches and Fortunetellers) that he had written as a dialogue between himself, the duke and another jurist. Like many early writers on witchcraft, Molitor accepted that the **heresy**, **apostasy**, and **idolatry** involved in making a **pact** with the **devil** were deserving of death. On the other hand, unlike Kramer, Molitor adopted the **skeptical** position of the **canon** *Episcopi* toward the activities and supernatural powers ascribed to witches. He argued that these were illusory and that witches could not raise **storms**, harm people, fly to **sabbaths**, or tell fortunes. As well as representing the continuation of the skeptical tradition of **demonology**, *De lamiis* is also important as the first witchcraft text to contain woodcuts of witches and their supposed activities, many of which became models for later artists of the early-modern period.

See also ART, WITCHCRAFT IN; NIGHT FLIGHT.

MONTAIGNE, MICHEL DE (1533–1595). One of the most important **French** philosophers of the early-modern period, Montaigne exhibited a powerful **skepticism** and uncertainty about the basis of human knowledge in almost every area, including **witchcraft**. His guiding motto was *que sais-je?* (what do I know?). In "On the Lame," published in the 2nd edition of *Essays* (1588), Montaigne observed that he had never seen a miracle or other supernatural event. He also mocked **demonologists** as delusional, and dismissed the old witches he had interviewed as insane or **possessed**. He concluded that it put a high value on one's opinions to have a man roasted alive because of them. Montaigne was attacked by his relative **Martín Del Rio** as an unbeliever, but defended by another witch-hunting relative, **Pierre de Lancre**, as consistently holding a position of doubt rather than truth.

MORA WITCHES. The great **Swedish witch-hunt** of 1668–1676 began in the county of Dalarna with the trials now associated with the village of Mora. The Mora trials became notorious because of the account written by the local vicar, Elaus Skragge, which was quickly translated into Dutch and **German** in 1670. In the summer of 1668, local officials were prompted to investigate the testimony of an 11-year-old girl that there was a local diabolical conspiracy. The investigation quickly spread as more **children** added to the story and some of the alleged witches were convicted and sentenced to death. The following year a royal commission was appointed to look into the matter. Several hundred children came forward with similar testimony about being kidnapped and spirited away to a **sabbath** held in a mythic location known as Blåkulla. Although the case certainly represents a major hunt by Scandinavian standards, the figures in the Mora trials have often been exaggerated. In all, some 60 suspects were interrogated, and 23 people were sentenced to death. These **executions** inspired other trials further afield, in the capital at Stockholm and even into Swedish possessions in Finland. In his discussions of the **Salem** trials, **Cotton Mather** used the Mora ones for comparison. He took his account from the additions made by Anthony Horneck to later editions of **Joseph Glanvill**'s *Saducismus Triumphatus* (first published in 1681).

MORGAN LE FEY. One of the major characters in the legends and literature surrounding the mythic King Arthur of Britain, Morgan le Fey (that is, Morgan the fairy) is depicted as a powerful **sorceress**. Morgan's character was inspired by pre-Christian Welsh mythology and, in the earliest stories recorded by Geoffrey of Monmouth and Chrétien de Troyes in the late 12th century, she appears as a **magical healer**. By the time the 15th-century author Thomas Malory wrote his *Le Morte d'Arthur*, however, she transformed into the Christian Arthur's half-sister and powerful **pagan** adversary, now her best-known role. Like the classical sorceresses **Circe**, **Hecate**, and **Medea**, Morgan provided a literary and artistic archetype for powerful and threatening female **magic**. Versions of Morgan le Fey also exist in the mythology surrounding Charlemagne and in Sicily, where she is known as Fata Morgana.

See also ART, WITCHCRAFT IN; FICTION, WITCHCRAFT IN.

MOSES. The story of Moses's and Aaron's defeat of the Egyptian pharaoh's magicians appears in the religious books of Judaism, Christianity, and **Islam**. In these stories, he is just the instrument through whom God demonstrated his power. Moses's apparent use of **magic** has, however, led some religious groups to adopt him as a magician. Two books, published jointly as the **grimoire** *Sixth and Seventh Books of Moses* in 1849, collect spells attributed to Moses. Although the title suggests a continuation of the Pentateuch, the first five books of the **Bible**, the spells can only be traced back to the 18th century. As a source of supposed Christian magic, however, the grimoire has influenced the beliefs and practices of religious groups and movements as diverse as **Hoodoo** practitioners in the American South, Rastafarianism, and Christian spiritualists in West **Africa**.

See also JEWS; NORTH AMERICA, WITCHCRAFT IN.

MURRAY, MARGARET (1863–1963). A British Egyptologist, archeologist, and anthropologist, early in the 20th century, Murray developed the theory that historical **witchcraft** was in fact the remnant of an ancient **pagan** fertility religion. Her ideas were viewed with **skepticism** in the academic community, but in the 1950s **Gerald Gardner**, the founder of modern witchcraft, or **Wicca**, was inspired by them.

Murray, born to British parents in Calcutta, studied Egyptology at the University of London and became a professional academic Egyptologist. She was also interested in anthropology, however, and especially in the history of witchcraft. In 1921, she published her first book on the subject, *The Witch-Cult in Western Europe*, in which she argued that witches really had existed in medieval and early-modern Europe, not as Christian **heretics** or devil-worshipers, but as clandestine practitioners of a pre-Christian fertility religion. She was inspired by the anthropologist James Frazer's theories about fertility cults in his famous book *The Golden Bough* (1890). In her second book on witchcraft, *The God of the Witches* (1931), she traced the history of the **Horned God**, a male pagan fertility deity. She claimed that this horned deity was the basis for the idea of the **devil** presiding over a witches' **sabbath**. Her most radical book, however, was her last, *The Divine King of England* (1954). Here she maintained that every English king from William the Conqueror in the 11th century to **James I** in the 17th was secretly a practitioner of the ancient fertility religion of witchcraft and that the deaths of many important figures in English history could be explained as ritual murders committed by this fertility cult.

Murray never advanced any strong evidence to support her theories, her arguments were based mostly on conjecture and coincidence (and in her final book, at least, on outright conspiracy theories), and her ideas were always controversial in the academic community. Since the publication of her final book in the 1950s, her ideas have been almost completely discredited. However, her theories were an important inspiration for modern witchcraft. In his book *Witchcraft Today*, for which Murray wrote the introduction, Gerald Gardner, the founder of modern witchcraft, maintained that he had discovered a surviving **coven** of traditional, hereditary witches. He claimed that he had been initiated into their ancient religion, which he intended to reintroduce to the modern world. For a time, the idea that witchcraft was a direct survival of an ancient pagan religion was an essential part of Wiccan belief. By the 1990s, however, in the face of mounting historical evidence to the contrary, most Wiccans had abandoned Murray's theory.

MUTI KILLINGS. *Muti* is a word derived from Zulu and refers to traditional medicine in much of southern **Africa**. Muti killings involve the murder of people, often **children**, for body parts that can be used in traditional medical and **witchcraft** concoctions. The killings are illegal, but said to be on the rise in South Africa. Similar killings have occurred in Tanzania, where albinos were being murdered in 2008 for the export of their body parts across southern and western Africa. It was claimed that these body parts were being used in witchcraft. There have also been high profile cases in the West. In 2002, the body of an unidentified boy was found mutilated in the River Thames in London, **England**. He was believed to have been the victim of a muti killing.

N

NAZIS AND WITCHCRAFT. From 1935, a group within Heinrich Himmler's *Schutzstaffel* (SS), known as the *H-Sonderkommando* (from *Hexen-Sonderkommando* or Special Witch Command), began to collate information about witch persecutions in **Germany** and, later, the occupied territories. The project ended in 1943, impeded by the course of World War II. The information the group uncovered in the historiography and archival sources was recorded on card indexes, most of which are now located in Poznan, **Poland**.

The aim of the group was to collect material that could be used in propaganda against both the Catholic and Protestant churches. In line with the racial **neo-paganism** espoused by Himmler, the *H-Sonderkommando* believed that witches were descendants of the Germanic race and adherents of a popular Germanic cult that had been rigorously persecuted as a **witchcraft** sect by Christian authorities against the will of the people. This view echoed that of **Margaret Murray**, who believed that witchcraft was essentially a **pagan** fertility religion, but did not ascribe any racial aspect to its persecution. In order to gain access to ecclesiastical archives, the members of *H-Sonderkommando* had to work in relative secrecy, dropping the word *Hexen* (Witches) from the command's name and posing as academics. Despite recording almost 34,000 cases, the project was a failure, partly because the volume of cases it uncovered was small in comparison to expectations (which ran into the millions), and partly because ordinary Germans clearly did participate in and, in many cases, clamor for the witch persecutions conducted by Christian authorities.

While the *H-Sonderkommando* records contain many errors and, in most cases, lack a sound historical context, they remain useful. They have brought to light cases that were previously unknown to historians, and the diligent cross-referencing of the index cards allows older, obscured references in the historiography to be clarified.

NECROMANCY. A form of **divination** that involves summoning the spirits of the dead, in the late-medieval and early-modern periods, necromancy came to mean demonic **magic**, and specifically a complex, learned form of ritual demonic invocation. This later confusion of meanings might have arisen from the Christian notion that the spirits of the dead, be they in heaven or hell, could not be summoned to return to earth; any sorcerer or diviner claiming to do so was in reality summoning **demons** who merely took the form of a dead person. The **Witch of Endor,** for example, who is described in the **Bible** as summoning the spirit of the dead prophet Samuel for King Saul, was thought by **Saint Augustine of Hippo** and later medieval authorities to have summoned a demon or the **devil** instead. Saint Jerome, however, believed that the apparition of the spirit was a hoax perpetrated by the so-called witch. **Demonologists** of the early-modern period, like **Jean Bodin,** tended to adopt Saint Augustine's explanation, while **skeptics** like **Reginald Scot** repeated versions of Saint Jerome's view.

In the earliest account of necromancy, in Homer's *Odyssey*, the sorceress **Circe** explains to Odysseus the rituals needed to consult with the spirit of the deceased seer Tiresias in preparation for his journey home. By the time Lucan wrote his epic *Pharsalia* in the mid-1st century, necromancy had become a wicked act performed by crones like **Erictho.** The discovery, in the 12th and 13th centuries, of a large number of classical, **Jewish,** and Arab texts describing learned magic practices interested Western European scholars, some of whom began to practice the necromantic rituals they found in them. Some of these rituals involved summoning demons. The obscure nature and ancient traditions of the texts meant, however, that the spread of necromancy in the later Middle Ages was restricted to the educated, usually clerical, elites.

The spread of necromantic practices did serve to increase ecclesiastical concern over demonic magic generally. In the 14th century, the Dominican inquisitor **Nicolau Eymeric** had books on necromancy burned because they inferred that their users were guilty of **idolatry** in their alleged worship of the spirits or demons they summoned, rather than merely commanding them. Eymeric's *Directorium inquisitorium* (Directory of Inquisitors) of 1376, among other works, helped pave the way for the demonization of common harmful **sorcery,** or *maleficium,* and the development of ideas of widespread demonic **witchcraft** in the centuries to come.

See also ANTIQUITY, WITCHCRAFT IN.

NEO-PAGANISM. In the second half of the 20th century, a wide variety of new religious systems emerged across Europe and **North America,** largely based on nature worship and new-age spirituality. They have tended to adopt ancient pre-Christian European religions, mainly varieties of Celtic and Norse **paganism,** as their antecedents. They do not, however, all claim to be directly descended from them. Modern **witchcraft,** or **Wicca,** comprises by far the largest number of neo-pagan movements.

Although they do not adhere to a single unified or coherent system of belief, most forms of neo-paganism share certain basic similarities. They arose after World War II, influenced by the work of **Gerald Gardner**, among others, and came to prominence in the 1960s as part of the response to the view that the traditional Western religions no longer adequately met modern spiritual needs and were in fact authoritarian and repressive, particularly toward **women**. Many varieties of neo-paganism therefore accord women and feminine spirituality an equal or superior status to men in their systems of belief and practice. Consequently, there is a strong historical link between the rise of neo-paganism, particularly Wicca, and the development of **feminist** movements in the 1960s and 1970s. Neo-pagans also tend to stress the worship of and a concern for nature, and thus their rise has been closely tied to that of modern environmental movements. **Starhawk**, for example, uses her spiritual influence to further the causes of both feminism and environmentalism. A general stress on individual spirituality and ritual practice means that most neo-pagans, whether modern witches or followers of modern **Satanism**, follow a basic creed, first advanced by the English magician and occultist **Aleister Crowley**: if it harms none, do what you will.

NEW ENGLAND, WITCHCRAFT IN. *See* NORTH AMERICA, WITCHCRAFT IN.

NIDER, JOHANNES (ca. 1385–1438). A Dominican friar, theologian, and religious reformer, Nider wrote some of the most extensive and important early accounts of **witchcraft** to appear in Europe in the first half of the 15th century. His *Formicarius* (The Anthill), a moralizing dialogue between a theologian and student that takes ants as its organizing image, written mostly in 1437 and early 1438, was very influential. It was printed in seven separate editions between the late 1400s and 1692, meaning that it was published throughout the entire period of the **witch-hunts**. In addition, it served as an important source of information for the later Dominican **Heinrich Kramer**, author of the *Malleus maleficarum*, first published in about 1487. The fifth book of the *Formicarius*, which deals specifically with "Witches and their Deceptions," was printed along with the *Malleus* in some later editions.

Born sometime in the early 1380s in the small town of Isny in Swabia in what is now southern **Germany**, Nider studied at Cologne and Vienna. He then attended the **Council of Basel**, where he began collecting many contemporary stories and examples of witchcraft that he would include in his *Formicarius*. In that work, he described witchcraft in much the form that it would take throughout the later period of the witch-hunts. Witches were evil sorcerers who performed harmful **sorcery**, or *maleficium*, with the aid of **demons**. They attained this power by surrendering themselves to Satan. Gathering at secret nocturnal conventicles (Nider never used the terms *synagogue* or *sabbath*), they worshiped a presiding demon or the **devil** himself, offered sacrifices to him, desecrated the cross and other religious objects, killed and ate babies and young **children**, and engaged in sexual **orgies**. Nider never described witches as flying to such gatherings, and elsewhere in the *Formicarius* he explicitly denied the reality of **night flight**, although he did not deny the basic power of demons to transport people through the air if they wished.

In another work, the *Preceptorium divinae legis* (Preceptor of Divine Law), Nider attempted to provide a guide to various problems of religious belief and practice based on the Ten Commandments. In this work, he included some important sections on demonic **magic** and witchcraft under the heading of the First Commandment, which stated that one should not worship any deities before the one Hebrew, and later Christian, God. Demonic invocation, magic, and witchcraft were thought by medieval theologians to entail the worship of demons and thus constituted **idolatry**.

One particularly important aspect of the witch stereotype that Nider developed was the presumption that **women** were more inclined toward witchcraft than men. In fact, Nider was the first learned authority to advance this position. Although he presented many examples of male witches, Nider described women as weaker than men in body, mind, and spirit. Thus, they were more prone to the seductions and temptations of the devil and submitted more quickly to his service than men. This basic line of argument would become much more pronounced in the extremely misogynist *Malleus maleficarum*.

NIGHT FLIGHT. Witches were widely supposed to have the power to fly through the air. In particular, they were thought to fly to their nocturnal gatherings, known as **sabbaths**. They often did so on **broomsticks**, staves, or occasionally on animals, and this became the standard image of the night flight, or transvection, of the witches. In Christian law and **demonology**, the idea was codified at least as early as the famous 10th-century **canon** *Episcopi*, but the beliefs on which the canon was based were much older and shared by diverse cultures.

In the story of Bel and the Dragon, told in the apocryphal *Additions to Daniel*, Habakkuk was carried by an angel from Judea to Chaldea to feed Daniel in the lion's den. In ancient and early-medieval Europe, the **Wild Hunt**, consisting of the dead or fairies, was believed to follow one of various deities or mythological figures, such as **Diana**, Odin, or **Herne the Hunter**. The hunt would presage disaster, and some traditions held that human beings who witnessed it could be dragged along in its wake. Sorceresses were described as transforming themselves into birds, such as owls or ravens, and **Morgan le Fey** possessed the ability to fly. In parts of 13th-century Europe, *bonae res* (good **women**) were believed to fly out at night on sticks, while the *malae res* (**evil** women) and *lamiae* rode on wolves as well as being associated with screech owls, evil birds that allegedly sucked on **children**'s blood, and the equally **cannibalistic Lilith**. Later, between 1574 and 1749, the *benandanti* of northern **Italy** explained to their prosecutors how they flew out in spirit to fight witches for the fertility of the next season's crops. Much of their beneficent activity was clearly associated with **shamanism**.

The canon *Episcopi* described groups of "wicked women, who . . . believe and profess that, in the hours of the night, they ride upon certain beasts with Diana, the goddess of the **pagans**, and an innumerable multitude of women, and in the silence of the night traverse great spaces of earth." The canon went on to state, however, that this belief was entirely false and that such supposed flight was only an illusion created by **demons**. Throughout the Middle Ages, such beliefs were often associated with the practice of **sorcery**, but authorities generally paid them little concern. Only in the 15th century, as the idea of the witches' sabbath began to develop, did the idea of night flight become particularly important. Such flight began to be regarded as the means by which witches would travel to their secret nocturnal gatherings. This meant, however, that if authorities wanted to regard the events of a sabbath as real, night flight also had to be real, and they had to disregard the tradition of the canon *Episcopi*. Some authorities decided that flight must still be an illusion, and so, therefore, must the entire sabbath, but they concluded that accused witches might still be condemned just for believing that they had taken part in such an event. Most authorities, however, were able to argue for the reality of night flight. Because the ability of demons to transport objects through the air was accepted, they argued that although such flight could sometimes be an illusion as stated in the canon *Episcopi*, there was no reason that, in other cases, it could not be entirely real.

The idea that witches fly at night features in the folklore concerning creatures like **Baba Yaga** and **Ole Higue**, and persist in the stereotypical image of witches recreated every **Halloween**.

NORTH AMERICA, WITCHCRAFT IN. Witchcraft has existed in North America since colonial times. The witch-hunt at **Salem**, Massachusetts, in 1692 marked the culmination of a series of much smaller witchcraft episodes in New England. This hunt was unusual in the level of **diabolism** attributed to the alleged witches, and the use of **spectral evidence**, making it more like a continental witch persecution than a large witch trial in **England**. While prominent Puritan ministers, like **Increase Mather** and his son **Cotton**, generally supported this outbreak of witchcraft prosecution, despite some doubts about the spectral evidence used, not all inhabitants of the colony were so credulous. A contemporary witchcraft episode in **Stamford**, Connecticut, did not end in a witch panic.

Witchcraft and similar practices also evolved, in the context of syncretistic religions and belief systems, through the use of **African** slaves and contact with the **Caribbean** and **South America**. **Hoodoo** developed in the American South among Irish sailors or African slaves, while there are strong pockets of **Voodoo** in the southern states, and Hispanic communities across North America in which **Santería**, for example, is practiced. The **Church of Wicca**, and other **Wiccan** and **neo-pagan** groups, are strong in the United States, more so than in England, where modern witchcraft began. This is due, in part, to the strong link that has developed between **feminism** and witchcraft in the work of the witches **Margot Adler** and **Starhawk**. The **Church of Satan** was also founded in the country in 1966. Despite a rich heritage of witchcraft, **magic**, and **sorcery**, the stereotypical European witch still dominates the imagery of **Halloween**.

NORTH BERWICK WITCHES. The trials of the so-called North Berwick witches are among the most famous in Scottish history, mainly because of the direct participation of the Scottish king, **James VI** (later also **James I of England**). The experience of these trials, held in 1590 and 1591, inspired the king to write his *Daemonologie* (Demonology), first published in 1597. The trials began when Gillis Duncan, a maid in the town of Tranent near Edinburgh, began practicing as a **healer**. Her employer was convinced that she must be a witch. She was interrogated, and the **devil's mark** was found on her throat. The use of **torture** on Gillis Duncan and those she denounced as fellow witches led to further arrests in East Lothian. Under torture, the witch suspects confessed to attending regular **sabbaths** in the coastal town of North Berwick, about 25 miles east of Edinburgh. They implicated the king's cousin, Francis, Earl of Bothwell, as their leader on whose behalf they attempted to kill the king. They tried to raise **storms** at sea as he journeyed back from **Denmark**, where he had gone to meet Princess Anne to whom he was betrothed. Later, they used wax images and **poison**. It seems that James was initially **skeptical** about **witchcraft**, but became convinced after some of the suspects were questioned in his presence. The trials of the North Berwick witches were described in *Newes from Scotland* (London, 1591) as propaganda to further James's claims to the English throne. They also provided the framework for other trials in **Scotland** in the 1590s.
See also DEMONOLOGY.

NORWAY, WITCHCRAFT IN. Witch trials in Norway took place while the country was under Danish rule. The most famous of these was that of **Anne Pedersdotter** of Bergen, the wife of the Lutheran theologian Absalon Pederssøn Beyer, who was executed in 1590. It was only after the promulgation of the Witchcraft Code of 1617, however, that mass persecution occurred. About 310 witches were executed in the country, mainly when Denmark was heavily engaged in warfare with its neighbors. Persecution was most intense in the sparsely populated northern county of Finnmark, where 30 percent of Norway's witches were executed. Interestingly, it was Norwegian rather than Sami **women** who were thought more likely to commit acts of harmful **sorcery**, or *maleficium*, in this county. Gradually, Danish **inquisitorial procedure** replaced the **accusatorial** process traditionally used in Norway, and, after a period of decline in witchcraft prosecution, the last witch was executed there in 1695.

See also EXECUTIONS; LAWS AGAINST WITCHCRAFT, EUROPEAN.

O

OBEAH. Like **Hoodoo**, **Santería**, and **Voodoo**, Obeah is a religion prac-ticed in the **Caribbean** and **South America**. It has its origins in the traditions of the Igbo people of West Africa, and was taken across the Atlantic by **African** slaves. Obeah consists of folk **magic**, **sorcery**, and other religious practices that are spiritualist, mystical, and **shamanistic** in character. While it can be beneficent or maleficent, Obeah is also used generally to describe a talisman or charm used for harmful magical purposes, and in some parts of the Caribbean is the name used for a witch or her spell. In West African **folklore**, obeah (or obia) is a monstrous animal sent by witches to kidnap young girls. The influential magician **Aleister Crowley** adopted the term *obeah* to mean an act of magic in his *Book of the Law* (1904).

See also CHILDREN, WITCHCRAFT AND.

OBSCENE KISS. The *osculum infame* or obscene kiss refers to the kiss witches were often thought to have to give the **devil** on his buttocks or anus as a sign of their homage and subservience to him while he presided over a witches' **sabbath**. A kiss was a typical sign of reverence in medieval society, and a kiss on the anus symbolized the profound inversion and obscenity entailed in **witchcraft**. Similar actions such as kissing **demons** or animals (the devil was often thought to preside over a sabbath in animal form) had earlier been attributed to medieval heretical groups.

OBSESSION. *See* POSSESSION, DEMONIC.

OINTMENTS. Supposedly magical ointments might consist of almost any grease-like substance spread over the body or some object. Historically, witches were thought to use ointments in many of their **magical** operations. The two chief uses of ointments were as **poison** to kill people or cause disease, and for **night flight**. Witches were commonly thought to know many recipes, often supposedly learned from the **devil** in the context of a witches' **sabbath**, for making poisonous ointments that they would then spread on people's skin to injure or kill them. Witches were also often thought to anoint themselves or various instruments such as **brooms** with other ointments in order to fly. Use of such ointments has led to speculation on the part of some scholars that at least some aspects of witchcraft can be attributed to the use of hallucinogenic compounds. Recipes for certain ointments supposedly used by witches are recorded in treatises on witchcraft. Some of these would clearly be toxic. Others, if spread on the skin, could produce a trance-like state and delusions of flight.

OLE HIGUE. In Guyana and Jamaica, the Ole Higue is a nocturnal female **vampire** who shares many characteristics with the early-modern witch and **Baba Yaga** of **Russian folklore**. By day, she appears as an old **woman** and is sometimes known as a witch. By night, she sheds her skin and flies through the air as a ball of fire. Finding a baby sleeping in its cradle, she sucks its blood before returning home. To rid themselves of the creature, villagers dress a baby in a blue nightgown, place rice and asafoetida (sometimes known as devil's dung because of its smell when raw) by the cradle, and cast a spell on the Ole Higue. The spell forces the Ole Higue to count the grains of rice, but she has to begin again each time she loses herself. At daybreak, the villagers can enter the house of the intended victim and beat the Ole Higue to death.

    See also CARIBBEAN WITCHCRAFT; CHILDREN, WITCHCRAFT AND; NIGHT FLIGHT.

OPERA, WITCHCRAFT IN. Witchcraft, sorcery, and **magic** have a long tradition in opera. Composers have based their works on classical literature, **folklore**, popular stories, and real events. There are, for example, a sorceress and two enchantresses in Henry Purcell's adaptation of the myth *Dido and Aeneas* (1689). Witches are also a feature of Giuseppe Verdi's *Macbeth* (1847), Richard Wagner's *Lohengrin* (1850), and Engelbert Humperdinck's *Hansel and Gretel* (1893). The 20th century saw operas based on real events. These have included *La Fiamma* (1934), Ottorino Respighi's work based on the case of **Anne Pedersdotter**, and, in 1961, an adaptation by Richard Ward of *The Crucible*, Arthur Miller's **play** about the **Salem** witch trials.

ORGIES. In medieval and early-modern Europe, witches were thought to be sexually driven and sexually promiscuous people. One of the main features of descriptions of the witches' **sabbath** was the participation of witches in sexual orgies with each other and with **demons** who were also present at these gatherings. The notion of people gathering in secret and engaging in wild, orgiastic rites was a common element of medieval clerical diatribes against most forms of **heresy**, carried over and applied also to witches when the concept of a diabolically organized, heretical cult of witches developed in the late Middle Ages. Certain aspects of the stereotype might have derived from surviving descriptions of ancient **pagan** fertility festivals, such as the Roman **Bacchanalia**. Within modern **witchcraft**, or **Wicca**, certain groups perform some rituals nude (*skyclad*, as it is often termed). This is thought to reduce inhibitions within the group and promote the flow of magical energies. Some critics of Wicca, however, fixate on such practices and continue to associate modern witchcraft with sexual immorality.

See also ANTIQUITY, WITCHCRAFT IN; SEXUALITY AND WITCH-CRAFT.

P

PACTS, DEMONIC. In medieval and early-modern Christian **demonology**, the notion of a pact with **demons** or the **devil**, either explicit or tacit, was an essential element of most forms of **sorcery**, and became one of the central crimes in cases of **witchcraft**. The roots of the Christian notion of the demonic pact are found in the **Bible**, chiefly Isaiah 28:15. The early-modern King James' Version translates the verse as: "We have made a covenant with death and with hell we are at agreement." The Latin term used in the medieval Vulgate is *pactum* (covenant; agreement). Early church fathers such as Origen (185–254) and **Saint Augustine of Hippo** (354–430) began to link the performance of **sorcery** and **divination** to pacts made with demons. Augustine in particular viewed the entire world in terms of a struggle between demonic and divine power, and he contrasted the **evil** of demonic **magic** starkly with the good and salvational power of divine miracle in his influential *City of God* and other works. Augustine's notions of demonic pacts would form the essential foundation on which all later Western Christian thought on this subject was based.

Although Augustine's view of demonic pacts entered into canon law during the early Middle Ages, demonic activity in the world was not then of major concern to Christian authorities. The legend of **Theophilus of Adana** (died ca. 538), who was released from his pact with the devil after repenting of it and receiving forgiveness from God through the intercession of the Virgin, became the model for dealing with such cases. Theophilus concluded his pact with the devil because he was jealous that he had not been raised to a bishopric. It was only in the 12th century that Christian authorities became increasingly concerned about demonic activity. In the 13th century, the theologian **Thomas Aquinas** began to develop further the notion of the demonic pact and its connections to demonic sorcery. By the end of the 14th century, the theologian and inquisitor **Nicolau Eymeric** was able to argue that all demonic sorcery necessarily involved the agreement and cooperation of demons. Sorcerers had to worship these demons and form pacts with them, either explicitly or implicitly, and so were guilty of **idolatry** and **heresy**. The most famous story of a sorcerer concluding a pact with a demon is that of the 16th-century magician **Faust**, but his end was not as happy as Theophilus's.

When the full stereotype of European witchcraft finally developed in the 15th century, the pact with the devil became central to the entire concept. Typically at a **sabbath**, new witches were thought to be required to renounce their faith and swear loyalty to the devil, usually sealing this with an **obscene kiss**. Increasingly, accounts came to describe a formal, written agreement signed by the witch, often in blood. In return, the witch was sometimes given money or some other token that ultimately proved to be worthless because it turned into excrement, leaves, or roof tiles. While Jeanne des Anges, the mother superior at the center of the **Loudun** possession case, was able to vomit up a demonic pact for the investigators, in the vast majority of witchcraft cases, the witch suspects were unable to produce their pact or quote directly from it, claiming that they could not or did not read it.

PAGANISM. The term *paganism* derives from the Latin words *pagus* (countryside) and *paganus* (rustic people, generally). Historically, it was used by Christian religious authorities to refer to any form of polytheistic religious belief, in contrast to the three main monotheistic religions of the West (Judaism, Christianity, and, later, **Islam**). As Christianity became the dominant religion in the Roman world of late **Antiquity**, it was found mainly in the cities. Early Christians therefore began to use the term *pagan* to describe those mainly living in the countryside who held to the older, polytheistic religions of the ancient world. During the Middle Ages, the term was extended to include Celtic, Germanic, and Slavic tribes that had not converted to Christianity.

The relationship between pagan religions, as they were understood by Christian authorities, and medieval and early-modern **witchcraft** is weak. Some of the alleged practices of pagan religions, such as sexual **orgies**, were later attributed to witchcraft. Other remnants of pre-Christian practice were incorporated, for example, into the **shamanistic** fertility rites practiced by the northern Italian *benandanti* who found themselves prosecuted as witches from the late 16th century. There is no evidence, however, to support the argument advanced by some scholars of the late 19th and early 20th centuries, most notably the British Egyptologist and anthropologist **Margaret Murray**, that historical witchcraft represented the covert but direct survival of pagan religion into the Christian era that was condemned as a cult of devil-worshiping witches. Although it was quickly dismissed by historians, Murray's argument did come to influence **Gerald Gardner**, the founder of modern witchcraft. or **Wicca**. Even within Wicca and modern **neo-paganism**, however, the idea that these early pioneers had rediscovered an authentic, ancient, pagan religion has largely been abandoned. Instead, most practitioners of modern witchcraft and neo-pagan religions recognize that they are developing new belief systems based on ancient, pagan models.

PARACELSUS (PHILIPPUS AUREOLUS THEOPHRASTUS BOMBAST VON HOHENHEIM) (1493–1541). A Swiss physician, natural philosopher, astrologer, and alchemist, Paracelsus was influenced by **Hermetic magic** and the **humanism** of Marsilio Ficino and Giovanni Pico della Mirandola, the uncle of **Gianfrancesco Pico della Mirandola**. The name Paracelsus means "beyond Celsus," the Roman physician and naturalist. Paracelsus attacked the Aristotelian natural philosophy and Galenic medicine that dominated university education in the 16th century, advocating instead a form of what might be called *natural magic* that blended **astrology**, **alchemy**, signs, observation, chemical intervention, wisdom, and virtue. He believed that occult properties and powers existed in natural substances and throughout the natural world, including the stars and planets, and that **cunning men and women**, as well as educated magicians and physicians, knew how to manipulate them in their magical **healing**.

Paracelsus wrote widely on magic and related activities, although most of his works were only published posthumously when his brand of natural philosophy became popular in the late 16th century. His most important treatise on witchcraft, *De sagis et eorum operibus* (On Witches and Their Works) formed part of his *De divinis operibus et secretis naturae* (On Divine Works and the Secrets of Nature, 1589). In it, he claimed that witches were born rather than seduced; they performed harmful **sorcery**, or *maleficium*, flew, and changed shape through their knowledge of the occult, or hidden, forces of nature. He also accepted the stereotype of the **sabbath** with its **orgies** and other demonic rites. Like the **skeptic Johann Weyer**, however, Paracelsus argued that witches should not be executed, but educated and taken care of.

Despite his connections with humanists like **Erasmus** and the later influence of his works, Paracelsus's acerbic personality meant that he died poor and unpublished. His life and works continued to divide opinion after his death. The English philosopher and statesman Francis Bacon was one of many admirers, and some Rosicrucians believed him to be the mythical alchemist Christian Rosenkreutz. The theologian and physician Thomas Erastus, on the other hand, condemned Paracelsus in 1571, and Johann Wolfgang von Goethe adopted him as a model for his **Faust**.

See also METAMORPHOSIS; NIGHT FLIGHT.

PEDERSDOTTER, ANNE (?–1590). The victim of perhaps the single most famous **witchcraft** accusation made in Scandinavia, Anne was the wife of the Lutheran theologian Absalon Pederssøn Beyer. It is not known exactly why she was first accused of witchcraft in 1575, but it may have had something to do with her husband's attempts to remove Roman Catholic imagery from the churches in Bergen, **Norway**, in accordance with Lutheran teachings. She was acquitted of these first witchcraft charges. Suspicions about Anne persisted, however, and she was tried and executed for the crime in 1590. Her trial has been the subject of a **play**, two **operas**, a novel and Carl Theodore Dreyer's **film** *Day of Wrath* (1943).

See also FICTION, WITCHCRAFT IN.

PENANGGAL. A type of female **vampire** found in Malaysian **folklore**, the penanggal (or penanggalan) shares the characteristics of early-modern **witches** and other mythical creatures, such as **Baba Yaga** or **Ole Higue**. She could be a **woman**, old or young, who has obtained beauty through black **magic** or other supernatural means, or a **midwife** who has broken a **pact** with the **devil** that she had concluded to gain supernatural powers. In another variant of the tale, the penanggal was once a priestess who was disturbed by a man while meditating in a ritual bath of vinegar. Whatever her origins, at night the penanggal flies as a detached head with hanging entrails in search of blood. She prefers the blood of pregnant women or newborn infants who, after the penanggal has sucked on them, are afflicted with a wasting disease. The blood from the penanggal's entrails will cause sores on the bodies it touches. The penanggal can be recognized by the odor of vinegar. Thorny leaves can be scattered over floors and around the vulnerable entrances to houses in order to trap or injure the penanggal by its exposed entrails. Once trapped, it can, like Ole Higue, be beaten to death.

See also ASIAN WITCHCRAFT; CHILDREN, WITCHCRAFT AND; NIGHT FLIGHT.

PENTAGRAM. The pentagram or pentacle, a five-pointed star usually inscribed within a circle, is an important religious symbol for modern **witchcraft**, or **Wicca**. The five points of the star are typically interpreted as representing the divine, or alternately humanity, in harmony with the four natural elements. This symbol has little association with historical witchcraft. Magical circles of various sorts, often with stars or other occult symbols inscribed within them, were frequently employed to perform ritual **magic**, especially ritual demonic magic or **necromancy**, in the medieval and early-modern periods. The use of such symbols was then revived in the modern era by occult groups such as the **Hermetic Order of the Golden Dawn**. An inverted pentagram (with a single point of the star facing down as opposed to the Wiccan pentagram in which the single points faces up) has also been adopted as the symbol of **Baphomet** by the modern **Church of Satan**, and this or similar symbols are frequently used by many groups practicing modern **Satanism**.

PERKINS, WILLIAM (1558–1602). A major English authority on **demonology**, **witchcraft**, and witch-hunting, Perkins was a fellow of Christ's College at Cambridge. His sermons on witchcraft were published posthumously as *A Discourse on the Damned Art of Witchcraft* (1608), and soon surpassed even the *Daemonologie* of **King James I** to become the standard authority on matters of witchcraft in **England** in the 17th century. **Cotton Mather** used his work as the basis of his justification of the **Salem** witch trials of 1692 in his *The Wonders of the Invisible World* (1693). Perkins relied heavily on the **Bible** for his condemnation of witchcraft, but rarely drew on earlier, continental authorities, with the notable exception of **Nicolas Rémy**, or contemporary witchcraft cases. The main foci of Perkins' *Discourse* were the **demonic pact** and popular superstitions. On the basis of these, he advocated the **execution** of every "good Witch" (**cunning man or woman**) because they led their clients further away from God under the pretense of doing good.

PICO DELLA MIRANDOLA, GIANFRANCESCO (1469–1533). A nephew of the more famous Renaissance philosopher Giovanni Pico della Mirandola, Gianfrancesco was also a **humanist** by training. He did not, however, share the **skepticism** about **witchcraft** that some humanists showed. In 1522 and 1523, he conducted witch trials in Mirandola, and based his *Strix sive de ludificatione daemonum* (The Witch, or the Deceptions of Demons, 1523) on that experience. In this dialogue, several characters debate the reality of witchcraft and then question an actual witch. In the end, the skeptical character in the dialogue is convinced of the error of his position and accepts the reality of witchcraft. Written in Latin, the work was translated into Italian as early as 1524. It was later published alongside works by other authors, including **Bartolomeo della Spina**.
    See also STRIX (STRIGA).

PLAYS, WITCHCRAFT IN. Periodically, witches and **witchcraft** have interested playwrights, particularly in the **England** of **James I**. At this time witch prosecution was steadily declining in the country. The most famous of these Jacobean plays was William Shakespeare's *Macbeth* (1605), in which Macbeth consults the three witches on the heath. Some of these plays were based on real-life events. *The Witch of Edmonton* (1621) by William Rowley, Thomas Dekker, and John Ford was a dramatic portrayal of the case of Elizabeth Sawyer, and Thomas Heywood and Richard Brome's *The Late*

Lancashire Witches (1634) was a melodrama of a case in 1633. Other plays of this period that feature witchcraft include John Marston's *The Wonder of Women, or the Tragedy of Sophonisba* (1606); Ben Jonson's *The Masque of Queens* (1609); *The Tempest* (1611), also by Shakespeare; and Thomas Middleton's *The Witch* (ca. 1612). Before 1600, when witch prosecution was at a peak in England, playwrights tended to avoid witchcraft and take **magic** and conjurers as their subject. Examples include the late Elizabethan plays *Friar Bacon and Friar Bungay* by Robert Grene and *Dr Faustus* by Christopher Marlowe. Goethe also wrote a play about **Faust** (various fragments, texts, and revisions, 1772–1832).

On occasion, witchcraft and magic have been used for political purposes in plays. John Bale's *Three Laws* (1538) and Dekker's *The Whore of Babylon* (1607) both linked witchcraft or magic to Catholicism. Arthur Miller's *The Crucible* (1953), his play about the **Salem** witch trials, is also an allegory of the McCarthyite Red Scare of the late 1940s and 1950s. *Vinegar Tom* (1976) by Caryl Churchill uses a story of witchcraft in the 17th century as a **feminist** critique of the discrimination against **women** in 20th-century Britain.

Hans Wiers-Jenssen's play about **Anne Pedersdotter** (1909) inspired both Ottorino Respighi's **opera** *La Fiamma* (1934) and Carl Theodore Dreyer's **film** *Day of Wrath* (1943). **Joan of Arc** has also been the subject of plays by Shakespeare, Friedrich Schiller, Bertolt Brecht, Jean Anouilh, and George Bernard Shaw. Another notable witchcraft play is Christopher Fry's *The Lady's Not for Burning* (1948).

See also LANCASHIRE WITCHES.

POISON. Historical witches and magicians were often accused of using poisons to harm or kill others. In a few cases, people accused of **witchcraft** may in fact have been skilled herbalists capable of producing very dangerous poisons. The root of the **mandrake** plant, for example, often associated with witchcraft, could be very toxic. The supposed link between witchcraft and poisoning was, however, usually more fantastic. Witches were often described as receiving various poisons, along with other magical **ointments**, from the devil at a witches' **sabbath**. They would use these poisons to kill or injure people at the **devil's** command. In the **Affair of the Poisons** in late-17th century France, the alleged use of poisons amounted to treason and Louis XIV had to regulate their availability.

The association of poison with witchcraft and **magic** was ancient. Both **Augustine of Hippo** and **Isidore of Seville** noted the double meanings of ancient Greek and Latin words related to poisoning and **sorcery**. In fact, the Latin word *veneficium* (poisonous substance; sorcery, witchcraft) came to be used for "witchcraft" in the legal terminology of parts of Europe.

See also ANTIQUITY, WITCHCRAFT IN.

POLAND, WITCHCRAFT IN. In the early-modern period, the Polish-Lithuanian Commonwealth incorporated Poland, Lithuania, and parts of Ukraine, Belarus, and Latvia. The number of **witchcraft** trials in Poland has been the subject of debate, but there appear to have been no more than a few thousand, at most. Although Polish was the first vernacular language into which the *Malleus maleficarum* was translated in 1614, the peak of witchcraft prosecution in the Commonwealth occurred between 1650 and 1750, when trials were declining throughout much of the rest of Europe, apart from **Hungary**. The trials were confined to the Catholic west of Poland rather than the Orthodox east of the wider Commonwealth. It is not clear why the Polish trials peaked when and where they did, but it seems probable that the wars and economic problems that beset the country in the mid-17th century left a culture of fear and suspicion that sometimes resulted in witchcraft accusations.

See also CHRONOLOGY OF WITCH-HUNTING.

POPULAR MUSIC, WITCHCRAFT IN. Along with **Hoodoo**, **Voodoo**, **magic**, **Halloween**, and **werewolves**, witches and **witchcraft** have attracted popular musicians of all genres, from blues and jazz to folk, rockabilly, and rock. Kip Tyler's "She's My Witch" (1958), The Eagles' "Witchy Woman" (1972), and The Cult's "The Witch" (used on the soundtrack to the **film** *Buffy the Vampire Slayer*, 1992) are typical in presenting the witch mainly as a lover or an object of lust. In "Season of the Witch" (1966), Donovan used witchcraft as a metaphorical explanation for the apparent strangeness of society at the time. Kate Bush, in "Waking the Witch" (1986), and Queen of the Stone Age, in "Burn the Witch" (2005), deal with accusations of witchcraft, and the **executions** of witches. Other bands, like Black Sabbath, have a longer-standing association with the **devil**, witchcraft, **evil**, and hell, in the **art** on the covers of their albums as much as the lyrics of their songs. In popular legend, the American blues singer and musician Robert Johnson made a **pact** with the devil at a crossroads, selling his soul for mastery of a devil-tuned guitar.

POSSESSION, DEMONIC. Referring to cases where a **demon** or the **devil** has supposedly entered a person's body and taken control over physical actions and to some extent the mind and personality. Possession, and its near equivalent obsession, in which demons were thought to afflict people from outside of their bodies, was often associated with **witchcraft**. Witches were believed to be able to send demons to afflict people whom they wished to harm. In cases of possession, they often employed some item of bewitched food to convey the demonic spirit into the person. According to some authorities, apples were particularly useful for this sort of activity. In cases of obsession, the demon was sometimes thought to appear, visible only to the person it was afflicting, in the form of the witch herself. This formed the basis for some cases of **spectral evidence.**

During the Middle Ages, the church prescribed **exorcism** as a remedy for possession. The basis for the power of exorcism, as for possession itself, is found in the **Bible,** primarily the New Testament passages in Matthew 8:28–32, Mark 5:2–13, and Luke 8:27–33, in which Christ encounters a possessed man (or two possessed people in Matthew's account) and frees him by commanding the demons to enter a herd of swine, which then drowned themselves. In early Christianity, possession, and more so obsession, were often thought to be a sign of holiness. Much early Christian **demonology** was developed in the deserts of Egypt by hermit monks who frequently believed themselves to be assailed by, and in spiritual conflict, with demons. By the later Middle Ages and the early-modern period, possessed people were often thought to have been victims of witchcraft. Perhaps the most famous such case occurred in a convent in the French town of **Loudun,** where several nuns claimed to have been possessed because of the **sorcery** of a local priest. The charges were false and in fact were politically motivated, and the whole affair was a ruse, but the priest was, nevertheless, eventually burned at the stake. Another famous case linking possession to witchcraft occurred in **Salem,** Massachusetts, where a major **witch-hunt** began when several young girls began to exhibit signs of possession, obsession, and bewitchment.

Throughout the period of the witch-hunts, exorcism remained a common remedy for possession in Catholic lands, In Protestant countries, where the clergy had abandoned the formal rite of exorcism, people resorted to prayer. In addition, to free themselves from supposed demonic assault, people often turned to a variety of common spells and charms that could be acquired from **cunning men and women.** The causes of possession could vary, from outright deception as in the Loudun case, and possibly in the case of Salem as well, to real mental illness or dementia. Authorities did recognize that some cases of apparent possession might be caused by such factors, and many **skeptical** authorities, such as **Johann Weyer,** argued that many aspects of witchcraft and demonic activity were in fact signs of physical diseases and should be treated medically, not spiritually.

PRAETORIUS, JOHANNES (1630–1680). A **German** poet and prolific writer of collections of myths and fairy tales, Johannes Praetorius (a Latinized version of Hans Schulte, his name) published a compilation of **witchcraft** beliefs and stories, *Blockes-Berges Verrichtung* (Performance at the Blocksberg), in 1668. Set on and around the Blocksberg, now more commonly known as the **Brocken,** as the central meeting place of German witches, Praetorius brought together an encyclopedic knowledge of witchcraft beliefs from an eclectic mix of sources. He reported all the stereotypical activities associated with witches: **pacts** with the **devil**; **night flights**; **sabbaths**; harmful **sorcery**, or *maleficium*; **orgies** involving witches, the devil and **incubi and succubi**; changeling **children**; and shape-shifting. He also reported stories of ghosts and spirits as well a "furious army" of the dead similar to a **wild hunt**. His sources included believers and **skeptics**, Catholics and Protestants, ranging from **Heinrich Kramer** to **Johann Weyer** by way of **Johann Geiler von Kaysersberg**, **Ulrich Molitor**, **Jean Bodin**, and **Nicolas Rémy**.

As well as being an uncritical compendium of beliefs as they stood at the end of the witch-hunts, *Blockes-Berges Verrichtung* was illustrated with a highly developed scene of a witches' sabbath. Praetorius's work also influenced Johann Wolfgang von Goethe's depiction of the **Walpurgisnacht** scene in *Faust*.

See also ART, WITCHCRAFT IN; METAMORPHOSIS.

PRICKING. A method of detecting witches during the period of the major European **witch-hunts** was to prick the skin of suspects with a needle or some sharp object. Witches were often thought to have dead areas of skin that would not bleed and were insensitive to pain. Such an area of flesh was evidence of the **devil's mark**, a spot where the **devil** had branded the witch in his service. The process of pricking was especially humiliating because it required the suspected witch, usually a **woman**, to disrobe before authorities. Such marks were generally thought to be located on very private and thus easily concealed areas of the body, such as near genitalia, although they could be found anywhere and were even thought to move around the body.

PROTESTANT REFORMATION. *See* REFORMATION.

Q

QUIMBANDA. Practitioners of Quimbanda reject the overt Catholic influences on both **Macumba**, the syncretic religion from which Quimbanda emerged, and Umbanda, preferring instead to highlight its more **African** aspects. It is practiced in Brazil and is usually associated with elaborate rituals for the purposes of revenge or **love magic**. The use of marginal places and animal sacrifices, sometimes deliberately to harm others, makes it seem darker than other Afro-Brazilian religions and more akin to **witchcraft**.

See also SOUTH AMERICA, WITCHCRAFT IN.

R

REFORMATION. The Protestant and Catholic Counter-Reformations of the 16th century impacted on early-modern witch beliefs and **witch-hunting** in complex ways. The Protestant Reformation began in the early 16th century, when there were few witch-hunts of any consequence. Protestant leaders like **Martin Luther** and, later, **Jean Calvin** rejected many aspects of medieval theology and canon law, but they did not directly challenge the 15th-century concept of diabolical **witchcraft** or the **demonology** on which it rested. It was only from the mid-16th century that preachers and theologians, like **Lambert Daneau**, began to write specifically Protestant demonologies and treatises on witchcraft. Such Protestants were concerned about the power of the **devil** to assail human beings. It was this concern that drove the severe witch-hunts in Calvinist **Scotland** and Puritan **New England** and informed the writings of **King James VI**, **William Perkins**, and **Cotton Mather**, among others. Witch trials also occurred in Protestant territories where authorities encountered thriving pagan communities, as happened in the **Swedish** colonization of Finland.

There existed, however, a moderate Protestant view of witchcraft, expressed in the 16th century by **Johannes Weyer** and **Reginald Scot**, that was **skeptical** about the reality of witchcraft. This skepticism accounts for the relatively low rates of witchcraft prosecution in many parts of Protestant Europe.

The confessional strife that led to religious warfare across Europe contributed to the general feeling of crisis that sustained witch beliefs and witch-hunting. It was only in parts of **France** and the **German Empire**, however, where Catholics and Protestants lived in close proximity, that it contributed directly to witch persecution. The intense witch-hunts in early 17th-century Catholic **Eichstätt**, for example, were part of the prince-bishop's reform agenda. In other territories of Catholic Europe that avoided the direct political and social challenges of competing confessions, such as **Spain**, the prosecuting authorities remained skeptical about witchcraft, and witch-hunting continued to be mild, sporadic, or nonexistent.

RÉMY, NICOLAS (ca. 1530–1612). An important jurist and demonologist who claimed personally to have condemned over 900 witches in trials over a 10-year period in Lorraine, Rémy is the author of *Daemonolatria* (Demonolatry), first published in 1595. *Daemonolatria* became a major treatise on **witchcraft** and **demonology** in the early 17th century, ranking in importance with those of **Jean Bodin**, on whose work Rémy relied, and **Martín Del Rio**. The authority of Rémy's treatise was augmented by the author's extensive personal experience of witches and the conduct of witch trials.

Rémy was born into a family of lawyers in Charmes in the duchy of Lorraine, and studied law at the university in Toulouse. After serving in **France** from 1563 until 1570, he returned to Lorraine, where he soon became a privy councilor to the duke and later his attorney general. It was in this period that Rémy claimed to have sentenced over 900 witches, although this number cannot be confirmed from surviving records and he himself only mentions 128 witches by name. He seems to have become concerned about witchcraft in 1582, when his oldest son died only shortly after Rémy had refused alms to an old beggar **woman**. Convinced that she was a witch who had murdered his son, he put her on trial. As a judge and, from 1591, the attorney general in Lorraine, he was able to instigate further witch trials. In 1592, plague struck the city of Nancy, and Rémy left for his country estate, where he began composing the treatise based on his experiences. After he returned to the ducal court and during the career of his successor, his son Claude-Marcel, witch prosecution remained high in the duchy.

Daemonolatria is important for reasserting the power of **demons** through their **pacts** with witches, demonstrating the religious and secular reasons for persecuting witches, and insisting on the immunity of civic magistrates from acts of witchcraft, harmful **sorcery**, or *maleficium*, and even the temptations of demons.

RENAISSANCE. *See* HUMANISM.

RUSSIA, WITCHCRAFT IN. While several grand princes and tsars of early-modern Russia feared that they or their wives had been attacked by **witchcraft** and **magic**, there seem to have been no outbreaks of mass **witch-hunting** on the scale experienced in the **German Empire**, **France**, or even **England** and **Scotland**. In total, there were only about 500 cases of witchcraft prosecuted in the late 16th century and throughout the 17th and 18th centuries; these cases resulted in about 100 **executions**. The Russian Orthodox church did not develop a strong **demonology**, preferring to treat witchcraft and magic as **pagan** beliefs that required lesser punishments than execution. Secular witchcraft legislation was also weak and ambiguous. In general, accused witches in Russia tended to be **healers** or other types of **cun-**

ning men and women, or they exhibited criminal or disobedient behavior. Most Russian witches prosecuted before the courts were **male**, but the reasons for this are unclear. **Baba Yaga**, a **folkloric** witch, remains a popular figure in modern Russian culture.

See also LAWS AGAINST WITCHCRAFT, EUROPEAN.

S

SABBATH, WITCHES'. The idea that witches gathered together to worship the **devil** at a sabbath developed in the 15th century as **demonologists** began to argue that **witchcraft** was a **heresy** rather than an illusion and, like the heresy of the **Waldensians**, needed to be eradicated from Christian society. Although the sabbath did not feature in the most notorious witch-hunting manual, **Heinrich Kramer**'s *Malleus maleficarum* of about 1486, it became a commonplace of witchcraft confessions, and one of the most widely disseminated visual representations of the witchcraft heresy. In the most fully developed versions of the sabbath, such as those depicted in the illustrations to **Pierre de Lancre**'s *Tableau de l'inconstance de mauvais anges et démons* (Description of the Inconstancy of Evil Angels and Demons) of 1612 and **Johannes Praetorius**'s *Blockes-Berges Verrichtung* (Performance at the Blocksberg) of 1668, the God-given order of the world was turned totally upside down: the witches worshiped the **devil**, who sometimes appeared as a black **cat**, goat, or other animal, rather than God; they offered him the *osculum infame*, or **obscene kiss**, in place of the kiss of fealty, humility, or peace; they engaged in sexual **orgies** with each other and with **demons**; they murdered babies and young **children**, and **cannibalized** them or boiled their flesh and bones into magical powders or **ointments** with which they could practice harmful **sorcery**, or *maleficium*; they raised **storms** to destroy crops or people (like King **James VI** of **Scotland**); and they desecrated the Eucharist and other religious artifacts. They tended to arrive at night, flying to far-flung places like the Blocksberg (known now as the **Brocken**) in the Harz Mountains where a great sabbath was supposedly held annually on *Walpurgisnacht*; and they worshiped in numbers ranging from 10 or 20 to several thousand, rather than the consistent 13 of a **coven** (a number that has no historical basis).

Many elements of the sabbath derived from Christian propaganda that had been used against previous heretical groups, like the Waldensians, and also **Jews**. Once **Nicolau Eymeric** had provided the definitive theological argument that demonic **magic** necessarily entailed the worship of demons and must, therefore, be always heretical, the idea that there was a witch cult that worshiped in secret could evolve. The **Errores Gazariorum** (Errors of the Gazarii) referred to such gatherings of witches as *synagogues* and described them in horrible detail. By 1458, the inquisitor **Nicholas Jacquier** was using the term *sabbath* to describe them in his *Flagellum haereticorum fascinariorum* (Scourge of the Heretical Witches). As well as being influenced by these and other demonologies, the artists' depictions of sabbaths drew on the confessions of witches as they were reported in pamphlets and broadsheets. These confessions were usually forced out of the witch suspects by the persistent use of leading questions and **torture**. The confessions reinforced the demonologists' view that there was a witch sect that needed to be destroyed. In the process of their descriptions of the sabbaths, the alleged witches were therefore also forced to name the people they had seen at them. In this way, individual trials could escalate into **witch-hunts**.

The discrete elements of the sabbath, as it had been applied to all heretics by Christian demonologists, had their origins in earlier religious propaganda and spiritual practice. Early Christians had been accused by **pagan** Roman authorities, for example, of worshiping the head of a donkey. The idea of **night flight** may have derived from archaic **shamanistic** practices in which shamans traveled in a trance at night to engage in spirit battles to secure the fertility of the land for the forthcoming year. These practices are related to the **Wild Hunt**, and seem to have survived in the beliefs of groups like the *benandanti* of northern **Italy**.

The idea of night flight, which was essential to the concept of the sabbath, proved to be problematic for demonologists. The **canon** *Episcopi* stated that night flight, like the fact of witchcraft, was only an illusion caused by demons. For this reason, some **skeptical** authorities argued that the sabbath was only a diabolical illusion. Other demonologists reasoned that if witchcraft was real, then witches could easily use magic to fly to their gatherings on **brooms** or animals such as goats. They themselves could create an illusion to make it appear to their spouses that they were still asleep in their beds.

See also ART, WITCHCRAFT IN.

SAINT OSYTH WITCH TRIALS. In February 1582, in the port of Saint Osyth in Essex, **England**, the magistrate Brian Darcy began investigating accusations of **witchcraft** laid against Ursula Kemp, a local **healer** and **midwife**. This investigation soon led to others, and a minor witch panic broke out in the town and surrounding villages. At the end of the investigations, two **women**, Kemp and Elizabeth Bennett, were executed, four were reprieved, two were discharged, and two were acquitted. The only **male witch** accused was not tried. Darcy's investigations were reported in the lengthy pamphlet *A True and Just Record of the Information, Examination and Confession of all the Witches, taken at St. Osyth in the County of Essex* (1582) before the trials had been concluded. The pamphlet is remarkable for revealing Darcy's treatment of witchcraft as a *crimen exceptum*, or exceptional crime, and his reading of **Jean Bodin**'s *De la démonomanie des sorciers* (1580). Darcy presumed the guilt of the accused, threatened them with **execution** if they did not confess (which would not have been possible because he was not trying them, and he had no power to commute a sentence in English law), and allowed **spectral evidence** given by **children**. The fates of the witch suspects suggest that the local juries were **skeptical** of the veracity of the evidence in several cases. The Saint Osyth pamphlet, along with his knowledge of witch trials in Kent, provoked **Reginald Scot** to write his *Discoverie of Witchcraft* (1584). In 1921, two skeletons were discovered in Saint Osyth with rivets driven through their knees and elbows. The treatment of the corpses has given rise to the suggestion that these skeletons are those of Kemp and Bennett, but there is no other evidence to support it.

SALAZAR FRÍAS, ALONSO DE (ca. 1564–1635). A cleric and inquisitor in **Spain**, in 1609 Salazar Frías was appointed to the regional inquisitorial tribunal in Logroño in the Basque lands in northern Spain. Numerous witch trials had been conducted at Logroño, resulting in many hundreds of confessions and convictions. Salazar Frías, however, expressed considerable **skepticism** regarding the procedures used in these trials, and was gravely concerned that convictions were being obtained from inconclusive evidence and forced confessions. The *Suprema*, the central council of the Spanish **Inquisition** in Madrid, directed him to undertake an inspection of the courts throughout the region for which his tribunal was responsible. In an investigation in 1611 and 1612, he confirmed his suspicions that many witch trials were being conducted improperly. As a result of his report, the *Suprema* issued a directive to all inquisitorial tribunals throughout Spain, instructing them to enforce stricter procedures in witch trials conducted under their jurisdiction. This careful application of proper legal procedure helped to reduce significantly the number of witch trials, and especially the number of convictions and executions for **witchcraft**, in Spanish lands.

See also INQUISITORIAL PROCEDURE.

SALEM, WITCHCRAFT AT. The most severe, important, and certainly most famous case of **witch-hunting** in Colonial **North America** took place in the summer of 1692 at Salem, Massachusetts. The panic started when some young girls began to exhibit strange symptoms after playing at fortune telling, and ended with 19 people executed by hanging and one being pressed to death for refusing to enter a plea. Two more of the accused died while in jail, and a total of more than 100 people were imprisoned. Although witch trials were by no means unknown in New England in the 17th century, the events at Salem were extremely severe given the overall size of the population involved. The 19 **executions** constituted well over half of all executions for **witchcraft** in the New England colonies for the entire century.

This major outbreak of witch-hunting began when several girls, including the daughter of the minister of Salem Village, Samuel Parris, began to play at **divination**, trying to learn the identities of their future husbands. Shortly thereafter they began to exhibit nervous symptoms that the people of Salem took to be evidence of demonic **possession** and bewitchment. The symptoms grew worse and spread to other girls and young **women**. Under questioning, the girls accused three women—Sarah Goode, Sarah Osborne, and a West Indian slave named Tituba—of having bewitched them. Goode and Osborne denied the charges, but Tituba, for reasons unknown, confessed to having dealings with the devil. In the wake of this confession, fear grew and accusations multiplied, spreading from Salem Village to the larger Salem Town and coming to the attention of clergy in Boston, where **Cotton Mather** and other leading ministers debated the matter. They expressed caution and the need for reliable evidence. Mather was especially concerned about the reliance on **spectral evidence**, in which victims claimed to have seen the spectral shape of a witch, invisible to others, tormenting them. Nevertheless, these ministers did nothing to halt the trials and in fact encouraged local authorities to root out all potential witches. The first execution took place on 10 June 1692, and the last on 22 September.

After the executions, however, the severity of the hunt created a backlash. Many people became concerned about the use of evidence in the trials, and **skepticism** about the girls' initial accusations grew. Ultimately, even **Increase Mather**, the father of Cotton Mather, preached the need for restraint in witch trials arguing that it was better for a true witch to go free than for an innocent person to be killed. Because of this backlash, the trials at Salem effectively marked the end of witch-hunting in New England.

See also STAMFORD WITCHES.

SAMHAIN. Now a religious festival of darkness or the dead in the calendars of some branches of modern **witchcraft**, or **Wicca**, and **neo-paganism**, Samhain was originally a Celtic festival celebrating the end of harvest and the beginning of winter. Its **pagan** origins are unclear, but by the eighth century it had become associated with the Christian All Saints' Eve, or **Halloween**, a time of year when people in parts of the Celtic world dressed up in disguise, made candle lanterns from turnips, and played pranks on neighbors. These activities and the association with the dead continue in the modern celebration of Halloween.

SANDERS, ALEX (1926–1988). The self-proclaimed "King of the Witches," Alex Sanders was an important figure in the early development of modern **witchcraft**, or **Wicca**, in **England**. He founded the so-called Alexandrian tradition of witchcraft, which differed from the Gardnerian tradition derived from the founder of modern witchcraft, **Gerald Gardner**.

According to Sanders' own account, his grandmother was a hereditary witch, that is, one whose knowledge of witchcraft had been passed down through her family. When he was seven, she initiated him into the ancient religion of the witches. His later writings on witchcraft, however, reveal the strong influence of the works of Gerald Gardner and others in the Gardnerian tradition. Sanders claimed that these similarities were because Gardner himself had taken many elements from hereditary witchcraft, and he, Sanders, actually represented a more genuine tradition. Sanders sought publicity to an even greater extent than Gardner did, and he helped to generate much media interest in Wicca in the late 1960s and 1970s. Although Alexandrian witchcraft is rather clearly derived from the original Gardnerian tradition, Sanders introduced some important new elements. He stressed ritual **magic** much more than Gardner did, and developed more formal and elaborate rites. Some have referred to the Alexandrian tradition as "high church" witchcraft.

SANTERÍA. Like **Voodoo** and **Macumba**, Santería is a syncretistic religion in which West **African** spirits and deities have been assimilated with Roman Catholic saints and other religious figures. Santería developed first among African slaves brought to the Americas and forced to convert to Catholicism. The religion is now widespread in many parts of Latin America and also in **North American** cities with large Hispanic populations. Many people see no conflict or difficulty in practicing Santería and Catholicism together. In Santería, deities are known as *orishas*. They are powerful and sometimes capricious in nature. The sacrifice of animals to the *orishas* is a major element of the religion. Typical sacrifices include chickens and roosters, pigeons and doves, and even goats and pigs. **Cats** and dogs are often rumored to be used when casting harmful spells. In the United States, this practice arouses strong opposition from people who suspect that these animals are tortured before they are killed, or who fear that pets might be stolen for sacrifice.

Santería is infused with magical practices, including **divination**, and priests communicate with ancestors and deities by means of a **shaman**-like trance. The *orishas* can be propitiated to **heal** illness, to provide good luck, to incite **love**, or for many other positive purposes. Practitioners of harmful **magic** or **witchcraft** supposedly also exist, however. These people are often known as *mayomberos* or "black witches." They are creatures who frequent graveyards and often employ body parts of dead bodies in their spells. The principal tool of the *mayomberos* is a magical **cauldron** known as a *nganga*, in which such parts can be mixed with other magical ingredients. Like the witches described by European **demonologists** during the **witch-hunts,** *mayomberos* are often considered to be in league with the **devil.**

See also CARIBBEAN WITCHCRAFT.

SATANISM. In broad terms, Satanism is simply the worship of Satan, one of many names ascribed to the Christian **devil**, and it has long been associated with **witchcraft**. It did, however, gain a more specific meaning as a coherent system of beliefs in the 20th century. In the medieval and early-modern periods, many Christian authorities believed that all witches were in league with the devil, whether or not they were **skeptical** of the reality of witchcraft. The illusions described in the early-medieval **canon** *Episcopi* could only occur because the witches had turned away from God and been tempted and deluded by the devil. The witches persecuted at the time of great **witch-hunts**, on the other hand, were believed to have been taught their harmful **sorcery**, or *maleficium*, after making **pacts** with, and actively worshiping, the devil at their secret, nocturnal **sabbaths**. In doing so, they were guilty of **heresy**, **idolatry**, and **apostasy**. The witches' confessions drawn out under leading questions and **torture** only served to reinforce this belief among witch-hunters. There is, however, no evidence that any large, organized Satanic group existed until recent times.

In the modern period, Satanism is still sometimes used to refer to the supposed worship of the Christian devil. Allegations of the existence of Satanist groups worshiping the devil through animal or human sacrifice, and other activities, occur regularly throughout the Western world. Many of the activities detailed in such allegations—secret gatherings of a conspiratorial cult worshiping the devil, performing obscene rites and engaging in sexual **orgies**, and harming or murdering **children**—are reminiscent of historical accusations of witchcraft. No credible evidence has ever been uncovered, however, that any such large, organized form of Satanism really exists.

Modern Satanism can also refer to actual, organized, and open Satanist groups, the largest and most famous of which is the **Church of Satan**, founded in San Francisco in the 1960s. These groups, however, do not really worship Satan in the sense of the **evil**, immoral Christian devil. Rather, such groups reject the Christian moral structure entirely and replace it with the principles of personal freedom, individuality, and pleasure (often specifically carnal pleasure), which they believe Christianity has wrongly condemned and associated with evil. Such groups adhere to their own strict, although non-Christian, moral code, and absolutely forbid the use of animal, let alone human, sacrifice or any form of nonconsensual sexual activity, such as the sexual molestation of children.

Although modern witches are sometimes accused of some aspects of Satanism, devil-worship and the myths surrounding it are antithetical to modern witchcraft, or **Wicca**. While modern Satanists and Wiccans share a rejection of Christianity and both practice and believe in the real efficacy of some forms of **magic**, they do not have anything to do with one another, and indeed the two groups generally have little respect for one another. It may be that the extreme hedonism of modern, organized Satanism accounts for its relatively small size when compared with the larger and growing Wiccan traditions.

See also PENTAGRAM.

SCOT, MICHAEL (ca. 1175–1235). A scholar in the service of the **German** emperor Frederick II, Scot was interested in **magic** and occult learning, especially in systems of **astrology**. He devised categories of permissible and impermissible magic and **divination**, and he wrote about and described methods of demonic invocation, although he was careful to condemn such practices. Despite this care, he developed a dark reputation as a powerful demonic sorcerer, something that often developed around medieval scholars with interests in the occult.

SCOT, REGINALD (1538–1599). One of the earliest and fullest skeptics of **witchcraft**, Scot published his *Discoverie of Witchcraft* in 1584. It was at the time one of only a handful of books written on the subject in the English language. Scot's background and life are obscure. Although he attended Oxford University, he did not stay to receive his degree, and lived mostly in the manner to which he was born as a country gentleman in Kent. His interest in witchcraft seems to have been a reaction to the witch trials he witnessed in his home county and the pamphlet report of the witchcraft investigations in **Saint Osyth** in Essex. His attack on the work of **Jean Bodin** and the apparent rejection of the spirit world in the *Discoverie* suggest that he may also have been provoked by a spiritual outlook often associated with the Family of Love.

In his *Discoverie*, Scot went beyond mere criticism of the procedures and methods of witch trials, to which many other critics of **witch-hunting** limited themselves both before and after him. Instead, he attacked the very basis of the idea of witchcraft: the witches' **pact** with the **devil** in exchange for the ability to perform demonic **sorcery**. Using new translations of the **Bible**, Scot maintained that the devil had no real power in the physical world, and so even those who truly believed themselves to be witches were incapable of performing any of the acts for which they were held guilty. In fact, Scot felt that most people convicted for witchcraft were either entirely innocent victims of local prejudices against the elderly or trial procedures, especially the use of **torture**, that virtually guaranteed conviction, or they were senile or deluded in some way. There were some witches, he maintained, who did work real harm, but they did so through natural means such as **poison** and not through supernatural demonic powers. He also observed that there were some frauds who claimed to have supernatural power for their own gain. In his **skepticism**, and especially his arguments about possible natural and especially medical causes for witchcraft, he was influenced by another skeptical writer, **Johann Weyer**.

Scot's *Discoverie* was attacked by **King James VI** of **Scotland** in his *Daemonologie* (1597) and other contemporaries like **William Perkins**. One of James's first acts on acceding to throne of **England** was to have Scot's book burned by the public executioner. The *Discoverie* did not reappear until 1651, but its very publication suggests that Scot's skeptical view had some support in England.

SCOTLAND, WITCHCRAFT IN. Until the Witchcraft Act of 1563, **witchcraft** was a sin dealt with solely by the Kirk (Church) in Scotland. The Witchcraft Act did not, however, provoke a witch panic. It was only in the 1590s that the first major outbreak of **witch-hunting** occurred in the country. The **North Berwick Witches**, as they have become known, were accused of various acts of harmful **sorcery**, or *maleficium*, in 1591, notably creating **storms**, allegedly as part of a seditious plot to kill the king, **James VI**, on his way back from Denmark with his new queen. Although indifferent or **skeptical** at first, James was persuaded that there was a plot, and, through the use of **torture** and special commissions, witch-hunting was allowed to continue for the next few years. James based his *Daemonologie* (1597) on the North Berwick episode. At the time of the Restoration of Charles II as king of **England**, **Ireland**, and Scotland in 1660, witch-hunting re-emerged. In the peak years of 1661 and 1662, about 300 witches were **executed** in Scotland. Many of these witches had been identified by professional witch **prickers**, 10 of whom were later prosecuted for fraud. As elsewhere in the British Isles, belief in witchcraft, **magical healing**, and similar practices continued despite the repeal of witchcraft legislation in 1736.

See also LAWS AGAINST WITCHCRAFT, EUROPEAN.

SEXUALITY AND WITCHCRAFT. Historically, **witchcraft** has always been viewed as a highly sexually charged act. Throughout the era of the great **witch-hunts**, witches were commonly thought to engage in sexual activity with **demons** in the form of **incubi and succubi**. Sexual **orgies** were a centerpiece of the witches' **sabbath**, and as a sign of their subservience and degradation, witches were often thought to have sex with the **devil** himself. Many authorities, notably **Heinrich Kramer** in the *Malleus maleficarum* (ca. 1486), considered that sexual lust and the desire for carnal pleasures were among the chief reasons people became witches, and this was also thought to be one of the reasons why far more **women** became witches than men. Women were generally considered to be weaker than men, driven more by their appetites and lusts, and far more susceptible to carnal temptations. Sexual relations with demons or the devil were not, however, thought to be pleasurable in most cases, and the sexual organs of these creatures were generally described as being as cold as ice. Sexuality also plays an important role in modern witchcraft, or **Wicca**, although here in an entirely positive way. Much Wiccan belief centers on aspects of natural fertility, and sexual energy, properly channeled, is thought to play an important part in many magical rituals.

See also MALE WITCHES.

SHAMANISM. An aspect of many ancient religious systems, shamanism describes a variety of practices in which individuals enter an ecstatic state and believe that they are able to encounter and interact with spirits and spiritual forces. In recent years, increasing evidence has been uncovered linking certain aspects of historical **witchcraft** to shamanism. The elements of **night flight** and communion with spiritual forces that characterized the witches' **sabbath** were at least partly grounded in recollections of older religious beliefs and practices—the Roman **Bacchanalia** festivities or the Germanic concept of the **Wild Hunt**, for example—that were probably themselves rooted in archaic shamanistic practices. The most famous example of shamanistic practices interacting with Christian notions of witchcraft was the case of the Italian ***benandanti***. In the modern period, practitioners of modern witchcraft, or **Wicca**, and other forms of **neo-paganism** sometimes incorporate aspects of shamanism into their beliefs and rituals.

SHTRIGA. In Albanian **folklore**, a *shtriga* is a **vampiric** witch who attacks **children**, often because she cannot bear them herself. As the name suggests the *shtriga* is a descendant of the ancient **strix**, but she also shares characteristics with similar female creatures in other cultures, such as **Baba Yaga**, **Ole Higue**, and **Penanggal**. A *shtriga* sucks the blood of infants while they sleep at night and then leaves as a flying insect. She is also believed to possess the **evil eye**. Salt, garlic, and a strong belief in God are among the means of protecting oneself from the *shtriga*. She can be captured and killed at the threshold of a house.

SIMON MAGUS. In the **Bible**, the most famous magician in the New Testament is Simon Magus of Samaria, who is described encountering Peter and John, the apostles of Christ, in Acts 8:9–24. When Simon sees that they can bestow the spirit of God on someone by laying on their hands, he offers them money to receive this power, but Peter refuses him and urges him to pray for forgiveness. In apocryphal biblical literature, the rivalry between Simon Magus and the apostle Peter, also called Simon Peter, was amplified. In the so-called Acts of Peter, for example, Simon uses his **magic** to simulate bringing a dead man back to life, but only Peter is able truly to revive him. Then Simon announces that he will fly up to heaven, but at a word from Peter, he comes crashing to the earth. Later medieval commentators made clear that Simon Magus was being borne aloft by **demons** that Peter was able to dispel. In the Middle Ages, Simon Magus became the archetype of the demonic magician or necromancer. Because ideas about **necromancy** served as an important basis for later notions of diabolical **witchcraft**, he also became a warning to alleged practitioners of harmful **sorcery**, or *maleficium*.

SKEPTICISM. Witchcraft beliefs were never uniform across Europe, and there were always people, including theologians, lawyers, judges, and physicians, who were skeptical of elements of the witch stereotype, the conduct of witch trials, or even the entire concept of witchcraft. Following the tradition of the early **canon** *Episcopi*, which stated that **night flight** was only a delusion caused by the **devil**, some authorities doubted the reality of this and other aspects of witchcraft. **Ulrich Molitor**, for example, believed that the large gatherings of witches, known as **sabbaths**, must also be a delusion. This form of skepticism had little effect on the overall course of **witchhunting** because people could still be condemned for believing that they had engaged in diabolical worship and other activities at the sabbath, even if these were considered to be only illusory.

A second form of early skepticism was medical or scientific in tone. In his *De occulta philosophia* (1531 and 1533), **Agrippa von Nettesheim** argued that the witches' beliefs resulted from their senility. His pupil, **Johann Weyer**, expanded on this view in *De praestigiis daemonum* (On the Tricks of Devils, 1563), diagnosing both the witches' beliefs and the illnesses attributed to their harmful **sorcery**, or *maleficium*, as disorders of the humors in the body. Humoral theory was the basis of medicine at this time, and Weyer's diagnoses were therefore natural. Weyer also argued that demonologists had mistranslated and misinterpreted the **biblical** words and stories, such as the **Witch of Endor**, commonly associated with witchcraft. While Weyer's medical and philological arguments influenced **Reginald Scot** in the 1580s, **Joseph Glanvill**, one of the early fellows of the Royal Society in the late 17th century, could still attempt to prove scientifically the existence of witchcraft and the spirit world.

Legal skepticism focused on the procedures of witch trials, especially the unrestricted use of **torture** in many areas. Agrippa, the Spanish inquisitor **Alonso de Salazar Frías**, and the German Jesuit **Friedrich Spee** all argued that leading questions and torture could end in the conviction and **execution** of innocent people and the escalation of small-scale trials into witch-hunts. Of these, only Salazar Frías had the most direct influence on the course of witchcraft prosecution, and very few witches were executed in **Spain** and its territories after 1612. Spee was not so successful, but his contemporaries, like his fellow Jesuit **Adam Tanner**, were soon able to help curtail witch persecution in **Germany**. Even some advocates of witch-hunting, such as **Increase Mather** after the **Salem** witch trials of 1692, were forced to advise against witch prosecution in order to prevent the further loss of innocent life.

Of course, there were always some people who were fully skeptical of the reality of witchcraft. Later authorities, including **Balthasar Bekker**, **Francis Hutchinson**, and **Christian Thomasius**, developed the work of Weyer and Scot, denying that the devil had extensive power over the physical world or that human beings could enter into **pacts** with **demons**. They thus undermined the very foundations of the idea of witchcraft as it was conceived in medieval and early-modern Europe. Throughout the period of the witch-hunts, such thinkers were a decided minority and often themselves faced persecution because of their more liberal ideas, although the witchcraft depicted in much **art** and in **plays**, as well as the tendency for juries to acquit witch suspects in **England**, suggests that skepticism at a popular level could always be expressed. By the end of the 17th century, however, and certainly by the time of the **Bavarian War of the Witches** in the 1760s, the full skeptical views prevailed among most learned commentators.

See also HOBBES, THOMAS (1588–1679); LOOS, CORNELIUS (1546–1593); MALEBRANCHE, NICOLAS (1638–1715); MONTAIGNE, MICHEL DE (1533–1595); PARACELSUS (PHILIPPUS AUREOLUS THEOPHRASTUS BOMBAST VON HOHENHEIM) (1493–1541).

SORCERY. The term *sorcery* is frequently used as a synonym or near synonym for **magic** or **witchcraft**. While the meanings of these words are often vague and certainly overlap, some distinctions can be drawn. First, *sorcery* is often used to describe low magic, that is, common or unlearned magic. Sorcery is supposedly performed by simple words and actions, whereas forms of high or learned magic are supposedly performed by complex and highly ritualized verbal formulas and ceremonies. In Europe during the medieval and early-modern periods, complex, ritualized demonic magic was often termed *necromancy* and was thought to be quite distinct from common sorcery or witchcraft. Sorcery can also carry implications of negative or harmful magic. In this sense, of connoting simple (or low) and harmful magic, the term *sorcery* is very close to the term *witchcraft*. It is worth noting that the English word *sorcery* derives from the French *sorcellerie*, which means both sorcery and witchcraft. Likewise, the common Latin term to describe harmful sorcery during the Middle Ages and early-modern period, *maleficium*, also came to mean *witchcraft*.

Nevertheless, the concept of sorcery can be usefully distinguished from witchcraft in several ways. First, *sorcery* does not always carry the connotation of negative or harmful magic. The term can sometimes be used to describe positive forms of magic, such as **magical healing** or magical means of prognostication and **divination**. Some scholars, notably anthropologists studying **African witchcraft**, have distinguished sorcery from witchcraft by arguing that sorcery involves certain performed actions (spoken words or gestures) along with the use of certain material objects to obtain desired supernatural effects while witchcraft draws on some inherent power found in the witch herself. Under this definition, anyone can learn to be a sorcerer, but one must be born a witch. This distinction, while useful when applied to African and other societies, is not as helpful when applied to medieval or early-modern Europe. During the period of the great **witch-hunts**, witches were believed actively to learn how to perform witchcraft from **demons** or from the **devil**, and anyone could become a witch. But witches were also regarded as being in certain ways inherently **evil** and corrupt because of the **pacts** they made with the devil and their **apostasy** from the true faith.

SOUCOUYANT. A witch **vampire** of the **Caribbean**, notably Trinidad and Guadeloupe, the soucouyant is very much like **Ole Higue** and **Loogaroo**. She lives as an old **woman** by day, but sheds her skin at night, turning into a fireball as she goes out in search of blood. She can enter homes through any small aperture, such as a keyhole or crack. An unfortunate victim can turn into a soucouyant herself if too much blood is taken, or she might die. In a transaction that mirrors the making of the **devil's mark** in early-modern **demonology**, the soucouyant uses the blood to buy magical powers from a **devil**. Like Ole Higue, a soucouyant can be captured by distracting her with the compulsion to count grains of rice. The rice is left at night at a house or a crossroads. The soucouyant's skin is said to be prized because it is a potent ingredient in black **magic**.

SOUTH AMERICA, WITCHCRAFT IN. Little is currently known about witchcraft beliefs in South and Central America before the European conquests. As the colonies of **Spain** and Portugal became more settled, church and secular authorities began to take more of an interest in the spiritual beliefs of the mixed populations of indigenous Amerindians, European settlers, and **African** slaves. **Witchcraft** and **sorcery** were treated as superstitions, in line with the generally **skeptical** attitude of the Spanish and Portuguese **Inquisitions** that reserved jurisdiction over such cases through their local tribunals or officials. In New Spain, witchcraft seems to have been treated harshly until the institution of the Mexican Inquisition in 1571. The treatment of witchcraft was also more lenient in New Granada and Peru after the Cartagena Inquisition was established in 1610. Amerindians were excluded from the jurisdiction of the Spanish tribunals because they were not Christian. In Brazil, witchcraft barely featured among the cases referred to the Inquisition in Lisbon, Portugal. The superstitions encountered by the inquisitors tended to involve **love magic** and **magical healing**, often using the sacramentals and prayers of the church, performed by the poor or slaves. There seems also to have been a confusion of local beliefs for stereotypical European ones by some colonists, and a degree of syncretism among practitioners of magic. Such practitioners were, however, usually given light sentences, such as scourging. The mix of different peoples in this part of the New World led to the evolution of more clearly defined syncretic religions such as **Santería**, **Quimbanda**, and **Macumba**.

SPAIN, WITCHCRAFT IN. There were few **witchcraft** trials or **executions** in Spain at the height of the great **witch-hunts**, and most of these took place in local jurisdictions. Generally, however, witchcraft was prosecuted by the more cautious Spanish **Inquisition**, especially after **Alonso de Salazar Frías**'s investigation into the **Basque witch trials** of 1609. It regarded witchcraft more as a superstition along the **skeptical** lines described in the 10th-century **canon** *Episcopi* than a **heresy**. Such superstitions needed to be corrected, but not treated as a *crimen exceptum* (exceptional crime), which would have allowed inquisitors to relax their rules on the use of **torture**, or punished severely. The Inquisition observed this cautious approach in the Spanish colonial territories in **South America**. A skeptical attitude toward witchcraft can also be found in the early Spanish novel *La Celestina* and the work of the artist **Francisco de Goya**.

See also ART, WITCHCRAFT IN; FICTION, WITCHCRAFT IN.

SPANISH INQUISITION. *See* INQUISITION.

SPECTRAL EVIDENCE. Given the inherent secrecy in all aspects of the crime of **witchcraft**, finding substantial evidence on which convictions could be based was always a problem for authorities. The best evidence, of course, was the confession of the accused themselves, usually obtained through **torture**. Another possible form of evidence, however, was spectral evidence, in which other people testified to having seen the spectral image of the witch. Such evidence might be supplied by another accused witch, who would testify to having seen someone in attendance at a witches' **sabbath** (many authorities maintained that witches traveled to sabbaths only in spirit), or by victims who would testify to having seen the form of a witch tormenting them. Many authorities argued that, although these specters might not be the witch herself, God would never allow the **devil** or a **demon** to impersonate an innocent person while working **evil**. Others, however, were very **skeptical** of such testimony, and throughout the period of the **witch-hunts**, spectral evidence was never generally held to be as reliable as a confession. Perhaps the most famous case of spectral evidence occurred at **Salem**, Massachusetts, where a number of young girls who exhibited symptoms of **possession** testified that they were often tormented by witches in spectral forms that only they could see.

SPEE, FRIEDRICH (1591–1635). A **German** Jesuit, lyricist, and poet, Friedrich Spee became an important opponent of witch prosecution after holding the position of confessor to convicted witches during the intense **witch-hunt** in **Würzburg** in the early 17th century. He published his criticisms of popular superstitions and the excessive use of **torture** by judges in *Cautio criminalis seu de processibus contra sagas liber* (A Warning on Criminal Justice, or A Book on Witch Trials) in 1631. By 1660, the *Cautio criminalis* was circulating widely, having been translated into German, Dutch and French.

Spee was born in Kaiserswerth in the Rhineland and attended the Jesuit college in nearby Cologne. He entered the Jesuit order in 1611 and then studied at Würzburg and Mainz. In 1627, he returned to Würzburg as a professor of theology, just before persecution peaked in the territory. At this time, he began hearing the confessions of the condemned witches in prison and soon became fully convinced that most, if not all, were innocent of the crimes for which they were **executed**. Rather, they had succumbed to the excessive use of **torture**, permitted because **witchcraft** was considered a *crimen exceptum*. Spee also recognized that witch trials were often reactions to popular superstitious clamorings for action against witches, and that the use of torture to find out the names of the suspects' accomplices who had attended events like the witches' **sabbaths** only served to increase and perpetuate witch-hunting.

Spee published *Cautio criminalis* anonymously, but his authorship of the work was widely known in Jesuit and other learned circles. Although he did not deny the power of **demons** and the **devil** or the reality of witchcraft, his **skepticism** aroused opposition in many parts of Germany. Spee's work, like that of **Adam Tanner**, did, however, influence a new generation of Jesuits at the college in Ingolstadt to adopt a more skeptical attitude toward the subject than their older colleagues, who had advised the dukes of **Bavaria** and the prince-bishops of **Eichstätt** on the persecution of the alleged witch sect.

SPINA, ALFONSO DE (ca. 1420–1491). A Franciscan friar who converted from Judaism, Alfonso de Spina was a theologian at the university at Salamanca, and was personal confessor to King Juan II of Castile. Just prior to his death, he was appointed bishop of Thermopolis. Around 1459, he wrote a treatise entitled *Fortalicium fidei* (Fortress of the Faith), in which he discussed various threats to the faith, including **heretics, Jews,** Saracens, and **demons.** In the section on demons, he also discussed **witchcraft,** broadly following the **skepticism** of the earlier **canon *Episcopi*.** Although Alfonso de Spina was not the first clerical authority to describe witchcraft in the 15th century, and his treatment of this subject was more moderate than some, his work, printed in the 1460s, became the first published treatise to deal with the subject.

SPINA, BARTOLOMEO DELLA (ca. 1475–1546). A prominent Dominican friar and theologian, Spina studied in Bologna and Padua. He eventually became Master of the Sacred Palace in Rome, the chief theologian to the pope, and he was appointed by Pope Paul III to consider the important theological questions raised at the Council of Trent. He wrote three short works arguing for the reality of **witchcraft** and the real danger that witches represented. His major work in this area was his *Questio de strigibus* (Concerning Witches), published in 1523. Spina is important in **demonology** for his attempt to discredit the authority of the **canon *Episcopi*,** in which witchcraft is described as a delusion, and promote the **witch-hunting** manual *Malleus maleficarum* (Hammer of Witches), written by **Heinrich Kramer** in about 1486.

SPRENGER, JAKOB (ca. 1436/38–1495). Traditionally listed as one of the authors of the infamous late-medieval **witch-hunting** manual *Malleus maleficarum* (Hammer of Witches), Sprenger was a Dominican friar, theologian, and papal inquisitor active in the **German Empire** in the later 15th century. He was born in or around the city of Basel and studied in Cologne, where in 1475 he received his doctorate in theology. He then taught and served in several offices at the university in Cologne. He was also an important figure within the Dominican order. In 1472, he became prior of the Dominicans in Cologne, an office he held until 1482, when he was relieved in order to be able to undertake other duties as a papal inquisitor. From 1481, he conducted numerous **inquisitions** into **heresy** and **witchcraft** in the Rhineland, and later more generally across southern Germany. In this capacity, he worked with **Heinrich Kramer,** and it was to these two inquisitors specifically that **Pope Innocent VIII** directed his bull *Summis desiderantes affectibus,* ordering all local authorities to assist them in their pursuit of witches. In 1488, Sprenger was named to the office of provincial of the Dominican province of Teutonia, a position second only to the master general of the entire order in that region.

Although he is typically listed as an author, along with Heinrich Kramer, of the *Malleus maleficarum*, there is much evidence to suggest that Sprenger had little or nothing to do with the writing of this treatise on witchcraft. The strongest piece of evidence, only discovered in 1972, is a letter written by Sprenger's successor in the office of prior in Cologne, Servatius Fanckel. Fanckel knew Sprenger well and explicitly stated that he was in no way involved in writing the *Malleus*. Because Fanckel was, in fact, an admirer of that work, there is no reason to suppose that he had any motive to downplay any actual involvement Sprenger might have had. It seems likely that Sprenger's identification as the author of the *Malleus* arose because of his association with Kramer. As Sprenger's reputation as a theologian and prominent Dominican was greater than Kramer's, the addition of his name to the work could only add to its authority.

STAMFORD WITCHES. At the same time as the major **witch-hunt** in **Salem**, Massachusetts, was occurring, a smaller panic occurred in Stamford, Connecticut, leading to much different results. In the spring of 1692, a servant girl named Katherine Branch began to suffer from fits, and she accused a respected local matron, Elizabeth Clauson, of bewitching her. Eventually, five other local people were implicated as well. One fled to neighboring New York, and three others were quickly cleared of all charges. Clauson and another woman, Mercy Disborough, came under more severe scrutiny, but eventually Clauson was freed. Disborough was convicted and sentenced to death, but was later reprieved. Unlike in Salem, at Stamford authorities were **skeptical** of the accusations from the start, and no large panic ever developed within the community as a whole.

See also NORTH AMERICA, WITCHCRAFT IN.

STARHAWK (1951–). An important figure in modern **witchcraft**, also known as **Wicca**, Starhawk is an American witch, **feminist**, peace activist, and author. She has dedicated most of her life to teaching, developing rituals, working within various organizations, and spreading knowledge of Wicca and of **neo-paganism** more generally to as broad an audience as possible. Her most important work is her book *The Spiral Dance*, a reflection on and statement of Wiccan principles, practices, and beliefs. The book, originally published in 1979, the same year as **Margot Adler**'s influential *Drawing Down the Moon*, has been reissued in 10th- and 20th-anniversary editions.

Born into a Jewish family, Starhawk was raised in a strongly religious household and by her own assessment was a devoutly religious child. As she grew, however, she became deeply concerned with what she saw as the severely limited role allowed to **women** in traditional Judaism. Already by the time she entered college at the University of California at Los Angeles (UCLA), she had been exposed to various forms of neo-pagan beliefs and felt herself drawn toward this form of religiosity. While in college, she was exposed more fully to Wicca. She was attracted especially to the religion's focus on worship of the **Goddess** and to the elevated place it allowed to women. Upon graduating, she briefly entered UCLA's film school, but soon set about writing and traveling. Eventually, she began work on what would become *The Spiral Dance*, an account of Wiccan pseudo-history, beliefs, and practices. Starhawk's lyrical and evocative writing seemed to capture the essence of Wiccan religiosity, highlighting especially the compatibility of Wicca with feminist and environmentalist concerns. The success of her book helped to spark a surge in the overall success of Wicca as a growing religious movement. The book became an essential Wiccan text, supplanting to some degree the writings of the founder of modern witchcraft, **Gerald Gardner**, especially in America, where feminist and environmentalist elements within Wicca were more developed than in Great Britain and elsewhere.

Starhawk herself eschews any "authoritative" role in the Wiccan or larger neo-pagan traditions. Although she has been a member of several groups and covens, she has also developed and practiced her beliefs alone. Much of her knowledge and inspiration, she claims, comes from her own dreams and trance experiences. She adheres to most of the standard elements of the Wiccan tradition, however, as developed by Gerald Gardner and others. She is particularly credulous of the claim that modern witchcraft is a direct descendant of historical European witchcraft, which was supposedly an ancient, pre-Christian fertility religion, demonized and brutally persecuted by the Christian church (in *The Spiral Dance*, she originally claimed that around 9,000,000 people were executed for witchcraft in medieval and early-modern Europe, although in later editions she has been forced to admit that this figure is "probably high"). This interpretation of historical witchcraft was largely developed in the late-19th and early-20th centuries, most famously by the British Egyptologist and amateur anthropologist **Margaret Murray**. Murray's theories have since been completely discredited, and many modern witches now maintain that their religion is not a direct survival of ancient **pagan** beliefs, but rather a deliberate recreation of imagined forms of ancient religion. Starhawk herself, in later editions of *The Spiral Dance*, argues that Wiccan beliefs are not dependent on any real historical tradition for their validity. Nevertheless, she does persist in maintaining that the supposed history of the Wiccan faith as a truly ancient pagan religion is essentially true, if not accurate in all details.

STORMS AND STORM-RAISING. Affecting the weather and raising destructive storms was believed to be a common element of harmful **sorcery,** or *maleficium,* in Europe throughout the medieval and early-modern periods, and is a standard element of harmful **magic** around the world. Such weather magic was deemed particularly appropriate to witches and other demonic sorcerers by Christian authorities because, in Christian theology, **demons** were spiritual, airy creatures and could easily manipulate the element of air. The very earliest sources on **witchcraft** describe witches raising storms, especially lightning and hail, which could easily destroy crops and cause widespread damage to property across entire regions. The early authority **Johannes Nider** gave an account of a witch performing a demonic invocation and then having the demon raise a storm with lightning and hail, and the *Errores Gazariorum* (Errors of the Gazarii), another early source, described witches flying high into the Alps to chip off large blocks of ice from the mountains. They then let this ice fall as hail. One of the most famous examples of weather-working witchcraft came in the case of the **North Berwick Witches,** who supposedly raised several storms at sea in order to drown the **Scottish** king **James VI.**

STRAPPADO. One of the most common means of **torture** used on witches and others in the later Middle Ages and early-modern period was the strappado (from the Latin *strappare,* to pull). The wrists of a prisoner were bound behind his or her back with a rope attached to a pulley. He was then hoisted in the air. Often weights were attached to the prisoner's feet to increase the weight on the arms and shoulders, which frequently dislocated, causing extreme pain. The prisoner was then left hanging in this position while being interrogated by authorities. To increase the pain, the prisoner could be raised to a significant height and then dropped suddenly to within a few inches of the floor, exerting tremendous, sudden pressure on the arms and shoulders. In **Eichstätt,** at the request of the interrogators, the executioner would sometimes lift and drop a witch suspect a number of times in succession in what the scribe recorded as "rabbit jumps." The excessive and persistent use of the strappado only occurred in cases in territories where **witchcraft** was treated as a *crimen exceptum.*

STRIX (STRIGA). In classical mythology, *striges* (the plural of *strix* or *striga*) were malevolent nighttime monsters. The Latin *strix* literally meant screech owl, and the *striges* were believed to be birdlike creatures with great talons. They preyed especially on sleeping men and **children.** With men, they often turned themselves into beautiful **women** and had sexual intercourse (thereby showing a relation to **succubi**) before killing them. They were also **vampires,** sucking the blood from their victims. The image of the *strix* contributed to the later Christian idea of witches as women who flew at night and often murdered babies and young children. The word also became a term for *witch* in the medieval and early-modern periods.

SUCCUBI. *See* INCUBI AND SUCCUBI.

***SUMMIS DESIDERANTES AFFECTIBUS*, BULL.** *See* INNOCENT VIII, POPE (1432–1492).

SWEDEN, WITCHCRAFT IN. Sweden did not experience many **witchcraft** trials. The only intense **witch-hunt** occurred quite late, beginning in 1668 and ending in 1676; it was concentrated on the parish of **Mora**, but did eventually reach the capital Stockholm, and resulted in 23 **executions**. The hunt was notable for the number of accusations by **children**. **Cotton Mather** later compared the Mora trials with those in **Salem**, Massachusetts. The witch trials in Finland, a possession of Sweden in the early-modern period, tended to focus on men until the 1670s, when **women** were much more frequently accused of the crime. The early focus on **male witches** seems to have arisen less from their role in traditional Finnish and Lappish religion, which did have some **shamanistic** elements that were dying out, than because witchcraft accusations became a means to resolve disputes.

SWIMMING. A common, although by no means universal or universally accepted, method for identifying witches, swimming involved binding a suspected witch and immersing her in water. If she floated to the surface, she was judged to be guilty. If she managed to remain submerged for some period of time, she was deemed to be innocent. The procedure operated on the theory that water was a pure element and would reject any guilty person, causing them to float. Thus, the witch was bound not to prevent her from swimming to the surface, but from deliberately keeping herself submerged. Although some people could drown in the process of proving their innocence, normally the accused was not required to remain submerged for very long.

As a method to discover sorcerers, swimming was mentioned in the early Babylonian Code of Hammurabi (1792–1750 BCE). In Europe, it derived from notions of trial by ordeal that had been employed in early-medieval period but that were increasingly abandoned by courts with the steady adoption of **inquisitorial procedure** beginning in the 12th century. Clergymen were forbidden to participate in ordeals in 1215 by the Fourth Lateran Council, and throughout the late 16th and early 17th centuries, a number of authorities, including the *parlement* of Paris, made it illegal. It continued to be used in some lesser jurisdictions and in lynchings of suspected witches, including cases in **England** in 1751, Holland in 1823, and Danzig in 1836.

See also ANTIQUITY, WITCHCRAFT IN.

SWITZERLAND, WITCHCRAFT IN. Witch trials in the cantons of the Swiss Confederation, or Switzerland, mark the beginning and end of European **witch-hunting**. The **witchcraft** trials that occurred in Switzerland in the early 15th century, along with those in neighboring parts of **France** and **Italy**, brought together the classic elements of the witchcraft stereotype, notably the **pact** with, and worship of, the **devil** or **demons** (and therefore **apostasy**, **idolatry**, and **heresy**), the **night flight**, the witches' **sabbath**, and harmful **sorcery**, or *maleficium*. These trials were debated at the **Council of Basel**, and prompted **Hans Fründ**, **Johannes Nider**, and others, to write influential accounts of witchcraft prosecutions. Between these trials and the death of **Anna Göldi**, the last person in Europe to be executed for the crime, in 1782, some 3,500 people were executed for witchcraft in Switzerland. This figure represents the highest rate of **execution** for witchcraft per capita of any European country. As in the **German Empire**, it seems likely that local judiciaries, free from strong centralized control, were able to pursue witches without restraint whenever they believed them to be a threat to their communities.

T

TANNER, ADAM (1572–1632). A Jesuit critic of witch persecution, Adam Tanner joined the Society of Jesus in 1590 and studied at Dillingen and Ingolstadt, where he was appointed to the chair in scholastic theology in 1603. He was to spend much of the rest of his life teaching at the university there, during which time the duchy of **Bavaria**, in whose territory Ingolstadt lay, and the neighboring prince-bishoprics of **Bamberg**, **Eichstätt**, and **Würzburg**, experienced intense **witch-hunts**. Even though Tanner's colleagues at the university at Ingolstadt advised on the persecution of the witch sect in the region, he was not afraid to assert his own more moderate views. Like **Friedrich Spee**, whose work he influenced, Tanner was **skeptical** of the excessive use of **torture** to gain confessions, and acknowledged that, under duress, innocent people might be forced to confess to the crime of witchcraft. Unlike Spee, he argued that many real witches were prosecuted, but instead of being executed for **heresy**, they should be rehabilitated into the church.

TEMPLARS. The Knights of the Temple of Solomon, or Knights Templar, were a crusading, military order during the Middle Ages. The Templars originated around 1120 in the Holy Land as a small group of knights dedicated to defending the pilgrims. The order quickly grew in size and popularity, until the knights in the Holy Land were supported by a large Templar network spread across Western Europe. The Templars acquired vast amounts of land, usually through pious donations. After the fall of Acre, the last Christian outpost in the Holy Land, in 1291, the Templars no longer had a clear purpose, and their great wealth aroused opposition to the order. In 1307, the Templars in **France** were arrested on the order of King Philip IV. The charges ranged from **heresy** and sodomy to worshiping **demons**, but in reality the arrests were motivated by Philip's desire to disband the order and seize its tremendous wealth and property. **Torture** was applied, however, and confessions were extracted, although many Templars later recanted.

Under pressure from the French, in 1312 Pope Clement V officially suppressed the order, and in 1314 the grand master of the order, Jacques de Molay, was burned at the stake.

The Templars were never charged with **witchcraft**, and even charges of demonic **sorcery** did not figure significantly in their final condemnation. However, the dynamics of their arrest and trial, especially the use of torture to extract clearly false confessions, were reminiscent of later witch trials, and the trial of the Templars is often seen as foreshadowing in certain respects the persecution of witches that was to come.

THEOPHILUS OF ADANA, SAINT (?–ca. 538). The subject of the first recorded story of a **pact** with the **devil**, Theophilus of Adana humbly declined to become bishop of Adana, now in modern Turkey. The new bishop then deprived Theophilus of his position as archdeacon. In revenge, Theophilus made a pact with the devil, renouncing Christ and the Virgin Mary, which he signed in his own blood. In return, the devil gave him the bishopric. As he was nearing the end of his life, Theophilus began to regret the pact and fear for his soul, so he prayed to the Virgin Mary to intercede with God for him. The Virgin appeared to Theophilus twice, the first time after he had fasted for 40 days to tell him that she would intercede on his behalf, the second after 30 days fasting to grant him absolution. The devil then left the contract on Theophilus's chest while he was sleeping. Theophilus took the contract to the bishop whose action had caused him to be jealous and confessed his sin. In response, the bishop burned the contract and, released from its burden, Theophilus died. The story confirmed that pacts with the devil, such as those later contracted by witches, could be made in certain circumstances, although it offers a more hopeful outcome than many suspected witches were allowed. It also provides one of the bases for the legend of **Faust**.

THOLOSAN, CLAUDE (?–ca. 1450). The exact years of Claude Tholosan's life are unknown, but he served as chief magistrate of Briançonnais, the region around Briançon in Dauphiné, from 1426 until 1449. He was a layman and a secular official, although highly educated and clearly familiar with ecclesiastical canon law as well as certain aspects of theology. In the early 15th century, the Alpine regions of Dauphiné were the location of some of the earliest witch trials in European history, and in his capacity as chief judge, Tholosan personally conducted numerous trials for **witchcraft**. Around 1436, he wrote a treatise *Ut magorum et maleficiorum errores manifesti ignorantibus fiant* (That the Errors of Magicians and Witches May Be Made Clear to the Ignorant), based on his own experiences trying witches. Unknown for many years and only rediscovered in the late 1970s, this treatise takes its place beside the works of **Johannes Nider, Hans Fründ, Mar-**

tin Le Franc, and the anonymous *Errores Gazariorum* (Errors of the Gazarii), as one of the most important pieces of literature on witchcraft. It is particularly significant because, of all the early accounts, this is the only one for which the author had certain firsthand experiences with supposed witches.

Tholosan described witchcraft in terms fairly close to what would become the standard stereotype. Witches performed harmful **sorcery**, *maleficium*, through the agency of **demons**; they renounced their faith and worshiped Satan; they were members of a secret sect and gathered at regular secret meetings to worship the devil and engage in activity that would come to typify the witches' **sabbath** (although Tholosan, like most other early authorities, denied the reality of **night flight** to the sabbath). As a lay judge, Tholosan was also concerned to justify secular authority over the crime of witchcraft, which he did by equating the **apostasy** of witches to a kind of treason or *lèse-majesté* against God, which the secular prince, as the representative of divine justice and order on earth, was required to combat.

THOMASIUS, CHRISTIAN (1655–1728). The leading light of the Enlightenment in **Germany**, Thomasius was born at Leipzig and educated in law at the universities there and at Frankfurt on the Oder. He fled to Halle to avoid arrest for his controversial views on a range of subjects, and, in 1694, helped to found its university, becoming its rector in 1710. He became an important opponent of **torture** after his request for it to be applied in a case of **witchcraft** was overruled, and a committed **skeptic** about the existence of witchcraft after reading **Friedrich Spee**'s *Cautio criminalis* (1631).

TINCTORIS, JOHANNES (ca. 1400–1469). Born in Tournai, Tinctoris studied theology at the university in Cologne, where he became dean of the arts faculty, then later dean of theological faculty and ultimately rector of the university. Sometime before 1460, he returned to Tournai, where he wrote a *Tractatus de secta vaudensium* (Treatise on the Sect of Waldensians), based on sermons he had delivered. In the tract, *Waldensians* is used as a synonym for *witches*, and Tinctoris accuses them of participating in **sabbaths** and performing the *osculum infame*, or **obscene kiss**, on the backside of a **goat**. He also cites as evidence the **execution** by burning of 15 people convicted for the crime of **witchcraft** in Arras.

See also FRANCE, WITCHCRAFT IN.

TORQUEMADA (TURRECREMATA), JUAN DE (1388–1468). A Spanish prelate and uncle of the more famous Tomás de Torquemada, who was chief inquisitor of the **Spanish Inquisition** in the late 15th century, Juan de Torquemada spent most of his life in Rome. In a commentary on canon law written around 1450, he addressed the notion of the **night flight** of witches as described in the **canon** *Episcopi*, asserting that such flight was entirely an illusion and a deception of **demons**.

TORTURE. The legal use of torture to extract confessions in court cases has a long history in Europe. The controlled use of torture was justified under ancient Roman law. For most of the early Middle Ages, however, courts used **accusatorial procedure**, and guilt or innocence was determined by judicial ordeal, or in some cases trial by combat, in which God helped the innocent to prevail. With the gradual rediscovery of Roman law in the 11th and 12th centuries, and the adoption of **inquisitorial procedure** in many parts of Europe, the judicial use of torture increased. Torture was typically applied in cases where evidence and witnesses were lacking or further information was required, such as **heresy** and treason. Following this practice, in some parts of Europe, especially where **witchcraft** was prosecuted as a heresy, torture was used on witch suspects to force them to confess to the crime, provide details of their activities, and name their accomplices with whom they had attended **sabbaths** and other diabolical events. In these places, the normal constraints on the use of torture were relaxed because of the nature of the crime and the fact that it was treated as a *crimen exceptum*. This relaxation of normal practice meant that witch suspects could be subjected to exceptional forms of torture over long periods or for several sessions of interrogation in succession.

In the prince-bishopric of **Eichstätt**, for example, torture was used regularly, in some cases during every session of interrogation, to force information from the witch suspects. The first stage in the torture process in Eichstätt was to bring the executioner into the interrogation chamber. The knowledge of his skill and the fear of being tainted by his dishonorable touch could prompt a suspect to begin a confession, if only rarely. The next stage was to show the suspect the thumbscrews and place her thumbs in them. This was followed by tightening the screws to cause pain. If the thumbscrews did not force the suspect to begin or continue her confession, she was prepared for the **strappado**. The interrogators could then ask the executioner to raise the suspect, add weights to her feet, drop her nearly to the floor, or jerk her up and down. The process of torture could be continued until the interrogators were satisfied that they had a full confession, and would be resumed if the suspect retracted her testimony, offered contradictory details, or refused to confess any more. Torture was not meant to harm or mark the witch suspect permanently, and executioners were highly knowledgeable about the amount of physical abuse each body could withstand. Other forms of torture used against witches elsewhere in Europe included the boots, a wooden instrument into which wedges were hammered until the leg was crushed, and the witches' chair, a seat covered in spikes on which a suspect sat and which might be heated. The use of either of these forms was exceptional because of the danger to the suspect's body.

In places where witchcraft was prosecuted as a felony or the authorities were cautious or skeptical about the accusations of witchcraft brought before them, torture was used to a limited extent or not at all. The **Spanish Inquisition** reserved torture for cases in which they thought the suspect or witness was withholding information, but they would only use it once with the permission of the *Suprema* in Madrid. In **Scotland**, torture could be used only under warrant from the Privy Council. The issuing of warrants sustained the **witch-hunts** of the 1590s across the country following the **North Berwick** trials. In **England**, torture could only be used in cases of treason or where the state was in danger. Because witchcraft was treated as a felony in the kingdom, it was not permissible to torture witch suspects. This is not to suggest that torture was not used illegally in such places, as the **Matthew Hopkins** episode in mid-17th century England shows, but restrictions on its use prevented witch prosecutions from getting out of hand.

The use of torture in witchcraft cases provoked a legal form of **skepticism** among some commentators. **Friedrich Spee** argued in his *Cautio criminalis* (1631) that the witches whose spiritual confessions he had heard in **Würzburg** were really innocent and only confessed to the crime under torture. His contemporary and fellow Jesuit, **Adam Tanner**, and, later, the 18th-century **German** jurist **Christian Thomasius** were of the same opinion.

See also SWIMMING.

TRANSVECTION. *See* NIGHT FLIGHT.

TRIER, WITCH-HUNTS AT. A series of severe witch trials took place in the archbishopric of Trier, which was also an independent principality within the **German Empire**, over the course of about 12 years, from 1582 to 1594. The trials were largely directed by the suffragan bishop of Trier, **Peter Binsfeld**, under the overall authority of Prince-Archbishop Johann von Schönenburg. Binsfeld would later write an important treatise on **witchcraft** intended mainly to justify the trials at Trier. The accusations of witchcraft seem to have been sparked by years of inclement weather, poor harvests, and economic suffering in the region. The initial trials were conducted in secular court under the direction of the senior civic judge and vice governor of the city, **Dietrich Flade**. Unfortunately, Flade was less enthusiastic about **witch-hunting** than were the religious authorities, and ultimately he came to be suspected of witchcraft himself. He was tried and executed in 1589. The trials also aroused the opposition of the theologian **Cornelius Loos**, who wrote a treatise expressing his **skepticism** about witchcraft and the methods used in witch-hunting. Binsfeld took action against him as well. The treatise was suppressed, and Loos was banished to Brussels.

TRITHEMIUS, JOHANNES (1462–1516). A Benedictine monk, abbot of Sponheim and later St. Jacob's in **Würzburg**, Trithemius wrote two works dealing, at least in part, with **witchcraft**. In 1515, he published *Liber octo questionum* (Book of the Eight Questions), a set of answers to questions originally put to him in 1505 by the **German** emperor Maximilian I, two of which concerned witches. Earlier in 1508, Trithemius had written *Antipalus maleficiorum* (Testimony of Witches) at the request of the Elector of Brandenburg, which was dedicated to explicating the evils of witchcraft and how the Catholic church should deal with them.

Trithemius practiced natural **magic**, as distinct from demonic magic or **sorcery**, and claimed as his teachers the 13th-century Dominican friar **Albertus Magnus** and his own contemporary **Gianfrancesco Pico della Mirandola**. Both **Agrippa** and **Paracelsus** numbered among Trithemius's pupils.

V

VALIENTE, DOREEN (1922–1999). An early member of the movement of modern **witchcraft**, or **Wicca**, in **England**, Valiente was the chief disciple of the founder of modern witchcraft, **Gerald Gardner**. In the mid-1950s, she co-authored with him many of the basic Wiccan rituals and texts that shaped the development of the new religion. She also founded her own **coven**, which soon broke away from Gardner's overall control.

Born in London, Valiente became very interested in occultism and considered herself to have psychic abilities. She was introduced to Gerald Gardner, and in 1953 she was initiated by him into his coven. Gardner claimed that modern witchcraft was a direct survival of an ancient pre-Christian, **pagan** fertility religion; that he himself had been initiated into a coven of traditional, hereditary witches; and that he had learned of the rituals, practices, and beliefs of witchcraft from them. Valiente accepted these claims, although from her explorations of occultism, she recognized that many aspects of the practices Gardner described were based on other modern writings, such as those of the famous ritual magician and occultist **Aleister Crowley**. From 1954 until 1957, Valiente collaborated with Gardner on reworking the so-called **Book of Shadows**, the key text of Wiccan rituals. In particular, she endeavored to reduce those elements that were clearly drawn from Crowley and other occultist sources, to emphasize the role of the **Goddess**, and to shape witchcraft more into a modern **neo-pagan** religion. Eventually tiring of Gardner's overbearing influence, in 1957 Valiente formed her own coven and broke with Gardner. She continued to publish on the principles and practices of Wicca until her death in 1999.

VAMPIRES. There are two major connections between vampiric creatures and **witchcraft**. In classical mythology, creatures called *lamiae* and *striges* were monsters who haunted the night. *Lamiae* were thought to attack and kill **children**, often sucking their blood. *Striges* were bird-like creatures (the Latin *strix* means screech owl) that also sucked blood. They appear to have provided an early basis for the later medieval and early-modern stereotype of witches as murderers of children who flew through the night. In some regions of Europe during the period of the witch-hunts, both *lamia* and *strix* (or *striga*) were used as terms for *witch*. In addition to this association, another connection between witchcraft and vampires took shape in **Hungary** and other areas of the Balkans in the 18th century. Here it appears that popular belief in vampires gradually took over some of the social and cultural functions that belief in witchcraft had filled. As official willingness to prosecute witches declined, accounts of vampirism rose, and vampires came to be seen as a cause for much otherwise unexplainable misfortune, as witches had been earlier. Vampiric, witch-like creatures, like **Ole Higue**, **Penanggal**, the **shtriga**, and the **soucouyants**, can also be found in other cultures across the world.

VINETI, JEAN (?–ca. 1475). A Dominican friar, Vineti was first a professor of theology at the university in Paris and then an **inquisitor** at Paris and later at Carcassonne in the south of **France**. Around 1450, he wrote a treatise *Contra daemonum invocatores* (Against Invokers of Demons), in which he addressed the subject of **witchcraft**. Vineti was very credulous and was one of the first authorities, along with **Nicholas Jacquier** and **Johannes Hartlieb**, to present an extended argument against the tradition of the **canon** *Episcopi* that the **night flight** of witches to a **sabbath** was only an illusion. Vineti maintained that both night flight and the sabbath itself were entirely real.

VISCONTI, GIROLAMO (?–1477 OR 1478). A member of the princely family of Milan, Girolamo became a Dominican friar. In 1448, he was appointed to be a professor of logic at the university in Milan, and from 1465 until his death, he was the Dominican provincial, or head of the order, in the province of Lombardy. Sometime around 1460, he wrote *Lamiarum sive striarum opusculum* (Little Book on Witches—*lamia* and *strix* both being words that meant witch in **Italy** at this time). Here he argued both for the reality of witches and for the **heretical** nature of **witchcraft**, placing them under the jurisdiction of clerical **inquisitions**.

VOODOO. Developing originally among the slave populations of the **Caribbean** region, primarily in Haiti, Voodoo is a religion that consists of a complex blend of Christian and native African elements. In this syncretism, it is similar to **Macumba** and **Santería**; it should not be confused with **Hoodoo**. The word *Voodoo* derives from the West African *vodu*, meaning spirit or deity. It can alternately be given as *Voudou* or *Vodou*, and practitioners generally prefer this latter term, as *Voodoo* is often seen as carrying pejorative connotations, denoting some sort of system of black **magic** devoid of any religious meaning. In fact, it is incorrect to equate Voodoo purely with harmful magic, although such **sorcery**, and other practices associated with **witchcraft**, do have a place within the overall religious system of Voodoo.

The basis of Voodoo is worship of the *loa*, spirits that can exercise power in the world. Practitioners believe in the single great creator-god of Christianity, but also maintain that there are numerous other powerful spirits in the world. The *loa* represent a mixture of Christian saints and angels along with traditional African spirit-deities. The Catholic Church generally equates the *loa* with **demons** and sees Voodoo as a corruption of Christianity. Believers, however, regard it as an enrichment of Christianity and themselves as faithful Christians. The *loa* are neither wholly good nor entirely **evil**, and so humans can access their power for a variety of purposes. A particularly evil form of sorcery in Voodoo is the creation of zombies, animated corpses that will serve the sorcerer who creates them. The *loa* also serve, however, as benign spirits, and people pray to them for protection from harmful sorcery.

Ideas of evil sorcery within Voodoo share many elements in common with historical ideas of harmful magic and witchcraft in Europe, and probably derive partly from European influence along with traditional elements of **African witchcraft**. Sorcerers are often thought to carry babies and young **children** off to secret gatherings where they kill and devour them, or they break into homes at night and suck the blood from children while they sleep. They are also often believed to use magic **ointments** that they rub on their bodies in order to fly, just as historical European witches were often thought to do.

WALDENSIANS. Followers of a man named Valdes, a rich merchant in Lyon in the late 12th and early 13th centuries, the Waldensians became the most widespread and enduring of all medieval heretical groups. Seeking to lead an "apostolic life" of poverty and preaching, as described in Christ's instructions to his disciples in the **Bible**, the Waldensians were condemned by the medieval church for refusing to accept episcopal and papal authority (first the archbishop of Lyon and then Pope Alexander III refused to allow them, as untrained laymen, to preach), and the movement was branded a **heresy**. Waldensianism nevertheless persisted as a widespread movement in southern **France**, the **German Empire**, and **Italy** for the remainder of the Middle Ages. Waldensian groups eventually developed a number of unorthodox doctrines and practices, but they were never particularly associated with the practice of demonic **sorcery**. Then, in the 15th century, in the western Alpine regions of Savoy, Dauphiné, and certain cantons in western **Switzerland**, several trials that began as **inquisitions** into Waldensian heresy shifted into some of the first **witch-hunts** in Europe. In the French-speaking regions of these territories, the word for Waldensian, *Vaudois*, became an early term for witches, and certain documents described the supposed satanic sect of witches as ". . . *heresin illorum haereticorum modernorum Valdensium*" (the heresy of the new Waldensian heretics). There is, however, no credible evidence to suggest that actual Waldensian practice ever involved the worship of the **devil** or the practice of demonic **magic**.

WALPURGISNACHT. The night of 30 April, prior to the feast day of Saint Walburga (on 1 May), Walpurgisnacht was widely believed throughout Germanic and Scandinavian lands to be a time of particular celebration and revelry for witches. On this night, witches were believed to fly to remote mountaintops to participate in great witches' **sabbaths**. The most famous of these supposedly took place on the peak of the **Brocken** in the Harz Mountains in northern **Germany**. Walpurgisnacht coincided with Celtic and Germanic spring fertility festivals, and the supposed revelry of witches associated with this day may have derived at least partly from **pagan** religious celebrations later demonized by Christian authorities.

WARLOCK. Because, historically, most witches were thought to be **women**, an alternate term, *warlock*, is sometimes used in modern writings to designate a male witch. The word derives from an Old English term for an oath-breaker or traitor. By the mid-15th century, it had become associated with **witchcraft**, although it carried no gender connotations and could be used for either male or female witches. There seems to be no particular historical basis for the modern application of the term only to men. Among practitioners of modern witchcraft, or **Wicca**, the term *warlock* is little used. Male practitioners prefer to be called *witches* or *Wiccans*, just as female practitioners are.

WEATHER MAGIC. *See* STORMS AND STORM-RAISING.

WEBSTER, JOHN (1610–1682). A physician who had been a surgeon to the Parliamentary forces in the English Civil War, Webster wrote *The Displaying of Supposed Witchcraft* (1671) in response to **Joseph Glanvill**'s *Some Philosophical Considerations Touching Witches and Witchcraft* (1666), better known by the title of its later, posthumous edition *Saducismus Triumphatus* (1681), and Meric Casaubon's *Of Credulity and Incredulity* (1668). Webster argued that the evidence of most witnesses to **witchcraft** events was unreliable and unscientific, he sought natural causes for the apparent efficacy of spells, and dismissed the stories of witches' **familiars** as fictitious because **demons** were unable to perform unnatural feats. While he took a **skeptical**, scientific approach toward witchcraft and the supernatural, Webster was not an atheist. He simply believed that the **devil**, demons, and miracles were largely metaphorical. Although he was attacked in the 1681 edition of Glanvill's work, Webster's views did come to influence those of commentators like **Francis Hutchinson**.

WENHAM, JANE (?–1730). The last person to be convicted of **witchcraft** in **England**, Jane Wenham was arrested for harming a maidservant of the vicar of Walkern, Hertfordshire, by supernatural means. The judge in the case, Sir John Powell, attempted to undermine the prosecution case, but Wenham, who had a long-standing local reputation for witchcraft, was still convicted by the jury. Powell was, however, able to secure her reprieve. The case is also remarkable because it became a political issue. No fewer than eight pamphlets were published about it with Tories arguing for the reality of witchcraft and Wenham's alleged actions, and the **skeptical** Whigs dismissing them entirely.

WEREWOLVES. The belief in lycanthropy, the ability of certain people to transform themselves or be transformed into wolves, is ancient. In Christian Europe during the medieval and early-modern periods, many learned **demonologists** took the issue of lycanthropy quite seriously. Like **witchcraft**, transformation into a werewolf was regarded not just as a potentially harmful supernatural feat, but also as a sin against God, a willful abandonment of the divinely ordained human form and spirit. In many regions, suspected werewolves were often tried in much the same manner as were witches. In addition, witches were sometimes described as transforming themselves into wolves. Most authorities agreed that no such physical transformation of the human body could actually take place. However, a **demon** or the **devil** might closely superimpose the form of a wolf over the real body of a witch. Alternately, the transformation might simply be a demonic illusion or deception.

WEYER, JOHANN (1515–1588). A physician and scholar, Weyer was one of the first important opponents of **witch-hunting**. Not only did he argue that from a legal standpoint many witch trials were deeply flawed, but he also maintained on theological and philological grounds that much supposed **witchcraft** was impossible, or at least could not be the work of human witches. Nevertheless, he did not deny the reality or power of **demons** or of the **devil**, and so could not fully undermine the basic foundations on which the idea of witchcraft rested.

Born in Brabant in the Netherlands, Weyer grew up in a merchant family. At the age of 15 he went to live and study with **Agrippa**. It was probably Agrippa who first introduced Weyer to the Neoplatonic and **Hermetic** traditions of learned Renaissance magic. After leaving Agrippa, Weyer studied medicine at Paris and Orléans and then returned to the Low Countries as a practicing physician. He married and in 1550 took up the post he held for the rest of his life as the personal physician to the duke of Cleves, whose court was centered at Düsseldorf. Sometime after taking this position, he began to become concerned with the matter of witchcraft. Witch trials were at that time on the rise in the entire region of the lower Rhine. In response to this occurrence, Weyer produced his most important work, *De praestigiis daemonum* (On the Deceptions of Demons), first published in 1563. Here he went beyond the sort of judicial **skepticism** about witch trials that was already present in his day, namely that most prosecutions for witchcraft were improperly conducted and seriously flawed and thus often resulted in false convictions. Rather he denied the very possibility of witchcraft itself.

Weyer did not seek to deny the real existence or power of demons. Instead, he argued that demons could not be compelled by human beings to perform the sorts of acts that formed the basis of accusations of witchcraft. Drawing on his expertise as a physician, he demonstrated that many cases of witchcraft or demonic **possession** were better explained by medical conditions, such as senility or insanity. He also attacked the concept of the demonic **pact** between a witch and the devil or a lesser demon. Viewing this pact as a contract, he set out to prove that legally it could not exist. According to Roman law, which formed the basis for most European law codes at this time, a valid contract required good faith (*bona fides*) from both parties, and could not be entered into with malicious intent. Obviously, argued Weyer, no good faith could be expected from the devil.

Weyer's arguments, while powerful and logically coherent, did little to convince the many proponents of witch-hunts that their cause was unjust, or that the crime they opposed had no basis in reality. His writings aroused great controversy and were fiercely attacked by almost every later authority on witchcraft and **demonology**. As Weyer never made any attempt to deny the basic existence of the devil and his demons, or their power, he left his later opponents an obvious point from which to launch their attacks. Still, the extent to which he did deny the reality of witchcraft makes him virtually unique among early opponents of the witch-hunts.

WICCA. An alternate term for **witchcraft**, *Wicca* is the preferred term among many modern witches (or Wiccans). *Wicca* is an Old English word for witch or more accurately sorcerer, but modern Wiccans who prefer the word generally do so because it now carries none of the negative stereotypes attached to the terms witch and witchcraft. It should be noted, however, that many practitioners of modern witchcraft staunchly maintain the use of the words *witch* and *witchcraft* and insist that they will reclaim these words from the negative connotations that they now carry.

Modern witchcraft originated in the 1950s. The father of the movement, and for all intents and purposes the founder of modern witchcraft, was the Englishman **Gerald Gardner**. In 1939, Gardner, a student of various esoteric religions, supposedly joined a coven of witches in **England**. He claimed that this group was a remnant of an ancient **pagan** religion practicing rites that had been preserved from the distant past. During the medieval and early-modern periods, this religion had been persecuted by Christian authorities as demonic witchcraft, but in fact the religion was older than Christianity and had nothing to do with either the Christian god or the Christian **devil**. Fearing that the religion was now on the verge of dying out, in 1954 Gardner declared its existence and its principles openly in his book *Witchcraft Today*.

In maintaining that modern witchcraft was a direct survival of an ancient pagan religion, Gardner was following the theories of **Margaret Murray**. Murray's thesis has since been completely debunked, and there is no credible evidence that historical witchcraft was rooted in some clandestine pre-Christian religion, or that modern witchcraft has any links to such a religion. It is now clear that Gardner simply invented most of the tenets of modern witchcraft from his earlier studies of world religions.

Modern witchcraft is by no means a single, unified, or cohesive faith. There is no one central organization to govern beliefs and practices. The original form of witchcraft created by Gardner, now known as Gardnerian witchcraft, is only one among many different forms (although all forms follow at least the basic principles that Gardner established). In general, witches are organized into groups called **covens**. These are presided over by a high priestess assisted by a high priest. Most forms of modern witchcraft give **women** an equal or even a superior place to men in the religion. Similarly, the supreme Wiccan deity is dual, taking the form of the **Goddess** and the God (often known as the **Horned God**). Of the pair, the Goddess is generally held to be superior and is strongly associated with the earth and nature. Modern witchcraft stresses a respect for the natural world, and modern witches worship the Goddess and God in a variety of ceremonies, often conducted outdoors. Practitioners of modern witchcraft also believe that they can perform a variety of magical spells, but always with the strict understanding that they should never use their power to bring harm or misfortune to others.

Because of the prominent place given to the Goddess and to female practitioners, modern witchcraft quickly drew the attention of many **feminists**, who wanted to see in it an essentially feminine religion in contrast to the perceived patriarchal structures of traditional Western religions. In 1979, the American witch **Starhawk** published her book *The Spiral Dance*, which more than any other work marked the successful fusion of the formal structures and beliefs of witchcraft from the Gardnerian tradition with the notion of witchcraft as an expression of essential female spirituality. Especially in America, where the tradition of feminist witchcraft is stronger than in Britain, this book in large part replaced Gardner's *Witchcraft Today* to become the basic statement of the religion. Also in 1979, the journalist and practicing witch **Margot Adler** published her book *Drawing Down the Moon*. This was the first systematic study of the beliefs and origins of modern witchcraft. In it, Adler rejected the Gardnerian notion that modern witchcraft was a direct survival of a real, pre-Christian religion. Instead, she recognized (as do most Wiccans today) that this pseudo-history would be better regarded as a foundational myth, and she argued that this realization in no way weakened the force or value of modern witchcraft as a religion.

WILD HUNT. In Germanic and Celtic legend, the Wild Hunt consisted of a band of ghosts or spirits who would ride through the night. The hunt was usually led by a divine or semi-divine figure, either female, often called Holda or Berta, or male, often called **Herne the Hunter**. In Christian Europe during the Middle Ages, authorities often transformed the female leader of the Wild Hunt into the classical goddess **Diana**, herself a goddess of hunting whom Christian authorities regarded as a **demon**. In addition, the belief developed that groups of **women**, instead of the spirits of the dead, would ride with Diana. The most famous expression of this belief is found in the 10th century **canon** *Episcopi*. Although condemned by the canon as mere demonic deception, this belief was an important basis for the later notions of **night flight** and the witches' **sabbath**.

WILLIAM OF MALMESBURY (ca. 1095–1142). A well-known chronicler and historian, William of Malmesbury wrote two important accounts of the history of **England** up to the 12th century. In his history of the kings of England, *Gesta regum*, written around 1140, he included a brief account of the **Witch of Berkeley**, which later became very famous and circulated also outside of William's history for the remainder of the Middle Ages and into the early-modern period.

WITCH BOTTLE. A form of protective charm common especially in **England**, a witch bottle was a small glass bottle or a Bartmann, or Bellarmine, jug (named after Cardinal Robert Bellarmine) that contained a combination of human hair, urine, nail clippings, and magical counter-spells. Witch bottles were probably made by **cunning men or women** and could be used in a variety of ways. They could be buried under, or placed near, potentially vulnerable entrances to houses, such as thresholds, windows, and hearths, as a means to protect a household from attack by a witch. More specifically, they could be used by a victim of bewitchment as a form of counter-magic. In these instances, as well as being placed strategically in the house, they could be smashed or thrown onto a fire to break a spell and cause the witch who had cast it pain, injury or death.

WITCH DOCTOR. *See* CUNNING MEN AND WOMEN.

THE WITCH OF EDMONTON. Written by Thomas Dekker, John Ford, and William Rowley, the **play** *The Witch of Edmonton* was based on the case of Elizabeth Sawyer, who was executed as a witch in April 1621 and was performed before the end of the same year. Her story had been reported first by the minister and visitor to Newgate Gaol, Henry Goodcole, in the pamphlet *The Wonderful Discoverie of Elizabeth Sawyer*, who had met Elizabeth while she was in prison. The pamphlet and play differed in many respects, but most significantly in tone. Goodcole was entirely credulous of **witchcraft** and presented Sawyer as a real witch. The playwrights, however, seem to have been more **skeptical**. They represented the unfortunate witch as the victim of social marginalization and class prejudice who was innocent of the crime of which she was accused. The play proved popular, suggesting that the audiences who came to see it, like the **English** jurymen who often acquitted witch suspects, were sympathetic toward some alleged witches at this time.

WITCHCRAFT. The term *witchcraft* can be, and historically has been used to denote a variety of supposed practices. Most broadly, *witchcraft* refers to relatively simple forms of common or low **magic** (as opposed to learned or high magic, which is typically very complex and ritualistic, and is limited to an educated elite) used to harmful effect. In this sense, witchcraft is largely synonymous with **sorcery**. In Europe during the medieval and early-modern periods, the Latin term for harmful sorcery, *maleficium*, was also the most common term for *witchcraft*. Taken to mean simply the practice of such sorcery, witchcraft can be said to have existed in almost every human society throughout history. Some anthropologists differentiate witchcraft from sorcery by labeling as sorcery any common magical practices that supposedly operate through certain words or gestures, or through certain material objects. Witchcraft, on the other hand, supposedly operates through some power inherent in the witch herself. Thus, sorcery is a learned skill while witchcraft is an innate characteristic. This distinction, however, does not pertain to witchcraft as defined during the period of the major European **witch-hunts**.

During the period of the major witch trials in Western Europe in the 16th and 17th centuries, witchcraft was widely conceived to involve the practice of harmful sorcery, *maleficium*, which operated through demonic forces. Witches learned to perform such sorcery from **demons** or from the **devil**, to whom they swore their allegiance. Such sorcery was not the only element of witchcraft in this period, however, and in many respects it was not the most important element. Witchcraft was also believed to involve profound **diabolism**. In exchange for magical powers, witches abandoned the Christian faith and gave their worship to the devil instead. They entered into **pacts** with demons and gathered as members of organized cults at secret, nocturnal **sabbaths**. Here, witches were believed to desecrate sacred items such as the cross and Eucharist, to murder and **cannibalize** small **children**, and to engage in sexual **orgies** with each other and with attendant demons. For most Christian authorities, the **apostasy** and **idolatry** entailed in this image of witchcraft were far worse than whatever harmful sorcery witches might work. This conception of witchcraft only appeared in Europe late in the Middle Ages, primarily in the early 15th century. Being so closely bound up with specifically Christian notions of theology and **demonology**, witchcraft in this sense obviously cannot be said to have existed in any other world culture.

In the 20th century, *witchcraft* came to take on yet another meaning. Self-styled modern witches conceive of witchcraft as a religious system, based on pre-Christian, **pagan** models. Although some modern witches maintain that there is a connection between their practices and historical witchcraft in Europe, they have sought to distance themselves from the historically negative connotations of witchcraft, and thus modern witchcraft is often referred to as **Wicca** (an Old English term for sorcery) instead. Modern witchcraft does involve certain magical practices that modern witches believe have real power.

WITCH-HUNT. Although **witchcraft** can with some justification be seen as an almost perennial aspect of numerous pre-modern human cultures, and although witches were uniformly regarded within these cultures as **evil** and socially harmful individuals who needed to be punished or often eradicated, witch-hunting in the historical sense is limited to a specific period and place. In Europe, the full notion of diabolical witchcraft, that is, of the witch as someone who not only practiced harmful **sorcery**, or *maleficium*, against others, but who did so by means of **demons** and demonic power, and in league with the **devil**, only emerged in the early 15th century. In this new conception of witchcraft, the witch was not regarded as an individual practitioner of evil, but was believed to be a member of a **heretical** sect. Witches were thought to gather at regular nocturnal assemblies known as witches' **sabbaths**, where they would commit **idolatry** and **apostasy** by worshiping demons and surrendering their souls to the devil in exchange for magical powers. The belief that witches were members of a secret, conspiratorial, diabolical cult provided the necessary basis for true witch-hunts, that is, a series of connected witch trials that fed off each other and resulted in numerous **executions**.

The first real witch-hunts took place in lands in and around the western Alps. The period of major witch-hunting, however, occurred later, in the 16th and 17th centuries. Reliable figures for many regions are lacking, but across Europe probably around 100,000 people were put on trial for witchcraft during these centuries, and probably around 50,000 were executed. The frequency and severity of witch-hunting varied widely from region to region and from year to year across Europe. Nevertheless, some generalizations can be made. Central Europe, above all the lands of **Switzerland** and the **German Empire**, were clearly the heartland of the witch-hunts. Some of the earliest, as well as some of the latest, witch trials took place in Switzerland, and over half of all executions for witchcraft, around 26,000, took place in German lands. In other regions of Europe, witch-hunting was less intense. In

Spain and **Italy**, for example, witch-hunting was kept under control mainly by the Spanish and Roman **Inquisitions**, while in **England** and **Scotland**, witch-hunts were made more difficult because of certain legal controls and the fact that the notion of fully diabolical witchcraft described above never gained wide credence and most accusations continued to focus on simple *maleficium*.

Across Europe, witch-hunting seems to have been most widespread in those regions where effective, centralized legal bureaucracies were lacking. Witch-hunting depended to a large extent on a relatively localized atmosphere of panic, and large, distant bureaucracies tended to act more slowly and with greater caution. Most witch-hunts began with an accusation of *maleficium* made against some individual. A trial would be held, and in many cases the process ended there, with the conviction (or, less often, acquittal) of a single suspected witch. Because witches were believed to be members of diabolical cults, however, often an accused witch was required by her judges to name other witches. If she proved reluctant, **torture** could be used. Also, a single witch trial could encourage other people in the same locality to make further accusations.

Often the process would still remain relatively contained and would end with only a few executions, producing what might be termed a *mid-level hunt*. In some cases, however, the level of fear and panic generated in a community that felt itself to be under attack by diabolical forces could spiral out of control. Especially if the officials in charge of the legal proceedings shared in the local panic, new accusations could be generated almost indefinitely. With the liberal use of torture, confessions could be extracted from virtually anyone accused, and so there was no natural stop to the string of convictions and executions that could take place. Such major hunts typically ended only when the accusations came to be leveled against socially and politically powerful people, such as priests and ministers, civic officials, and their wives. Faced with the possibility of convicting such people, magistrates would finally realize that the process was out of control and put an end to the hunt.

See also CHRONOLOGY OF WITCH-HUNTING.

WITCH'S MARK. Also known as a witch's teat, a witch's mark could be any small mark, mole, wart, or bodily protuberance (including an actual third nipple) supposedly used by witches to suckle their demonic **familiars**, who were thought to crave human blood. In those areas where belief in the witch's mark prevailed, accused witches would be stripped and thoroughly searched, and almost any bodily mark or blemish could be seen as evidence of witchcraft. In the absence of any clear mark, scars might be seen as evidence of an attempt to cut off or remove the mark.

WOMEN AND WITCHCRAFT. The association of women with **witchcraft** is ancient and enduring. In **Antiquity**, goddesses like **Hecate** were patrons of **magic, sorcery**, and witchcraft. Like the sorceress **Erictho**, the vampiric **Lilith**, and striges and **lamia**, these magical female deities became as well known to European scholars during the Renaissance as the **Witch of Endor** in the **Bible** or **Morgan le Fey** in legend. Female witches still appear in **folklore** across the world and range from **Baba Yaga** in **Russia** to **Ole Higue** in the **Caribbean**, and **Yama-uba** in Japan to the **penanggal** in the Malaysia. The gender association is so strong that *warlock* and similar terms have been introduced to identify **male witches**.

It is no surprise, therefore, that during the period of the **witch-hunts** in Europe, about 75 percent of those accused of and executed for witchcraft were women. In some places, the proportion was much higher. It was only in places where men were associated with **pagan shamanistic** practices or were vulnerable to politicized witchcraft accusations, such as **Estonia** or Finland, then a territory of **Sweden**, that male witches were more common. In these places, women often became the primary victims of witch trials as the mainstream **demonology** asserted itself. This demonology, even in the more cautious form of the 10th-century **canon** *Episcopi*, assumed that women were more likely to be seduced into witchcraft, even if only as an illusory act, by the **devil** because they were intellectually and emotionally weaker. **Johannes Nider** developed this argument further at the very beginning of the European witch-hunts in the early 15th century. He was echoed by his **skeptical** contemporary **Martin Le Franc** in *Le champion des dames* (Defender of Women). Later in the century, **Heinrich Kramer** asserted in his *Malleus maleficarum* (Hammer of [Female] Witches) that "all witchcraft comes from carnal lust, which in women is insatiable." Few later demonologists were as explicitly misogynistic as Kramer, but the assumption that witchcraft was at least sex-related is found in the actions of witch interrogators, like those in the **German** prince-bishopric of **Eichstätt**, who pursued the women named as accomplices by female witch suspects, but did not act on the many alleged male accomplices named by the few male witches they tried and executed. Nevertheless, throughout the witch-hunts, victims of misfortune were more likely to accuse a woman of witchcraft than they were a man. The accusers were also frequently women themselves.

Accusations of women not only turned on their common association with all forms of low magic, notably **love magic** and **magical healing**, but also because they were being pushed to the margins of society in early-modern Europe. Demographic pressures, followed by the intensification of the so-called Little Ice Age (and the agrarian crises and inflationary cycles that it caused), made women who did not have the protection of a man much more vulnerable to accusations of witchcraft when things went wrong in a household or community. Their situation was not helped by a general hardening of attitudes toward post-menopausal women, the group hardest hit by the witch persecutions, and an apparent rise of individualism among the middling sorts who had previously been an important source of charity for poor women.

In modern witchcraft, or **Wicca**, the status of women has been entirely reversed from the historical stereotype of witchcraft. As a system of religious belief, Wicca propounds a complete equality between male and female, and exhibits a great respect especially for female generative powers. The religion identifies both a god (often known as the **Horned God**) and a **Goddess**, who represents nature and the earth. In theory, these deities are equal, but in practice an emphasis often falls on the Goddess. As Wicca spread in the 1960s and 1970s, some elements of the movement became closely associated with the **feminism** of that period. A key figure here was the influential Wiccan author **Starhawk**. Many practitioners are drawn to Wicca, at least in part, because of the positive emphasis it places on women, as opposed to what they perceive as the patriarchal and repressive nature of more traditional Western religions.

See also ASIAN WITCHCRAFT; STRIX (STRIGA).

WÜRZBURG, WITCH TRIALS AT. Like the other **German** prince-bishoprics of **Bamberg** and **Eichstätt**, Würzburg experienced a particularly intense series of **witch-hunts** in the late 16th and early 17th centuries. Over 1,200 people were executed for witchcraft in the territory, 300 of them in 1616 and 1617, and 900 between 1625 and 1630. The victims of the hunts were not typical. They included a councilor and 43 canons and vicars, several wives of men of authority, and 17 children. As in Bamberg, Eichstätt, and the powerful duchy of **Bavaria**, the prince-bishops conducted witch-hunts as part of a broader Catholic **Reformation** agenda, which included a hospital and a university as well as a general crackdown on all forms of **heresy**, superstition, and ungodliness. It is possible that the hunts were also a response to popular pressure for action following outbreaks of plague. The confiscation mandate issued in 1627 meant that the bishopric received 79,000 gulden from the **executions**. It was the confessions he heard as the witches' confessor in Würzburg that convinced **Friedrich Spee** that most, if not all, were the innocent victims of aggressive forms of **torture**, and prompted him to write his **skeptical** *Cautio criminalis* (A Warning on Criminal Justice, 1631). After the death of Prince-bishop Philipp Adolf von Ehrenberg in 1631, witch-hunting in the territory ceased.

Y

YAMA-UBA. In Japanese **folklore**, Yama-uba was a witch—or sometimes merely an *oni* (**demon**, ogre or troll)—who lived among the forests and mountains and fed on human beings, sometimes through an extra mouth on top of her head. She either seduced unwary travelers as a beautiful young **woman** or solicited their help in her natural form, that of an old crone, before devouring them. Occasionally, she traded knowledge of her skills in **sorcery** and **poisons** with humans, often in return for a victim to eat.

See also ASIAN WITCHCRAFT; CANNIBALISM.

Bibliography

CONTENTS

INTRODUCTION

This bibliography, like the dictionary as a whole, focuses primarily on the phenomenon of witchcraft in Christian Europe during the medieval and early-modern periods, and above all on the age of the great European witch-hunts from the 15th through the 17th centuries. The historical development of witchcraft in Europe was, however, shaped by traditions of magic—and by legal, intellectual, and social responses to magic—stretching back beyond the early Christian period into Antiquity. Witchcraft has also exerted a powerful influence on the modern world, being appropriated into modern occultist, neo-pagan, and Satanist movements. For this reason, the bibliography covers magic and witchcraft for virtually the full span of Western history. The basic organization of the bibliography is chronological, with some sections and subsections arranged thematically. Systems of harmful magic similar to those which existed in some parts of Europe historically are found in many other world cultures, and scholars taking an anthropological approach to the study of witchcraft have often made comparisons between the European and non-European aspects of this phenomenon. For this reason, sections on non-European witchcraft, taking in Africa, Asia, and the Americas, have been included here for comparative purposes.

It is neither possible nor desirable to append a comprehensive bibliography of witchcraft history to the dictionary. The subject has been studied seriously for well over a century, and been of interest to historians of one kind or another since the early 18th century. Earlier histories tended to take a dismissive or romantic view of witchcraft. Many historians, even in the late 1960s, viewed witchcraft as a peasant "superstition" that had somehow survived the rationalizing processes of the Renaissance and Scientific Revolution. In about 1970, Keith Thomas and his student Alan Macfarlane destroyed this notion by showing how intrinsic witchcraft beliefs were to the worldview of the Elizabethan and Stuart gentry in England. Romantics, on the other hand, interpreted late-medieval and early-modern witches as followers of an ancient pagan fertility cult. Margaret Murray, a British Egyptologist and anthropologist of the early 20th century, promoted this interpretation in a series of ever-more fantastical books. Murray was influenced by anthropologists like Sir James Frazer, but her work was soon debunked. Despite this, her work formed the basis of early attempts, notably by the founder of modern witchcraft, Gerald Gardner, to give his new movement a history. Although many Wiccans now accept that they are not following a religion with a recognizable history, Murray's interpretation is still sometimes repeated.

The histories of witchcraft "from below," from the point of view of ordinary people in early-modern England, written by Thomas and Macfarlane, provided the foundation for a more comprehensive series of historical studies of the subject across Europe. It helps, of course, that the witchcraft trials and witch-hunts were so extensive and unusual that suspects, their accusers, and witnesses, who would never have been given any voice, had their narratives about social discord recorded, however obscured by the questions of their interrogators or the hand of the scribe. As social and cultural history have developed to incorporate new perspectives and answer new questions, so new interpretations of witchcraft have been constructed. The most influential approaches, especially where they have grown out of women's or gender history, have adopted the questions and techniques of anthropology, psychoanalysis, and post-modern textual analysis. The scope of witchcraft history is, therefore, huge, and a complete bibliography of every study ever written would run into several volumes. Yet, the subject remains interesting, and in many ways as intractable as ever, as new questions pose themselves. Because of this florescence, this bibliography is limited largely to works from the last four-to-five decades. Earlier works have only been included if they are generally considered seminal by historians working in the field.

Scholarship on witchcraft is, of necessity, a truly international effort. Every country in Europe experienced witchcraft trials, if not full-scale witch-hunting, to some extent. Every country therefore has a national body of scholarship on the subject that will include important and innovative work. There have been major studies in German, French and English, focusing on the heartlands of witch-hunting, but there is extensive scholarship on the peripheral states of Europe (Estonia, Finland, Iceland), the Netherlands and Hungary, the Scandinavian countries, and Spain and Italy, where few witch trials occurred. As the present volume is intended for an English-speaking readership, English-language scholarship has been preferred as much as possible. It has been essential, however, to include scholarship in other languages, especially for regional studies.

Although a great deal of scholarly attention has been focused on witchcraft, the field is still dominated by narrow studies rather than comparative studies or broad syntheses. The emphasis of this bibliography is on books, which are typically more easily available and which are more often addressed to (or at least accommodating of) general readers, but a large number of scholarly articles are also listed. Where several articles have been published in a single volume, to save space and avoid needless pedantry, only the full volume is listed. To readers looking to begin their investigations or interested in a general overview, the following suggestions can be made. Probably the best single-volume survey of the entire history of magic and witchcraft in the Western world is Jeffrey Russell's *A History of Witchcraft*. Richard Kieckhefer's *Magic in the Middle Ages* is the best survey for that period, culminating in a consideration of the emergence of diabolic witchcraft and witch-hunting, which actually only appeared at the end of the Middle Ages. There exist several options for an English-language survey of the period of the witch-hunts proper, including Brian Levack's *The Witch-Hunt in Early Modern Europe*, Wolfgang Behringer's *Witches and Witch-Hunts*, and Malcolm Gaskill's *Witchcraft: A Very Short Introduction*. The six-volume series *Witchcraft and Magic in Europe*, edited by Bengt Ankarloo, offers a comprehensive and detailed chronological survey of the entire historical development of witchcraft in Western civilization from the ancient world to the 20th century.

A more thematic approach to the same time-span is taken by the four-volume *Encyclopedia of Witchcraft: The Western Tradition*, edited by Richard M. Golden. Both the individual volumes of the series and the entries in the encyclopedia have been written by experts in their particular area of witchcraft studies. *The Witchcraft Sourcebook*, edited by Brian Levack, complements the excellent earlier collection of primary sources in translation, covering the entire medieval and early-modern periods, *Witchcraft in Europe 400–1700*, edited by Alan Kors and Edward Peters.

PRIMARY SOURCES: COLLECTIONS AND TRANSLATIONS

Modern Editions and Translations

Bodin, Jean. *On the Demon-Mania of Witches*. Ed. Randy A. Scott and Jonathan L. Pearl. Toronto: Centre for Reformation and Renaissance Studies, 1995.

Boguet, Henry. *An Examen of Witches*. Ed. Montague Summers. Trans. E. A. Ashwin. 1929. Reprint, New York: Barnes and Noble, 1971.

Copenhaver, Brian P., ed. *Hermetica: The Greek Corpus Hermeticum and the Latin Asclepius in a New English Translation with Notes and Introduction*. Cambridge: Cambridge University Press, 1992.

Davidson, L. S., and J. O. Ward, eds. *The Sorcery Trial of Alice Kyteler: A Contemporary Account (1324) Together with Related Documents in English Translation, with Introduction and Notes*. Binghamton, N.Y.: Medieval and Renaissance Texts and Studies, 1993.

Del Rio, Martín. *Investigations into Magic*. Ed. P. G. Maxwell-Stuart. Manchester: Manchester University Press, 2000.

Guazzo, Francesco Maria. *Compendium Maleficarum*. Ed. Montague Summers. Trans E. A. Ashwin. 1929. Reprint, New York: Barnes and Noble, 1970.

Hopkins, Matthew. *The Discovery of Witches*. Ed. Montague Summers. London: Cayme, 1928.

Kramer, Heinrich. *Der Hexenhammer. Malleus Maleficarum. Kommentierte Neuübersetzung*. Ed. Günter Jerouschek and Wolfgang Behringer. Trans. Günter Jerouschek, Wolfgang Behringer, and Werner Tschacher. Munich: Deutsche Taschenbuch Verlag, 2000.

————. *The Hammer of Witches: A Complete Translation of the Malleus Maleficarum*. Ed. Christopher S. Mackay. Cambridge: Cambridge University Press, 2009.

————. *The Malleus Maleficarum*. Ed. P. G. Maxwell-Stuart. Manchester: Manchester University Press, 2007.

Lancre, Pierre de. *On the Inconstancy of Witches: Pierre de Lancre's Tableau de l'inconstance des mauvais anges et demons (1612)*. Ed. Gerhild Scholz Williams. Trans. Harriet Stone and Gerhild Scholz Williams. Tempe: Arizona Center for Medieval and Renaissance Studies, with Brepols, 2006.

Mammoli, Domenico, ed. *The Record of the Trial and Condemnation of a Witch, Mattueccia di Francesco, at Todi, 20 March 1428*. Res Tudertinae, vol. 14. Rome: n.p., 1972.

Rémy, Nicholas. *Demonolatry*. Ed. Montague Summers. Trans. E. A. Ashwin. 1930. Reprint, Secaucus, N.J.: University Books, 1974.

Schroeder, Friedrich-Christian, ed. *Die Peinliche Gerichtsordnung Kaiser Karls V. und des Heiligen Römischen Reichs von 1532. (Carolina)*. Stuttgart: Reclam, 2000.

Scot, Reginald. *The Discoverie of Witchcraft*. Ed. Montague Summers. 1930. Reprint, Washington, D.C.: Kaufman and Greenberg, 1995.

Spee, Friedrich [von]. *Cautio Criminalis, or a Book on Witch Trials*. Trans. Marcus Heller. Charlottesville: University of Virginia Press, 2003.

Weyer, Johann. *On Witchcraft: An Abridged Translation of Johann Weyer's De praestigiis daemonum*. Ed. Benjamin G. Kohl and H. C. Erik Midelfort. Trans. John Shea. Ashville, N.C.: Pegasus Press, 1998.

————. *Witches, Devils, and Doctors in the Renaissance: Johann Weyer, De Praestigiis Daemonum*. Ed. George Mora. Binghamton, N.Y.: Medieval and Renaissance Texts and Studies, 1991.

Edited Source Collections

Behringer, Wolfgang, ed. *Hexen und Hexenprozesse*. 3rd ed. Munich: Deutscher Taschenbuch Verlag, 1995.

Betz, Hans Dieter, ed. *The Greek Magical Papyri in Translation, including the Demotic Spells.* 2nd ed. Chicago: University of Chicago Press, 1992.

Boyer, Paul, and Stephen Nissenbaum, eds. *Salem-Village Witchcraft: A Documentary Record of Local Conflict in Colonial New England.* 2nd ed. Boston: Northeastern University Press, 1993.

———. *The Salem Witchcraft Papers: Verbatim Transcripts of the Legal Documents of the Salem Witchcraft Outbreak of 1692.* 3 vols. New York: Da Capo Press, 1977.

Corbin, Peter, and Douglas Sedge, eds. *Three Jacobean Witchcraft Plays.* Manchester, Eng.: Manchester University Press, 1986.

Elmer, Peter, ed. *English Witchcraft, 1560–1736,* vol. 4: *The Post-Reformation Synthesis and Its Opponents.* London: Pickering & Chatto, 2003.

———. *English Witchcraft, 1560–1736,* vol. 5: *The Later English Trial Pamphlets.* London: Pickering & Chatto, 2003.

Gager, John G., ed. *Curse Tablets and Binding Spells from the Ancient World.* Oxford: Oxford University Press, 1992.

Gaskill, Malcolm, ed. *English Witchcraft, 1560–1736,* vol. 3: *The Matthew Hopkins Trials.* London: Pickering & Chatto, 2003.

Gibson, Marion, ed. *Early Modern Witches: Witchcraft Cases in Contemporary Writing.* London: Routledge, 2000.

———. *English Witchcraft, 1560–1736,* vol. 2: *Early English Trial Pamphlets.* London: Pickering & Chatto, 2003.

———. *Witchcraft and Society in England and America, 1550–1750.* London: Continuum, 2003.

———. *Women and Witchcraft in Popular Literature, c. 1560–1715.* Aldershot, Eng.: Ashgate, 2007.

Hansen, Joseph, ed. *Quellen und Untersuchungen zur Geschichte des Hexenwahns und der Hexenverfolgung im Mittelalter.* 1901. Reprint, Hildesheim, Ger.: Georg Olms, 1963.

Henningsen, Gustav, ed. *The Salazar Documents: Inquisitor Alonso de Salazar Frías and Others on the Basque Witch Persecution.* Leiden: Brill, 2004.

Hill, Frances, ed. *The Salem Witch Trials Reader.* New York: Da Capo Press, 2000.

Hunter, Michael, ed. *The Occult Laboratory: Magic, Science and Second Sight in Late Seventeenth-Century Scotland.* Woodbridge, Eng.: Boydell & Brewer, 2001.

Kors, Alan, and Edward Peters, eds. *Witchcraft in Europe, 400–1700: A Documentary History.* 2nd ed. Philadelphia: University of Pennsylvania Press, 2001.

Larner, Christina, Christopher Hyde Lee, and Hugh V. McLachlan, eds. *A Source-Book of Scottish Witchcraft.* Glasgow: SSRC Project on Accusations and Prosecutions for Witchcraft in Scotland, 1977.

Lea, Henry Charles. *Materials toward a History of Witchcraft*. Ed. Arthur C. Howland. 3 vols. Philadelphia: University of Pennsylvania Press, 1939.

Levack, Brian P., ed. *The Witchcraft Sourcebook*. London: Routledge, 2002.

Luck, Georg, ed. *Arcana Mundi: Magic and the Occult in the Greek and Roman Worlds*. Baltimore, Md.: Johns Hopkins University Press, 1985.

Mandrou, Robert, ed. *Possession et sorcellerie au XVIIe siècle: Textes inédits*. Paris: Hachette, 1979.

Maxwell-Stuart, P. G., ed., *The Occult in Early Modern Europe: A Documentary History*. Basingstoke, Eng.: Palgrave Macmillan, 1999.

———. *The Occult in Medieval Europe, 500–1500: A Documentary History*. Basingstoke, Eng.: Palgrave Macmillan, 2005.

Normand, Lawrence, and Gareth Roberts, eds. *Witchcraft in Early Modern Scotland: James VI's Demonology and the North Berwick Witches*. Exeter: University of Exeter Press, 2000.

Ostorero, Martine, Agostino Paravicini Bagliani, and Kathrin Utz Tremp, eds. *L'imaginaire du sabbat: Edition critique des textes les plus anciens (1430 c.–1440 c.)*. Lausanne, Switz.: Université de Lausanne, 1999.

Rosen, Barbara, ed. *Witchcraft in England, 1558–1618*. Amherst: University of Massachusetts Press, 1991.

Sharpe, James, ed. *English Witchcraft, 1560–1736*, vol. 1: *Early English Demonological Works*. London: Pickering & Chatto, 2003.

———. *English Witchcraft, 1560–1736*, vol. 6: *The Final Debate*. London: Pickering & Chatto, 2003.

GENERAL STUDIES

General Surveys and Essay Collections

Ankarloo, Bengt, and Stuart Clark, eds. *Witchcraft and Magic in Europe*. 6 vols. Philadelphia: University of Pennsylvania Press, 1999–2003 (vol. 1: *Biblical and Pagan Societies*; vol. 2: *Ancient Greece and Rome*; vol. 3: *The Middle Ages*; vol. 4: *The Period of the Witch Trials*; vol. 5: *The Eighteenth and Nineteenth Centuries*; vol. 6: *The Twentieth Century*).

Bailey, Michael D. *Magic and Superstition in Europe: A Concise History from Antiquity to the Present*. Lanham, Md.: Rowman & Littlefield, 2007.

Behringer, Wolfgang. *Witches and Witch-Hunts: A Global History*. Cambridge: Polity, 2004.

Breslaw, Elaine G., ed. *Witches of the Atlantic World: A Historical Reader and Primary Sourcebook*. New York: New York University Press, 2000.

Caro Baroja, Julio. *The World of the Witches*. Trans. O. N. V. Glendinning. Chicago: University of Chicago Press, 1965.

Dülmen, Richard van, ed. *Hexenwelten. Magie und Imagination vom 16.–20. Jahrhundert*. Frankfurt: Fischer, 1987.

Ferreiro, Alberto, ed. *The Devil, Heresy, and Witchcraft: Essays in Honor of Jeffrey B. Russell*. Leiden: Brill, 1998.

Franklyn, Julian. *Death by Enchantment: An Examination of Ancient and Modern Witchcraft*. New York: Putnam, 1971.

Gaskill, Malcolm. *Witchcraft: A Very Short Introduction*. Oxford: Oxford University Press, 2010.

Jensen, Gary. *The Path of the Devil: Early Modern Witch Hunts*. Lanham, Md.: Rowman & Littlefield, 2006.

Klaits, Joseph. *Servants of Satan: The Age of the Witch Hunts*. Bloomington: Indiana University Press, 1985.

Klaniczay, Gábor, and Éva Pócs, eds. *Demons, Spirits, Witches*. 3 vols. Budapest: Central European University Press, 2005–2008.

Levack, Brian P. *The Witch-Hunt in Early Modern Europe*. 2nd ed. London: Longman, 1995.

Maxwell-Stuart, P. G. *Witchcraft: A History*. Basingstoke, Eng.: Tempus, 2001

———. *Witchcraft in Europe and the New World, 1400–1800*. Basingstoke, Eng.: Palgrave, 2001.

Muchembled, Robert, ed. *Magie et sorcellerie en Europe du Moyen Age à nos jours*. Paris: Colin, 1984.

Parés, Luis Nicolau, and Roger Sansi, eds. *Sorcery in the Black Atlantic*. Chicago: University of Chicago Press, 2011.

Quaife, G. R. *Godly Zeal and Furious Rage: The Witch in Early Modern Europe*. New York: St. Martin's Press, 1987.

Ravensdale, Tom, and James Morgan. *The Psychology of Witchcraft: An Account of Witchcraft, Black Magic, and the Occult*. New York: Arco, 1974.

Russell, Jeffrey Burton, and Brooks Alexander. *A New History of Witchcraft: Sorcerers, Heretics, and Pagans*. London: Thames & Hudson, 2007.

Scarre, Geoffrey. *Witchcraft and Magic in 16th and 17th Century Europe*. 2nd ed. Atlantic Highlands, N.J.: Humanities Press, 2001.

Schwaiger, Georg, ed. *Teufelsglaube und Hexenprozesse*. 4th ed. Munich: Beck, 1999.

Wilson, Stephen. *The Magical Universe: Everyday Ritual and Magic in Premodern Europe*. London: Hambledon, 2001.

Bibliographical and Historiographical Surveys

Barry, Jonathan, and Owen Davies, eds. *Palgrave Advances in Witchcraft Historiography*. Basingstoke, Eng.: Palgrave Macmillan, 2007.

Barstow, Anne. "On Studying Witchcraft as Women's History: A Historiography of the European Witch Persecutions." *Journal of Feminist Studies in Religion* 4 (1988): 7–19.

Behringer, Wolfgang. "Neue historische Literatur: Erträge und Perspektiven der Hexenforschung." *Historische Zeitschrift* 249 (1989): 619–40.

Crowe, Martha J., ed. *Witchcraft: Catalogue of the Witchcraft Collection in the Cornell University Library.* Millwood, N.Y.: KTO Press, 1977.

Franz, Günther, and Franz Irsigler, eds. *Methoden und Konzepte der historischen Hexenforschung.* Trier, Ger.: Spee, 1998.

Gijswijt-Hofstra, Marijke. "Recent Witchcraft Research in the Low Countries." In *Historical Research in the Low Countries*, ed. N. C. F. van Sas and Els Witte. The Hague: Nederlands Historisch Genootschap, 1992, 23–34.

Melton, J. Gordon. *Magic, Witchcraft, and Paganism in America: A Bibliography.* New York: Garland, 1982.

Midelfort, H. C. Erik. "Recent Witch Hunting Research, or Where Do We Go from Here?" *Papers of the Bibliographical Society of America* 62 (1968): 373–420.

———. "Witchcraft, Magic and the Occult." In *Reformation Europe: A Guide to Research*, ed. Steven Ozment. St. Louis, Mo.: Center for Reformation Research, 1982: 183–209.

Monter, E. William. "The Historiography of European Witchcraft: Progress and Prospects." *Journal of Interdisciplinary History* 2 (1972): 435–51.

Nugent, Donald. "Witchcraft Studies, 1959–1971: A Bibliographical Survey." *Journal of Popular Culture* 5 (1971): 710–25.

Whitney, Elspeth. "International Trends: The Witch 'She' / The Historian 'He': Gender and the Historiography of the European Witch-Hunts." *Journal of Women's History* 7 (1995): 77–101.

Encyclopedias and Reference Sources

Golden, Richard M., ed. *Encyclopedia of Witchcraft: The Western Tradition.* Santa Barbara, Calif.: ABC-Clio, 2006.

Greenwood, Susan. *The Encyclopedia of Magic and Witchcraft: An Illustrated Historical Reference to Spiritual Worlds.* London: Lorenz, 2001.

Grimassi, Raven. *Encyclopedia of Wicca and Witchcraft.* St. Paul, Minn.: Llewellyn, 2000.

Guiley, Rosemary Ellen. *The Encyclopedia of Witches and Witchcraft.* 2nd ed. New York: Checkmark, 1999.

Lewis, James R. *Witchcraft Today: An Encyclopedia of Wiccan and Neopagan Traditions.* Santa Barbara, Calif.: ABC-Clio, 1999.

Newell, Venetia. *The Encyclopedia of Witchcraft and Magic*. London: Hamlyn, 1974.

Pickering, David. *Cassell's Dictionary of Witchcraft*. London: Cassell, 1996.

Robbins, Rossell Hope. *The Encyclopedia of Witchcraft and Demonology*. New York: Crown, 1959.

WITCHCRAFT IN THE ANCIENT WORLD

Abusch, Tzvi. *Babylonian Witchcraft Literature: Case Studies*. Atlanta, Ga.: Scholars Press, 1987.

———. "The Demonic Image of the Witch in Standard Babylonian Literature: The Reworking of Popular Conceptions by Learned Exorcists." In *Religion, Science, and Magic in Concert and in Conflict*, ed. Jacob Neuser, Ernest S. Frerichs, and Paul Virgil McCracken Flesher. Oxford: Oxford University Press, 1989, 27–58.

———. "An Early Form of the Witchcraft Trial *Maqlû* and the Origin of a Babylonian Magical Ceremony." In *Lingering over Words: Studies in Ancient Near Eastern Literature in Honor of William L. Moran*, ed. Tzvi Abusch, John Huehnergard, and Piotr Steinkeller. Atlanta, Ga.: Scholars Press, 1990, 1–67.

———. "Mesopotamian Anti-Witchcraft Literature: Texts and Studies, Part I: The Nature of *Maqlû*, Its Character, Divisions, and Calendrical Setting." *Journal of Near Eastern Studies* 33 (1974): 251–62.

———. *Mesopotamian Witchcraft: Towards a History and Understanding of Babylonian Witchcraft Beliefs and Literature*. Leiden: Brill, 2002.

Aune, D. E. "Magic in Early Christianity." In *Aufsteig und Niedergang der römischen Welt* II.23.2, ed. Wolfgang Hasse. Berlin: Walter de Gruyter, 1980, 1507–57.

Barb, A. A. "The Survival of Magic Arts." In *The Conflict between Paganism and Christianity in the Fourth Century*, ed. Arnaldo Momigliano. Oxford: Clarendon, 1963, 100–25.

Bernand, André. *Sorciers grecs*. Paris: Fayard, 1991.

Brenk, Frederick E. "In the Light of the Moon: Demonology in the Early Imperial Period." In *Aufsteig und Niedergang der römischen Welt* II.16.3, ed. Wolfgang Hasse. Berlin: Walter de Gruyter, 1986, 2068–2145.

Ciraolo, Leda, and Jonathan Seidel, eds. *Magic and Divination in the Ancient World*. Leiden: Brill, 2002.

Clerc Jean-Benoît. *Homines Magici: Etude sur la sorcellerie et la magie dans la société romaine impériale*. Berlin: Peter Lang, 1995.

Cryer, Frederick H. *Divination in Ancient Israel and Its Near Eastern Environs: A Socio-Historical Investigation.* Sheffield, Eng.: Journal for the Study of the Old Testament Press, 1994.

Dickie, Matthew W. "Heliodorus and Plutarch on the Evil Eye." *Classical Philology* 86 (1991): 17–29.

———. *Magic and Magicians in the Greco-Roman World.* London: Routledge, 2001.

Faraone, Christopher A. "An Accusation of Magic in Classical Athens." *Transactions of the American Philological Association* 119 (1989): 149–60.

———. *Ancient Greek Love Magic.* Cambridge, Mass.: Harvard University Press, 1999.

———. "Binding and Burying the Forces of Evil: Defensive Use of 'Voodoo' Dolls in Ancient Greece." *Classical Antiquity* 10 (1991): 165–205.

———. "Deianira's Mistake and the Demise of Hericles: Erotic Magic in Sophocles' *Trachiniae.*" *Helios* 21 (1994): 115–35.

Faraone, Christopher A., and Dirk Obbink, eds. *Magika Hiera: Ancient Greek Magic and Religion.* Oxford: Oxford University Press, 1991.

Finkel, Irving L. "Necromancy in Ancient Mesopotamia." *Archiv für Orientforschung* 29–30 (1983–84): 1–17.

Frankfurter, David. "The Magic of Writing and the Writing of Magic: The Power of the Word in Egyptian and Greek Traditions." *Helios* 21 (1994): 189–221.

Garrett, Susan R. *The Demise of the Devil: Magic and the Demonic in Luke's Writings.* Minneapolis, Minn.: Fortress Publishing, 1989.

Graf, Fritz. *Magic in the Ancient World.* Trans. Franklin Philip. Cambridge, Mass.: Harvard University Press, 1997.

———. "The Magician's Initiation." *Helios* 21 (1994): 161–77.

———. "Medea, the Enchantress from Afar: Remarks on a Well-Known Myth." In *Medea: Essays on Medea in Myth, Literature, Philosophy, and Art,* ed. James J. Claus and Sarah Iles Johnston. Princeton, N.J.: Princeton University Press, 1997, 27–43.

Janowitz, Naomi. *Magic in the Roman World: Pagans, Jews and Christians.* London: Routledge, 2001.

Jeffers, Ann. *Magic and Divination in Ancient Palestine and Syria.* Leiden: Brill, 1996.

Luck, Georg. *Hexen und Zauberei in der römischen Dichtung.* Zurich: Artemis, 1962.

Meyer, Marvin, and Paul Mirecki, eds. *Ancient Magic and Ritual Power.* Leiden: Brill, 1995.

Michalowski, Piotr. "On Some Early Sumerian Magical Texts." *Orientalia* n.s. 54 (1985): 216–25.

Ogden, Daniel. *Greek and Roman Necromancy*. Princeton, N.J.: Princeton University Press, 2001.

———. *Magic, Witchcraft and Ghosts in the Greek and Roman Worlds: A Sourcebook*. 2nd ed. Oxford: Oxford University Press, 2009.

Pinch, Geraldine. *Magic in Ancient Egypt*. Austin: University of Texas Press, 1995.

Rabinowitz, Jacob. *The Rotting Goddess: The Origin of the Witch in Classical Antiquity*. New York: Autonomedia, 1998.

Reiner, Eric. *Astral Magic in Babylonia*. Philadelphia: American Philosophical Society, 1995.

Remus, Harold E. "Magic or Miracle: Some Second-Century Instances." *Second Century* 2 (1982): 127–56.

Rollins, S. "Women and Witchcraft in Ancient Assyria (c. 900–600 B.C.)." In *Images of Women in Antiquity*, ed. Averil Cameron and Amélie Kuhrt. Detroit, Mich.: Wayne State University Press, 1983, 34–45.

Schäfer, Peter, and Hans G. Klippenberg, eds. *Envisioning Magic: A Princeton Seminar and Symposium*. Leiden: Brill, 1997.

Scobie, Alex. "Strigiform Witches in Roman and Other Cultures." *Fabula* 19 (1978): 74–101.

Smith, Jonathan Z. "The Evil Eye in Mesopotamia." *Journal of Near Eastern Society* 51 (1992):19–32.

———. "Towards Interpreting Demonic Powers in Hellenistic and Roman Antiquity." *Aufsteig und Neidergang der römischen Welt* II.16.1, ed. Wolfgang Haase. Berlin: Walter de Gruyter, 1978, 425–39.

———. "The Wisdom of the Chaldeans: Mesopotamian Magic as Conceived by Classical Authors." In *East and West: Cultural Relations in the Ancient World*, ed. Tobias Fischer-Hansen. Copenhagen: Museum Tusculanum, 1988, 93–101.

Stratton, Kimberly B. *Naming the Witch: Magic, Ideology, and Stereotype in the Ancient World.* New York: Columbia University Press, 2007.

Thomsen, Marie-Louise. *Zauberdiagnose und Schwarze Magie in Mesopotamien*. Copenhagen: Carsten Niebuhr Institute for Ancient Near Eastern Studies, 1987.

Ulmer, Rivka. *The Evil Eye in the Bible and Rabbinic Literature*. Hoboken, N.J.: KTAV Publishing House, 1994.

Walters, Stanley D. "The Sorceress and Her Apprentice: A Case Study of an Accusation." *Journal of Cuneiform Studies* 23 (1970–71): 27–38.

Ward, John O. "Women, Witchcraft and Social Patterning in the Later Roman Lawcodes." *Prudentia* 13 (1981): 99–118.

WITCHCRAFT IN MEDIEVAL AND EARLY-MODERN EUROPE

Late Antiquity and Early Middle Ages

Brown, Peter. "Society and the Supernatural: A Medieval Change." *Daedalus* 104.2 (1975): 133–51.

———. "Sorcery, Demons and the Rise of Christianity: From Late Antiquity into the Middle Ages." In Peter Brown, *Religion and Society in the Age of St. Augustine*. New York: Harper and Row, 1972, 119–46.

Dukes, Eugene D. *Magic and Witchcraft in the Dark Ages*. Lanham, Md.: University Press of America, 1996.

Flint, Valerie I. J. *The Rise of Magic in Early Medieval Europe*. Princeton, N.J.: Princeton University Press, 1991.

Janowitz, Naomi. *Icons of Power: Ritual Practice in Late Antiquity*. University Park: Pennsylvania State University Press, 2002.

Markus, Robert A. "Augustine on Magic: A Neglected Semiotic Theory." *Revue des études augustiniennes* 40 (1994): 375–88.

Meens, Rob. "Magic and the Early Medieval World View." In *Community, the Family, and the Saint: Patterns of Power in Early Medieval Europe*, ed. Joyce Hill and Mary Swan. Turnhout, Bel.: Brepols, 1998, 285–95.

Murray, Alexander. "Missionaries and Magic in Dark-Age Europe." *Past and Present* 136 (1992): 186–205.

Riché, Pierre. "La magie à l'époque carolingienne." *Comptes rendus des séances de l'Académie des Inscriptions et Belles-lettres* 1 (1973): 127–38.

Schäfer, Peter. "Jewish Magical Literature in Late Antiquity and the Early Middle Ages." *Journal of Jewish Studies* 41 (1990): 75–91.

Smelik, K. A. D. "The Witch of Endor: 1 Samuel 28 in Rabbinic and Christian Exegesis till 800 A.D." *Vigiliae Christianae* 33 (1979): 160–79.

Thee, Francis C. R. *Julius Africanus and the Early Christian View of Magic*. Tübingen, Ger.: Mohr, 1984.

Ward, John O. "Witchcraft and Sorcery in the Later Roman Empire and the Early Middle Ages: An Anthropological Comment." *Prudentia* 12 (1980): 93–108.

The Middle Ages

Bailey, Michael D. "The Disenchantment of Magic: Spells, Charms, and Superstition in Early European Witchcraft Literature." *American Historical Review* 111 (2006): 383–404.

———. "From Sorcery to Witchcraft: Clerical Conceptions of Magic in the Later Middle Ages." *Speculum* 76 (2001): 960–90.

Barber, Malcolm. *The Trial of the Templars*. Cambridge: Cambridge University Press, 1978.

Blauert, Andreas, ed. *Ketzer, Zauberer, Hexen: Die Anfänge der europäischen Hexenverfolgungen*. Frankfurt: Suhrkamp, 1990.

Bologne, Jean-Claude. *Du flambeau au bûcher: Magie et superstition au Moyen Age*. Paris: Plon, 1993.

Boudet, Jean-Patrice. "La genèse médiévale de la chasse aux sorcières: Jalons en vue d'une relecture." In *Le mal et le diable: Leurs figures à la fin du Moyen Age*, ed. Nathalie Nabert. Paris: Beauchesne, 1996, 34–52.

Cohn, Norman. *Europe's Inner Demons: The Demonization of Christians in Medieval Christendom*. Rev. ed. Chicago: University of Chicago Press, 2000.

Deane, Jennifer Kolpacoff. *A History of Medieval Heresy and Inquisition*. Lanham, Md.: Rowman & Littlefield, 2011.

Habiger-Tuczay, Christa. *Magie und Magier im Mittelalter*. Munich: Diedrichs, 1992.

Hansen, Joseph. *Zauberwahn, Inquisition und Hexenprozess im Mittelalter und die Entstehung der grossen Hexenverfolgung*. 1900. Reprint, Aalen, Ger.: Scientia, 1964.

Harmening, Dieter. "Magiciennes et sorcières: La mutation du concept de magie à la fin du Moyen Age." *Heresis* 13–14 (1989): 421–45.

———. *Superstitio: Überlieferungs- und theoriegeschichtliche Untersuchungen zur kirchlich-theologischen Aberglaubensliteratur des Mittelalters*. Berlin: Schmidt, 1979.

———. *Zauberei im Abendland: Vom Anteil der Gelehrten am Wahn der Leute: Skizzen zur Geschichte des Aberglaubens*, Würzburg, Ger.: Königshausen & Neumann, 1991.

Harvey, Margaret. "Papal Witchcraft: The Charges against Benedict XIII." In *Sanctity and Secularity: The Church and the World*, ed. Derek Baker. Oxford: Blackwell, 1973, 109–16.

Jones, William R. "Political Uses of Sorcery in Medieval Europe." *The Historian* 34 (1972): 670–87.

Kieckhefer, Richard. "Erotic Magic in Medieval Europe." In *Sex in the Middle Ages: A Book of Essays*, ed. Joyce E. Salisbury. New York: Garland, 1991, 30–55.

———. *European Witch Trials: Their Foundations in Popular and Learned Culture, 1300–1500*. Berkeley: University of California Press, 1976.

———. *Forbidden Rites: A Necromancer's Manual of the Fifteenth Century*. University Park: Pennsylvania State University Press, 1998.

———. "The Holy and the Unholy: Sainthood, Witchcraft, and Magic in Late Medieval Europe." *Journal of Medieval and Renaissance Studies* 24 (1994): 355–85. Reprinted in *Christendom and Its Discontents: Exclusion, Persecution and Rebellion, 1000–1500*, ed. Scott L. Waugh and Peter D. Diehl. Cambridge: Cambridge University Press, 1996, 310–37.

———. *Magic in the Middle Ages*. Cambridge: Cambridge University Press, 1989.

———. "Mythologies of Witchcraft in the Fifteenth Century." *Magic, Ritual, and Witchcraft* 1 (2006): 79–108.

———. "The Specific Rationality of Medieval Magic." *American Historical Review* 99 (1994): 813–36.

Lecouteux, Claude. *Fées, sorcières et loups-garous au Moyen Age*. Paris: Imago, 1992.

Maier, Anneliese. "Eine Verfügung Johannes XXII. über die Zuständigkeit der Inquisition für Zaubereiprozesse." *Archivum Fratrum Praedicatorum* 22 (1952): 226–46. Reprinted in Anneliese Maier, *Ausgehendes Mittelalter: Gesamelte Aufsätze zur Geistesgeschichte des 14. Jahrhunderts*. 3 vols. Rome, 1964–77, 2:59–80.

Manselli, Raoul. *Magia e stregoneria nel medio evo*. Turin: Giappichelli, 1976.

Mormando, Franco. *The Preacher's Demons: Bernardino of Siena and the Social Underworld of the Early Italian Renaissance*. Chicago: University of Chicago Press, 1999.

Murray, Alexander. "Medieval Origins of the Witch-Hunt." *The Cambridge Quarterly* 7 (1976): 63–74.

Peters, Edward. *The Magician, the Witch, and the Law*. Philadelphia: University of Pennsylvania Press, 1978.

Rose, Elliot. *A Razor for a Goat: Problems in the History of Witchcraft and Diabolism*. 1962. Reprint, Toronto: University of Toronto Press, 1989.

Russell, Jeffrey Burton. "Medieval Witchcraft and Medieval Heresy." In *On the Margin of the Visible: Sociology, the Esoteric, and the Occult*, ed. Edward A. Tiryakian. New York: Wiley, 1974, 179–89.

———. *Witchcraft in the Middle Ages*. Ithaca, N.Y.: Cornell University Press, 1972.

Russell, Jeffrey B., and Mark W. Wyndham. "Witchcraft and the Demonization of Heresy." *Mediaevalia* 2 (1976): 1–21.

Tucker, Elizabeth. "Antecedents of Contemporary Witchcraft in the Middle Ages." *Journal of Popular Culture* 14 (1980): 70–78.

The Era of the Witch-Hunts

Ankarloo, Bengt, and Gustav Henningsen, eds. *Early Modern European Witchcraft: Centres and Peripheries*. Oxford: Oxford University Press, 1990.

Barry, Jonathan, Marianne Hester, and Gareth Roberts, eds. *Witchcraft in Early Modern Europe: Studies in Culture and Belief*. Cambridge: Cambridge University Press, 1996.

Bechtel, Guy. *Le sorcier et l'Occident: La destruction de la sorcellerie en Europe des origines aux grands bûchers*. Paris: Plon, 1997.

Becker, Gabriele, et al. *Aus der Zeit der Verzweiflung: Zur Genese und Aktualität des Hexenbilds*. Frankfurt: Suhrkamp, 1976.

Behringer, Wolfgang. "Kinderhexenprozesse: Zur Rolle von Kindern in der Geschichte der Hexenverfolgung." *Zeitschrift für historische Forschung* 16 (1989): 31–47.

———. "Weather, Hunger and Fear: Origins of the European Witch-Hunts in Climate, Society and Mentality." *German History* 13 (1995): 1–27.

Ben-Yehuda, Nachman. "The European Witch Craze of the Fourteenth to Seventeenth Centuries: A Sociologist's Perspective." *American Journal of Sociology* 86 (1980): 1–31.

———. "Problems Inherent in Socio-Historical Approaches to the European Witch-Craze." *Journal for the Scientific Study of Religion* 20 (1981): 326–38.

———. Witchcraft and the Occult as Boundary Maintenance Devices." In *Religion, Science, and Magic in Concert and in Conflict*, ed. Jacob Neusner, Ernest S. Frerichs, and Paul Virgil McCracken Flesher. Oxford: Oxford University Press, 1989, 229–60.

Bever, Edward. "Old Age and Witchcraft in Early Modern Europe." In *Old Age in Preindustrial Society*, ed. Peter N. Stearns. New York: Holmes and Meier, 1982, 150–90.

———. *The Realities of Witchcraft and Popular Magic in Early Modern Europe: Culture, Cognition and Everyday Life*. Basingstoke, Eng.: Palgrave Macmillan, 2008.

Blécourt, Willem de. "Witch Doctors, Soothsayers and Priests: On Cunning Folk in European Historiography and Tradition." *Social History* 19 (1994): 285–303.

Briggs, Robin. *Witches and Neighbors: The Social and Cultural Context of European Witchcraft*. 2nd ed. New York: Viking, 2002.

Clark, Stuart. "Inversion, Misrule and the Meaning of Witchcraft." *Past and Present* 87 (1980): 98–127.

———. *Thinking with Demons: The Idea of Witchcraft in Early Modern Europe*. Oxford: Clarendon, 1997.

Clark, Stuart, ed. *Languages of Witchcraft: Narrative, Ideology and Meaning in Early Modern Culture*. New York: St. Martin's Press, 2001.

Currie, Elliott P. "Crimes without Criminals: Witchcraft and Its Control in Renaissance Europe." *Law and Society Review* 3 (1968): 7–32.

Davies, Owen, and Willem de Blécourt, eds. *Beyond the Witch Trials: Witchcraft and Magic in Enlightenment Europe*. Manchester, Eng.: Manchester University Press, 2004.

Edwards, Kathryn A., ed. *Werewolves, Witches, and Wandering Spirits: Traditional Beliefs and Folklore in Early Modern Europe*. Kirksville, Mo.: Truman State University Press, 2002.

Eiden, Herbert, and Rita Voltmar, eds. *Hexenprozesse und Gerichtspraxis*. Trier, Ger.: Paulinus, 2001.

Eliade, Mircea. "Some Observations on European Witchcraft." *History of Religions* 14 (1975): 149–72. Reprinted in Mircea Eliade, *Occultism, Witchcraft, and Cultural Fashions: Essays in Comparative Religions*. Chicago: Chicago University Press, 1976, 69–92.

Hook, Dale. "The Great European Witch-Hunts: A Historical Perspective." *American Journal of Sociology* 88 (1983): 1270–74.

Honegger, Claudia, ed. *Die Hexen der Neuzeit: Studien zur Sozialgeschichte eines kulturellen Deutungsmusters*. Frankfurt: Suhrkamp, 1978.

Horsley, Richard A. "Further Reflections on Witchcraft and European Folk Religion." *History of Religions* 19 (1979).

———. "Who Were the Witches? The Social Roles of the Accused in the European Witch-Trials." *Journal of Interdisciplinary History* 9 (1979): 689–715.

Larner, Christina, "*Crimen Exceptum*? The Crime of Witchcraft in Europe." In *Crime and the Law: The Social History of Crime since 1500*, ed. V. A. C. Gatrell, Bruce Lenman, and Geoffrey Parker. London: Europa, 1980, 49–75.

———. *Witchcraft and Religion: The Politics of Popular Belief*. Ed. Alan Macfarlane. Oxford: Blackwell, 1984.

Levack, Brian. "The Great Witch-Hunt." In *Handbook of European History, 1400–1600: Late Middle Ages, Renaissance, and Reformation*, 2 vols., ed. Thomas A. Brady Jr., Heiko A. Oberman, and James D. Tracy. Leiden: Brill, 1994–95, 2:607–40.

Maxwell-Stuart, P. G. *Witch Hunters: Professional Prickers, Unwitchers and Witch Finders of the Renaissance*. Stroud, Eng.: Tempus, 2003.

Midelfort, H. C. Erik. "Were There Really Witches?" In *Transition and Revolution: Problems and Issues of European Renaissance and Reformation History*, ed. Robert M. Kingdon. Minneapolis, Minn.: Burgess, 1974, 189–205.

———. "Witch Hunting and the Domino Theory." In *Religion and the People, 800–1700*, ed. James Obelkevich. Chapel Hill: University of North Carolina Press, 1979, 277–88, 323–25.

Monter, E. William, ed. *European Witchcraft*. New York: Wiley, 1969.

———. "French and Italian Witchcraft." *History Today* 30 (November 1980): 31–35.

———. *Ritual, Myth and Magic in Early Modern Europe*. Athens: Ohio University Press, 1983.

Muchembled, Robert. *Le roi et le sorcière: L'Europe des bûchers (XVe–XVIIe siècle)*. Paris: Desclée, 1993.

———. *Le sorcière au village: XVe–XVIIIe siècle*. Paris: Gallimard, 1979.

Nugent, Donald. "The Renaissance and/of Witchcraft." *Church History* 40 (1971): 69–78.

Oldridge, Darren, ed. *The Witchcraft Reader*. London: Routledge, 2002.

Oplinger, Jon. *The Politics of Demonology: The European Witchcraze and the Mass Production of Deviance*. London: Associated University Presses, 1990.

Scribner, Robert W. "Magic, Witchcraft, and Superstition." *Historical Journal* 37 (1994): 219–30.

———. "The Reformation, Popular Magic, and the 'Disenchantment of the World.'" *Journal of Interdisciplinary History* 23 (1992–93): 475–94.

Segl, Peter, et al. *Hexenglaube und Hexenverfolgungen: Eine kritische Bilanz*. Augsburg, Ger.: Akademie-Publikationen, 1989.

Stephens, Walter. "Incredible Sex: Witches, Demons, and Giants in the Early Modern Imagination." In *Monsters in the Italian Literary Imagination*, ed. Keala Jewel. Detroit, Mich.: Wayne State University Press, 2001, 153–76.

Stokes, Laura Patricia. *Demons of Urban Reform: Early European Witch Trials and Criminal Justice, 1430–1530*. Basingstoke, Eng.: Palgrave Macmillan, 2011.

Thurston, Robert W. *Witch, Wicce, Mother Goose: The Rise and Fall of the Witch Hunts in Europe and North America*. New York: Longman, 2001.

Trevor-Roper, H. R. *The European Witch-Craze of the Sixteenth and Seventeenth Centuries and Other Essays*. New York Harper, 1969.

Waite, Gary K. *Heresy, Magic and Witchcraft in Early Modern Europe*. Basingstoke, Eng.: Palgrave, 2003.

The Witches' Sabbath

Bailey, Michael D. "The Medieval Concept of the Witches' Sabbath." *Exemplaria* 8 (1996): 419–39.

Durrant, Jonathan. "The *Osculum Infame*: Heresy, Secular Culture and the Image of the Witches' Sabbath." In *The Kiss in History*, ed. Karen Harvey. Manchester, Eng.: Manchester University Press, 2005, 36–61.

Ginzburg, Carlo. *Ecstasies: Deciphering the Witches' Sabbath*. Trans. Raymond Rosenthal. New York: Pantheon, 1991.

———. "The Witches' Sabbat: Popular Cult or Inquisitorial Stereotype?" In *Understanding Popular Culture: Europe from the Middle Ages to the Nineteenth Century*, ed. Steven L. Kaplan. Berlin: Mouton, 1984, 39–51.

Jacques-Chaquin, Nicole, and Maxime Préaud, eds. *Le sabbat des sorciers en Europe (XVe–XVIIIe siècles)*. Grenoble, France: Millon, 1994.

Klaniczay, Gábor. "Der Hexensabbat im Spiegel von Zeugenaussagen in Hexen-Prozessen." *Zeitschrift für Kulturwissenschaft* 5 (1993): 31–54.

Paravicini Bagliani, Agostino, Kathrin Utz Tremp, and Martine Ostorero. "Le sabbat dans les Alpes: Les prémices médiévales de la chasse aux sorcières." In *Sciences: Raison et déraisons*. Lausanne, Switz.: Payot, 1994, 67–89.

Tschacher, Werner. "Der Flug durch die Luft zwischen Illusionstheorie und Realitätsbeweis: Studien zum sog. Kanon Episcopi und zum Hexenflug." *Zeitschrift der Savigny-Stiftung für Rechtsgeschichte* 116, Kan. Abt. 85 (1999): 225–76.

Witchcraft, Medicine, and Disease

Andreski, Stanislav. "The Syphilitic Shock: A New Explanation of the 'Great Witch Craze' of the 16th and 17th Centuries in the Light of Medicine and Psychiatry." *Encounter* 58 (1982): 7–26.

Bever, Edward. "Witchcraft Fears and Psychosocial Factors in Disease." *Journal of Interdisciplinary History* 30 (2000): 573–90.

Davies, Owen. *Cunning Folk: Popular Magic in English History*. London: Hambledon, 2003.

Estes, Leland. "The Medical Origins of the European Witch Craze: A Hypothesis." *Journal of Social History* 17 (1983): 271–84.

Geyer-Kordesch, Johanna. "Whose Enlightenment? Medicine, Witchcraft, Melancholia and Pathology." In *Medicine in the Enlightenment*, ed. Roy Porter. Amsterdam: Rodopi, 1994, 113–27.

Harner, Michael J. "The Role of Hallucinogenic Plants in European Witchcraft." In *Hallucinogens and Shamanism*, ed. Michael J. Harner. Oxford: Oxford University Press, 1973, 125–50.

King, L. S. "Friedrich Hoffmann and Some Medical Aspects of Witchcraft." *Clio Medica* 9 (1974): 299–309.

———. "Witchcraft and Medicine: Conflicts in the Early Eighteenth Century." In *Circa Tiliam: Studiae historiae medicinae Gerrit Arie Lindeboom septuagenaria oblata.* Leiden: Brill, 1974, 122–39.

Müller-Ebeling, Claudia, Christian Rätsch, and Wolf-Dieter Storl. *Witchcraft Medicine: Healing Arts, Shamanic Practices, and Forbidden Plants.* Trans. Annabel Lee. Rochester, Vt.: Inner Traditions, 2003.

Nemec, Jaroslav. *Witchcraft and Medicine, 1484–1793.* Washington, D.C.: U.S. Department of Health, Education, and Welfare, 1974.

Piomelli, Daniele, and Antonio Pollio. "'In upupa o strige': A Study in Renaissance Psychotropic Plant Ointments." *History and Philosophy of the Life Sciences* 16 (1994): 241–73.

Schoeneman, Thomas J. "Criticisms of the Psychopathological Interpretation of the Witch-Hunts: A Review." *American Journal of Psychiatry* 139 (1982): 1028–32.

———. "The Role of Mental Illness in the European Witch Hunts of the Sixteenth and Seventeenth Centuries: An Assessment." *Journal of the History of Behavioral Sciences* 13 (1977): 337–51.

———. "The Witch Hunt as a Cultural Change Phenomenon." *Ethos* 3 (1975): 529–54.

Sidky H. *Witchcraft, Lycanthropy, Drugs, and Disease: An Anthropological Study of the European Witch-Hunts.* New York: Peter Lang, 1997.

Várkonyi, Agnes. "Connections between the Cessation of Witch Trials and the Transformation of the Social Structure Related to Medicine." *Acta Ethnographica* 37 (1991–1992): 426–71.

Women, Gender, and Witchcraft

Ahrendt-Schulte, Ingrid, Dieter R. Bauer, Sönke Lorenz, and Jürgen Michael Schmidt, eds. *Geschlecht, Magie und Hexenverfolgung.* Bielefeld, Ger.: Verlag für Regionalgeschichte, 2002.

Apps, Lara, and Andrew Gow. *Male Witches in Early Modern Europe.* Manchester, Eng.: Manchester University Press, 2003.

Bailey, Michael D. "The Feminization of Magic and the Emerging Idea of the Female Witch in the Late Middle Ages." *Essays in Medieval Studies* 19 (2002): 120–34.

Barstow, Anne Llewellyn. *Witchcraze: A New History of the European Witch Hunts.* San Francisco: Pandora, 1994.

Blöcker, Monica. "Frauenzauber-Zauberfrauen." *Zeitschrift für schweizerische Kirchengeschichte* 76 (1982): 1–39.

Coudert, Allison P. "The Myth of the Improved Status of Protestant Women: The Case of the Witchcraze." In *The Politics of Gender in Early Modern Europe*, ed. Jean R. Brink, Allison P. Coudert, and Maryanne C. Horowitz. Kirksville, Mo.: Sixteenth Century Journal Publishers, 1989, 61–94.

Dienst, Heide. "Zur Rolle von Frauen im magischen Vorstellungen und Praktiken—nach ausgewählten mittelalterlichen Quellen." In *Frauen in Spätantike und Frühmittelalter: Lebensbedingungen-Lebensnormen-Lebensformen*, ed. Werner Affeldt. Sigmaringen, Ger.: Thorbecke, 1990, 173–94.

Dinzelbacher, Peter. *Heilige oder Hexen? Schicksale auffälliger Frauen im Mittelalter und Frühneuzeit*. Munich: Artemis, 1995.

Ehrenreich, Barbara, and Deirdre English. *Witches, Midwives and Nurses: A History of Women Healers*. New York: Feminist Press, 1973.

Garrett, Clarke. "Women and Witches: Patterns of Analysis." *Signs* 3 (1977): 461–70.

Harley, David. "Historians as Demonologists: The Myth of the Midwife-Witch." *Social History of Medicine* 3 (1990): 1–26.

Heinemann, Evelyn. *Witches: A Psychoanalytical Exploration of the Killing of Women*. Trans. Donald Kiraly. London: Free Association Books, 2000.

Hester, Marianne. *Lewd Women and Wicked Witches: A Study of the Dynamics of Male Domination*. London: Routledge, 1992.

Holmes, Clive. "Women: Witnesses and Witches." *Past and Present* 140 (1993): 45–78.

Horsley, Ritta Jo, and Richard A. Horsley. "On the Trail of the 'Witches': Wise Women, Midwives and the European Witch Hunts." In *Women in German Yearbook 3: Feminist Studies and German Culture*, ed. Mariane Buckhard and Edith Waldstein. Washington D.C.: University of America Press, 1987, 1–28.

Jackson, Louise. "Witches, Wives and Mothers: Witchcraft Persecution and Women's Confessions in Seventeenth-Century England." *Women's History Review* 4 (1995): 63–84.

James-Raoul, Danièle. "La femme maléfique dans la literature Romanesque de la fin du Moyen Age." In *Le mal et le diable: Leurs figures à la fin du Moyen Age*, ed. Nathalie Nabert. Paris: Beauchesne, 1996, 11–33.

Kittell, Ellen E. "Toward a Perspective on Women, Sex, and Witches in the Later Middle Ages." In *Von Menschen und ihren Zeichen: Sozialhistorische Untersuchungen zum Spätmittelalter und zur Neuzeit*, ed. Ingrid Matschinegg et al. Bielefeld, Ger.: Verlag für Regionalgeschichte, 1990, 13–40.

Klaniczay, Gábor. "*Miraculum* und *maleficium*: Einige Überlegungen zu den weiblichen Heiligen des Mittelalters in Mitteleuropa." *Wissenschaftskolleg Jahrbuch* (1990/1991): 220–48.

Labouvie, Eva. "Männer im Hexenprozeß: Zur Sozialanthropologie eines 'männlichen' Verständnisses von Hexerei." *Geschichte und Gesellschaft* 16 (1990): 56–78.

McLachlan, Hugh. "Witchcraft and Antifeminism." *Scottish Journal of Sociology* 4 (1980): 141–66.

Monter, E. William. "The Pedestal and the Stake: Courtly Love and Witchcraft." In *Becoming Visible: Women in European History*, ed. Renate Bridenthal and Claudia Koonz. Boston: Houghton Mifflin, 1977, 119–36.

Opitz, Claudia, ed. *Der Hexenstreit: Frauen in der frühneuzeitlichen Hexenverfolgung*. Freiburg, Ger.: Herder, 1995.

Purkiss, Diane. *The Witch in History: Early Modern and Twentieth-Century Representations*. London: Routledge, 1996.

Roper, Lyndal. *Oedipus and the Devil: Witchcraft, Sexuality and Religion in Early Modern Europe*. London: Routledge, 1994.

———. *Witch Craze: Terror and Fantasy in Baroque Germany*. New Haven, Conn.: Yale University Press, 2006.

Rowlands, Alison, ed. *Witchcraft and Masculinities in Early Modern Europe*. Basingstoke, Eng.: Palgrave Macmillan, 2009.

Schulte, Rolf. *Man as Witch: Male Witches in Central Europe*. Trans. Linde Froome-Döring. Basingstoke, Eng.: Palgrave Macmillan, 2009.

Walinski-Kiehl, Robert. "Males, 'Masculine Honor,' and Witch Hunting in Seventeenth-Century Germany." *Men and Masculinities* 6 (2004): 254–71.

Weston, L. M. C. "Women's Medicine, Women's Magic: The Old English Metrical Childbirth Charms." *Modern Philology* 92 (1995): 279–93.

Williams, Selma R., and Pamela Williams Adelman. *Riding the Nightmare: Women and Witchcraft from the Old World to Colonial Salem*. New York: Harper, 1978.

Willis, Deborah. *Malevolent Nurture: Witch-Hunting and Maternal Power in Early Modern England*. Ithaca, N.Y.: Cornell University Press, 1995.

Magic and Occult Science in the Era of the Witch-Hunts

Cook, John W. "Magic, Witchcraft, and Science." *Philosophical Investigations* 6 (1983): 2–36.

Copenhaver, Brian P. "Scholastic Philosophy and Renaissance Magic in the *De vita* of Marsilio Ficino." *Renaissance Quarterly* 37 (1984): 632–80.

Couliano, Ioan P. *Eros and Magic in the Renaissance*. Chicago: University of Chicago Press, 1987.

Easlea, Brian. *Witch Hunting, Magic and the New Philosophy: An Introduction to the Debates of the Scientific Revolution 1450–1750*. Atlantic Highlands, N.J.: Humanities Press, 1980.

Gouk, Penelope. *Music, Science and Natural Magic in Seventeenth-Century England*. New Haven, Conn.: Yale University Press, 1999.

Hunter, Michael. "New Light on the "Drummer of Tedworth": Conflicting Narratives of Witchcraft in Restoration England." *Historical Research* 78 (2005): 311–53.

Idel, Moshe. "The Magical and Neoplatonic Interpretation of the Kabbala in the Renaissance." In *Jewish Thought in the Sixteenth Century*, ed. Bernard D. Cooperman. Cambridge, Mass.: Harvard University Press, 1984, 186–242.

Jobe, Thomas Harmon. "The Devil in Restoration Science: The Glanvill-Webster Witchcraft Debate." *Isis* 72 (1981): 343–56.

León-Jones, Karen Silva de. *Giordano Bruno and the Kabbalah: Prophets, Magicians, and Rabbis*. New Haven, Conn.: Yale University Press, 1997.

Mebane, John S. *Renaissance Magic and the Return of the Golden Age: The Occult Tradition and Marlowe, Jonson, and Shakespeare*. Lincoln: University of Nebraska Press, 1989.

Merkel, Ingrid, and Allen G. Debus, eds. *Hermeticism and the Renaissance: Intellectual History and the Occult in Early Modern Europe*. Washington D.C.: Folger Shakespeare Library, 1988.

Shumaker, Wayne. *The Occult Sciences in the Renaissance*. Berkeley: University of California Press, 1972.

Tambiah, Stanley Jeyaraja. *Magic, Science, Religion, and the Scope of Rationality*. Cambridge: Cambridge University Press, 1990.

Walker, D. P. *Spiritual and Demonic Magic from Ficino to Campanella*. 1958. Reprint University Park: Pennsylvania State University Press, 2000.

Woolley, Benjamin. *The Queen's Conjurer: The Science and Magic of Dr. John Dee, Advisor to Queen Elizabeth I*. New York: Holt, 2001.

Yates, Frances A. *The Art of Memory*. Chicago: University of Chicago Press, 1966.

———. *Giordano Bruno and the Hermetic Tradition*. Chicago: University of Chicago Press, 1964.

———. "The Hermetic Tradition in Renaissance Science." In *Art, Science, and History in the Renaissance*, ed. Charles S. Singleton. Baltimore, Md.: Johns Hopkins University Press, 1967, 255–74.

———. *The Occult Philosophy in the Elizabethan Age*. London: Routledge, 1979.

———. *The Rosicrucian Enlightenment*. London: Routledge, 1972.

Zambelli, Paola. *L'ambigua natura della magia: Filosofi, streghe, riti nel Rinascimento*. 2nd ed. Venice: Marsilio, 1996.

———. "Magic and Radical Reformation in Agrippa of Nettesheim." *Journal of the Warburg and Courtauld Institutes* 39 (1976): 69–103.

————. *White Magic, Black Magic in the European Renaissance: From Ficino, Pico, Della Porta to Trithemius, Agrippa, Bruno.* Leiden: Brill, 2007.

Zika, Charles. *Reuchlin und die okkulte Tradition der Renaissance.* Sigmaringen, Ger.: Thorbecke, 1998.

REGIONAL STUDIES OF WITCHCRAFT

British Isles (England, Ireland, Scotland, Wales)

Almond, Philip. *The Witches of Warboys: An Extraordinary Story of Sorcery, Sadism and Satanic Possession in Elizabethan England.* London: I. B. Tauris, 2007.

Anderson, Alan, and Raymond Gordon. "Witchcraft and the Status of Women: The Case of England." *The British Journal of Sociology* 29 (1978): 171–84.

Bostridge, Ian. *Witchcraft and Its Transformations, c.1650–c.1750.* Oxford: Clarendon, 1997.

Byrne, Patrick. *Witchcraft in Ireland.* Cork, Ireland: Mercier, 1975.

Clark, Stuart, and P. T. J. Morgan. "Religion and Magic in Elizabethan Wales: Robert Hilland's Dialogue on Witchcraft." *Journal of Ecclesiastical History* 27 (1976): 31–46.

Cowan, Edward J. "The Darker Vision of the Scottish Renaissance: The Devil and Francis Stewart." In *Renaissance and Reformation in Scotland,* ed. Ian B. Cowan and Duncan Shaw. Edinburgh: Scottish Academic Press, 1983, 125–40.

Crawford, Jane. "Evidence for Witchcraft in Anglo-Saxon England." *Medium Aevum* 32 (1963): 99–116.

Darr, Orna Alyagon. *Marks of an Absolute Witch: Evidentiary Dilemmas in Early Modern England.* Aldershot, Eng.: Ashgate, 2011.

Deacon, Richard. *Matthew Hopkins: Witch-Finder General.* London: Muller, 1976.

Durston, Gregory. *Witchcraft and Witch Trials: A History of English Witchcraft and Its Legal Perspectives, 1542–1736.* Chichester, Eng.: Barry Rose Law, 2000.

Gaskill, Malcolm. "The Devil in the Shape of a Man: Witchcraft, Conflict and Belief in Jacobean England." *Historical Research* 71 (1998): 142–71.

————. *Witchfinders: A Seventeenth-Century Tragedy.* London: John Murray, 2005.

Geis, Gilbert, and Ivan Bunn. *A Trial of Witches: A Seventeenth-Century Witchcraft Prosecution.* London: Routledge, 1997.

Gibson, Marion. *Reading Witchcraft: Stories of Early English Witches.* London: Routledge, 1999.

Goodare, Julian, ed. *The Scottish Witch-Hunt in Context.* Manchester, Eng.: Manchester University Press, 2002.

Goodare, Julian, Lauren Martin, and Joyce Miller, eds. *Witchcraft and Belief in Early Modern Scotland.* Basingstoke, Eng.: Palgrave Macmillan, 2008.

Gregory, Annabel. "Witchcraft, Politics and 'Good Neighbourhood' in Early Seventeenth-Century Rye." *Past and Present* 133 (1991): 31–66.

Griffiths, Bill. *Aspects of Anglo-Saxon Magic.* Hockwold-cum-Wilton, Eng.: Anglo-Saxon Books, 1996.

Guskin, Phyllis J. "The Context of Witchcraft: The Case of Jane Wenham (1712)." *Eighteenth Century Studies* 15 (1981): 48–71.

Harley, David. "Mental Illness, Magical Medicine and the Devil in Northern England, 1650–1700." In *The Medical Revolution of the Seventeenth Century,* ed. R. K. French and A. Wear. Cambridge: Cambridge University Press, 1989, 114–44.

Holmes, Clive. "Popular Culture? Witches, Magistrates and Divines in Early Modern England." In *Understanding Popular Culture: Europe from the Middle Ages to the Nineteenth Century,* ed. Steven Kaplan. Berlin: Mouton, 1984, 85–111.

Hutton, Ronald. *Witches, Druids and King Arthur.* London: Hambledon, 2003.

Jolly, Karen Louise. "Anglo-Saxon Charms in the Context of a Christian World View." *Journal of Medieval History* 11 (1985): 279–93.

———. "Magic, Miracle, and Popular Practice in the Early Medieval West: Anglo-Saxon England." In *Religion, Science, and Magic in Concert and Conflict,* ed. Jacob Neusner, Ernest S. Frerichs, and Paul Virgil McCracken Flesher. Oxford: Oxford University Press, 1989, 166–82.

———. *Popular Religion in Late Saxon England: Elf Charms in Context.* Chapel Hill: University of North Carolina Press, 1996.

Kelly, H. A. "English Kings and the Fear of Sorcery." *Medieval Studies* 39 (1977): 206–38.

Lapoint, E. C. "Irish Immunity to Witch-Hunting, 1534–1711." *Éire-Ireland* 27 (1992): 76–92.

Larner, Christina. *Enemies of God: The Witch-Hunt in Scotland.* Baltimore, Md.: Johns Hopkins University Press, 1981.

Levack, Brian. "The Great Scottish Witch-Hunt of 1661–1662." *Journal of British Studies* 20 (1980): 90–108.

———. "Possession, Witchcraft and the Law in Jacobean England." *Washington and Lee University Law Review* 52 (1995): 1613–40.

MacDonald, Michael, ed. *Witchcraft and Hysteria in Elizabethan England: Edward Jorden and the Mary Glover Case.* London: Routledge, 1991.

Macfarlane, Alan. *Witchcraft in Tudor and Stuart England: A Regional and Comparative Study.* 1970. Reprint London: Routledge, 1999.

Maxwell-Stuart, P. G. *An Abundance of Witches: The Great Scottish Witch-Hunt.* Stroud, Eng.: Tempus, 2005.

———. "The Fear of the King is Death: James VI and the Witches of East Lothian." In *Fear in Early Modern Society*, ed. William C. Naphy and Penny Roberts. Manchester, Eng.: Manchester University Press, 1997, 209–25.

———. *Satan's Conspiracy: Magic and Witchcraft in Sixteenth-Century Scotland.* East Linton, Scotland: Tuckwell Press, 2001.

McLachlan, Hugh V. ed. *The Kirk, Satan and Salem: The History of the Witches of Renfrewshire.* Glasgow, Scotland: The Grimsay Press, 2006.

Meaney, A. L. "Women, Witchcraft and Magic in Anglo-Saxon England." In *Superstition and Popular Medicine in Anglo-Saxon England*, ed. D. G. Scragg. Manchester, Eng.: Manchester University Press, 1989, 9–40.

Newton, John, and Jo Bath, eds. *Witchcraft and the Act of 1604.* Leiden: Brill, 2008.

Normand, Lawrence, and Gareth Roberts. *Witchcraft in Early Modern Scotland: James VI's Demonology and the North Berwick Witches.* Exeter, Eng.: University of Exeter Press, 2000.

Peel, Edgar, and Pat Southern. *The Trials of the Lancashire Witches: A Study of Seventeenth-Century Witchcraft.* 3rd ed. Nelson, Eng.: Hendon, 1985.

Poole, Richard, ed. *The Lancashire Witches: Histories and Stories.* Manchester, Eng.: Manchester University Press, 2002.

Rushton, Peter. "Women, Witchcraft, and Slander in Early Modern Europe: Cases from the Church Courts of Durham." *Northern History* 18 (1982): 116–32.

Sawyer, Ronald C. "'Strangely handled in all her lyms': Witchcraft and Healing in Jacobean England." *Journal of Social History* 22 (1989): 461–85.

Sharpe, James. *The Bewitching of Anne Gunter: A Horrible and True Story of Deception, Witchcraft, Murder, and the King of England.* London: Profile, 1999.

———. *Instruments of Darkness: Witchcraft in Early Modern England.* Philadelphia: University of Pennsylvania Press, 1996.

———. "Witchcraft and Women in Seventeenth-Century England: Some Northern Evidence." *Continuity and Change* 6 (1991): 179–99.

———. *Witchcraft in Early Modern England.* London: Longman, 2001.

———. *Witchcraft in Seventeenth-Century Yorkshire: Accusations and Counter-Measures.* York, Eng.: Bothwick Institute of Historical Research, 1992.

Stavreva, Kirilka. "Fighting Words: Witch-Speak in Late Elizabethan Docu-fiction." *Journal of Medieval and Early Modern Studies* 30 (2000): 309–38.

Stoyle, Mark. *The Black Legend of Prince Rupert's Dog: Witchcraft and Propaganda during the English Civil War.* Exeter, Eng.: University of Exeter Press, 2011.

Suggett, Richard. *A History of Witchcraft and Magic in Wales.* Stroud, Eng.: Tempus, 2008.

Swales, J. K., and Hugh V. McLachlan. "Witchcraft and the Status of Women." *British Journal of Sociology* 30 (1979): 349–58.

Thomas, Keith. *Religion and the Decline of Magic.* New York: Scribner's, 1971.

Tourney, Garfield. "The Physician and Witchcraft in Restoration England." *Medical History* 16 (1972): 143–55.

Unsworth, C. R. "Witchcraft Beliefs and Criminal Procedure in Early Modern England." In *Legal Record and Historical Reality*, ed. Thomas Glyn Watkin. London: Hambledon, 1989.

Valletta, Frederick. *Witchcraft, Magic, and Superstition in England, 1640–70.* Aldershot, Eng.: Ashgate, 2000.

Wilby, Emma. *Cunning Folk and Familiar Spirits: Shamanistic Visionary Traditions in Early Modern British Witchcraft and Magic.* Brighton, Eng.: Sussex Academic Press, 2005.

———. *The Visions of Isobel Gowdie: Magic, Witchcraft, and Dark Shamanism in Seventeenth-Century Scotland.* Brighton, Eng.: Sussex Academic Press, 2010.

Eastern Europe

Kazhdan, Alexander. "Holy and Unholy Miracle Workers." In *Byzantine Magic*, ed. Henry Maguire. Washington D.C.: Dumbarton Oaks, 1995, 73–82.

Kivelson, Valerie A. "Male Witches and Gendered Categories in Seventeenth-Century Russia." *Comparative Studies in Society and History* 45 (2003): 606–31.

———. "Through the Prism of Witchcraft: Gender and Social Change in Seventeenth-Century Muscovy." In *Russia's Women: Accommodation, Resistance, Transformation*, ed. Barbara Evans Clements, Barbara A. Engel, and Christine D. Worobec. Berkeley: University of California Press, 1991, 74–94.

Klaniczay, Gábor. *The Uses of Supernatural Power.* Ed. Karen Margolis. Trans. Susan Singerman. Princeton, N.J.: Princeton University Press, 1990.

Klaniczay, Gábor, and Éva Pócs, eds. *Witch-Beliefs and Witch-Hunting in Central and Eastern Europe*. Special issue of *Acta Ethnographica Hungarica* 37 (1991–92).

Plakans, Andrejs. "Witches and Werewolves in Modern Livonia." In *Rättea: En Festskrift till Bengt Ankarloo*, ed. Lars M. Andersson et al. Lund, Norway: Nordic Academic Press, 2000, 255–71.

Pócs, Éva. *Between the Living and the Dead: A Perspective on Witches and Seers in the Early Modern Age*. Trans. Szilvia Rédey and Michael Webb. Budapest: Central European University Press, 1999.

———. *Fairies and Witches at the Boundary of South-Eastern and Central Europe*. Helsinki: Suomalainen Tiedenkatemia, 1989.

Ryan, W. F. *The Bathhouse at Midnight: A Historical Survey of Magic and Divination in Russia*. University Park: Pennsylvania State University Press, 1999.

Tazbir, Janusz. "Hexenprozesse in Polen." *Archiv für Reformationsgeschichte* 71 (1980): 280–307.

Wyporska, Wanda. "Witchcraft, Arson, and Murder—The Turek Trial of 1652." *Central Europe* 1 (2003): 41–54.

Zguta, Russell. "The Ordeal by Water (Swimming of Witches) in the East Slavic World." *Slavic Review* 82 (1977): 220–30.

———. "Was There a Witch-Craze in Muscovite Russia?" *Southern Folklore Quarterly* 40 (1977): 119–27.

———. "Witchcraft and Medicine in Pre-Petrine Russia." *Russian Review* 37 (1978): 438–48.

———. "Witchcraft Trials in Seventeenth-Century Russia." *American Historical Review* 82 (1977): 1187–1207.

France and the Low Countries

Bordes, Françoise. *Sorciers et sorcières: Procès de sorcellerie en Gascogne et Pays Basque*. Toulouse, France: Edition Privat, 1999.

Briggs, Robin. *Communities of Belief: Culture and Social Tensions in Early Modern France*. Oxford: Clarendon, 1989.

———. "Witchcraft and Popular Mentality in Lorraine, 1580–1630." In *Occult and Scientific Mentalities in the Renaissance*, ed. Brian Vickers. Cambridge: Cambridge University Press, 1984, 337–49.

———. "Women as Victims? Witches, Judges and the Community." *French History* 5 (1991): 438–50.

Clark, Stuart. "The 'Gendering' of Witchcraft in French Demonology: Misogyny or Polarity?" *French History* 5 (1991): 426–37.

Delcambre, Etienne. *Le concept de sorcellerie dans le Duché de Lorraine au XVIe et au XVIIe siècle.* 3 vols. Nancy, France: Société d'archéologie lorraine, 1948–51.

Diedler, Jean-Claude. *Démons et sorcières en Lorraine: Le bien et le mal dans les communautés rurales de 1550 à 1660.* Paris: Messene, 1996.

Dupont-Bouchat, Marie-Sylvie, ed. *La sorcellerie dans les Pays-Bas sous l'Ancien Régime: Aspects juridiques, institutionnels et sociaux.* Courtrai, Belgium: UGA, 1987.

———. "Sorcellerie et superstition: L'attitude de l'Eglise dans les Pays-Bas, XVIe–XVIIIe siècle." In *Magie, sorcellerie, parapsychologie,* ed. Hervé Hasquin. Brussels: Université de Bruxelles, 1984, 61–83.

Dupont-Bouchat, Marie-Sylvie, Willem Frijhoff, and Robert Muchembled, eds. *Prophètes et sorciers dans les Pays-Bas XVIe–XVIIIe siècle.* Paris: Hachette, 1978.

Garrett, Clarke. "Witches and Cunning Folk in the Old Regime." In *The Wolf and the Lamb: Popular Culture in France from the Old Regime to the Twentieth Century,* ed. Jacques Beauroy, Marc Betrand, and Edward T. Gargan. Sarasota, Calif.: Anma Libri, 1976, 53–64.

Gauvard, Claude. "Paris, le Parlement et la sorcellerie au milieu du XVe siècle." In *Finances, pouvoirs et mémoire: Mélanges offerts à Jean Favier.* Paris: Fayard, 1999, 85–111.

Gijswijt-Hofstra, Marijke. "The European Witchcraft Debate and the Dutch Variant." *Social History* 15 (1990): 181–94.

———. "Witchcraft in the Northern Netherlands." In *Current Issues in Women's History,* ed. Ariana Angerman et al. London: Routledge, 1974, 75–92.

Gijswijt-Hofstra, Marijke, and Willem Frijhoff, eds. *Witchcraft in the Netherlands: From the Fourteenth to the Twentieth Century.* Trans. Rachel M. J. van der Wilden-Fall. Rotterdam: Universitaire Pers Rotterdam, 1991.

Jacques-Chaquin, Nicole, and Maxime Préaud. *Les sorciers du carroi de Marlou: Un procès de sorcellerie en Berry (1582–1583).* Grenoble, France: Millon, 1996.

Klaits, Joseph. "Witchcraft Trials and Absolute Monarchy in Alsace." In *Church, State, and Society under the Bourbon Kings of France,* ed. Richard M. Golden. Lawrence, Kans.: Coronado Press, 1982, 148–72.

Le Roy Ladurie, Emmanuel. *Jasmin's Witch.* Trans. Brian Pierce. New York: George Braziller, 1987.

———. *Montaillou: The Promised Land of Error.* Trans. Barbara Bray. New York: George Braziller, 1978.

Mandrou, Robert. *Magistrats et sorciers en France au XVIIe siècle: Une analyse de psychologie historique.* Paris: Seuil, 1968.

Monter, E. William. *Judging the French Reformation: Heresy Trials by Six-teenth Century Parlements*. Cambridge, Mass.: Harvard University Press, 1999.

———. "Toads and the Eucharist: The Male Witches of Normandy, 1564–1660." *French Historical Studies* 20 (1997): 563–95.

Muchembled, Robert. *Les derniers bûchers: Un village de Flandre et ses sorcières sous Louis XIV*. Paris: Ramsay, 1981.

———. *Popular Culture and Elite Culture in France, 1400–1750*. Trans. Lydia Cochrane. Baton Rouge: Louisiana State University Press, 1985.

———. *Sorcières, justice et société aux 16e et 17e siècles*. Paris: Imago, 1987.

———. "Witchcraft, Popular Culture, and Christianity in the Sixteenth Cen-tury, with an Emphasis upon Flanders and Artois." In *Ritual, Religion, and the Sacred: Selections from the Annales: Economies, Sociétiés, Civilisa-tions*, vol. 7, ed. Robert Forster and Orest Ranum, trans. Elborg Forster and Patricia M. Ranum. Baltimore, Md.: Johns Hopkins University Press, 1982, 213–36.

———. "The Witches of the Cambrésis: The Acculturation of the Rural World in the Sixteenth and Seventeenth Centuries." In *Religion and the People, 800–1700*, ed. James Obelkevich. Chapel Hill: University of North Carolina Press, 1979, 221–76, 315–23.

Oates, Caroline, "The Trial of a Teenage Werewolf, Bordeaux, 1603." *Crim-inal Justice History* 9 (1988): 1–29.

Paravy, Pierrette. *De la Chrétienté romaine à la Réforme en Dauphiné: Evêques, fidèles et déviants (vers 1340–vers 1530)*. 2 vols. Rome: École française de Rome, 1993.

———. "Faire Croire: Quelques hypothèses de recherche basées sur l'étude des procès de sorcellerie du Dauphiné au XVe siècle." In *Faire Croire: Modalités de la diffusion et la reception des messages religieux du XIIe au XVe siècle*. Rome: École française de Rome, 1981, 119–30.

———. "Streghe e stregoni nella società del Delfinato nel XV secolo." In *Poteri carismatici e informali: Chiesa e società medioevali*, ed. Agostino Paravicini Bagliani and André Vauchez. Palermo, Italy: Sellerio, 1992, 78–92.

Rapley, Robert. *A Case of Witchcraft: The Trial of Urbain Grandier*. Mon-treal, Canada: McGill-Queen's University Press, 1998.

Rochelandet, Brigitte. *Sorcières, diables et bûchers en Franche-Comté aux XVIe et XVIIe siècles*. Besançon, France: Cêtre, 1997.

Soman, Alfred. "Decriminalizing Witchcraft: Does the French Experience Furnish a European Model?" *Criminal Justice History* 10 (1989): 1–22.

———. " La décriminalisation de la sorcellerie en France." *Histoire, écono-mie et société* 4 (1985): 179–203.

————. "The Parlement of Paris and the Great Witch Hunt (1565–1640)." *Sixteenth Century Journal* 9 (1978): 31–44.

————. *Sorcellerie et justice criminelle: Parlement de Paris (16e–18e siècles).* London: Variorum, 1992.

————. "Trente procès de sorcellerie dans le Perche (1566–1624)." *L'orne litéraire* 8 (1986): 42–57.

————. "Witch Lynching at Juniville." *Natural History* 95 (1986): 6–15.

Somerset, Anne. *The Affair of the Poisons: Murder, Infanticide and Satanism at the Court of Louis XIV.* London: Weidenfeld and Nicolson, 2003.

Villette, Pierre. *La sorcellerie et sa repression dans le nord de la France.* Paris: Pensée universelle, 1976.

Wilkins, Kay S. "Attitudes to Witchcraft and Demonic Possession in France during the Eighteenth Century." *Journal of European Studies* 3 (1973): 348–62.

German Lands

Ahrendt-Schulte, Ingrid. *Zauberinnen in der Stadt Horn (1554–1603): Magische Kultur und Hexenverfolgung in der Frühen Neuzeit.* Frankfurt: Campus, 1997.

Alfing, Sabine. *Hexenjagd und Zaubereiprozesse in Münster: Vom Umgang mit Sündenböcken in den Krisenzeit des 16. und 17. Jahrhunderts.* Münster, Ger.: Waxmann, 1991.

Baumgarten, Achim B. *Hexenwahn und Hexenverfolgung im Naheraum: Ein Beitrag zur Sozial- und Kulturgeschichte.* Frankfurt: Peter Lang, 1987.

Behringer, Wolfgang. *Mit dem Feuer vom Leben zum Tod: Hexengesetzgebung in Bayern.* Munich: Hugendubel, 1988.

————. *Shaman of Oberstdorf: Chonrad Stoeckhlin and the Phantoms of the Night.* Trans. H. C. Erik Midelfort. Charlottesville: University of Virginia Press, 1998.

————. *Witchcraft Persecutions in Bavaria: Popular Magic, Religious Zealotry and Reason of State in Early Modern Europe.* Trans. J. C. Grayson and David Lederer. Cambridge: Cambridge University Press, 1998.

Beier-de Haan, Rosemarie, Rita Voltmer, and Franz Irsigler, eds. *Hexenwahn: Ängste der Neuzeit.* Berlin: Minerva Farnung, 2002.

Benedikter, Hans. *Hexen und Zauberer in Tirol.* Bozen, Italy: Athesia, 2000.

Brauner, Sigrid. *Fearless Wives and Frightened Shrews: The Construction of the Witch in Early Modern Germany.* Ed. Robert H. Brown. Amherst: University of Massachusetts Press, 1995.

Degn, Christian, Hartmut Lehmann, and Dagmar Unverhau, eds. *Hexenprozesse: Deutsche und skandinavische Beiträge* Neumünster, Ger.: Wachholz, 1983.

Dillinger, Johannes. *"Evil People"*: *A Comparative Study of Witch Hunts in Swabian Austria and the Electorate of Trier*. Trans. Laura Stokes. Charlottesville: University of Virginia Press, 2009.

Dillinger, Johannes, Thomas Fritz, and Wolfgang Mährle. *Zum Feuer verdammt: Die Hexenverfolgungen in der Grafschaft Hohenberg, der Reichsstadt Reutlingen und der Fürstpropstei Ellwangen*. Stuttgart, Ger.: Steiner, 1998.

Durrant, Jonathan B. *Witchcraft, Gender and Society in Early Modern Germany*. Leiden: Brill, 2007.

Gebhard, Horst Heinrich. *Hexenprozesse im Kurfürstentum Mainz des 17. Jahrhunderts*. Aschaffenburg, Ger.: Geschichts- und Kunstverein Aschaffenburg, 1989.

Gehm, Britta. *Die Hexenverfolgung im Hochstift Bamberg und das Eingreifen des Reichshofrates zu ihrer Beendigung*. Hildesheim, Ger.: Georg Olms, 2000.

Hsia, R. Po-chia. *The Myth of Ritual Murder: Jews and Magic in Reformation Germany*. New Haven, Conn.: Yale University Press, 1988.

Jerouschek, Günter. *Die Hexen und ihr Prozess: Die Hexenverfolgung in der Reichsstadt Esslingen*. Esslingen, Ger.: Stadtarchiv, 1992.

Koppenhöfer, Johanna. *Die Mitleidlose Gesellschaft: Studien zu Verdachtsgenese. Ausgrenzungsverhalten und Prozessproblematik im frühneuzeitlichen Hexenprozeß in der alten Grafschaft Nassau unter Johann VI. und der späteren Teilgrafschaft Nassau-Dillenburg (1559–1687)*. Frankfurt: Peter Lang, 1995.

Kunstmann, Hartmut H. *Zauberwahn und Hexenprozesse in der Reichsstadt Nürnberg*. Nuremberg, Ger.: Stadtarchiv, 1970.

Kunze, Michael. *Highroad to the Stake: A Tale of Witchcraft*. Trans. William E. Yuill. Chicago: Chicago University Press, 1987.

Labouvie, Eva. *Verbotene Künste: Volksmagie und ländlicher Aberglaube in den Dorfgemeinde des Saarraumes (16.–19. Jahrhundert)*. St. Ingbert, Ger.: Röhrig, 1992.

———. *Zauberei und Hexenwerk: Ländlicher Hexenglaube in der Frühen Neuzeit*. Frankfurt: Fischer, 1991.

Lambrecht, Karen. *Hexenverfolgung und Zaubereiprozesse in den schlesischen Territorien*. Cologne: Böhlau, 1995.

Lehmann, Hartmut. "The Persecution of Witches as Restoration of Order: The Case of Germany, 1590s–1650s." *Central European History* 21 (1988): 107–21.

Lorenz, Sönke. *Aktenversendung und Hexenprozess: Dargestellt am Beispiel der Juristenfakultäten Rostock und Greifswald (1570/82–1630)*. 2 vols. Frankfurt: Peter Lang, 1982–83.

———, ed. *Hexen und Hexenverfolgung im deutschen Südwesten*. Ostfildern bei Stuttgart, Ger.: Cantz, 1994.

Lorenz, Sönke, and Dieter Bauer, eds. *Das Ende der Hexenverfolgung.* Stuttgart, Ger.: Franz Steiner, 1995.

Midelfort, H. C. Erik. "Heartland of the Witchcraze: Central and Northern Europe." *History Today* 31 (February, 1981): 27–31.

———. *Hexenverfolgung: Beiträge zur Forschung, unter besonderer Berücksichtigung des südwestdeutschen Raumes.* Würzburg, Ger.: Königshausen & Neumann, 1995.

———. *A History of Madness in Sixteenth-Century Germany.* Stanford, Calif.: Stanford University Press, 1999.

———. "Witchcraft and Religion in Sixteenth-Century Germany: The Formation and Consequences of an Orthodoxy." *Archiv für Reformationsgeschichte* 62 (1971): 266–78.

———. *Witch Hunting in Southwestern Germany, 1562–1684: The Social and Intellectual Foundations.* Stanford, Calif.: Stanford University Press, 1972.

Niederstätter, Alois, and Wolfgang Scheffknecht, eds. *Hexe oder Hausfrau: Das Bild der Frau in der Geschichte Vorarlbergs.* Sigmaringendorf, Ger.: Glock & Lutz, 1991.

Pohl, Herbert. *Zauberglaube und Hexenangst im Kurfürstentum Mainz: Ein Beitrag zur Hexenfrage im 16. und beginnenden 17. Jahrhundert.* 2nd ed. Stuttgart, Ger.: Franz Steiner, 1998.

Renczes, Andrea. *Wie löscht man eine Familie aus? Eine Analyse Bamberger Hexenprozesse.* Pfaffenweiler, Ger.: Centaurus, 1990.

Roper, Lyndal. "Evil Imaginings and Fantasies: Child-Witches and the End of the Witch Craze." *Past and Present* 167 (2000): 107–39.

Rowlands, Alison. "Witchcraft and Old Women in Early Modern Germany." *Past and Present* 173 (2001): 50–89.

———. "Witchcraft and Popular Religion in Early Modern Rothenburg ob der Tauber." In *Popular Religion in Germany and Central Europe, 1400–1800,* ed. Bob Scribner and Trevor Johnson. New York: St. Martin's Press, 1996, 101–18, 245–49.

———. *Witchcraft Narratives in Germany: Rothenburg 1561–1652.* Manchester, Eng.: Manchester University Press, 2003.

Rummel, Walter. *Bauern, Herren und Hexen: Studien zur Sozialgeschichte sponheimischer und kurtrierischer Hexenprozesse, 1574–1664.* Göttingen, Ger.: Vandenhoeck & Ruprecht, 1991.

Saatkamp, Marielies. *Bekandt daß sie ein Zaubersche were: Zur Geschichte der Hexenverfolgung im Westmünsterland.* Vreden, Ger.: Landeskundliches Institut Westmünsterland, 1994.

Sabean, David Warren. "The Sacred Bond of Unity: Community through the Eyes of a Thirteen-Year-Old Witch (1683)." In David Warren Sabean, *The Power in the Blood: Popular Culture and Village Discourse in Early Modern Germany.* Cambridge: Cambridge University Press, 1984, 94–112.

Schmidt, Jürgen Michael. *Glaube und Skepsis: Die Kurpfalz und die abendländische Hexenverfolgung 1446–1685.* Bielefeld, Ger.: Verlag für Regionalgeschichte, 2000.

Schormann, Gerhard. *Der Krieg gegen die Hexen: Das Ausrottungsprogramm des Kurfürsten von Köln.* Göttingen, Ger.: Vandenhoeck & Ruprecht, 1991.

———. *Hexenprozesse in Deutschland.* 3rd ed. Göttingen, Ger.: Vandenhoeck & Ruprecht, 1996.

———. *Hexenprozesse in Nordwestdeutschland.* Hildesheim, Ger.: Lax, 1977.

Schwillus, Harald. *Kleriker im Hexenprozeß: Geistliche als Opfer der Hexenprozesse des 16. und 17. Jahrhunderts in Deutschland.* Würzburg, Ger.: Echter Verlag, 1992.

Scribner, Robert W. "Magic and the Formation of Protestant Popular Culture in Germany." In R. W. Scribner, *Religion and Culture in Germany (1400–1800)*, ed. Lyndal Roper. Leiden: Brill, 2001, 323–45.

———. "Magie und Aberglaube: Zur volkstümlichen sakramentalischen Denkart in Deutschland am Ausgang des Mittelalters." In *Volksreligion im hohen und späten Mittelalter*, ed. Peter Dinzelbacher and Dieter R. Bauer. Paderborn, Ger.: Schöningh, 1990, 253–73.

———. "Witchcraft and Judgement in Reformation Germany." *History Today* 40 (April, 1990): 12–19.

Thieser, Bernd. *Die Oberpfalz im Zusammenhang des Hexenprozessgeschehens im süddeutschen Raum während des 16. und 17. Jahrhundert.* Bayreuth, Ger.: Hagen, 1987.

Tschaikner, Manfred. *"Damit das Böse ausgerottet werde": Hexenverfolgungen im Vorarlberg im 16. und 17. Jahrhundert.* Bregenz, Austria: Vorarlberger Autoren Gesellschaft, 1992.

Valentinitsch, Helfried, ed. *Hexen und Zauberer: Die grosse Verfolgung—ein europäisches Phänomen in der Steiermark.* Graz, Austria: Leykam, 1987.

Voltmer, Rita. "Zwischen Herrschaftskrise, Wirtschaftsdepression und Jesuitenpropaganda: Hexenverfolgungen in der Stadt Trier (15.–17. Jahrhundert)." *Jahrbuch für westdeutsche Landesgeschichte* 27 (2001): 37–107.

Walinski-Kiehl, Robert S. "The Devil's Children: Child Witch-Trials in Early Modern Germany." *Continuity and Change* 11 (1996): 171–89.

———. "'Godly States': Confessional Conflict and Witch-Hunting in Early Modern Germany." *Mentalities* 5 (1988): 13–24.

Walz, Rainer. *Hexenglaube und magische Kommunikation im Dorf der frühen Neuzeit: Die Verfolgungen in der Graftschaft Lippe*. Paderborn, Ger.: Schöningh, 1993.

Wilbertz, Gisela, Gerd Schwerhoff and Jürgen Scheffler, eds. *Hexenverfolgungen und Regionalgeschichte: Die Grafschaft Lippe im Vergleich*. Bielefeld, Ger.: Verlag für Regionalgeschichte, 1994.

Zeck, Mario. *"Im Rauch gehn Himmel geschüggt": Hexenverfolgungen in der Reichsstadt Rottweil*. Stuttgart, Ger.: Ibidem Velag, 2000.

Italy, Portugal, and Spain

Bertolin, Silvia, and Ezio Emerico Gerbore. *La stregoneria nella Valle d'Aosta medievale*. Quart, Italy: Musumeci, 2003.

Bertolotti, Maurizio. "The Ox's Bones and the Ox's Hide: A Popular Myth, Part Hagiography and Part Witchcraft." Trans. Eren Branch. In *Microhistory and the Lost Peoples of Europe*, ed. Edward Muir and Guido Ruggiero. Baltimore, Md.: Johns Hopkins University Press, 1991, 42–70.

Blécourt, Willem de. "Spuren einer Volkskultur oder Dämonisierung? Kritische Bemerkungen zu Ginzburgs 'Die Benandanti'." *Kea: Zeitschrift für Kulturwissenschaft* 5 (1993): 17–29.

Bonomo, Giuseppe. *Caccia alle streghe: Le credenza nelle streghe dal sec. XIII al XIX con particolare riferimento all'Italia*. 3rd ed. Palermo, Italy: Palumbo, 1986.

Brucker, Gene A. "Sorcery in Early Renaissance Florence." *Studies in the Renaissance* 10 (1963): 7–24.

Cassar, Carmel. "Witchcraft Beliefs and Social Control in Seventeenth-Century Malta." *Journal of Mediterranean Studies* 3 (1993): 316–34.

———. *Witchcraft, Sorcery, and the Inquisition: A Study of Cultural Values in Early Modern Malta*. Msida, Malta: Mireva, 1996.

Centini, Massimo. *Streghe, roghi e diavoli: I processi di stregoneria in Piemonte*. Cuneo, Italy: L'arciere, 1995.

Corrêa De Melo, M. C. "Witchcraft in Portugal during the Eighteenth Century, Analysed through the Accusations of the Tribunal do Santo Oficio de Evora." In *Transactions of the Eighth International Congress on the Enlightenment*, Studies on Voltaire and the Eighteenth Century, vol. 303. Oxford: Voltaire Foundation, 1992, 573–78.

Dall'Olio, Guido. "Tribunali vescovili, Inquisizione romana e stregoneria." In *Il piacere del testo: Saggi e studi per Albano Biondi*, vol. 1. Ed. Adriano Prosperi. Rome: Bulzoni, 2001, 63–82.

Decker, Rainer. "Entstehung und Verbreitung der römischen Hexenprozessinstruktion." In *Inquisition, Index, Zensur: Wissenkulturen der Neuzeit im Widerstreit*, ed. Hubert Wolf. Paderborn, Ger.: Schöningh, 2001, 159–75.

Deutscher, Thomas. "The Role of the Episcopal Tribunal of Novara in the Suppression of Heresy and Witchcraft, 1563–1615." *Catholic Historical Review* 77 (1991): 403–21.

Di Simplicio, Oscar. *Autunno della stregoneria: Maleficio e Magia Nell'Italia Moderna.* Bologna, Italy: Il Mulino, 2005.

———. *Inquisizione, stregoneria, medicina: Siena e il suo stato (1580–1721).* Siena, Italy: Il Leccio, 2000.

———. "Witchcraft and Infanticide." *Acta Istria* 11 (2003): 48–88.

Fiume, Giovanna. "The Old Vinegar Lady, or the Judicial Modernization of the Crime of Witchcraft." Trans. Margaret A. Gallucci. In *History from Crime,* ed. Edward Muir and Guido Ruggiero. Baltimore, Md.: Johns Hopkins University Press, 1994, 65–87.

Gari Lacruz, Ángel. *Brujería e Inquisición en Aragón en la primera mitad del siglo XVII.* Zaragoza, Spain: Diputación General de Aragón, 1991.

———. "Variedad de competencias en el delito de brujería 1600–1650 en Aragón." In *La Inquisición Española: Nueva vision, nueva horizonte,* ed. Joaquín Perez Villanueva. Madrid: Siglo Veintiuno, 1980, 319–27.

Gemmo, Roberto. *Streghe e magia: Episodi di opposizione religiosa popolare sulle Alpi del Seicento.* Biella, Italy: ELF, 1994.

Gentilcore, David. "The Church, the Devil and the Healing Activities of Living Saints in the Kingdom of Naples after the Council of Trent." In *Medicine and the Reformation,* ed. Ole Peter Grell and Andrew Cunningham. London: Routledge, 1993, 134–55.

———. *From Bishop to Witch: The System of the Sacred in Early Modern Terra d'Otranto.* Manchester, Eng.: Manchester University Press, 1992.

———. *Healers and Healing in Early Modern Italy.* Manchester, Eng.: Manchester University Press, 1998.

Gil del Rio, Alfredo. *Inquisición y brujería.* Madrid: Casset, 1992.

Ginzburg, Carlo. *The Night Battles: Witchcraft and Agrarian Cults in the Sixteenth and Seventeenth Centuries.* Trans. John Tedeschi and Anne Tedeschi. Baltimore, Md.: Johns Hopkins University Press, 1983.

———. "Witchcraft and Popular Piety: Notes on a Modenese Trial of 1519." In Carlo Ginzburg, *Clues, Myths, and the Historical Method.* Trans. John Tedeschi and Anne Tedeschi. Baltimore, Md.: Johns Hopkins University Press, 1989, 1–16.

Guggino, Elsa. *La magia in Sicilia.* Palermo, Italy: Sellerio, 1978.

Haliczer, Gustav. *Inquisition and Society in the Kingdom of Valencia, 1478–1834.* Berkeley: University of California Press, 1990.

Henningsen, Gustav. "The Greatest Witch-Trial of All: Navarre, 1609–14." *History Today* 30 (November, 1980): 36–39.

———. *The Witches' Advocate: Basque Witchcraft and the Spanish Inquisition.* Reno: University of Nevada Press, 1980.

Loriga, Sabine. "A Secret to Kill the King: Magic and Protection in Piedmont in the Eighteenth Century." Trans. Margaret A. Gallussi and Corrada Biazzo Curry. In *History from Crime*, ed. Edward Muir and Guido Ruggiero. Baltimore, Md.: Johns Hopkins University Press, 1994, 88–109.

Martin, Ruth. *Witchcraft and the Inquisition in Venice, 1550–1650*. Oxford: Oxford University Press, 1989.

Monter, E. William. *Frontiers of Heresy: The Spanish Inquisition from the Basque Lands to Sicily*. Cambridge: Cambridge University Press, 1990.

Mormando, Franco. "Bernardino of Siena, Popular Preacher and Witch-Hunter: A 1426 Witch Trial in Rome." *Fifteenth Century Studies* 24 (1998): 84–118.

———. *The Preacher's Demons: Bernardino of Siena and the Social Underworld of Early Renaissance Italy*. Chicago: University of Chicago Press, 1999.

Nardon, Franco. *Benandanti e inquisitori nel Friuli del Seicento*. Trieste, Italy: Università di Trieste, 1999.

O'Neil, Mary. "Magical Healing, Love Magic and the Inquisition in Late Sixteenth-Century Modena." In *Inquisition and Society in Early Modern Europe*, ed. Stephen Haliczer. Totowa, N.J.: Barnes and Noble, 1987, 88–114.

———. "*Sacerdote ovvero strione*: Ecclesiastical and Superstitious Remedies in 16th-Century Italy." In *Understanding Popular Culture: Europe from the Middle Ages to the Nineteenth Century*, ed. Steven Kaplan. Berlin: Mouton, 1984, 53–83.

Paton, Bernadette. "'To the Fire, to the Fire! Let Us Burn a Little Incense to God': Bernardino, Preaching Friars, and *Maleficio* in Late Medieval Siena." In *No Gods Except Me: Orthodoxy and Religious Practice in Europe, 1200–1600*, ed. Charles Zika. Parkville, Australia: University of Melbourne History Department, 1991, 9–14.

Romeo, Giovanni. *Inquisitori, esorcisti e streghe nell'Italia della Controriforma*. Florence: Sansoni, 1990.

Ruggiero, Guido. *Binding Passions: Tales of Magic, Marriage and Power at the End of the Renaissance*. Oxford: Oxford University Press, 1993.

———. "The Strange Death of Margarita Marcellini: *Male*, Signs, and the Everyday World of Pre-Modern Medicine." *American Historical Review* 106 (2001): 1141–58.

Sánchez Ortega, M. H. "Sorcery and Eroticism in Love Magic." In *Cultural Encounters: The Impact of the Inquisition in Spain and the New World*, ed. Mary Elizabeth Perry and Anne J. Cruz. Berkeley: University of California Press, 1991, 58–92.

———. "Women as a Source of 'Evil' in Counter-Reformation Spain." In *Culture and Control in Counter-Reformation Spain*, ed. Anne J. Cruz and Mary Elizabeth Perry, Minneapolis: University of Minnesota Press, 1992, 196–215.

Scully, Sally. "Marriage or a Career? Witchcraft as an Alternative in Seventeenth-Century Venice." *Journal of Social History* 28 (1995): 857–76.

Tausiet, María. *Ponzona en los ojos: Brujería y superstición en Aragón en el siglo XVI*. Zaragoza, Spain: Institucíon Fernando el Católico, 2000.

Tedeschi, John. "The Roman Inquisition and Witchcraft: An Early 17th-Century 'Instruction' on Correct Trial Procedure." *Revue de l'histoire des religions* 200 (1983): 163–88.

Villarín, Juan. *La hechiceria en Madrid: Brujas, maleficios, encantamientos y sugestiones de la villa y corte*. Madrid: Avapiés, 1993.

Walker, Timothy, D. *Doctors, Folk Medicine and the Inquisition: The Repression of Magical Healing in Portugal during the Enlightenment*. Leiden: Brill, 2005.

Zabala, Mikel. *Brujería e inquisición en Bizkaia (siglos XVI y XVII)*. Bilbao, Spain: Ekain, 2000.

Zanelli, Giuliana. *Streghe e società: Nell'Emilia e Romagna del cinqueseicento*. Ravenna, Italy: Longo, 1992.

Scandinavia

Degn, Christian, Hartmut Lehmann, and Dagmar Unverhau, eds. *Hexenprozesse: Deutsche und skandinavische Beiträge*. Neumünster, Ger.: Wachholz, 1983.

Ellison, R. C. "The Kirkjuból Affair: A Seventeenth-Century Icelandic Witchcraft Case Analysed." *The Seventeenth Century* 8 (1993): 217–43.

Gent, Jacqueline van. *Magic, Body and the Self in Eighteenth-Century Sweden*. Leiden: Brill, 2008.

Granqvist, Karin. "'Thou shalt have No Other Gods before Me' (Exodus 20:3): Witchcraft and Superstition Trials in Seventeenth- and Eighteenth-Century Swedish Lapland." In *Kulturkonfrontation I Lappmarken*, ed. P. Sköld and K. Kram. Umeå, Sweden: Kulturgräns Norr, 1998, 13–29.

Hagen, Rune. "The Witch-Hunt in Early Modern Finnmark." *Acta Borealia* 1 (1999): 43–62.

Henningsen, Gustav. "Witch Hunting in Denmark." *Folklore* 93 (1982): 131–37.

Jochens, Jenny. "*Hexerei eller Blind Allarm*: Recent Scandinavian Witchcraft Studies." *Scandinavian Studies* 65 (1993): 103–13.

————. "Magie et différences des sexes dans les mythes et la société germanico-nordique." *Cahiers de civilisation médiévale, Xe–XII siècles* 36 (1993): 375–89.

————. "Old Norse Magic and Gender." *Scandinavian Studies* 63 (1993): 305–17.

Johansen, Jens Christian V. "Superstition and Witchcraft in Reformation Scandinavia." In *The Scandinavian Reformation: From Evangelical Movement to Institutionalisation of Reform*, ed. Ole Peter Grell. Cambridge: Cambridge University Press, 1995, 179–211.

————. "Witchcraft, Sin and Repentance: The Decline of Danish Witchcraft Trials." *Acta Ethnographica* 37 (1991–1992): 413–23.

Miller, W. I. "Dreams, Prophecy and Sorcery: Blaming the Secret Offender in Medieval Iceland." *Scandinavian Studies* 58 (1986): 101–23.

Mitchell, S. A. "Nordic Witchcraft in Transition." *Scandia* 63 (1997): 17–33.

Morris, Katherine. *Sorceress or Witch? The Image of Gender in Medieval Iceland and Northern Europe*. Lanham, Md.: University Press of America, 1991.

Neronen, M. "'Envious Are All the People, Witches Watch at Every Gate': Finnish Witches and Witch Trials in the 17th Century." *Scandinavian Journal of History* 18 (1993): 77–91.

Sörlin, Per. "The Blåkulla Story: Absurdity and Rationality." *Arv. Nordic Yearbook of Folklore* 53 (1997): 131–52

————. *"Wicked Arts": Witchcraft and Magic Trials in Southern Sweden, 1635–1734*. Leiden: Brill, 1998.

Toivo, Raisa Maria. *Witchcraft and Gender in Early Modern Society: Finland and the Wider European Experience*. Aldershot, Eng.: Ashgate, 2008.

Willumsen, Liv Helene. "Witchcraft of the High North: The Finnmark Witchcraft Trials in the Seventeenth Century." *Scandinavian Journal of History* 22 (1997): 199–221.

Switzerland

Andenmatten, Bernard, and Kathrin Utz Tremp. "De l'hérésie à la sorcellerie: L'inquisiteur Ulric de Torrenté OP (vers 1420–1445) et l'affermissement de l'inquisition en Suisse romande." *Revue écclesiastique Suisse* 86 (1992): 69–119.

Binz, Louis. "Les débuts de la chasse aux sorcières dans le diocèse de Genève." *Bibliothèque d'Humanisme et de Renaissance* 59 (1997): 561–81.

Blauert, Andreas. *Frühe Hexenverfolgungen: Ketzer- Zauberei- und Hexenprozesse des 15. Jahrhunderts*. Hamburg, Ger.: Junius, 1989.

―――. "Hexenverfolgung in einer spätmittelalterlichen Gemeinde: Der Beispiel Kriens/Luzern um 1500." *Geschichte und Gesellschaft* 16 (1990): 8–25.

Blöcker, Monica. "Ein Zaubereiprozess im Jahre 1028." *Schweizerische Zeitschrift für Geschichte* 29 (1979): 533–55.

Borst, Arno. "The Origins of the Witch-Craze in the Alps." In Arno Borst, *Medieval Worlds: Barbarians, Heretics, and Artists in the Middle Ages.* Trans. Eric Hansen. Chicago: University of Chicago Press, 1992, 101–22.

Broye, Christian. *Sorcellerie et superstitions à Genève, XVIe–XVIIIe siècles.* Geneva: Concepte Moderne, 1990.

Burghartz, Susanna. "The Equation of Women and Witches: A Case Study of Witchcraft Trials in Lucerne and Lausanne in the Fifteenth and Sixteenth Centuries." In *The German Underworld: Deviants and Outcasts in German History,* ed. Richard J. Evans. London: Routledge, 1988, 57–74.

Choffat, Pierre-Han. *La sorcellerie comme exutoire: Tensions et conflicts locaux, Dommartin 1524–1528.* Lausanne, Switz.: Université de Lausanne, 1989.

Kamber, Peter. "La chasse aux sorciers et aux sorcières dans le Pays de Vaud: Aspects quantitatifs (1581–1620)." *Revue historique vaudoise* 90 (1982): 21–33.

Maier, Eva. *Trente ans avec le diable: Une nouvelle chasse aix sorciers sur la Riviera lémanique (1477–1484).* Lausanne, Switz.: Université de Lausanne, 1996.

Mazzali, Tiziana. *Il martirio delle streghe: Una nuova dramatica testimonianza dell'Inquisizione laica del Seicento.* Milan: Xenia, 1988.

Modestin, Georg. "Der Teufel in der Landschaft: Zur Politik der Hexenverfolgungen im heutigen Kanton Freiburg von 1440 bis 1470." *Freiburger Geschichtsblätter* 76 (1999): 81–122.

―――. *Le diable chez l'évêque: Chasse aux sorciers dans le diocèse de Lausanne (vers 1460).* Lausanne, Switz.: Université de Lausanne, 1999.

―――. "Wozu brauch man Hexen? Herrschaft und Verfolgung in Châtel-Saint-Denis (1444–1465)." *Freiburger Geschichtsblätter* 77 (2000): 107–29.

Monter, E. William. "Patterns of Witchcraft in the Jura." *Journal of Social History* 5 (1971): 1–29.

―――. *Witchcraft in France and Switzerland: The Borderlands during the Reformation.* Ithaca, N.Y.: Cornell University Press, 1976.

―――. "Witchcraft in Geneva, 1537–1662." *Journal of Modern History* 43 (1971): 179–204.

Ostorero, Martine. *"Folâtrer avec les démons": Sabbat et chasse aux sorciers à Vevey (1448).* Lausanne, Switz.: Université de Lausanne, 1995.

Pfister, Laurence. *L'enfer sur terre: Sorcellerie à Dommartin (1498).* Lausanne, Switz.: Université de Lausanne, 1997.

Schatzmann, Niklaus. *Verdorrende Bäume und Brote wie Kuhfladen: Hexen-prozesse in der Leventia 1431–1459 und die Anfänge der Hexenverfolgungen auf der Alpensüdseite.* Zurich: Chronos, 2003.

Strobino, Sandrine. *Françoise sauvée des flammes? Une Valaisanne accusée de sorcellerie au XVe siècle.* Lausanne, Switz.: Université de Lausanne, 1996.

Taric Zumsteg, Fabienne. *Les sorciers à l'assaut du village Gollion (1615–1631).* Lausanne, Switz.: Zèbre, 2000.

Utz Tremp, Kathrin. "Ist Glaubenssache Frauensache? Zu den Anfängen der Hexenverfolgungen im Freiburg (um 1440)." *Freiburger Geschichtsblätter* 72 (1995): 9–50.

North America

Adams, Gretchen A. *The Specter of Salem: Remembering the Witch Trials in Nineteenth-Century America.* Chicago: University of Chicago Press, 2010.

Boyer, Paul, and Stephen Nissenbaum. *Salem Possessed: The Social Origins of Witchcraft.* Cambridge, Mass.: Harvard University Press, 1974.

Breslaw, Elaine G. *Tituba, Reluctant Witch of Salem: Devilish Indians and Puritan Fantasies.* New York: New York University Press, 1996.

Brown, David C. "The Case of Giles Cory." *Essex Institute Historical Collections* 121 (1985): 162–81.

Caporael, Linda R. "Ergotism: Satan Loosed in Salem?" *Science* 192 (1976): 21–26.

Carlson, Laurie Winn. *A Fever in Salem: A New Interpretation of the New England Witch Trials.* Chicago: Ivan R. Dee, 1999.

Demos, John Putnam. *Entertaining Satan: Witchcraft and the Culture of Early New England.* Oxford: Oxford University Press, 1982.

———. "John Godfrey and His Neighbors: Witchcraft and the Social Web in Colonial Massachusetts." *William and Mary Quarterly* 33 (1976): 242–65.

———. "Underlying Themes in the Witchcraft of Seventeenth-Century New England." *American Historical Review* 75 (1970): 1311–26.

Drake, Frederick C. "Witchcraft in the American Colonies, 1647–62." *American Quarterly* 20 (1968): 694–725.

Erikson, Kai T. "The Witches of Salem Village." In *On the Margin of the Visible: Sociology, the Esoteric and the Occult,* ed. Edward A. Tiryakian. New York: Wiley, 1974, 209–14.

Fox, Sanford J. *Science and Justice: The Massachusetts Witchcraft Trials.* Baltimore, Md.: Johns Hopkins University Press, 1968.

Games, Alison. *Witchcraft in Early North America.* Lanham, Md.: Rowman & Littlefield, 2010.

Gildrie, Richard P. "The Salem Witchcraft Trials as a Crisis of Popular Imagination." *Essex Institute Historical Collections* 128 (1992): 270–85.

———. "Visions of Evil: Popular Culture, Puritanism, and the Massachusetts Witchcraft Crisis of 1692." *Journal of American Culture* 8 (1985): 17–33.

Godbeer, Richard. *The Devil's Dominion: Magic and Religion in Early New England.* Cambridge: Cambridge University Press, 1992.

———. *Escaping Salem: The Other Witch Hunt of 1692.* Oxford: Oxford University Press, 2005.

Gregg, Larry. *The Salem Witch Crisis.* New York: Praeger, 1992.

Hall, David D. "Witchcraft and the Limits of Interpretation." *New England Quarterly* 59 (1985): 253–81.

———. *Worlds of Wonder, Days of Judgement: Popular Religious Belief in Early New England.* New York: Knopf, 1989.

Hansen, Chadwick. "Andover Witchcraft and the Causes of the Salem Witchcraft Trials." In *The Occult in America: New Historical Perspectives*, ed. Howard Kerr and Charles L. Crow. Urbana: University of Illinois Press, 1983, 38–57.

———. *Witchcraft at Salem.* New York: George Braziller, 1969.

Harley, David. "Explaining Salem: Calvinist Psychology and the Diagnosis of Possession." *American Historical Review* 101 (1996): 307–30.

Heyman, Christine L. "Specters of Subversion, Societies of Friends: Dissent and the Devil in Provincial Essex County." In *Saints and Revolutionaries: Essays on Early American History*, ed. David Hall, John M. Murrin, and Thad W. Tate. New York: Norton, 1984, 38–74.

Hill, Frances. *A Delusion of Satan: The Full Story of the Salem Witch Trials.* New York: Doubleday, 1995.

Hoffer, Peter Charles. *The Devil's Disciples: Makers of the Salem Witchcraft Trials.* Baltimore, Md.: Johns Hopkins University Press, 1996.

———. *The Salem Witchcraft Trials: A Legal History.* Lawrence: University Press of Kansas, 1997.

Kamensky, Jane. "Words, Witches and Women Trouble: Witchcraft, Disorderly Speech and Gender Boundaries in Puritan New England." *Essex Institute Historical Collections* 128 (1992): 286–306.

Karlsen, Carol F. *The Devil in the Shape of a Woman: Witchcraft in Colonial New England.* New York: Norton, 1987.

Kences, James E. "Some Unexplored Relationships of Essex County Witchcraft to the Indian Wars of 1675 and 1689." *Essex Institute Historical Collections* 20 (1984): 179–212.

Kibbey, Ann. "Mutations of the Supernatural: Witchcraft, Remarkable Providences, and the Power of Puritan Men." *American Quarterly* 34 (1982): 125–48.

Kluckhorn, Clyde. *Navaho Witchcraft*. 1944. Reprint, Boston: Beacon Press, 1967.

Norton, Mary Beth. *In the Devil's Snare: The Salem Witchcraft Crisis of 1692*. New York: Knopf, 2002.

Owen, Dennis E. "Spectral Evidence: The Village Witchcraft Cosmology of Salem Village in 1692." In *Essays in the Sociology of Perceptions*, ed. Mary Douglas. London: Routledge, 1982.

Pearl, Jonathan L. "Witchcraft in New France in the Seventeenth Century: The Social Aspects." *Historical Reflections* 4 (1977): 191–205.

Reis, Elizabeth. *Damned Women: Sinners and Witches in Puritan New England*. Ithaca, N.Y.: Cornell University Press, 1997.

———. "The Devil, the Body, and the Feminine Soul in Puritan New England." *Journal of American History* 82 (1995): 15–36.

———, ed. *Spellbound: Women and Witchcraft in America*. Wilmington, Del.: Scholarly Resources, 1998.

Rosenthal, Bernard. *Salem Story: Reading the Witch Trials of 1692*. Cambridge: Cambridge University Press, 1993.

Simmons, Mark. *Witchcraft in the Southwest: Spanish and Indian Supernaturalism on the Rio Grande*. Lincoln: University of Nebraska Press, 1974.

Taylor, John M. *The Witchcraft Delusion: The Story of Witchcraft Persecutions in Seventeenth-Century New England, Including Original Trial Transcripts*. New York: Gramercy, 1995.

Walker, Deward E., ed. *Witchcraft and Sorcery of the American Native Peoples*. Moscow: University of Idaho Press, 1989.

Weisman, Richard. *Witchcraft, Magic and Religion in Seventeenth Century Massachusetts*. Amherst: University of Massachusetts Press, 1984.

Werking, Richard H. "'Reformation Is Our Only Preservation': Cotton Mather and Salem Witchcraft." *William and Mary Quarterly* 29 (1972): 281–90.

South and Central America

Behar, R. "Sexual Witchcraft, Colonialism, and Women's Powers: Views from the Mexican Inquisition." In *Sexuality and Marriage in Colonial Latin America*, ed. Anunción Lavrin. Lincoln: University of Nebraska Press, 1989, 178–206.

Ceballos Gómez, Diana Luz. *Hechicería, brujería e Inquisición en el Nuevo Reino de Granada: Un duelo de imaginarios*. Bogotá: Universidad Nacional de Colombia, 1194.

Cervantes, Fernando. *The Devil in the New World: The Impact of Diabolism in New Spain*. New Haven, Conn.: Yale University Press, 1994.

————. "The Devils of Querétaro: Scepticism and Credulity in Late Seventeenth-Century Mexico." *Past and Present* 130 (1991).

Gareis, Iris. "'Brujos' y 'brujas' en el antiguo Perú: Apariencia y realidad en las fuentes históricas." *Revista de Indias* 53 (1993): 583–613.

————. "Una bucólica andina: Curanderos y brujos en la costa norte del Perú (siglo XVIII)." In *En el nombre del Señor: Shamanes, demonios y curanderos del norte del Perú*, ed. Luis Millones and Moises Lemlij. Lima, Peru: Biblioteca Peruana de Psicoanálisis, 1994, 211–30.

Henningsen, Gustav. "The Diffusion of Magic in Colonial America." In *Clashes of Culture: Essays in Honour of Niels Steensgaard*, ed. J. C. V. Johansen, E. Ladevig Petersen, and Henrik Stevnsborg, Odense, Denmark: Odense University Press, 1992, 160–78.

————. "La evangelización negra: Difusión de la magia europea por la América colonial." *Revista de la Inquisición* 3 (1994): 9–27.

Silverblatt, Irene. *Moon, Sun, and Witches: Gender Ideologies and Class in Inca and Colonial Peru*. Princeton, N.J.: Princeton University Press, 1987.

Souza, Laura de Mello e. *The Devil and the Land of the Holy Cross: Witchcraft, Slavery, and Popular Religion in Colonial Brazil*. Trans. Diane Grosklaus Whitty. Austin: University of Texas Press, 2004.

Africa

Abrahams, Ray. "A Modern Witchhunt among the Lango of Uganda." *Cambridge Anthropology* 10 (1985): 32–45.

————, ed. *Witchcraft in Contemporary Tanzania*. Cambridge: University of Cambridge, African Studies Centre, 1994.

Ashforth, Adam. *Witchcraft, Violence, and Democracy in South Africa*. Chicago: University of Chicago Press, 2005.

Crais, Clifton. *Magic, State Power and the Political Imagination in South Africa*. Cambridge: Cambridge University Press, 2002.

Crawford, J. R. *Witchcraft and Sorcery in Rhodesia*. Oxford: Oxford University Press, 1967.

Debrunner, Hans W. *Witchcraft in Ghana: A Study of the Belief in Destructive Witches and Its Effect on the Akan Tribes*. 2nd ed. Accra, Ghana: Presbyterian Book Depot, 1961.

Douglas, Mary. "Witch Beliefs in Central Africa." *Africa* 37 (1967): 72–80.

Evans-Pritchard, E. E. *Witchcraft, Oracles and Magic among the Azande*. 2nd ed. Oxford: Clarendon, 1950.

Fisiy, Cyprian F., and Peter Geschiere. "Judges and Witches, or How Is the State to Deal with Witchcraft? Examples from Southeastern Cameroon." *Cahiers d'études africaines* 118 (1990): 135–56.

———. "Sorcery, Witchcraft, and Accumulation—Regional Variation in South West Cameroon." *Critique of Anthropology* 11 (1991): 251–78.

Geschiere, Peter. *The Modernity of Witchcraft: Politics and the Occult in Postcolonial Africa.* Trans. Peter Geschiere and Jane Rothman. Charlottesville: University of Virginia Press, 1997.

Hammond-Tooke, W. D. "The Cape Nguni Witch Familiar as a Mediatory Construct." *Man* n.s. 9 (1974): 128–36.

Harnischfeger, Johannes. "State Decline and the Return of Occult Powers: The Case of Prophet Eddy in Nigeria." *Magic, Ritual, and Witchcraft* 1 (2006): 56–78.

———. "Witchcraft and the State in South Africa." *Anthropos* 95 (2000): 99–112.

Harris, Grace. "Possession, 'Hysteria' in a Kenyan Tribe." *American Anthropologist* 59 (1957): 1046–66.

Harwood, Alan. *Witchcraft, Sorcery and Social Categories among the Safwa.* Oxford: Oxford University Press, 1970.

Jackson, Michael D. "Structure and Event: Witchcraft Confession among the Kuranko." *Man* 10 (1975): 387–403.

Marwick, Max G. "Another Modern Anti-Witchcraft Movement in East Central Africa." *Africa* 20 (1950): 100–12.

———. "The Continuance of Witchcraft Beliefs." In *Africa in Transition,* ed. Prudence Smith. London: Reinhardt, 1958, 106–14.

———. "The Social Context of Cewâ Witch Beliefs." *Africa* 22 (1952): 120–22.

———. *Sorcery in Its Social Setting: A Study of the Northern Rhodesian Cewâ.* Manchester, Eng.: Manchester University Press, 1965.

Middleton, John, and E. H. Winter, eds. *Witchcraft and Sorcery in East Africa.* New York: Praeger, 1963.

Moore, Henrietta, and Todd Sanders, eds. *Magical Interpretation, Material Realities: Modernity, Witchcraft and the Occult in Postcolonial Africa.* London: Routledge, 2001.

Nadel, S. F. "Witchcraft in Four African Societies." *American Anthropologist* 54 (1952): 18–29.

Nicolini, Beatrice, ed. *Studies in Witchcraft, Magic, War and Peace in Africa: 19th and 20th Centuries.* Lewiston, N.Y.: Edwin Mellen, 2006.

Niehus, Isak A. *Witchcraft, Power and Politics: Exploring the Occult in the South African Lowveld.* Cape Town, S.A.: Sterling, 2001.

Ogembo, Justus M. *Contemporary Witch-Hunting in Gusii, Southwestern Kenya.* Lewiston, N.Y.: Edwin Mellen, 2006.

Reynolds, Barrie. *Magic, Divination, and Witchcraft among the Barotse of Northern Rhodesia.* Berkeley: University of California Press, 1963.

Rodlach, Alexander. *Witches, Westerners, and HIV: AIDS and Cultures of Blame in Africa.* Walnut Creek, Calif.: Left Coast Press, 2006.

Schapera, Isaac. "Sorcery and Witchcraft in Bechuanaland." *African Affairs* 51 (1952): 41–52.

Smith, James Howard. *Bewitching Development: Witchcraft and the Reinvention of Development in Neoliberal Kenya*. Chicago: University of Chicago Press, 2008.

Willis, R. G. "Kamcape: An Anti-Sorcery Movement in South-West Tanzania." *Africa* 38 (1968): 1–15.

Wyllie, R. W. "Introspective Witchcraft among the Effutu of Southern Ghana." *Man* n.s. 8 (1973): 74–79.

Asia, Oceania, and the Middle East

Fortune, Reo Franklin. *Sorcerers of Dobu: The Social Anthropology of the Dobu Islanders of the Western Pacific*. London: Routledge, 1963.

Kuhn, Philip A. *Soulstealers: The Chinese Sorcery Scare of 1768*. Cambridge, Mass.: Harvard University Press, 1990.

Obeyesekere, Gananath. "Sorcery, Premeditated Murder, and the Canalization of Aggression in Sri Lanka." *Ethnography* 14 (1975): 1–23.

Savage Smith, Emilie, ed. *Magic and Divination in Early Islam*. Aldershot, Eng.: Ashgate, 2004.

Ter Haar, Barend J. *Telling Stories: Witchcraft and Scapegoating in Chinese History*. Leiden: Brill, 2005.

Watson, C. W., and Roy Ellen, eds. *Understanding Witchcraft and Sorcery in Southeast Asia*. Honolulu: University of Hawaii Press, 1993.

THE DEVIL AND DEMONOLOGY, AND POSSESSION AND EXORCISM

Almond, Philip C. *Demonic Possession and Exorcism in Early Modern England: Contemporary Texts and Their Cultural Contexts*. Cambridge: Cambridge University Press, 2004.

Boureau, Alain. *Satan the Heretic: The Birth of Demonology in the Medieval West*. Trans. Teresa Lavender Fagan. Chicago: University of Chicago Press, 2006.

Caciola, Nancy. "Mystics, Demoniacs, and the Physiology of Spirit Possession in Medieval Europe." *Comparative Studies in Society and History* 42 (2000): 268–306.

Certeau, Michel de. *The Possession at Loudun*. Trans Michael B. Smith. Chicago: University of Chicago Press, 1996.

Clark, Stuart. "The Rational Witchfinders: Consensus, Demonological Naturalism and Popular Superstitions." In *Science, Culture, and Popular Belief in Renaissance Europe*, ed. Stephen Pumfrey, Paolo L. Rossi, and Maurice Slawinski. Manchester, Eng.: Manchester University Press, 1991, 225–38.

———. "The Scientific Status of Demonology." In *Occult and Scientific Mentalities in the Renaissance*, ed. Brian Vickers. Cambridge: Cambridge University Press, 1984, 351–74.

Dendle, Peter. *Satan Unbound: The Devil in Old English Narrative Literature*. Toronto: University of Toronto Press, 2001.

De Waardt, Hans, and Jürgen Michael Schmidt, eds. *Dämonische Besessenheit: Zur Interpretation eines kulturhistorischen Phänomens*. Bielefeld, Ger.: Verlag für Regionalgeschichte, 2005.

Elliott, Dyan. *Fallen Bodies: Pollution, Sexuality, and Demonology in the Middle Ages*. Philadelphia: University of Pennsylvania Press, 1999.

———. "Seeing Double: John Gerson, the Discernment of Spirits, and Joan of Arc." *American Historical Review* 107 (2002): 26–54.

Ferber, Sarah. *Demonic Possession and Exorcism in Early Modern France*. London: Routledge: 2004.

Ferguson, Everett. *Demonology of the Early Christian World*. Lewiston, N.Y.: Mellen, 1984.

Finlay, Anthony. *Demons! The Devil, Possession and Exorcism*. London: Blanford, 1999.

Frankfurter, David. *Evil Incarnate: Rumors of Demonic Conspiracy and Satanic Abuse in History*. Princeton, N.J.: Princeton University Press, 2006.

Gérest, Claude. "Der Teufel in der theologischen Landschaft der Hexenjäger des 15. Jahrhunderts." *Concilium* 2 (1975): 173–83.

Goddu, André. "The Failure of Exorcism in the Middle Ages." *Soziale Ordnung im Selbstverständnis des Mittelalters* 12 (1980): 540–57.

Haag, Herbert. *Teufelsglaube*. Tübingen, Ger.: Katzmann, 1972.

Jelsma, Auke. "The Devil and Protestantism." In Auke Jelsma, *Frontiers of the Reformation: Dissidence and Orthodoxy in Sixteenth-Century Europe*. Aldershot, Eng.: Ashgate, 1998, 25–39.

Kelly, Henry Ansgar. *The Devil, Demonology and Witchcraft: The Development of Christian Beliefs in Evil Spirits*. Rev. ed. New York: Doubleday, 1974.

Kirsch, Irving. "Demonology and Science during the Scientific Revolution." *Journal of the History of Behavioral Sciences* 16 (1980): 359–68.

Kreiser, B. Robert. "The Devils of Toulon: Demonic Possession and Religious Politics in Eighteenth-Century Provence." In *Church, State, and Society under the Bourbon Kings of France*, ed. Richard M. Golden. Lawrence, Kans.: Coronado Press, 1982, 173–221.

Lecouteux, Claude. *Démons et genies du terroir au Moyen Age*. Paris: Imago, 1995.

Maggi, Armando. *In the Company of Demons: Unnatural Beings, Love, and Identity in the Italian Renaissance*. Chicago: University of Chicago Press, 2006.

———. *Satan's Rhetoric: A Study of Renaissance Demonology*. Chicago: University of Chicago Press, 2001.

Maxwell-Stuart, P. G. *Satan: A Biography*. Stroud, Eng.: Amberley, 2008.

Midelfort, H. C. Erik. "Catholic and Lutheran Reactions to Demonic Possession in the Late Seventeenth Century: Two Case Histories." *Daphnis* 15 (1986): 623–48.

———. "The Devil and the German People: Reflections on the Popularity of Demon Possession in Sixteenth-Century Germany." In *Religion and Culture in the Renaissance and Reformation*, ed. Steven Ozment, Kirksville, Mo.: Sixteenth Century Journal Publishers, 1989, 99–119.

Muchembled, Robert. *A History of the Devil: From the Middle Ages to the Present*. Cambridge: Polity, 2003.

Neumann, Almut. *Verträge und Pakte mit dem Teufel: Antike und mittelalterliche Vorstellungen im "Malleus maleficarum."* St. Ingbert, Ger.: Röhrig Universitätsverlag, 1997.

Newman, Barbara. "Possessed by the Spirit: Devout Women, Demoniacs, and the Apostolic Life in the Thirteenth Century." *Speculum* 73 (1998): 733–70.

Nicholls, David. "The Devil in Renaissance France." *History Today* 30 (November, 1980): 25–30.

Nischan, Bodo. "The Exorcism Controversy and Baptism in the Late Reformation." *Sixteenth Century Journal* 18 (1987): 31–51.

Oldridge, Darren. *The Devil in Early Modern England*. Stroud, Eng.: Sutton, 2000.

Pagels, Elaine. *The Origin of Satan*. New York: Random House, 1995.

Pearl, Jonathan L. *The Crime of Crimes: Demonology and Politics in France 1560–1620*. Waterloo, Ont.: Wilfred Laurier University Press, 1999.

Petzoldt, Ruth, and Paul Neubauer, eds. *Demons: Mediators between This World and the Other: Essays on Demonic Beings from the Middle Ages to the Present*. Frankfurt: Peter Lang, 1998.

Russell, Jeffrey Burton. *The Devil: Perceptions of Evil from Antiquity to Primitive Christianity*. Ithaca, N.Y.: Cornell University Press, 1977.

———. *Lucifer: The Devil in the Middle Ages*. Ithaca, N.Y.: Cornell University Press, 1984.

———. *Mephistopheles: The Devil in the Modern World*. Ithaca, N.Y.: Cornell University Press, 1986.

———. *Satan: The Early Christian Tradition*. Ithaca, N.Y.: Cornell University Press, 1981.

Sluhovsky, Moshe. "The Devil in the Convent." *American Historical Review* 107 (2002): 1378–1411.

Spanos, Nicholas P., and Jack Gottlieb. "Demonic Possession, Mesmerism, and Hysteria: A Social Psychological Perspective on Their Historical Interrelations." *Journal of Abnormal Psychology* 88 (1979): 527–46.

Stanford, Peter. *The Devil: A Biography*. London: Mandarin, 1996.

Stephens, Walter. *Demon Lovers: Witchcraft, Sex, and the Crisis of Belief*. Chicago: University of Chicago Press, 2002.

Veenstra, Jan R. "Stretching the Imagination: Demons between Man's Body and Soul." In *Tradition and Innovation in an Era of Change*, ed. Rudolf Suntrup and Jan R. Veenstra. Frankfurt: Peter Lang, 2001, 203–25.

Walker, Anita M., and Edmund H. Dickerman. "'A Woman under the Influence': A Case of Alleged Possession in Sixteenth-Century France." *Sixteenth Century Journal* 22 (1991): 535–54.

Walker, D. P. "Demonic Possession used as Propaganda in the Later 16th Century." In *Scienze, credenze occulte, livelli di cultura: Convegno internazionale di studi (Firenze, 26–30 giugno, 1980)*. Florence, Italy: Olschki, 1982, 237–48.

———. *Unclean Spirits: Possession and Exorcism in France and England in the Late Sixteenth and Early Seventeenth Centuries*. Philadelphia: University of Pennsylvania Press, 1981.

Walzel, Diana Lynn. "Sources of Medieval Demonology." *Rice University Studies* 60 (1974): 83–99.

THEORISTS OF WITCHCRAFT, AND TREATISES AND LITERATURE ON WITCHCRAFT

Anglo, Sydney. "Melancholia and Witchcraft: The Debate between Wier, Bodin, and Scot." In *Folie et déraison à la Renaissance*. Brussels: Université de Bruxelles, 1976, 209–28.

———, ed. *The Damned Art: Essays in the Literature of Witchcraft*. London: Routledge, 1977.

Attfield, Robin. "Balthasar Bekker and the Decline of the Witch-Craze: The Old Demonology and the New Philosophy." *Annals of Science* 42 (1988): 383–95.

Bailey, Michael D. *Battling Demons: Witchcraft, Heresy, and Reform in the Late Middle Ages*. University Park: Pennsylvania State University Press, 2003.

Bonney, Françoise. "Autour de Jean Gerson: Opinions de théologiens sur les superstitions et la sorcellerie au début de XVe siècle." *Le Moyen Age* 77 (1971): 85–98.

Brauner, Sigrid. "Martin Luther on Witchcraft: A True Reformer?" In *The Politics of Gender in Early Modern Europe*, ed. Jean R. Brink, Allison P. Coudert, and Maryanne C. Horowitz. Kirksville, Mo.: Sixteenth Century Journal Publishers, 1989, 29–42.

Broedel, Hans Peter. *The Malleus Maleficarum and the Construction of Witchcraft: Theology and Popular Belief.* Manchester: Manchester University Press, 2003.

Camerlynck, Elaine. "Féminité et sorcellerie chez les théoriciens de la démonologie à la fin du Moyen Age: Etude du *Malleus maleficarum.*" *Renaissance and Reformation* n.s. 7 (1983): 13–25.

Caro Baroja, Julio. "Martín del Rio y sus *Disquisiciones mágicas.*" In Julio Caro Baroja, *El señor inquisidor y ostras vidas por oficio.* Madrid: Alianza, 1968, 171–96.

Classen, Albrecht. "The End of the Middle Ages? Criticism of Sorcery and Witchcraft through Johann Weyer in his *De Praestigiis Daemonum* of 1583." In *Zauberer und Hexen in der Kultur des Mittelalters*, ed. Danielle Buschinger and Wolfgang Spiewok. Greifswald, Ger.: Reinecke, 1994, 27–43.

Darst, David H. "Witchcraft in Spain: The Testimony of Martín de Castañega's Treatise on Superstition and Witchcraft (1529)." *Proceedings of the American Philosophical Society* 123 (1979): 298–322.

Decker, Rainer. "Spee und Tanner aus der Sicht eines römischen Kardinal-Inquisitors." *Spee Jahrbuch* 6 (1999): 45–52.

Estes, Leland L. "Reginald Scot and His *Discoverie of Witchcraft*: Religion and Science in Opposition to the European Witch Craze." *Church History* 52 (1983): 444–56.

Fürbeth, Frank. *Johannes Hartlieb: Untersuchungen zu Leben und Werk.* Tübingen, Ger.: Niemeyer, 1992.

Haustein, Jörg. *Martin Luthers Stellung zur Zauber- und Hexenwesen.* Stuttgart, Ger.: Kohlhammer, 1990.

Henningsen, Gustav. "The Papers of Alsonso de Salazar Frias: A Spanish Witchcraft Polemic, 1610–14." *Temenos* 5 (1969): 85–106.

Herzig, Tamar. "The Demons' Reaction to Sodomy: Witchcraft and Homosexuality in Gianfrancesco Pico della Mirandola's *Strix.*" *Sixteenth Century Journal* 34 (2003): 53–72.

Horowitz, Maryanne Cline. "Montaigne versus Bodin on Ancient Tales of Demonology." *Proceedings of the Annual Meeting of the Western Society for French History* 16 (1989): 103–10.

Houdard, Sophie. *Les sciences du diable: Quatre discours sur la sorcellerie (XVe–XVIIe siècle).* Paris: Editions du Cerf, 1992.

Jensen, Peter. "Calvin and Witchcraft." *Reformed Theological Review* 34 (1975): 76–86.

Lange, Ursula. *Untersuchungen zu Bodins "Démonomanie."* Frankfurt: Klostermann, 1970.

Lehmann, Hartmut, and Otto Ulbricht, eds. *Vom Unfug des Hexen-Processes: Gegner der Hexenverfolgungen von Johann Weyer bis Friedrich Spee.* Wiesbaden, Ger.: Harrossowitz, 1992.

Lehrich, Christopher I. *The Language of Demons and Angels: Cornelius Agrippa's Occult Philosophy.* Leiden: Brill, 2003.

Leutenbacher, Siegfried. *Hexerei- und Zaubereidelikt in der Literatur von 1450 bis 1550: Mit Hinweis auf der Praxis im Herzogtum Bayern.* Berlin: Schweitzer, 1972.

Midelfort, H. C. Erik. "Johannes Weyer and the Transformation of the Insanity Defense." In *The German People and the Reformation*, ed. R. Po-chia Hsia. Ithaca, N.Y.: Cornell University Press, 1988, 234–61.

Monter, E. William. "Inflation and Witchcraft: The Case of Jean Bodin." In *Action and Conviction in Early Modern Europe: Essays in Memory of E. H. Harbison*, ed. Theodore K. Rabb and Jerrold E. Seigel. Princeton, N.J.: Princeton University Press, 1969, 371–89.

Paravy, Pierrette. "A propos de la gènese médiévale des chasses aux sorcières: Le traité de Claude Tholosan, juge dauphinois (vers. 1436)." In *Mélanges de l'École Française de Rome: Moyen Ages-Temps Modernes* 91 (1979): 333–79.

Pearl, Jonathan L. "Bodin's Advice to Judges in Witchcraft Cases." *Proceedings of the Annual Meeting of the Western Society for French History* 16 (1989): 95–102.

———. "Humanism and Satanism: Jean Bodin's Contributions to the Witchcraft Crisis." *Canadian Review of Sociology and Anthropology* 19 (1982): 541–48.

Petersohn, Jürgen. "Konziliaristen und Hexen: Ein unbekannter Brief des Inquisitors Heinrich Institoris an Papst Sixtus IV. aus dem Jahre 1484." *Deutsches Archiv für Erforschung des Mittelalters* 44 (1988): 120–60.

Rummel, Walter. "Friedrich Spee und das Ende der kurtrierischen Hexenprozesse." *Jahrbuch für westdeutsche Landesgeschichte* 15 (1989): 105–16.

Segl, Peter. "Der Hexenhammer: Eine Quelle der Alltags- und Mentalitätsgeschichte." In *Mentalität und Gesellschaft im Mittelalter: Gedenkschrift für Ernst Werner*, ed. Sabine Tanz. Frankfurt: Peter Lang, 1993, 127–54.

———, ed. *Der Hexenhammer: Entstehung und Umfeld des "Malleus Maleficarum" vom 1487.* Cologne: Böhlau, 1988.

———. "'Malefice . . . non . . . sunt . . . heretice nuncupande': Zu Heinrich Kramers Widerlegung der Ansichten *aliorum inquisitorum in viuersis regnis hispanie.*" In *Papstum, Kirche und Recht im Mittelalter: Festschrift für Horst Fuhrmann*, ed. Hubert Mordek. Tübingen, Ger.: Niemeyer, 1991, 369–82.

Stephens, Walter. "Tasso and the Witches." *Annali d'Italianistica* 12 (1994): 181–202.

———. "Witches Who Steal Penises: Impotence and Illusion in *Malleus maleficarum.*" *Journal of Medieval and Early Modern Studies* 28 (1998): 495–529.

Taylor, Steven M. "Le procès de la sorcellerie chez Martin Le Franc: *Le Champion des Dames*, Livre IV." In *Zauberer und Hexen in der Kultur des Mittelalters*, ed. Danielle Buschinger and Wolfgang Spiewok. Greifswald, Ger.: Reineke, 1994, 203–12.

Tschacher, Werner. *Der Formicarius des Johannes Nider von 1437/38: Studien zu den Anfängen der europäischen Hexenverfolgungen im Spätmittelalter.* Aachen, Ger.: Shaker, 2000.

Veenstra, Jan. *Magic and Divination at the Courts of Burgundy and France: Text and Context of Laurens Pignon's "Contre les devineurs" (1411).* Leiden: Brill: 1998.

Webster, Charles. *From Paracelsus to Newton: Magic and the Making of Modern Science.* Cambridge: Cambridge University Press, 1982.

West, Robert H. *Reginald Scot and Renaissance Writings on Witchcraft.* Boston: Twayne, 1984.

Williams, Gerhild Scholz. *Defining Dominion: The Discourses of Magic and Witchcraft in Early Modern France and Germany.* Ann Arbor: University of Michigan Press, 1995.

Wilson, Eric. "Institoris at Innsbruck: Heinrich Institoris, the *Summis Desiderantes* and the Brixen Witch-Trial of 1485." In *Popular Religion in Germany and Central Europe, 1400–1800*, ed. Bob Scribner and Trevor Johnson. New York: St. Martin's Press, 1996, 87–100, 239–45.

Wunder, Heide. "Friedrich von Spee and die verfolgten Frauen." In *Die politische Theologie Friedrich von Spees*, ed. Doris Brockmann and Peter Eicher. Munich: Fink, 1991, 119–32.

Zenz, Emil. " Cornelius Loos—ein Vorlaufer Friedrich von Spees im Kampf gegen den Hexenwahn." *Kurtrierisches Jahrbuch* 21 (1981): 146–53.

Ziegler, Wolfgang. *Möglichkeiten der Kritik am Hexen- und Zauberwesen im ausgehenden Mittelalter: Zeitgenössische Stimmen und ihre soziale Zuhörigkeit.* 2nd ed. Cologne: Böhlau, 1973.

WITCHCRAFT IN ART

Davidson, Jane P. "Great Black Goats and Evil Little Women: The Image of the Witch in Sixteenth-Century German Art." *Journal of the Rocky Mountain Medieval and Renaissance Society* 6 (1985): 141–57.

―――. *The Witch in Northern European Art, 1470–1750.* Freren, Ger.: Luca, 1987.

―――. "Wolves, Witches and Werewolves." *Journal of the Fantastic in the Arts* 2 (1990): 47–68.

Hoak, Dale. "Art, Culture, and Mentality in Renaissance Society: The Meaning of Hans Baldung Grien's *Bewitched Groom* (1544)." *Renaissance Quarterly* 38 (1985): 488–510.

―――. "Witch-Hunting and Women in the Art of the Renaissance." *History Today* 31 (February, 1981): 22–26.

Hults, Linda C. "Baldung and the Witches of Freiburg: The Evidence of Images." *Journal of Interdisciplinary History* 18 (1987–88): 249–76.

―――. "Baldung's 'Bewitched Groom' Revisited: Artistic Temperament, Fantasy and the 'Dream of Reason'." *Sixteenth Century Journal* 15 (1984): 259–79.

―――. "Hans Baldung Grien's 'Weather Witches' in Frankfurt." *Pantheon: Internationale Zeitschrift für Kunst* 40 (1982): 124–30.

―――. *The Witch as Muse: Art, Gender, and Power in Early Modern Europe.* Philadelphia: University of Pennsylvania Press, 2005.

Link, Luther. *The Devil: The Archfiend in Art from the Sixth to the Sixteenth Century.* New York: Abrams, 1996.

Mesenzeva, Charmain. "Der Behexte Stallknecht des Hans Baldung Griens." *Zeitschrift für Kunstgeschichte* 44 (1981): 57–61.

Schade, Sigrid. *Schadenzauber und die Magie des Körpers: Hexenbilder der Frühen Neuzeit.* Worms, Ger.: Wernersche Verlagsgesellschaft, 1983.

Sullivan, Margaret A. "The Witches of Dürer and Hans Baldung Grien." *Renaissance Quarterly* 53 (2000): 333–401.

Swan, Claudia. *Art, Science, and Witchcraft in Early Modern Holland: Jacob de Gheyn II (1565–1629).* Cambridge: Cambridge University Press, 2005.

Zika, Charles. *The Appearance of Witchcraft.* London: Routledge, 2009.

―――. *Exorcising Our Demons: Magic, Witchcraft and Visual Culture in Early Modern Europe.* Leiden: Brill, 2003.

―――. "Images of Circe and Discourses of Witchcraft, 1480–1580." *Zeitenblicke: Online-Journal für die Geschichtswissenschaften* 1 (2002).

―――. "'Magie'—'Zauberei'—'Hexerei': Bildmedien und kultereller Wandel." In *Kulturelle Reformation: Sinnreformation im Umbruch, 1400–1600*, ed. Bernhard Jussen and Craig Koslofsky. Göttingen, Ger.: Vandenhoeck & Ruprecht, 1999, 317–82.

WITCHCRAFT IN THE MODERN WORLD

Magic and Superstition after the Witch-Hunts

Argyrou, Vassos. "Under a Spell: The Strategic Use of Magic in Greek Cypriot Society." *American Ethnologist* 20 (1993): 256–71.

Blécourt, Willem de, and Owen Davies, eds. *Witchcraft Continued: Popular Magic in Modern Europe*. Manchester, Eng.: Manchester University Press, 2004.

Conrad, John L. "Bulgarian Magic Charms: Ritual, Form, and Content." *Slavic and East European Journal* 31 (1987): 548–62.

———. "Magic Charms and Healing Rituals in Contemporary Yugoslavia." *Southeastern Europe* 10 (1983): 99–120.

Davies, Owen. "Cunning-Folk in England and Wales during the Eighteenth and Nineteenth Centuries." *Rural History* 8 (1997): 91–107.

———. "Cunning Folk in the Medical Market-Place during the Nineteenth Century." *Medical History* 43 (1999): 55–73.

———. "Hag-Riding in Nineteenth-Century West Country England and Modern Newfoundland: An Examination of an Experience-Centred Witchcraft Tradition." *Folk Life* 35 (1996–97): 36–53.

———. "Healing Charms in Use in England and Wales 1700–1950." *Folklore* 107 (1996): 19–32.

———. "Methodism, the Clergy, and the Popular Belief in Witchcraft and Magic." *History* 82 (1997): 252–65.

———. "Newspapers and the Popular Belief in Witchcraft and Magic in the Modern Period." *Journal of Social History* 30 (1997): 597–617.

———. *Witchcraft, Magic and Culture, 1736–1951*. Manchester, Eng.: Manchester University Press, 1999.

Denier, Marie-Claude. "Sorciers, présages et croyances magiques en Mayenne aux XVIIIe et XIXe siècles." *Annales de Bretagne et de Pays de l'Ouest (Anjou, Maine, Touraine)* 97 (1990): 115–32.

Devlin, Judith. *The Superstitious Mind: French Peasants and the Supernatural in the Nineteenth Century*. New Haven, Conn.: Yale University Press, 1987.

Favret-Saada, Jeanne. *Deadly Words: Witchcraft in the Bocage*. Trans. Catherine Cullen. Cambridge: Cambridge University Press, 1980.

———. "Unbewitching as Therapy." *American Ethnologist* 16 (1989): 40–56.

Gaskill, Malcolm. *Hellish Nell: Last of Britain's Witches*. New York: HarperCollins, 2002.

Gibbons, B. J. *Spirituality and the Occult: From the Renaissance to the Modern Age*. London: Routledge, 2001.

Greenwood, Susan. *Magic, Witchcraft and the Otherworld: An Anthropology*. Oxford: Berg, 2000.

Krzwynska, Tanya. *A Skin for Dancing In: Possession, Witchcraft and Voodoo in Film*. London: Flicks Books, 2000.

Lorenz, Sönke, Dieter R. Bauer, Wolfgang Behringer, and Jürgen Michael Schmidt, eds. *Himmlers Hexenkartothek: Das Interesse des Nationalsozialismus an der Hexenverfolgung*. Bielefeld, Ger.: Verlag für Regionalgeschichte, 1999.

Maple, Eric. *Superstition and Superstitions*. London: W. H. Allen, 1971.

Monroe, John Warne. *Laboratories of Faith: Mesmerism, Spiritualism, and the Occultism in Modern France*. Ithaca, N.Y.: Cornell University Press, 2008.

———. "The Way We Believe Now: Modernity and the Occult." *Magic, Ritual and Witchcraft* 2 (2007): 68–78.

Oates, Caroline, and Juliette Woods. *A Coven of Scholars: Margaret Murray and Her Working Methods*. London: Folklore Society, 1998.

Owen, Alex. *The Darkened Room: Women, Power and Spiritualism in Late Nineteenth Century England*. Philadelphia: University of Pennsylvania Press, 1990.

Oxbrow, Mark. *Halloween: From Pagan Ritual to Party Night*. Oxford: Oxford University Press, 2001.

Schier, Barbara. "Hexenwahn und Hexenverfolgung: Rezeption and politische Zurichtung eines kulturwissenschaftlichen Themas im Dritten Reich." *Bayerische Jahrbuch für Volkskunde* (1990): 43–115.

Schiffmann, Aldona Christina. "The Witch and the Crime: The Persecution of Witches in Twentieth-Century Poland." *ARV: Scandinavian Yearbook of Folklore* 43 (1987): 147–65.

Schöck, Inge. *Hexenglaube in der Gegenwart: Empirische Untersuchungen in Südwestdeutschland*. Tübingen, Ger.: Vereinigung für Volkskunde, 1978.

Sebald, Hans. "Nazi Ideology Redefining Deviants: Witches, Himmler's Witch-Trial Survey, and the Case of the Bishopric of Bamberg." *Deviant Behaviour* 10 (1989): 253–70.

———. *Witch Children*. Amherst, N.Y.: Prometheus, 1995.

———. *Witchcraft: The Heritage of a Heresy*. New York: Elsevier, 1978.

Soman, Alfred. "Sorcellerie, justice criminelle, et société dans la France moderne." *Histoire, économie, et société* 12 (1993): 177–218.

Traimond, Bernard. *Le pouvoir de la maladie: Magie et politique dans les Landes de Gascogne, 1750–1826*. Bordeaux, France: Université de Bordeaux, 1988.

Worobec, Christine D. *Possessed: Women, Witches, and Demons in Imperial Russia*. DeKalb: Northern Illinois University Press, 2001.

———. "Witchcraft Beliefs and Practices in Prerevolutionary Russian and Ukrainian Villages." *Russian Review* 54 (1995): 165–87.

Modern Wicca, Neo-Paganism, and Satanism

Adler, Margot. *Drawing Down the Moon: Witches, Druids, Goddess-Worshippers, and Other Pagans in America Today*. Rev. ed. Boston: Beacon, 1986.

Bovenschen, Silvia. "The Contemporary Witch, the Historical Witch, and the Witch Myth: The Witch, Subject to the Appropriation of Nature and the Object of Domination of Nature." *New German Critique* 15 (1978): 83–119.

Butler, Alison. *Victorian Occultism and the Making of Modern Magic: Invoking Tradition*. Basingstoke, Eng.: Palgrave Macmillan, 2011.

Clifton, Chas S. *Her Hidden Children: The Rise of Wicca and Paganism in America*. Lanham, Md.: AltaMira Press, 2006.

Coleman, Kristy S. *Re-Riting Women: Dianic Wicca and the Feminine Divine*. Lanham, Md.: AltaMira Press, 2009.

Crowley, Vivienne. *Wicca: The Old Religion in the New Millennium*. Rev. ed. London: Thorsons, 1996.

Culpepper, Emil Erwin. "Contemporary Goddess Theology: A Sympathetic Critique." In *Shaping New Vision: Gender and Values in American Culture*, ed. Clarissa W. Atkinson, Constance H. Buchanan, and Margaret R. Miles. Ann Arbor, Mich.: UMI Research Press, 1987, 51–71.

Eller, Cynthia. *Living in the Lap of the Goddess: The Feminist Spirituality Movement in America*. Boston: Beacon, 1995.

Fritscher, Jack. *Popular Witchcraft: Straight from the Witch's Mouth*. 2nd ed. Madison: University of Wisconsin Press, 2004.

Gardner, Gerald. *Witchcraft Today*. New York: Citadel, 1954.

Harmening, Dieter, ed. *Hexen Heute: Magische Traditionen und neue Zutaten*. Würzburg, Ger.: Königshausen & Neumann, 1991.

Hutton, Ronald. *The Triumph of the Moon: A History of Modern Pagan Witchcraft*. Oxford: Oxford University Press, 1999.

Johnston, Hannah E. ed. *The New Generation Witches: Teenage Witchcraft in Contemporary Culture*. Aldershot, Eng.: Ashgate, 2007.

Kelly, Aidan. *A History of Modern Witchcraft, 1939–1964*. St. Paul, Minn.: Llewellyn, 1991.

King, Francis. *Ritual Magic in England, 1887 to the Present Day*. London: Spearman, 1970.

Klassen, Chris. *Storied Selves: Shaping Identity in Feminist Witchcraft*. Lanham, Md.: Lexington Books, 2008.

La Fontaine, Jean. *Speak of the Devil: Tales of Satanic Abuse in Contemporary England.* Cambridge: Cambridge University Press, 1998.

Leek, Sibyl. *The Complete Art of Witchcraft.* New York: Penguin, 1971.

Lewis, James R., ed. *Magical Religion and Modern Witchcraft.* Albany: State University of New York Press, 1996.

Luhrmann, T. M. *Persuasions of the Witch's Craft: Ritual Magic in Contemporary England.* Cambridge, Mass.: Harvard University Press, 1989.

Medway, Gareth J. *Lure of the Sinister: The Unnatural History of Satanism.* New York: New York University Press, 2001.

Owen, Alex. *The Place of Enchantment: British Occultism and the Culture of the Modern.* Chicago: University of Chicago Press, 2004.

Partridge, Christopher H. *The Re-Enchantment of the West.* 2 vols. London: T & T Clark International, 2004–2005.

Pearson Joanne. *Religion and the Return of Magic: Wicca as Esoteric Spirituality.* Lancaster, Eng.: University of Lancaster, 2000.

Pearson, Joanne, Richard Roberts, Geoffrey Samuel, and Joanne Overend, eds. *Nature Religions Today: Paganism in the Modern World.* Edinburgh: Edinburgh University Press, 1998.

Salomonsen, Jane. *Enchanted Feminism: Ritual, Gender and Divinity among the Reclaiming Witches of San Francisco.* London: Routledge, 2002.

Sanders, Maxine. *Fire Child: The Life and Magic of Maxine Sanders, 'Witch Queen'.* Oxford: Mandrake, 2007.

Starhawk. *The Spiral Dance: A Rebirth of the Ancient Religion of the Great Goddess.* 20th anniversary ed. San Francisco: Harper, 1999.

Truzzi, Marcello. "The Occult Revival as Popular Culture: Some Random Observations of the Old and Nouveau Witch." *Sociological Quarterly* 13 (1972): 16–36.

Valiente, Doreen. *The Rebirth of Witchcraft.* Custer, Wash.: Phoenix Publishing, 1989.

Wise, Constance. *Hidden Circles in the Web: Feminist Wicca, Occult Knowledge, and Process Thought.* Lanham, Md.: AltaMira Press, 2008.

ANTHROPOLOGICAL, HISTORICAL, AND COMPARATIVE STUDIES

Abrahams, Ray. *Vigilant Citizens: Vigilantism and the State.* Oxford: Polity, 1998.

Douglas, Mary, ed. *Witchcraft Confessions and Accusations.* London: Tavistock, 1970.

Hammond-Tooke, W. D. "Urbanization and the Interpretation of Misfortune: A Quantitative Analysis." *Africa* 40 (1970): 25–39.

Kennedy, John G. "Psychological and Social Explanations of Witchcraft." *Man* 2 (1967): 216–25.

Lehmann, Arthur C., and James E. Myers, eds. *Magic, Witchcraft, and Religion: An Anthropological Study of the Supernatural*. Palo Alto, Calif.: Mayfield, 1985.

Lewis, I. M. *Ecstatic Religion: An Anthropological Study of Spirit Possession and Shamanism*. Harmondsworth, Eng.: Penguin, 1971.

Mair, Lucy. *Witchcraft*. New York: McGraw-Hill, 1969.

Marwick, Max G. "The Study of Witchcraft." In *The Craft of Social Anthropology*, ed. A. L. Epstein. London: Tavistock, 1967, 231–44.

———, ed. *Witchcraft and Sorcery: Selected Readings*. 2nd ed. New York: Penguin, 1982.

———. "Witchcraft as a Social Strain-Gauge." *Australian Journal of Science* 26 (1964): 263–68.

Newell, Venetia, ed. *The Witch Figure: Folklore Essays by a Group of Scholars in England Honouring the 75th Birthday of Katharine M. Briggs*. London: Routledge, 1973.

Parrinder, Geoffrey. *Witchcraft: European and African*. New York: Barnes and Noble, 1963.

Turner, Victor W. "Witchcraft and Sorcery: Taxonomy versus Dynamics." *Africa* 34 (1964): 314–24.

About the Authors

Jonathan Durrant completed his Ph.D. in witchcraft and gender at the University of London. He is currently a senior lecturer the University of Glamorgan, Wales, where he teaches courses on early-modern history. His research interests include the experience of witchcraft in Germany and England, concepts of masculinity and other forms of identity among early-modern soldiers, particularly during the Thirty Years War (1618–49), and representations of early-modern history on film. He is the author of *Witchcraft, Gender and Society in Early Modern Germany* (2007).

Michael D. Bailey received his Ph.D. from Northwestern University, Illinois, where he specialized in medieval and early-modern European history. He now teaches medieval history at Iowa State University. His principal research interests focus on the history of magic, witchcraft, and superstition in Europe. Among his publications are *Battling Demons: Witchcraft, Heresy, and Reform in the Late Middle Ages* and *Magic and Superstition in Europe: A Concise History from Antiquity to the Present*, as well as numerous articles on these topics. He was also one of the founding co-editors of the interdisciplinary journal *Magic, Ritual, and Witchcraft*.